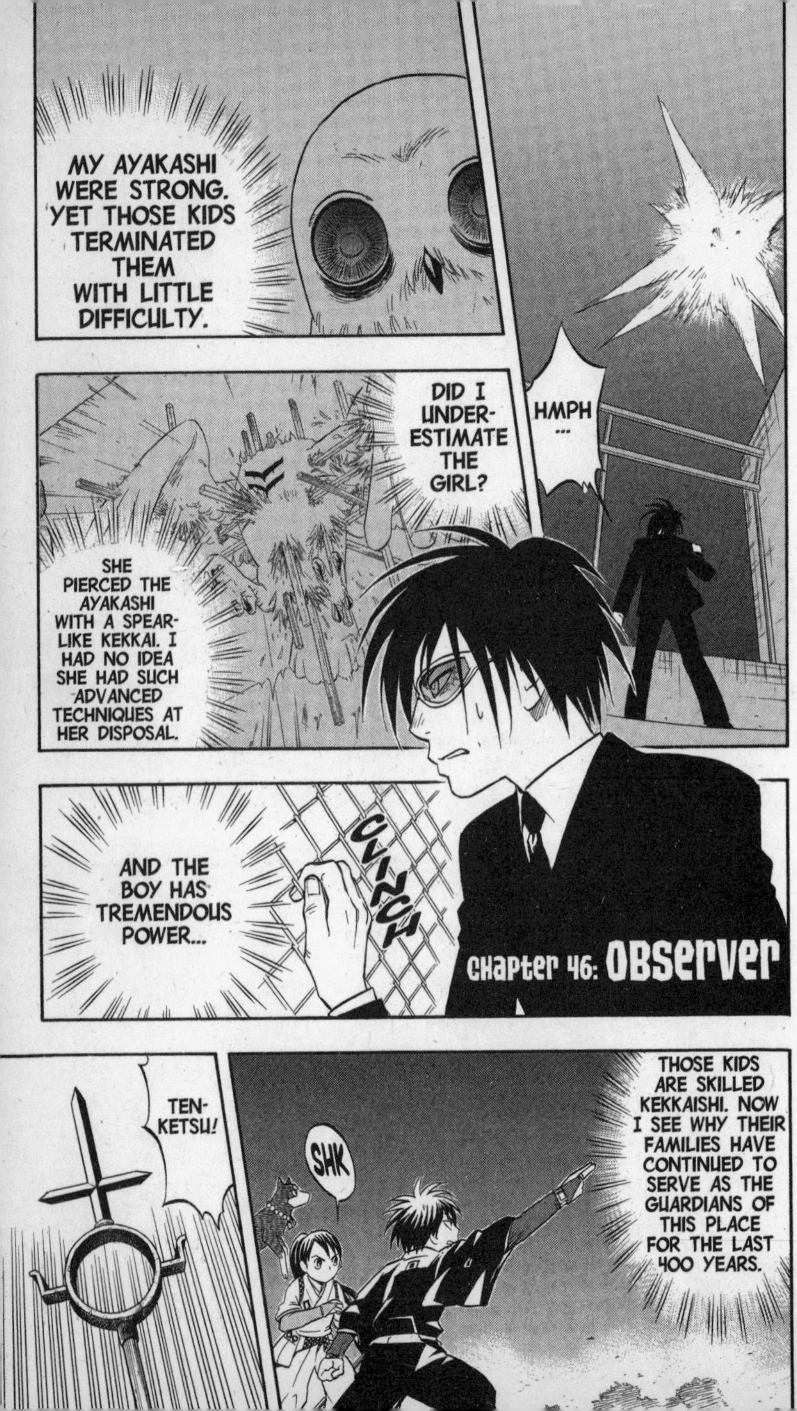
HMPH...
MY AYAKASHI WERE STRONG. YET THOSE KIDS TERMINATED THEM WITH LITTLE DIFFICULTY.
DID I UNDER-ESTIMATE THE GIRL?
SHE PIERCED THE AYAKASHI WITH A SPEAR-LIKE KEKKAI. I HAD NO IDEA SHE HAD SUCH ADVANCED TECHNIQUES AT HER DISPOSAL.
CLINCH
AND THE BOY HAS TREMENDOUS POWER...
Chapter 46: Observer
THOSE KIDS ARE SKILLED KEKKAISHI. NOW I SEE WHY THEIR FAMILIES HAVE CONTINUED TO SERVE AS THE GUARDIANS OF THIS PLACE FOR THE LAST 400 YEARS.
SHK
TEN-KETSU!

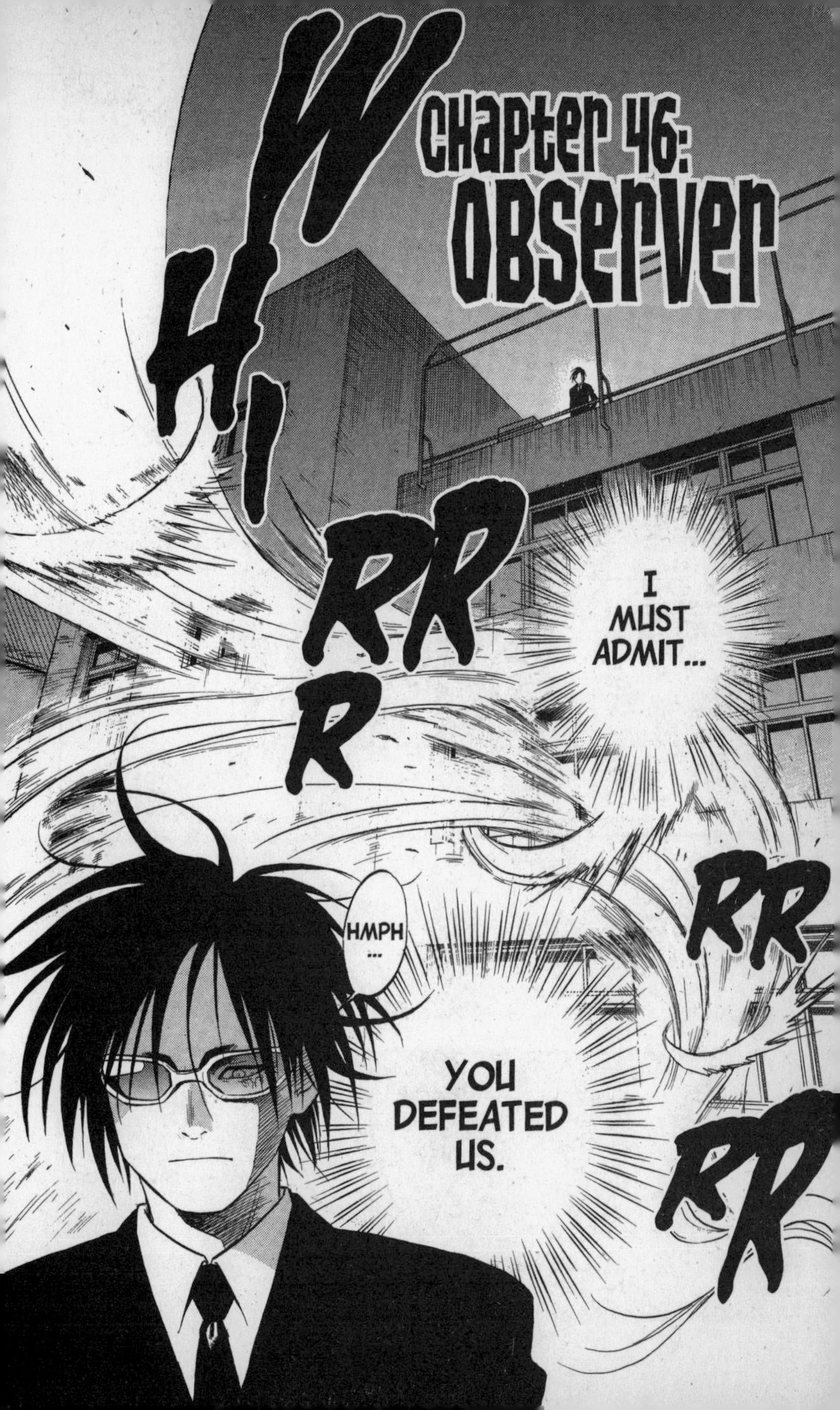
Chapter 46:
Observer
WHIRRR
I MUST ADMIT...
RRRR
HMPH...
YOU DEFEATED US.

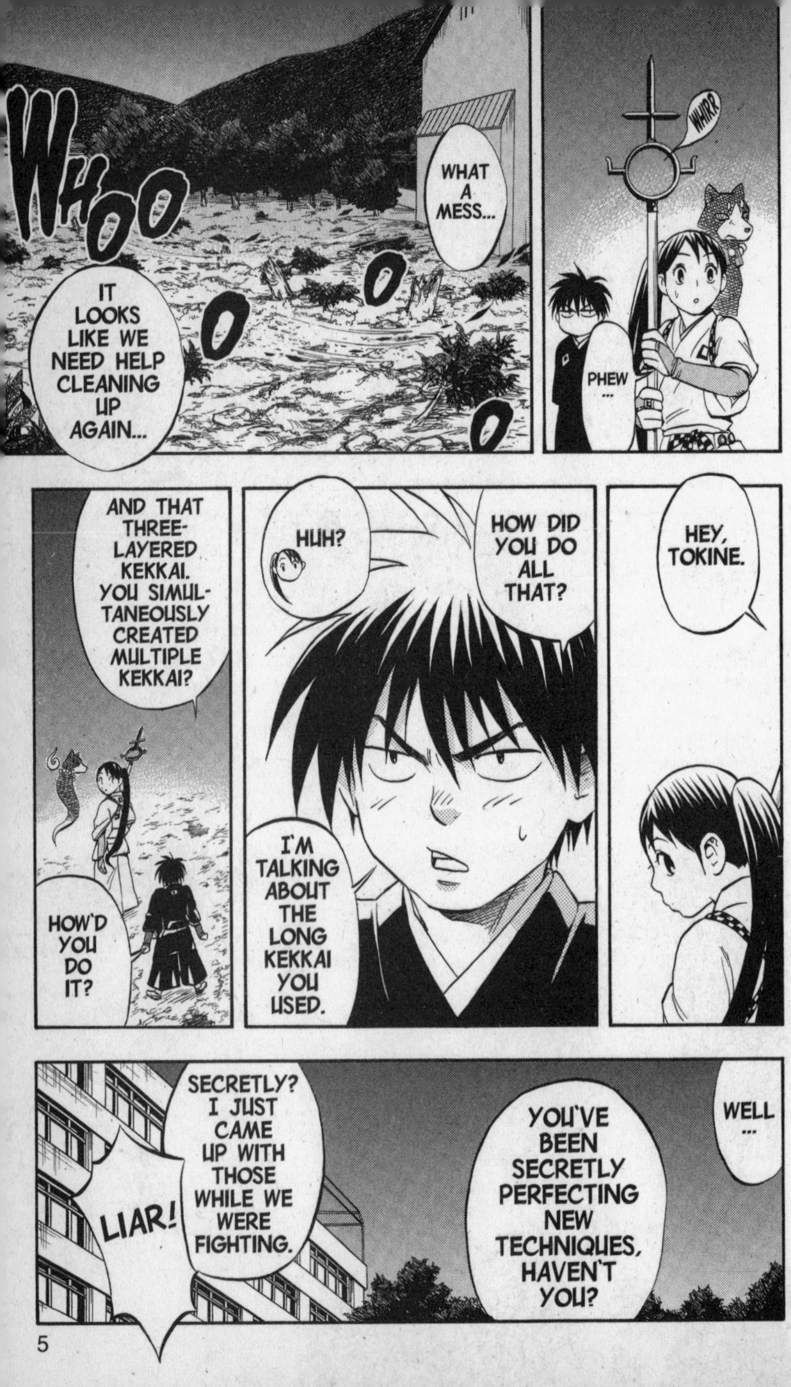
WHIRR
PHEW...
WHAT A MESS...
WHOOOOOO
IT LOOKS LIKE WE NEED HELP CLEANING UP AGAIN...
HEY, TOKINE.
HOW DID YOU DO ALL THAT?
HUH?
I'M TALKING ABOUT THE LONG KEKKAI YOU USED.
AND THAT THREE-LAYERED KEKKAI. YOU SIMULTANEOUSLY CREATED MULTIPLE KEKKAI?
HOW'D YOU DO IT?
WELL...
YOU'VE BEEN SECRETLY PERFECTING NEW TECHNIQUES, HAVEN'T YOU?
SECRETLY? I JUST CAME UP WITH THOSE WHILE WE WERE FIGHTING.
LIAR!

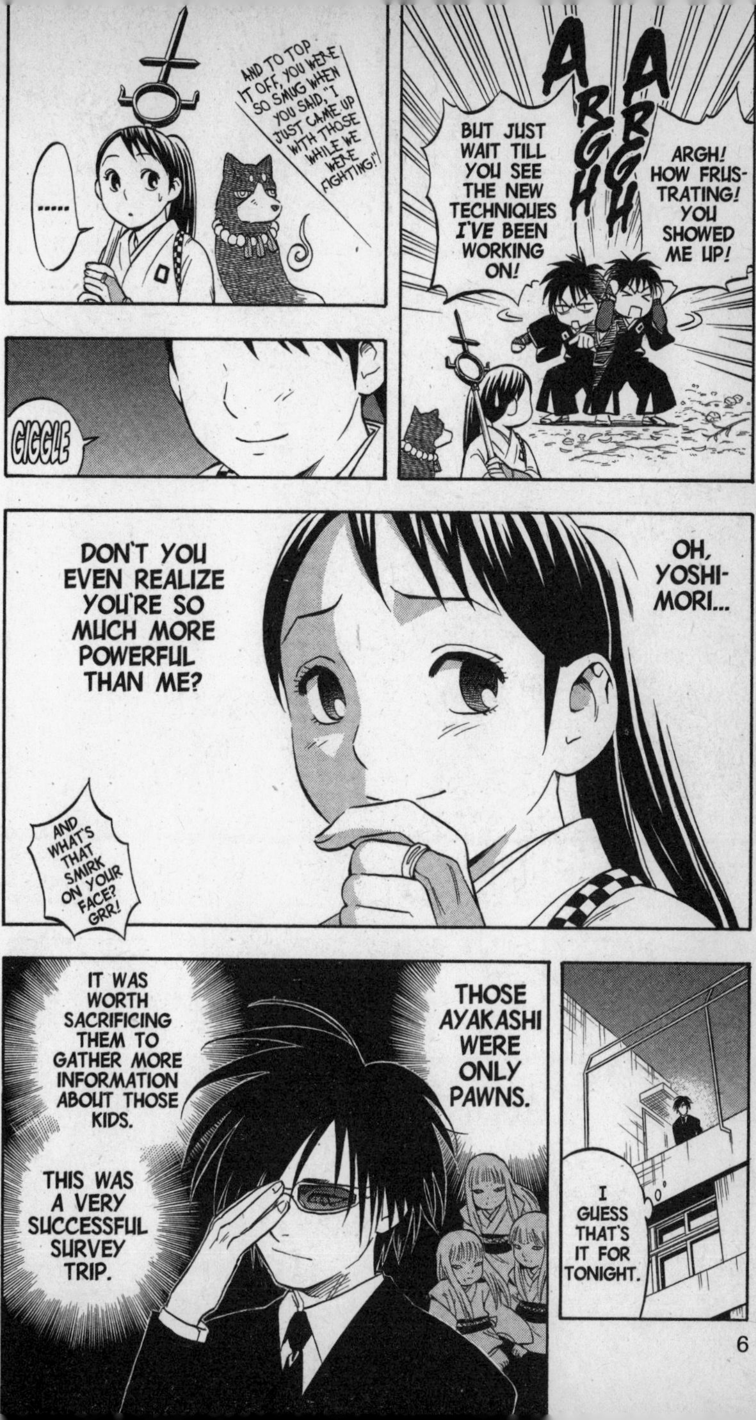
AARGH AARGH
ARGH! HOW FRUSTRATING! YOU SHOWED ME UP!
BUT JUST WAIT TILL YOU SEE THE NEW TECHNIQUES *I'VE* BEEN WORKING ON!
AND TO TOP IT OFF, YOU WERE SO SMUG WHEN YOU SAID, "I JUST CAME UP WITH THOSE WHILE WE WERE FIGHTING!"
......
GIGGLE
OH, YOSHIMORI...
DON'T YOU EVEN REALIZE YOU'RE SO MUCH MORE POWERFUL THAN ME?
AND WHAT'S THAT SMIRK ON YOUR FACE? GRR!
I GUESS THAT'S IT FOR TONIGHT.
THOSE AYAKASHI WERE ONLY PAWNS.
IT WAS WORTH SACRIFICING THEM TO GATHER MORE INFORMATION ABOUT THOSE KIDS.
THIS WAS A VERY SUCCESSFUL SURVEY TRIP.

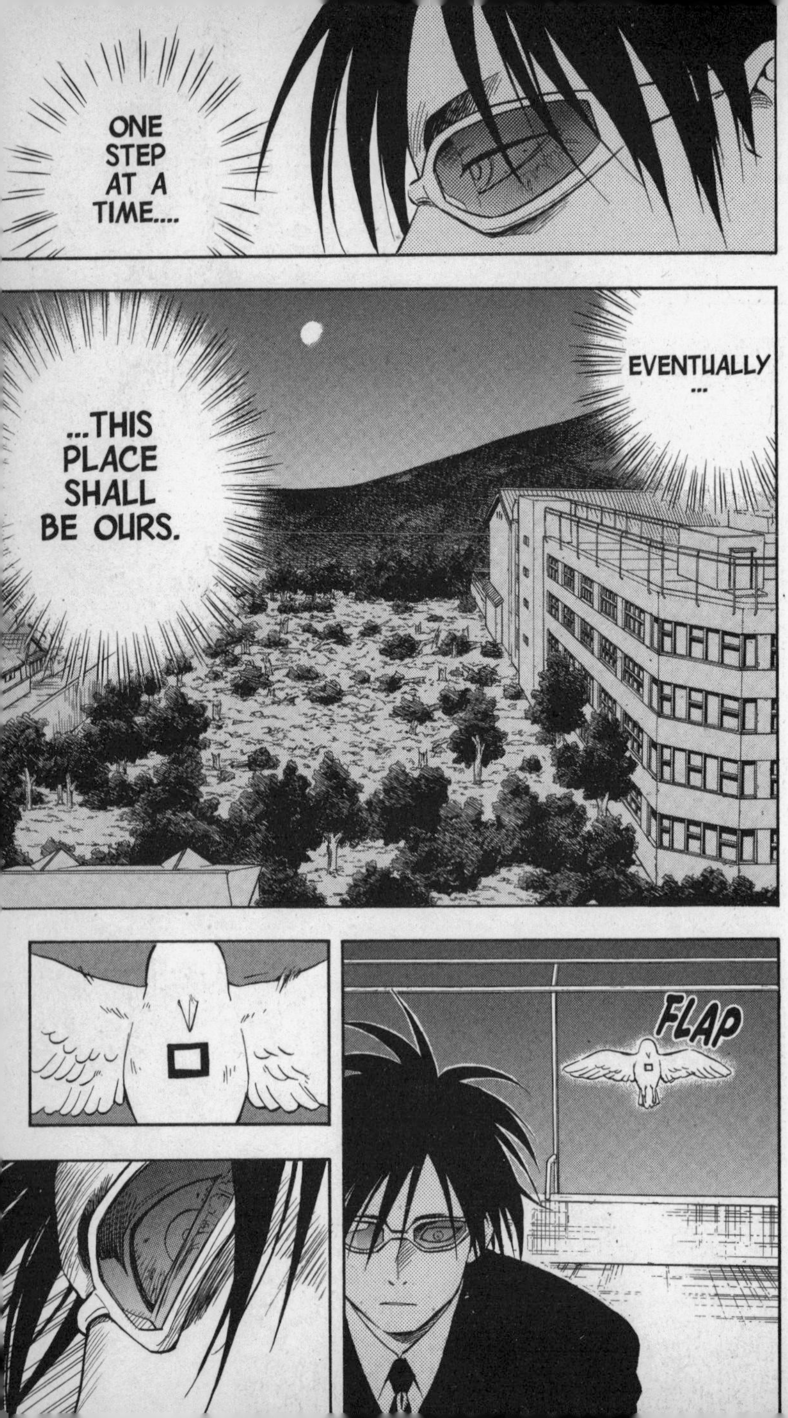
ONE STEP AT A TIME....
EVENTUALLY ...
...THIS PLACE SHALL BE OURS.
FLAP

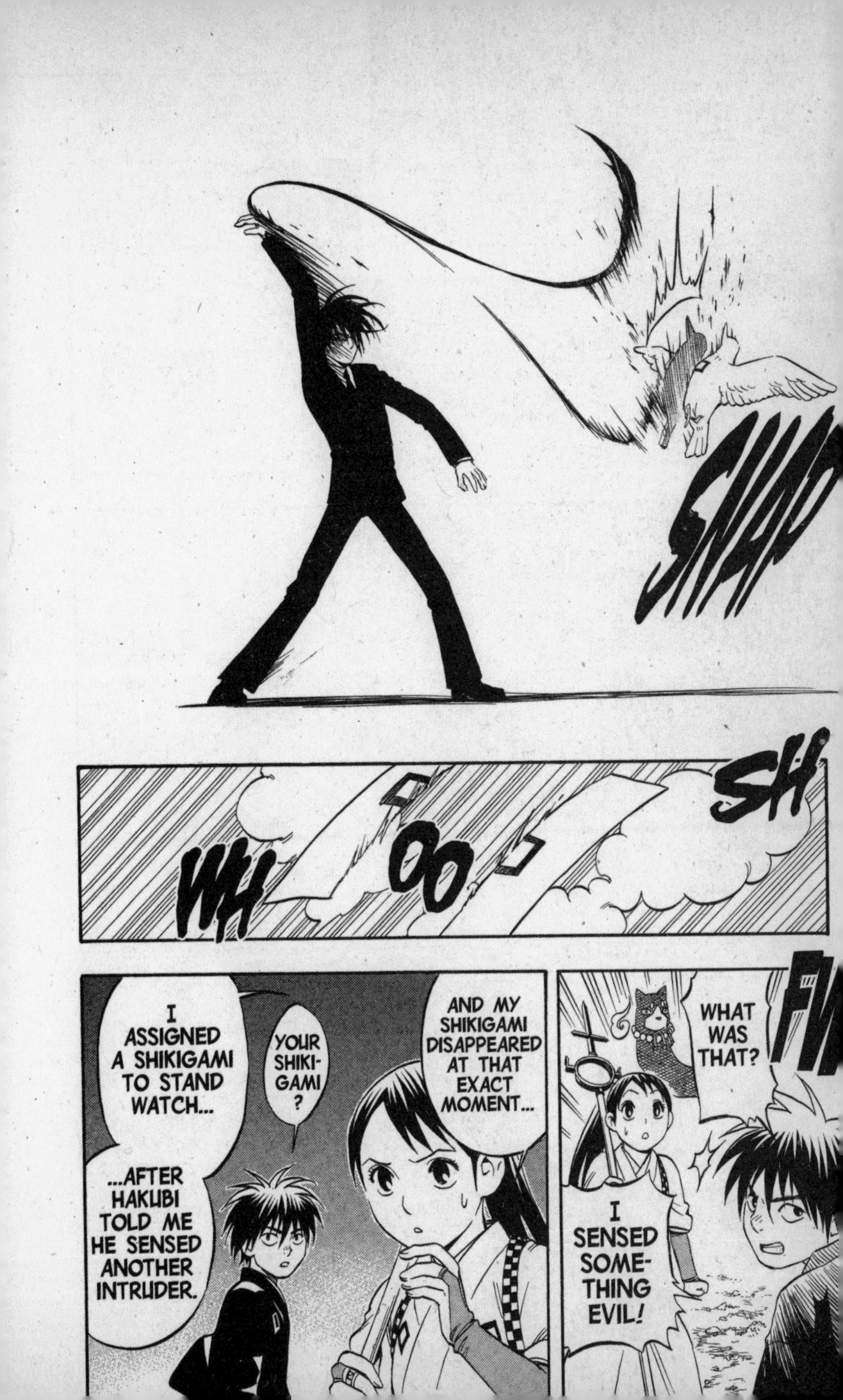
SNAP
WH OO SH
WHAT WAS THAT?
FW
I SENSED SOMETHING EVIL!
I ASSIGNED A SHIKIGAMI TO STAND WATCH...
YOUR SHIKIGAMI?
AND MY SHIKIGAMI DISAPPEARED AT THAT EXACT MOMENT...
...AFTER HAKUBI TOLD ME HE SENSED ANOTHER INTRUDER.

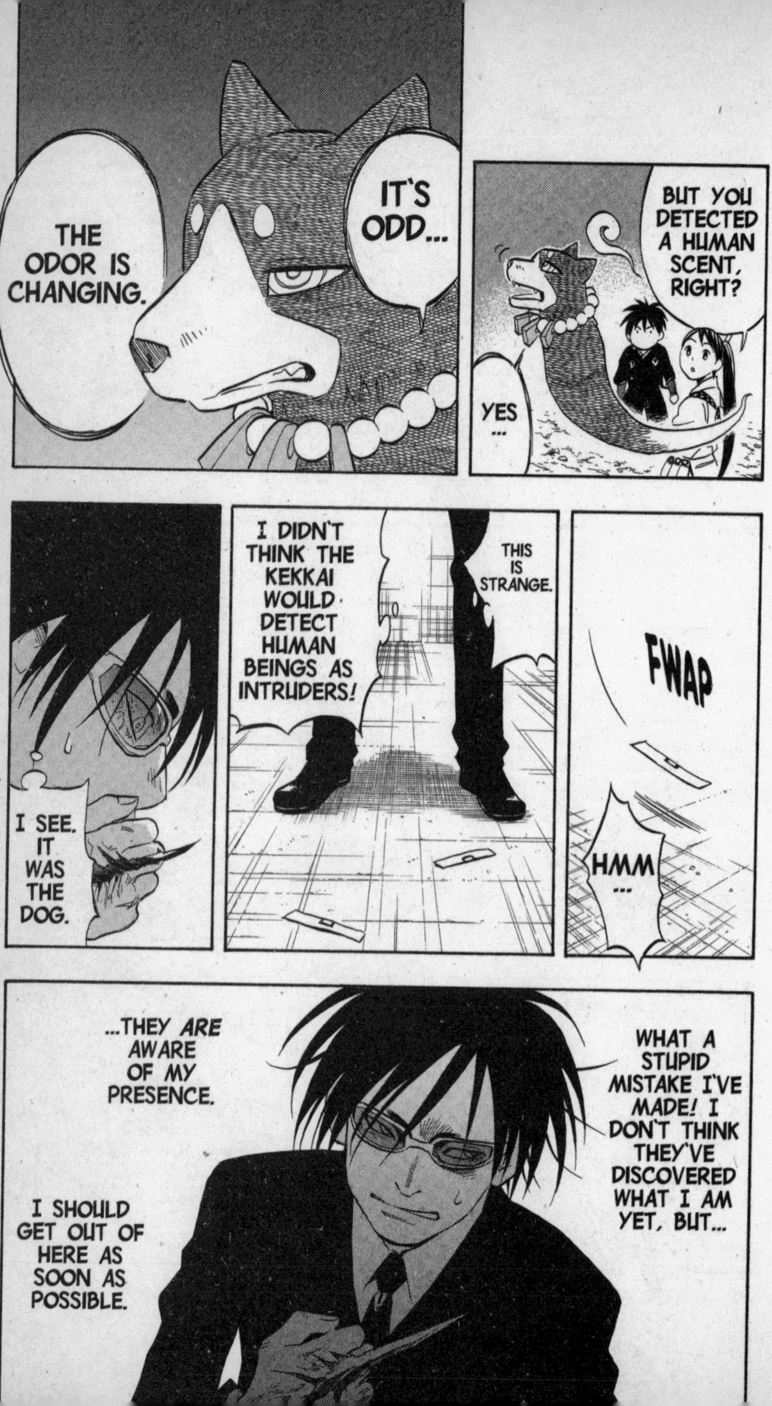
BUT YOU DETECTED A HUMAN SCENT, RIGHT?
YES ...
IT'S ODD...
THE ODOR IS CHANGING.
FWAP
HMM ...
THIS IS STRANGE.
I DIDN'T THINK THE KEKKAI WOULD DETECT HUMAN BEINGS AS INTRUDERS!
I SEE. IT WAS THE DOG.
WHAT A STUPID MISTAKE I'VE MADE! I DON'T THINK THEY'VE DISCOVERED WHAT I AM YET, BUT...
...THEY ARE AWARE OF MY PRESENCE.
I SHOULD GET OUT OF HERE AS SOON AS POSSIBLE.

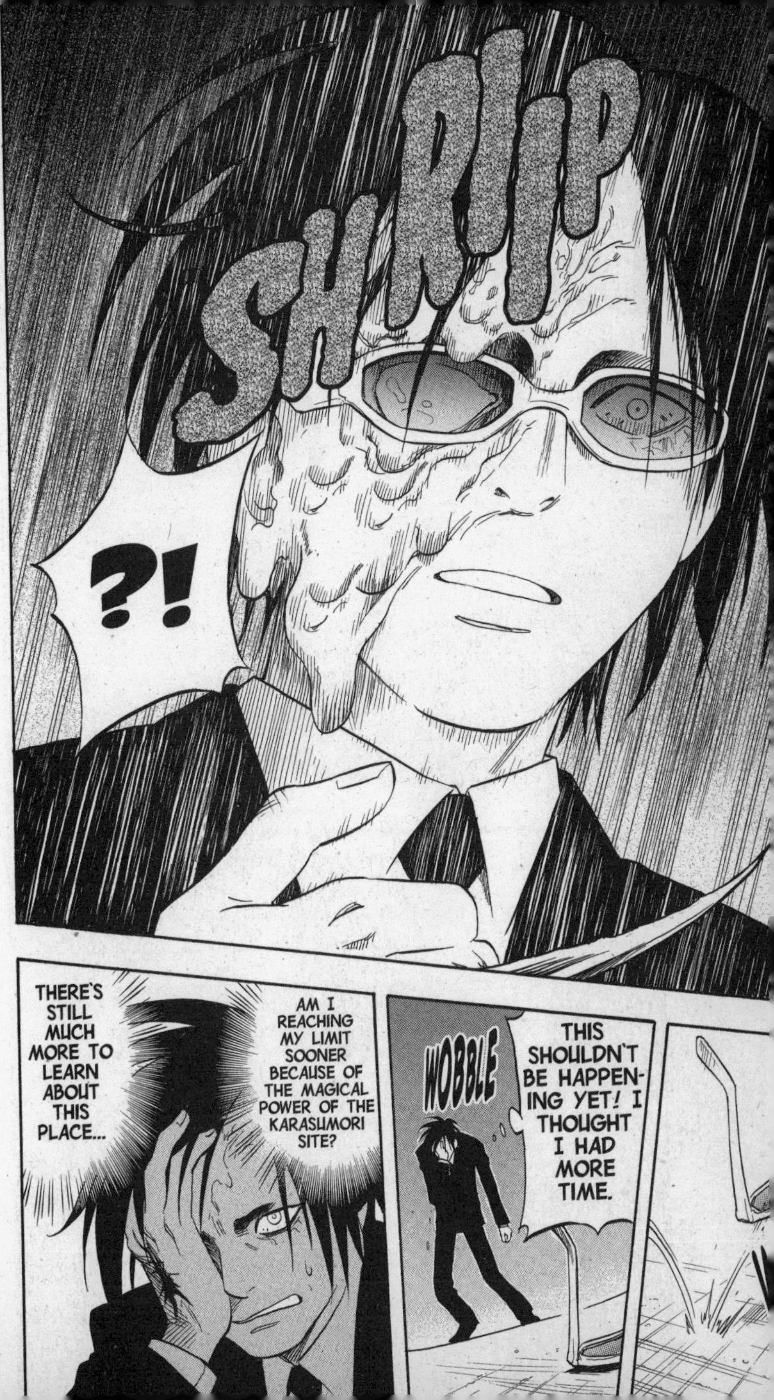
SHRLIP
?!
WOBBLE
THIS SHOULDN'T BE HAPPENING YET! I THOUGHT I HAD MORE TIME.
AM I REACHING MY LIMIT SOONER BECAUSE OF THE MAGICAL POWER OF THE KARASUMORI SITE?
THERE'S STILL MUCH MORE TO LEARN ABOUT THIS PLACE...

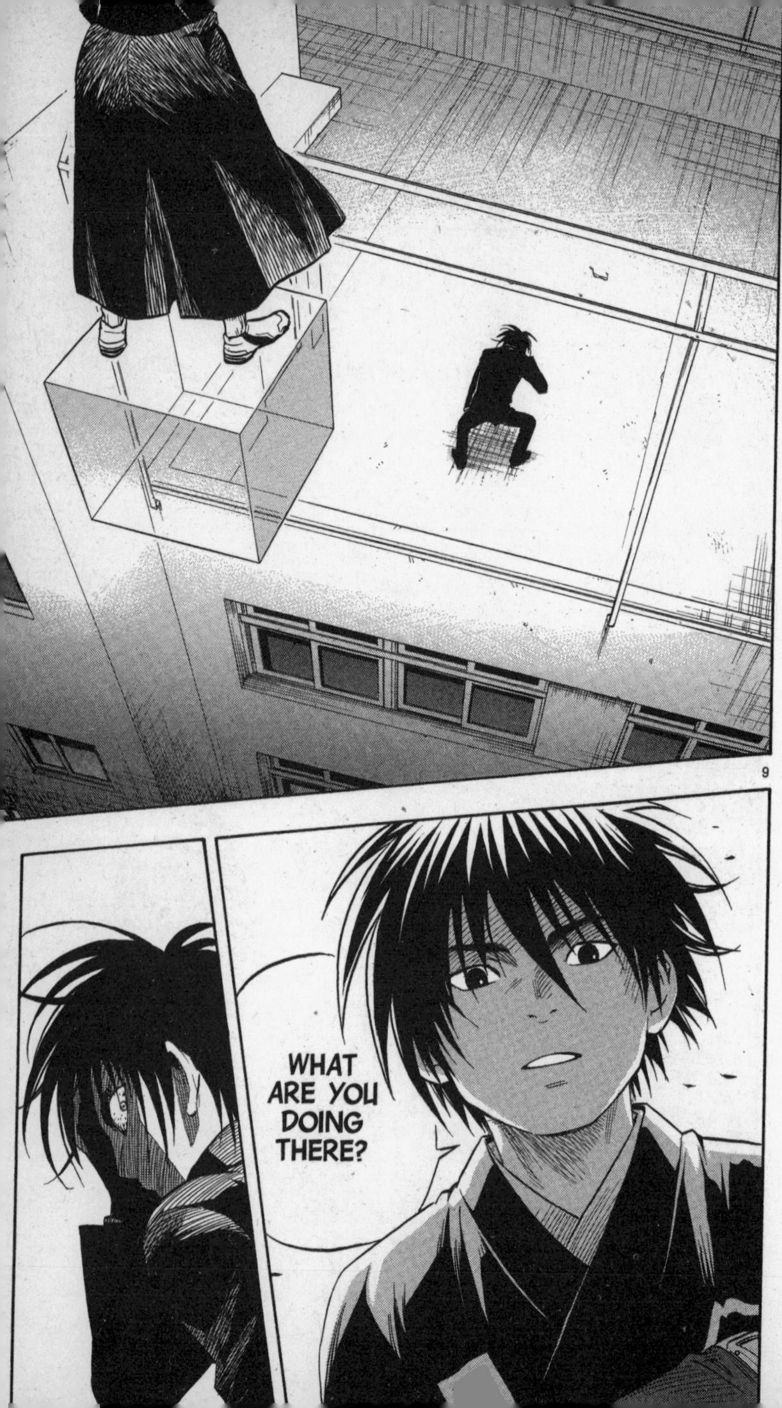
WHAT ARE YOU DOING THERE?

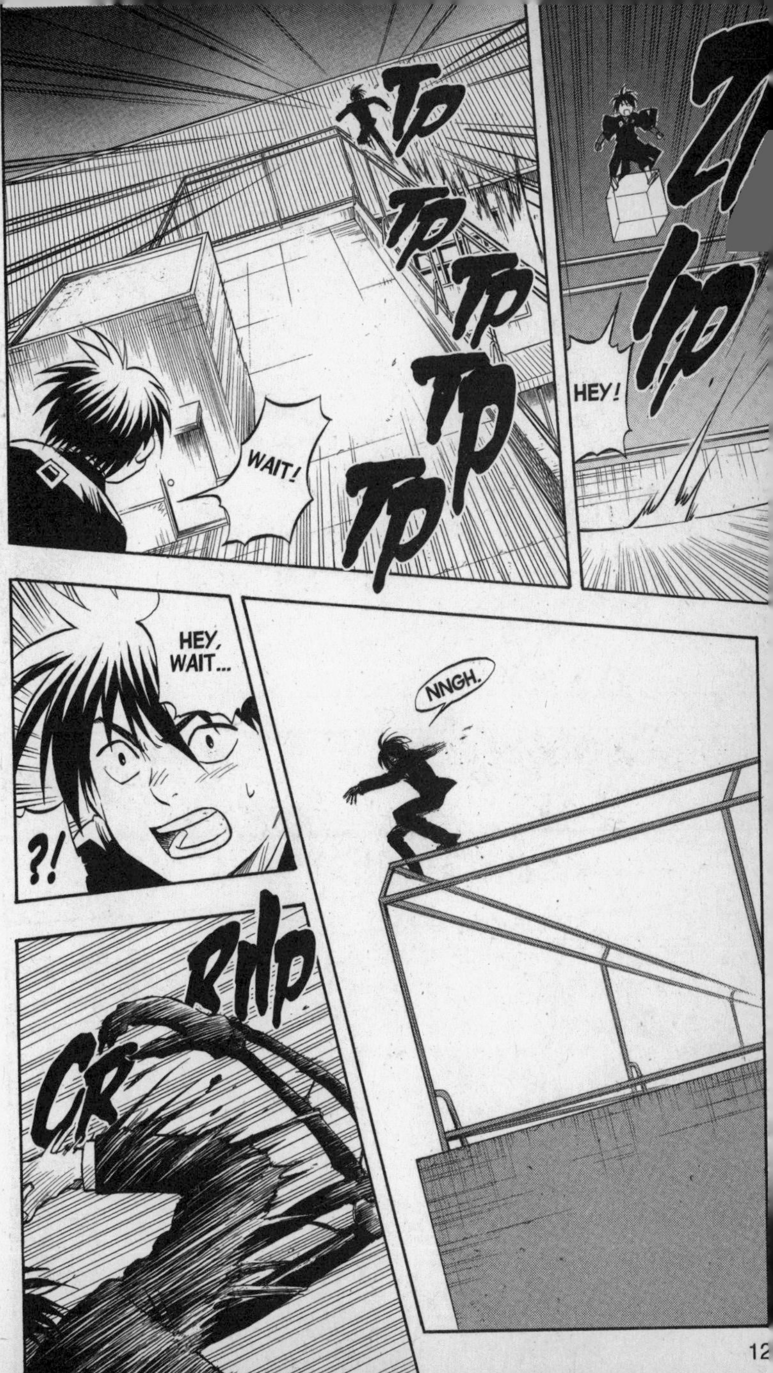
ZIP
HEY!
TP
TP
TP
TP
TP
WAIT!
NNGH.
HEY, WAIT...
?!
RIP
CR

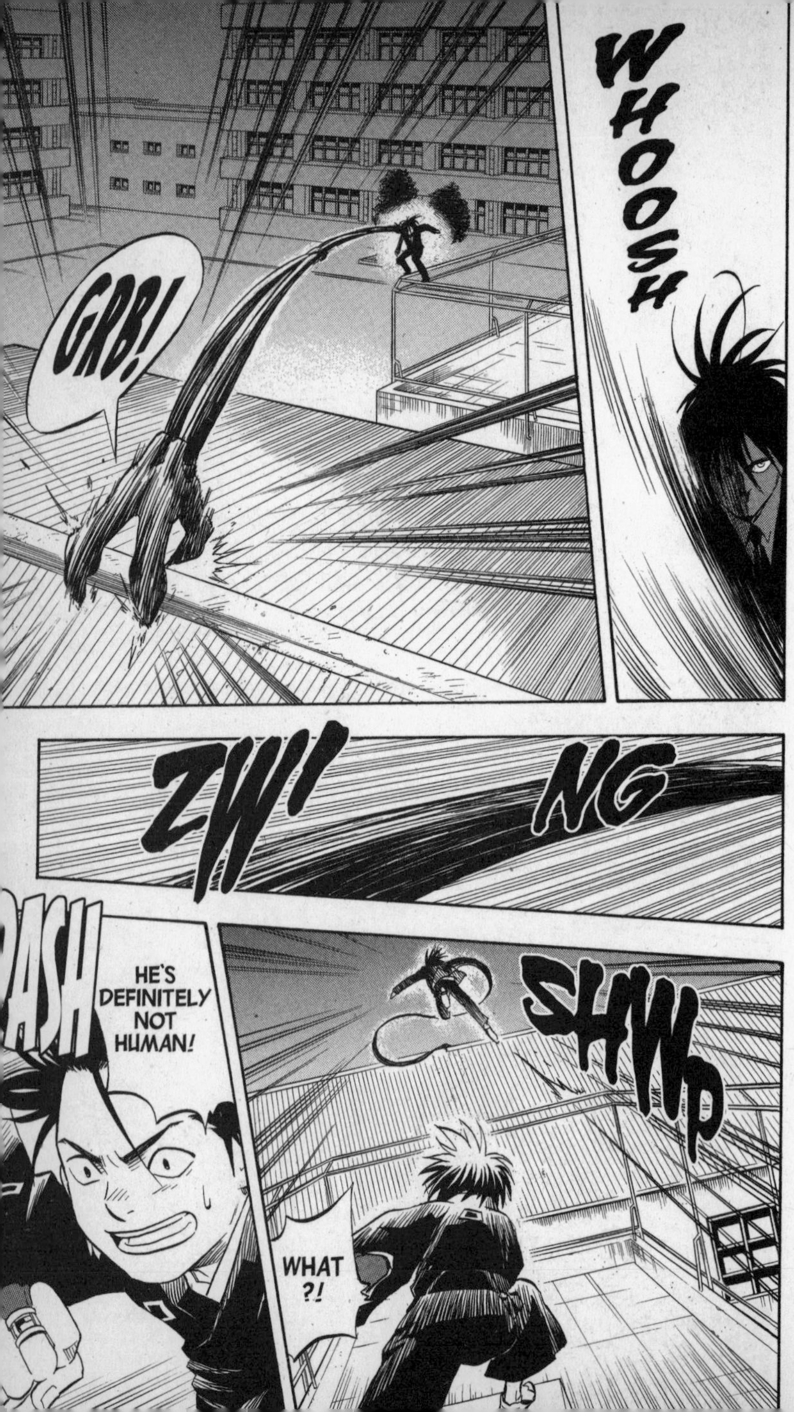
WHOOSH
GRB!
ZWING
SHWIP
WHAT ?!
ASH
HE'S DEFINITELY NOT HUMAN!

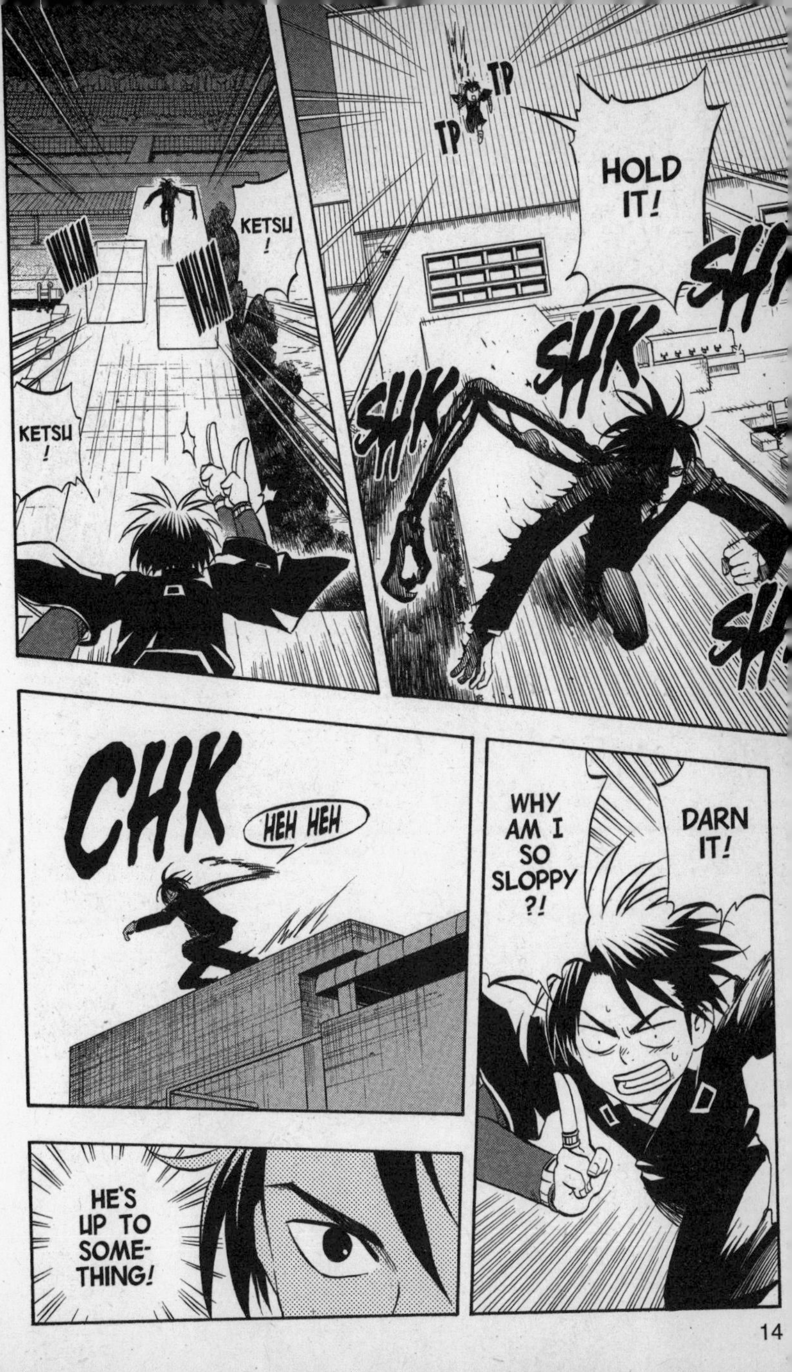
HOLD IT!
TP
TP
SHK
SHK
KETSU!
KETSU!
DARN IT!
WHY AM I SO SLOPPY?!
CHK
HEH HEH
HE'S UP TO SOME-THING!

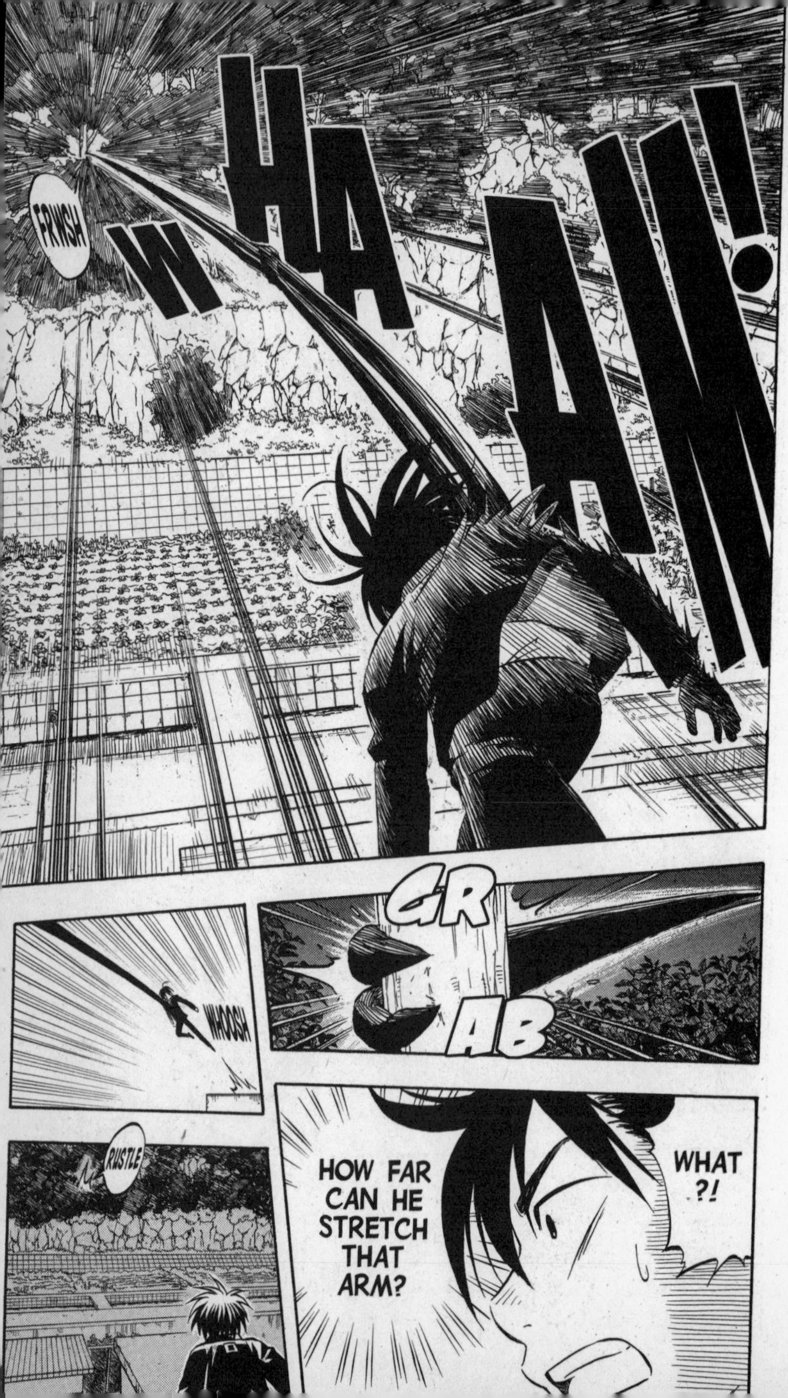

WHAAAN!
FRWSH
GRAB
WHOOSH
WHAT?!
HOW FAR CAN HE STRETCH THAT ARM?
RUSTLE

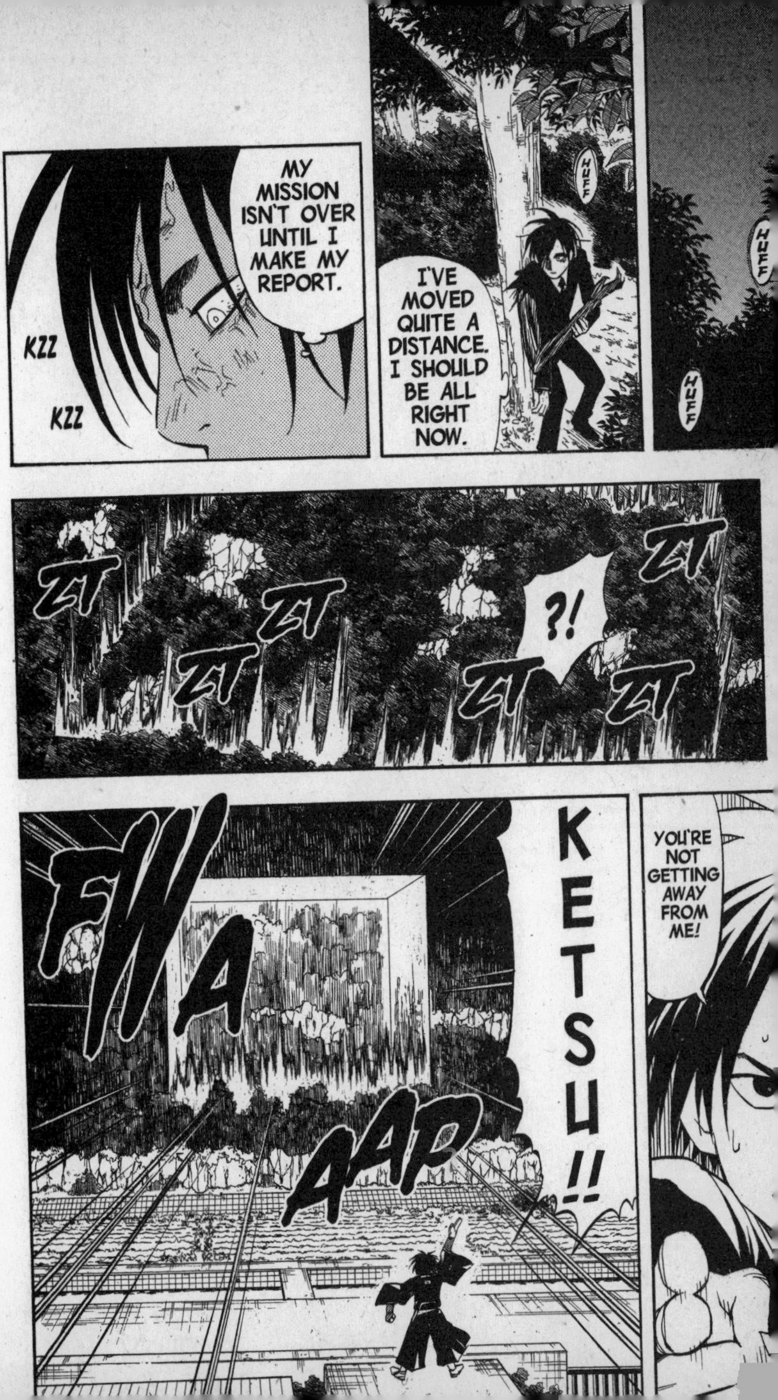
HUFF
HUFF
HUFF
I'VE MOVED QUITE A DISTANCE. I SHOULD BE ALL RIGHT NOW.
MY MISSION ISN'T OVER UNTIL I MAKE MY REPORT.
KZZ
KZZ
ZT
?!
ZT
ZT
ZT
ZT
ZT
YOU'RE NOT GETTING AWAY FROM ME!
KETSU!!
FWAAAP

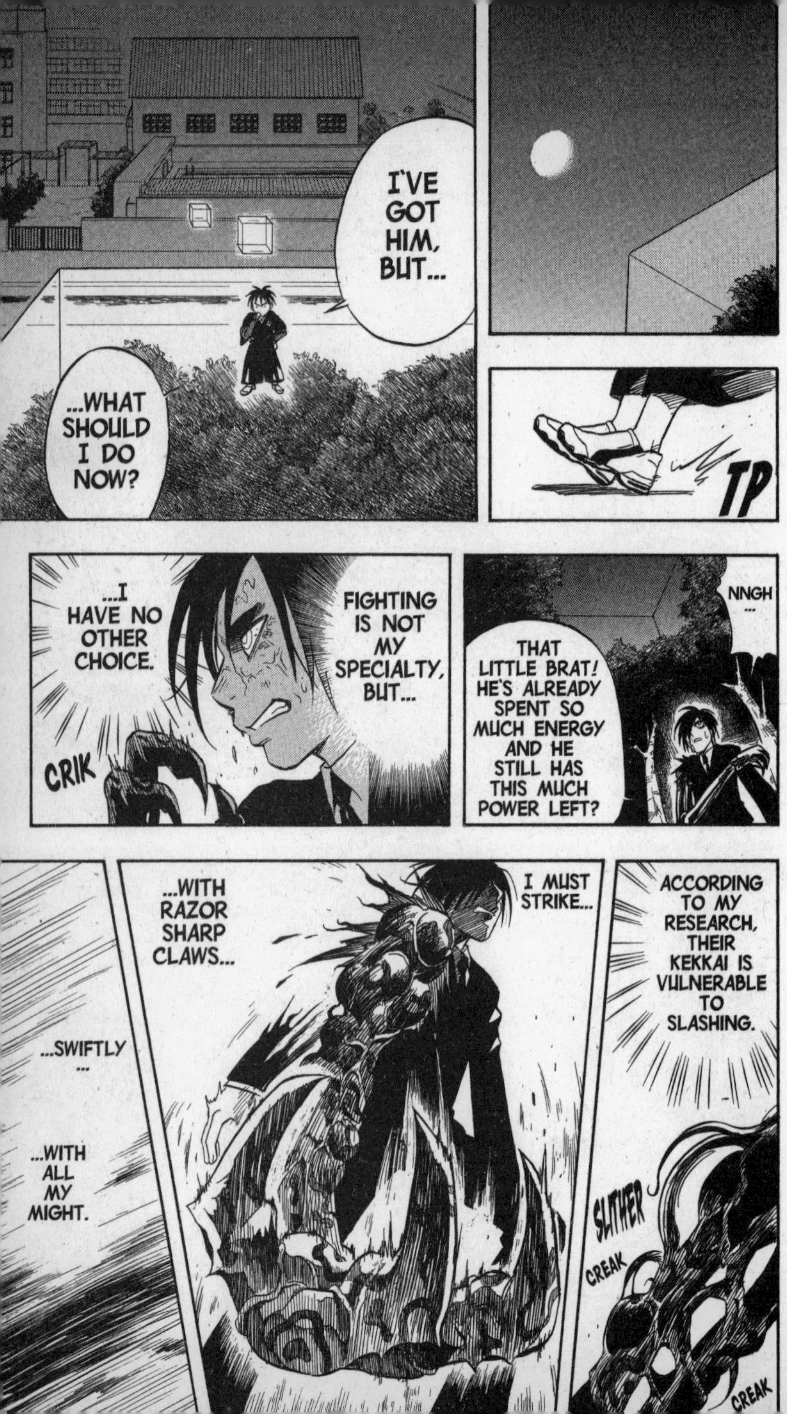
TP
I'VE GOT HIM, BUT...
...WHAT SHOULD I DO NOW?
NNGH ...
THAT LITTLE BRAT! HE'S ALREADY SPENT SO MUCH ENERGY AND HE STILL HAS THIS MUCH POWER LEFT?
FIGHTING IS NOT MY SPECIALTY, BUT...
...I HAVE NO OTHER CHOICE.
CRIK
ACCORDING TO MY RESEARCH, THEIR KEKKAI IS VULNERABLE TO SLASHING.
SLITHER
CREAK
CREAK
I MUST STRIKE...
...WITH RAZOR SHARP CLAWS...
...SWIFTLY ...
...WITH ALL MY MIGHT.

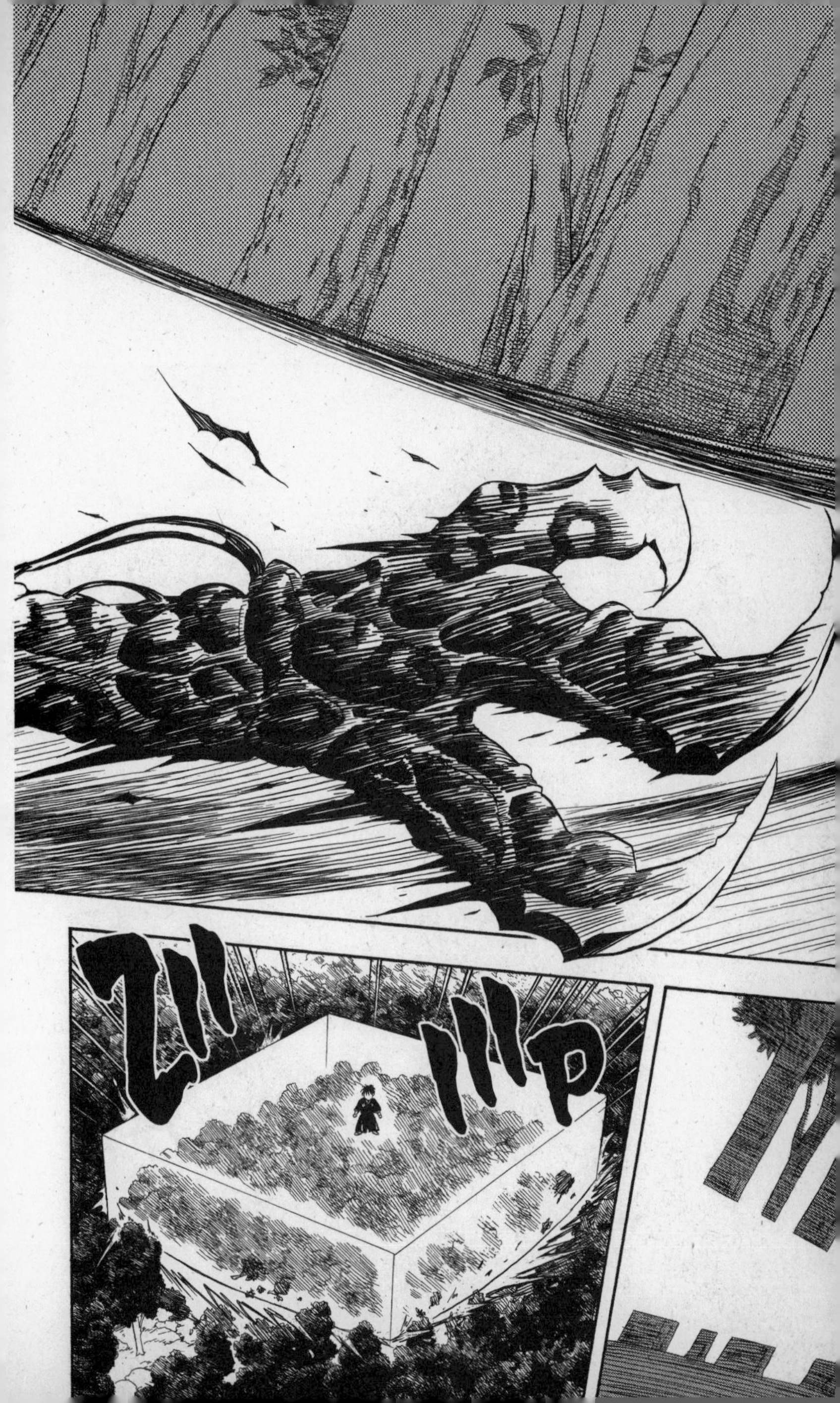
ZIIIIIP

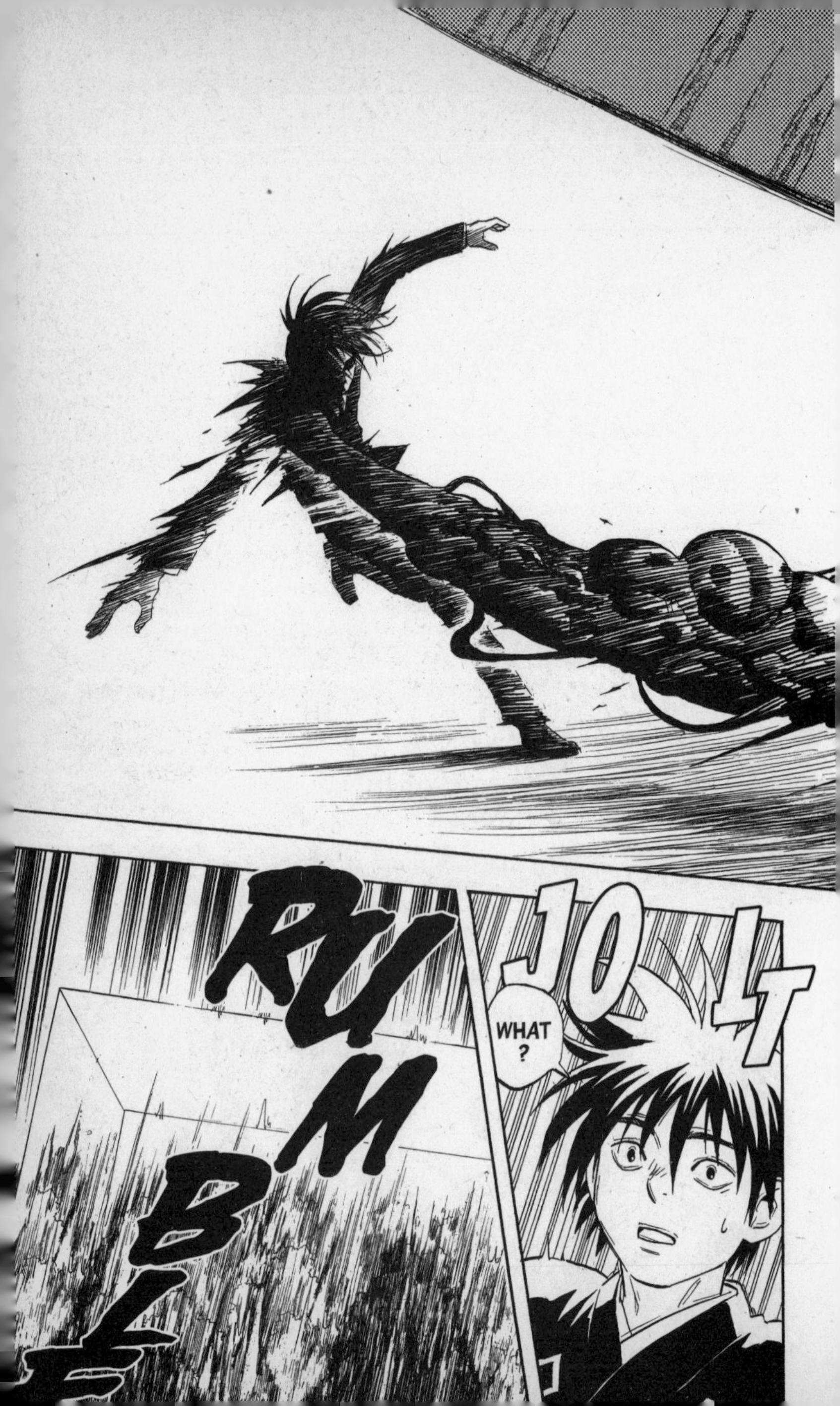
JOLT
WHAT?
RUMBLE

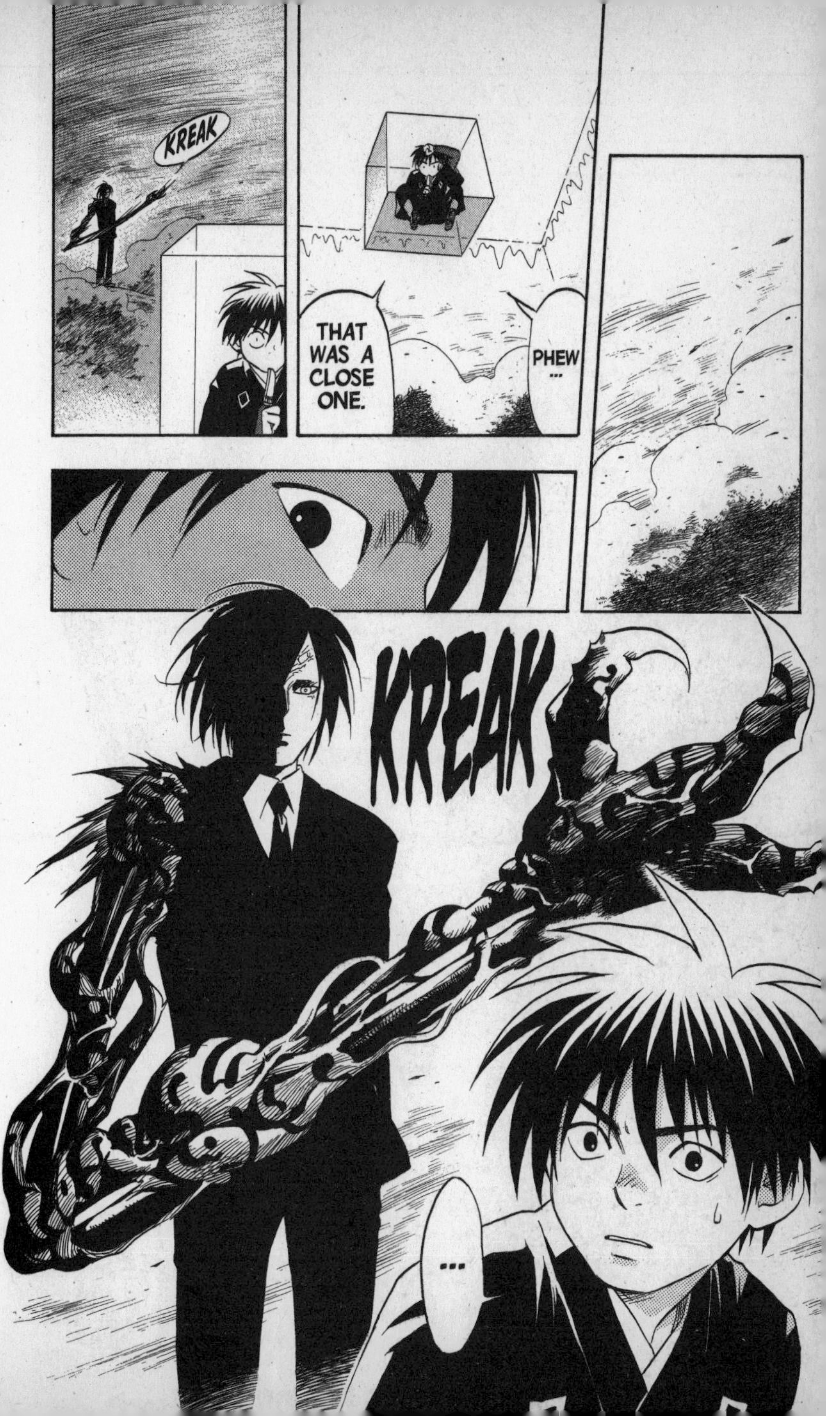
PHEW...
THAT WAS A CLOSE ONE.
KREAK
KREAK
...

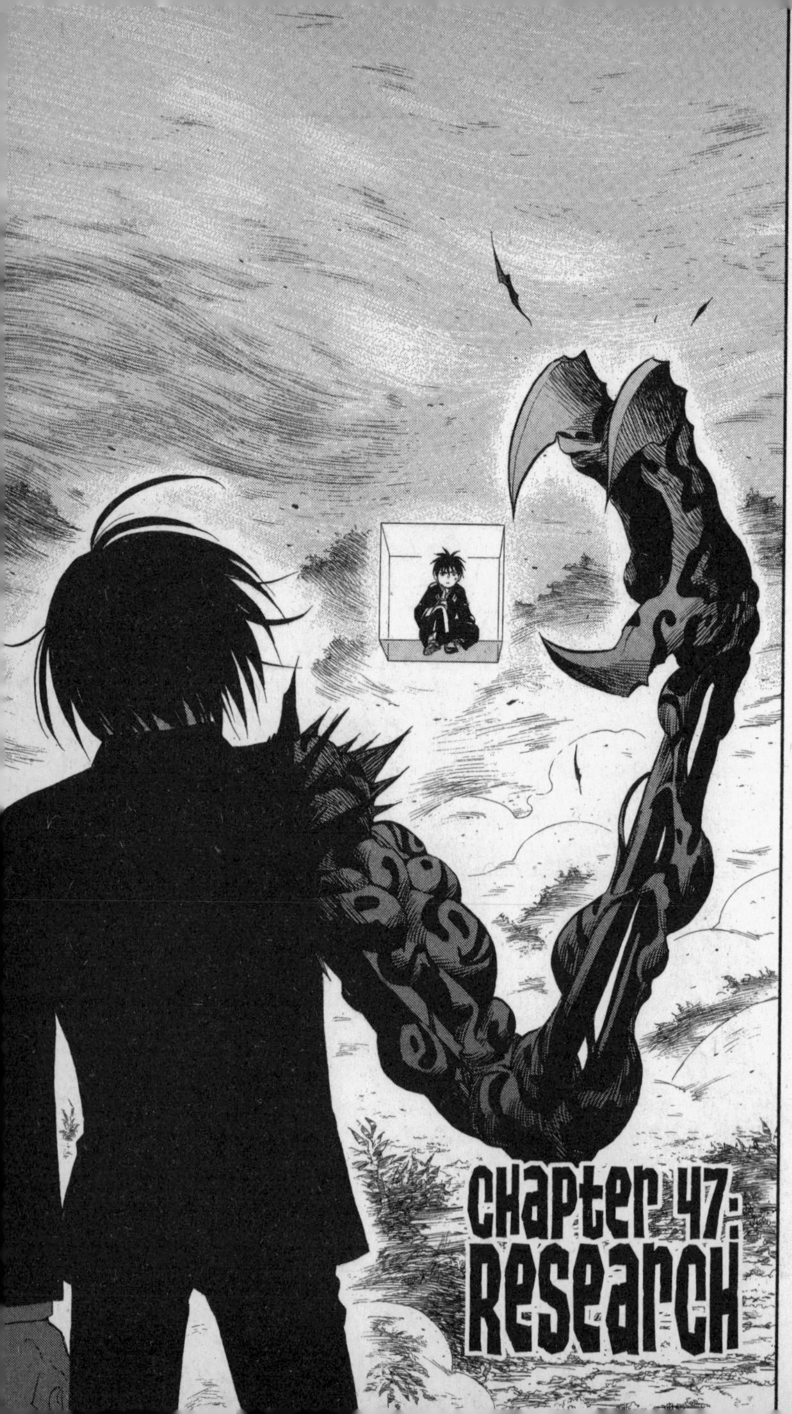
Chapter 47:
Research

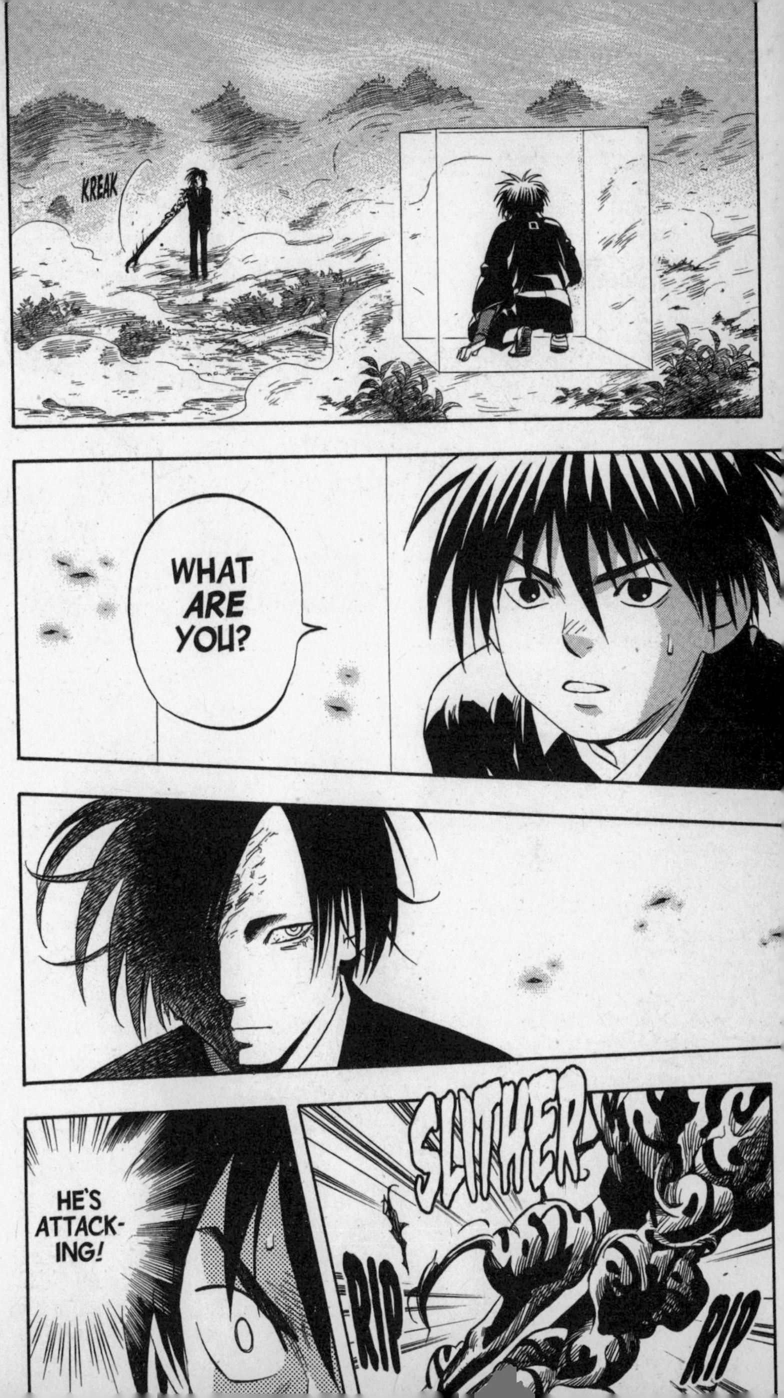
KREAK
WHAT ARE YOU?
SLITHER
RIP
RIP
HE'S ATTACK-ING!

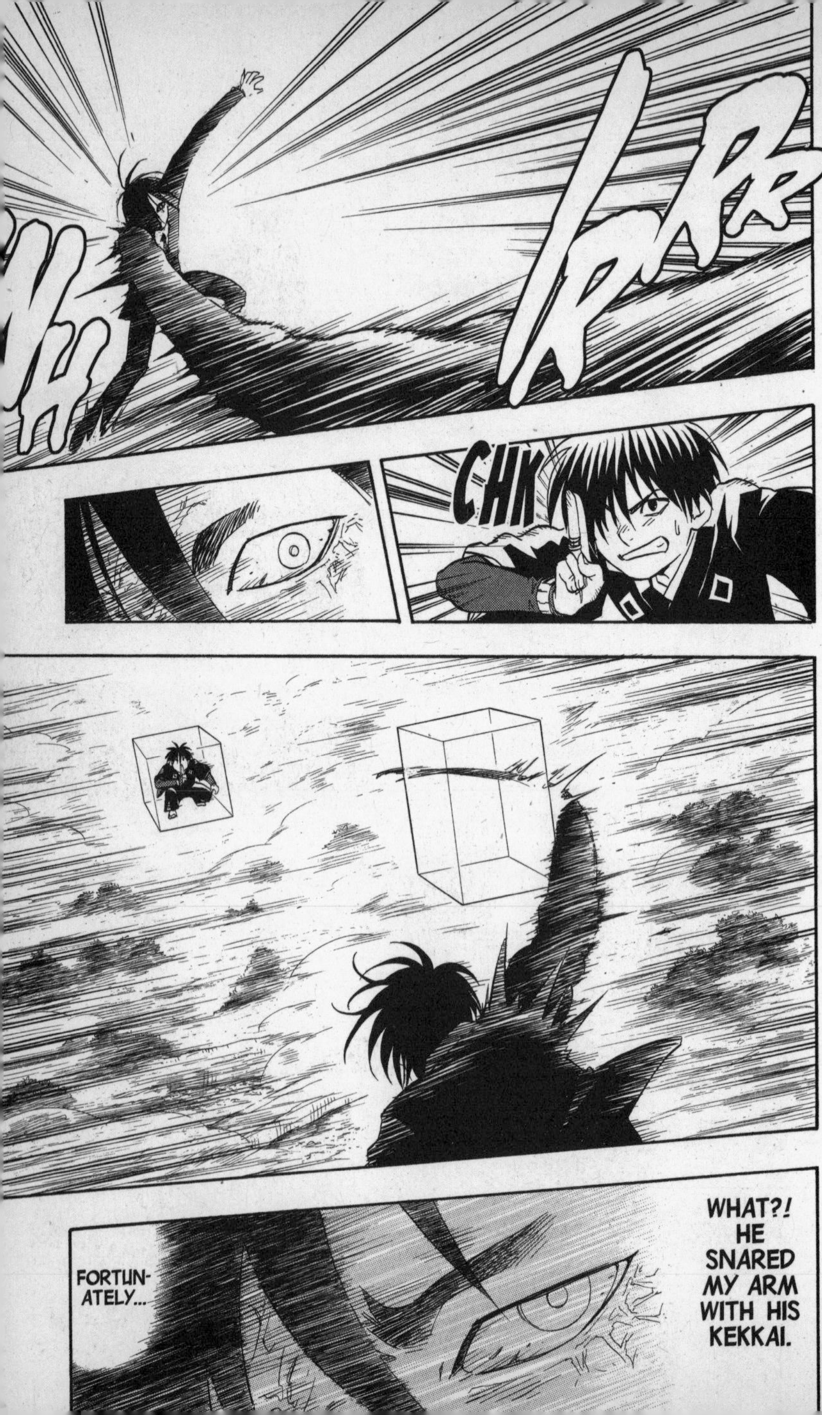
CHK
WHAT?! HE SNARED MY ARM WITH HIS KEKKAI.
FORTUN-ATELY...

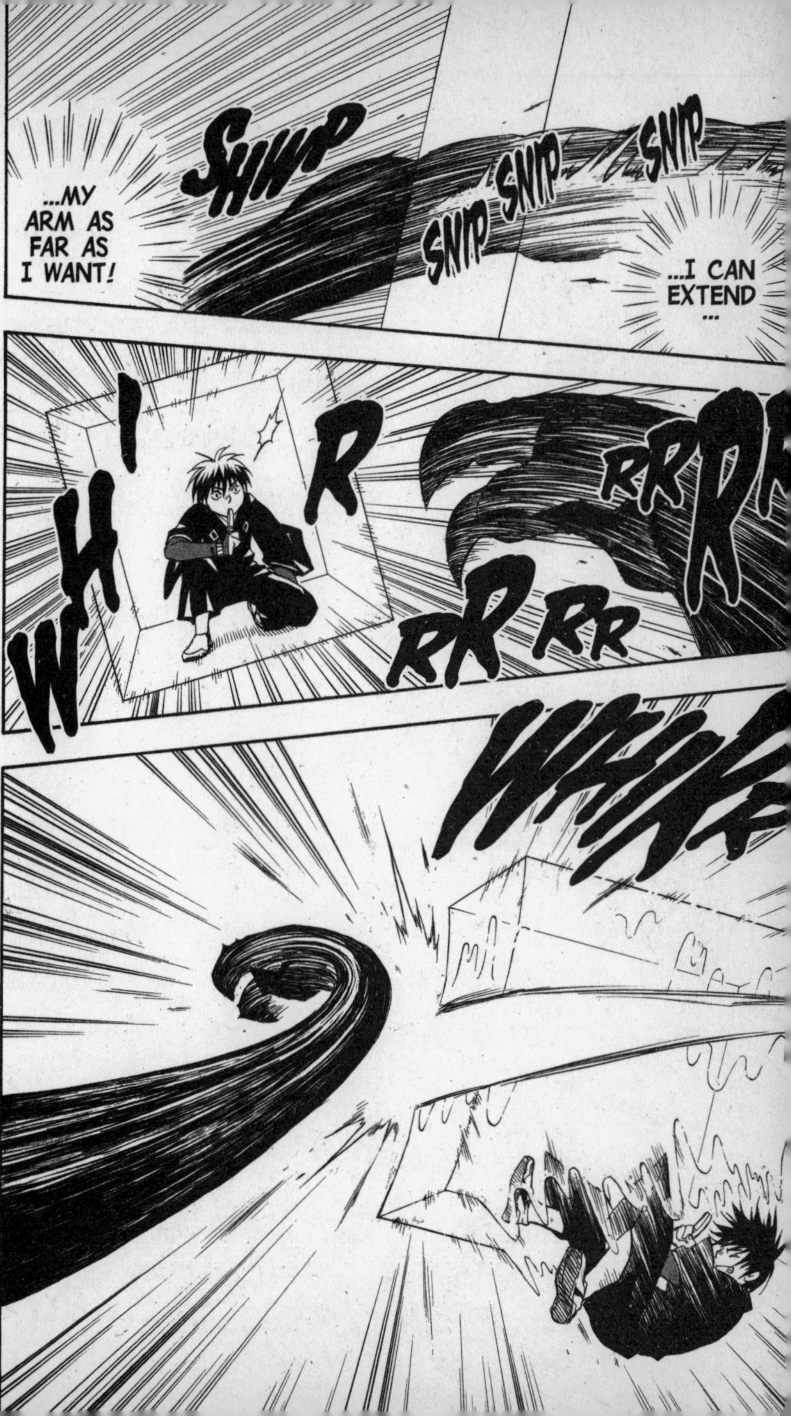

SNIP
...I CAN EXTEND ...
SNIP SNIP
SHWIP
...MY ARM AS FAR AS I WANT!
RRRR
RRRRR
WHIR
WHAK

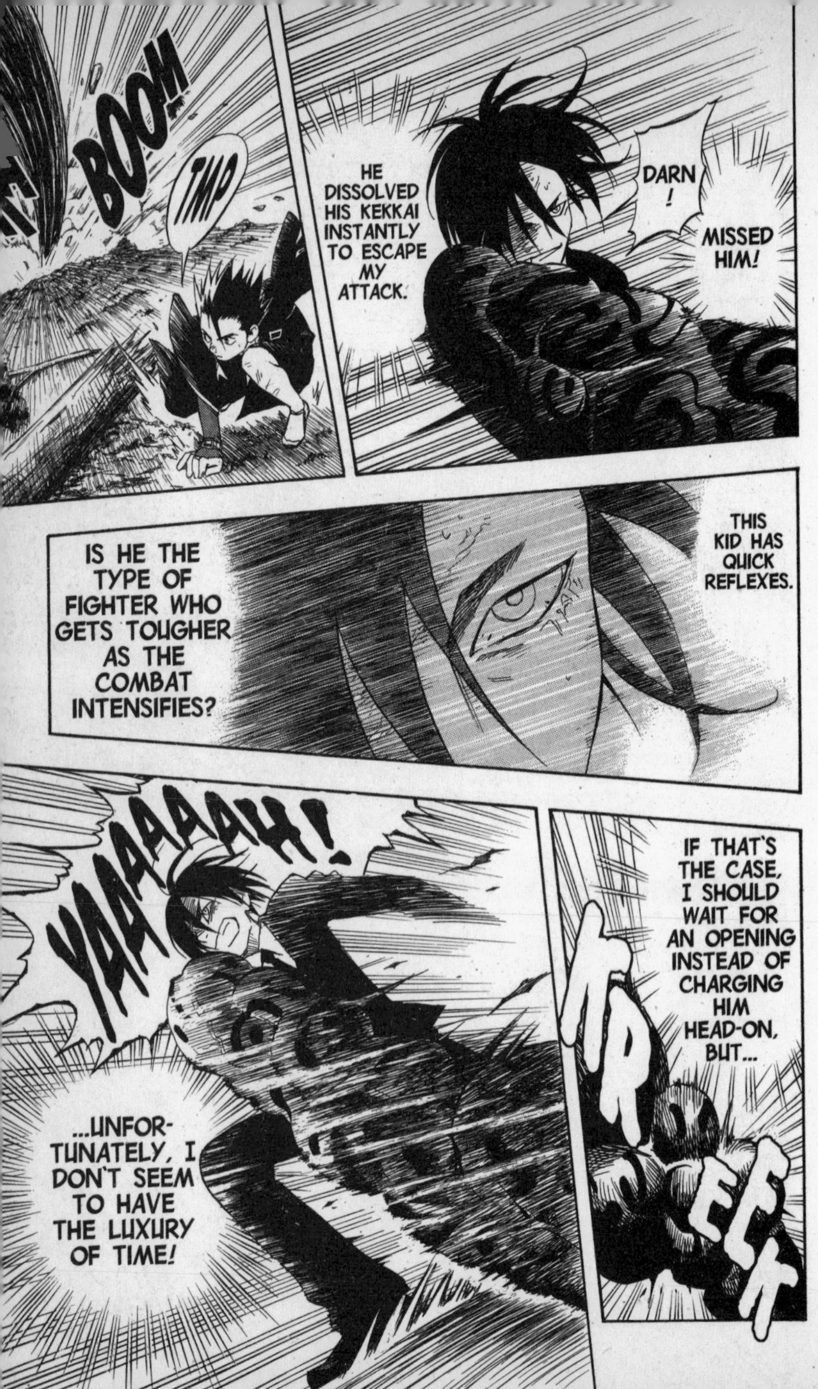
DARN!
MISSED HIM!
HE DISSOLVED HIS KEKKAI INSTANTLY TO ESCAPE MY ATTACK.
BOOM
TMP
THIS KID HAS QUICK REFLEXES.
IS HE THE TYPE OF FIGHTER WHO GETS TOUGHER AS THE COMBAT INTENSIFIES?
IF THAT'S THE CASE, I SHOULD WAIT FOR AN OPENING INSTEAD OF CHARGING HIM HEAD-ON, BUT...
YAAAAAAH!
...UNFORTUNATELY, I DON'T SEEM TO HAVE THE LUXURY OF TIME!

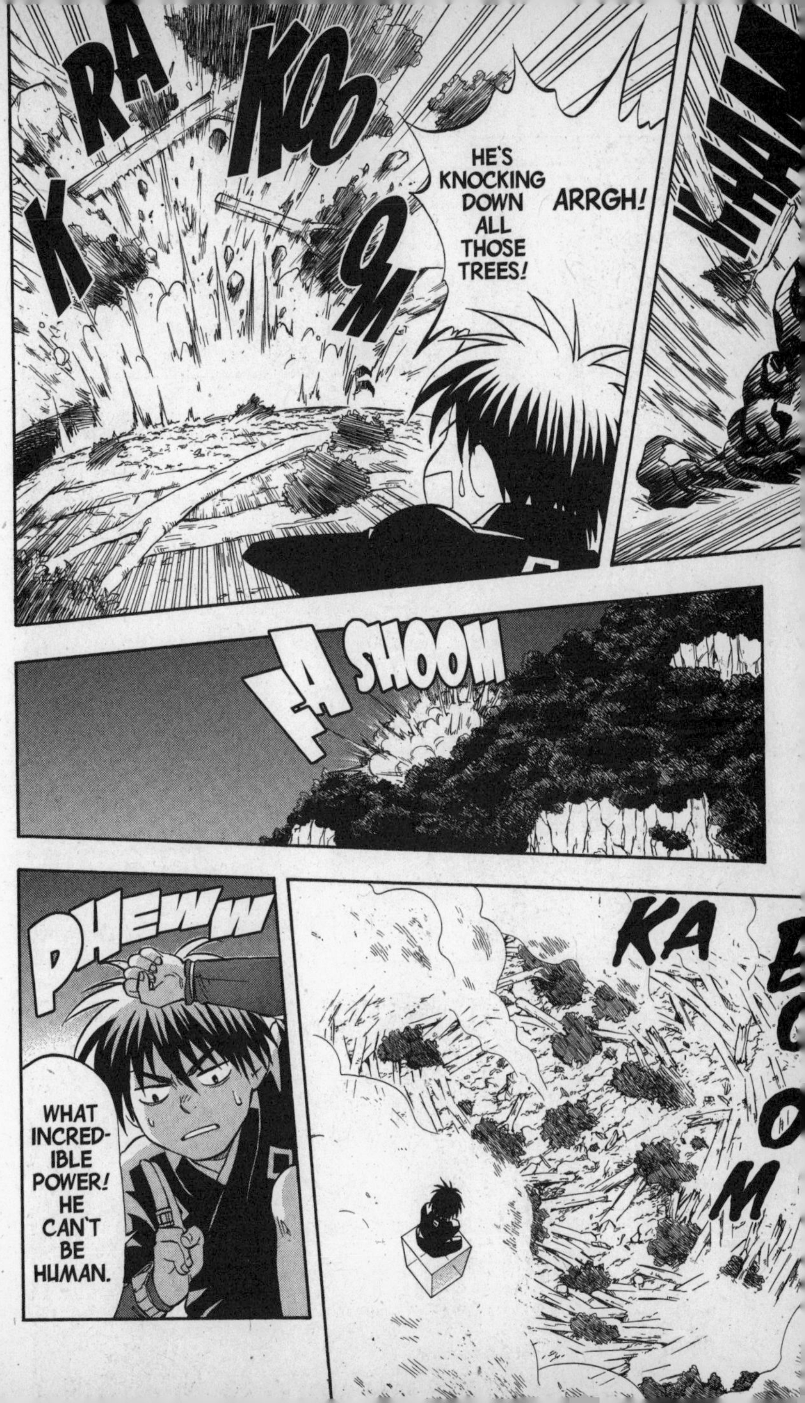

WHAM
KRAKOOOM
ARRGH!
HE'S KNOCKING DOWN ALL THOSE TREES!
FASHOOM
KA
PHEWW
WHAT INCRED-IBLE POWER! HE CAN'T BE HUMAN.

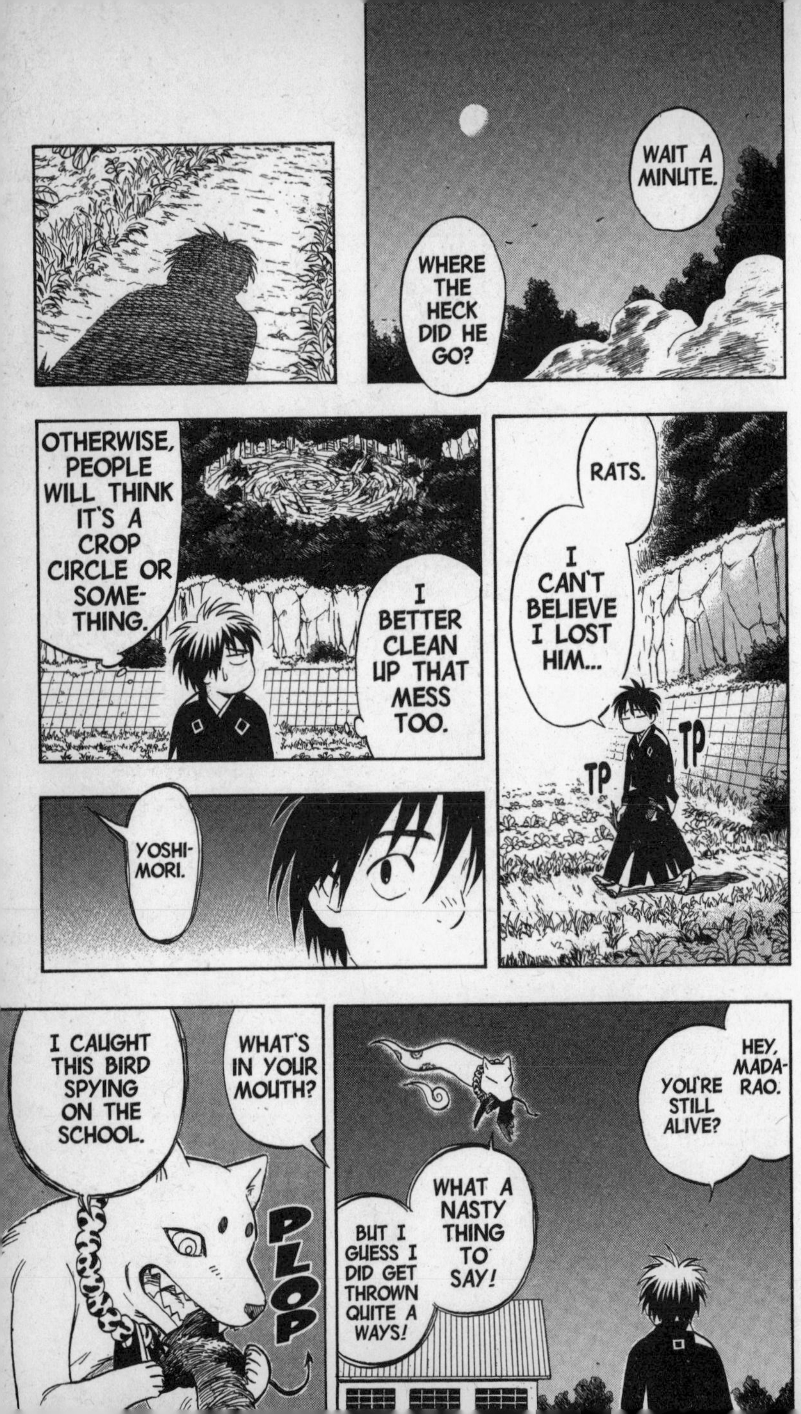
WAIT A MINUTE.
WHERE THE HECK DID HE GO?
RATS.
I CAN'T BELIEVE I LOST HIM...
TP
TP
I BETTER CLEAN UP THAT MESS TOO.
OTHERWISE, PEOPLE WILL THINK IT'S A CROP CIRCLE OR SOME-THING.
YOSHI-MORI.
HEY, MADA-RAO.
YOU'RE STILL ALIVE?
WHAT A NASTY THING TO SAY!
BUT I GUESS I DID GET THROWN QUITE A WAYS!
WHAT'S IN YOUR MOUTH?
I CAUGHT THIS BIRD SPYING ON THE SCHOOL.
PLOP

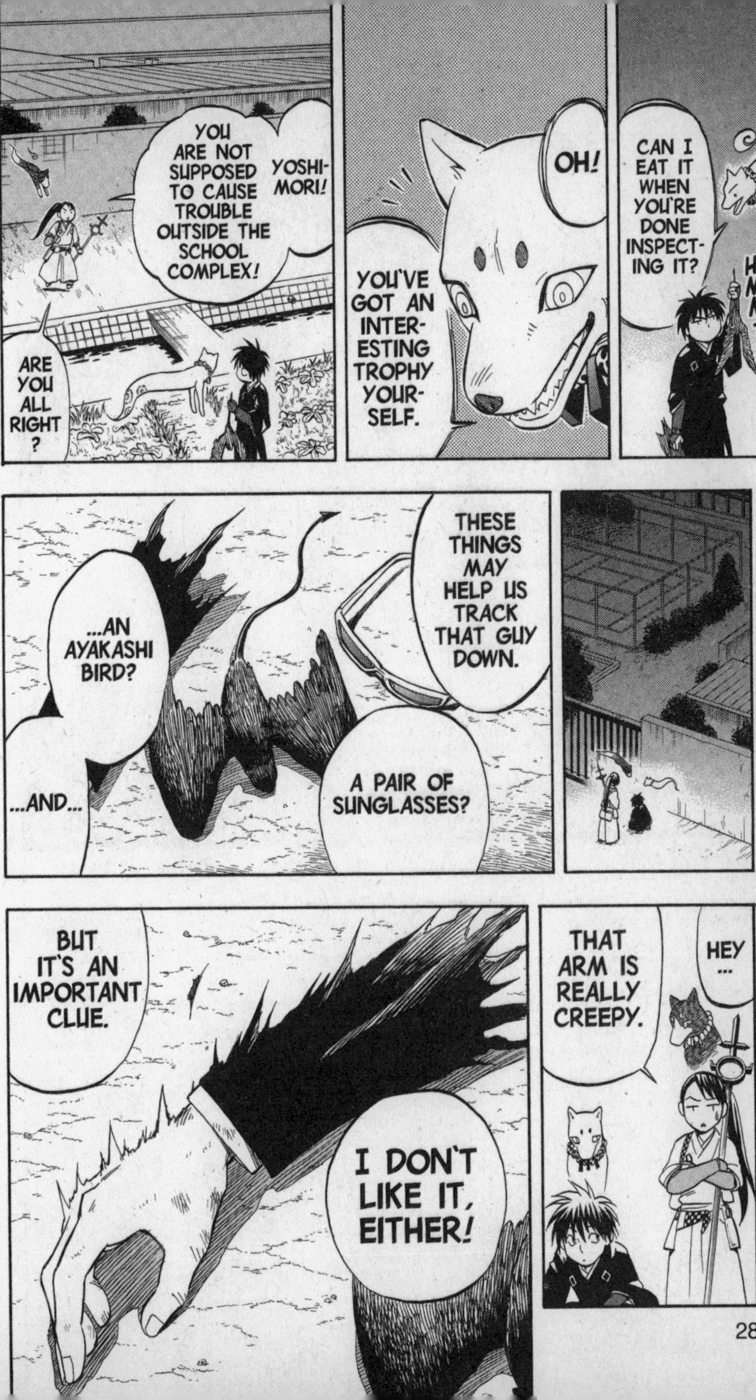
CAN I EAT IT WHEN YOU'RE DONE INSPECTING IT?
HMM...
OH!
YOU'VE GOT AN INTERESTING TROPHY YOURSELF.
YOSHIMORI!
YOU ARE NOT SUPPOSED TO CAUSE TROUBLE OUTSIDE THE SCHOOL COMPLEX!
ARE YOU ALL RIGHT?
THESE THINGS MAY HELP US TRACK THAT GUY DOWN.
...AN AYAKASHI BIRD?
...AND...
A PAIR OF SUNGLASSES?
HEY...
THAT ARM IS REALLY CREEPY.
BUT IT'S AN IMPORTANT CLUE.
I DON'T LIKE IT, EITHER!

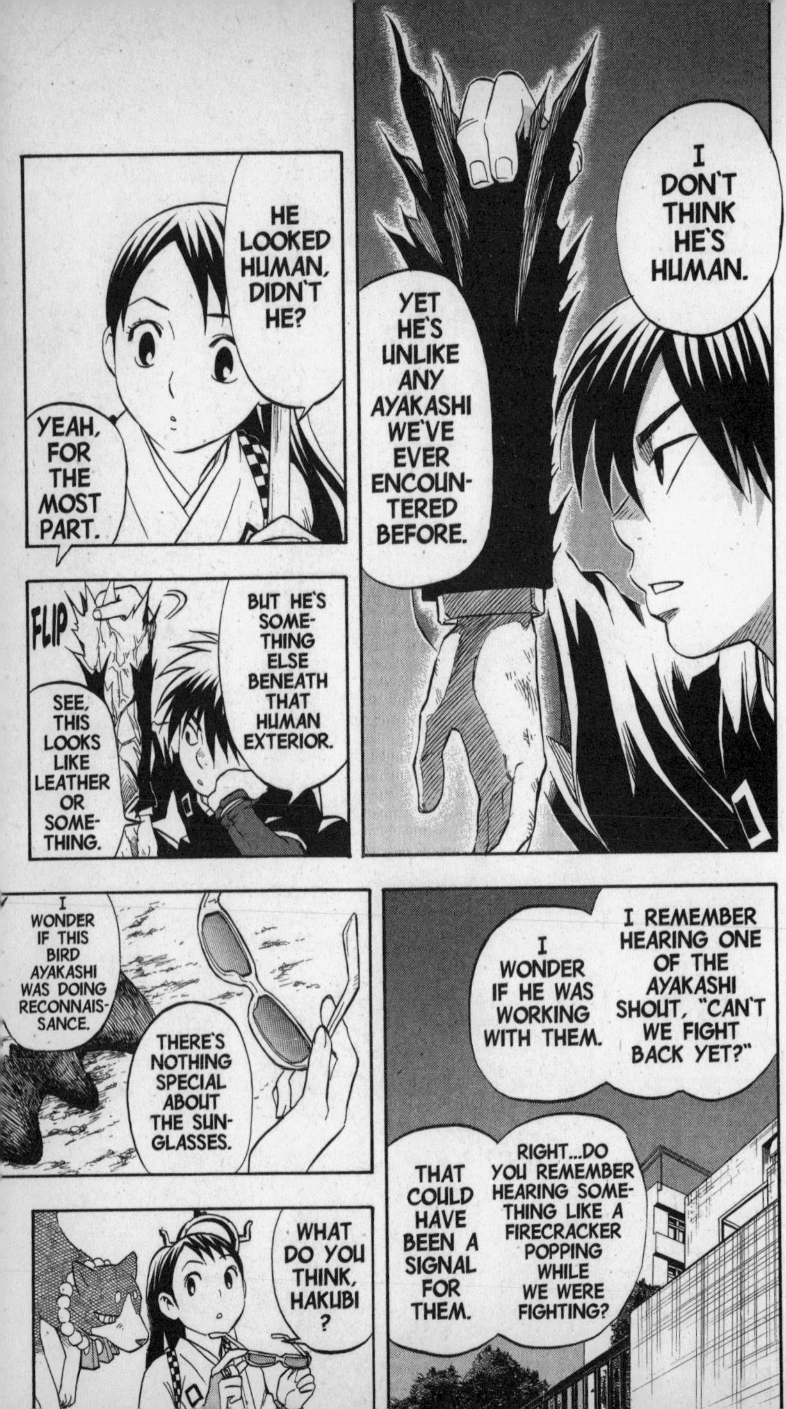

I DON'T THINK HE'S HUMAN.
YET HE'S UNLIKE ANY AYAKASHI WE'VE EVER ENCOUNTERED BEFORE.
HE LOOKED HUMAN, DIDN'T HE?
YEAH, FOR THE MOST PART.
FLIP
BUT HE'S SOMETHING ELSE BENEATH THAT HUMAN EXTERIOR.
SEE, THIS LOOKS LIKE LEATHER OR SOMETHING.
I REMEMBER HEARING ONE OF THE AYAKASHI SHOUT, "CAN'T WE FIGHT BACK YET?"
I WONDER IF HE WAS WORKING WITH THEM.
RIGHT...DO YOU REMEMBER HEARING SOMETHING LIKE A FIRECRACKER POPPING WHILE WE WERE FIGHTING?
THAT COULD HAVE BEEN A SIGNAL FOR THEM.
I WONDER IF THIS BIRD AYAKASHI WAS DOING RECONNAISSANCE.
THERE'S NOTHING SPECIAL ABOUT THE SUNGLASSES.
WHAT DO YOU THINK, HAKUBI?

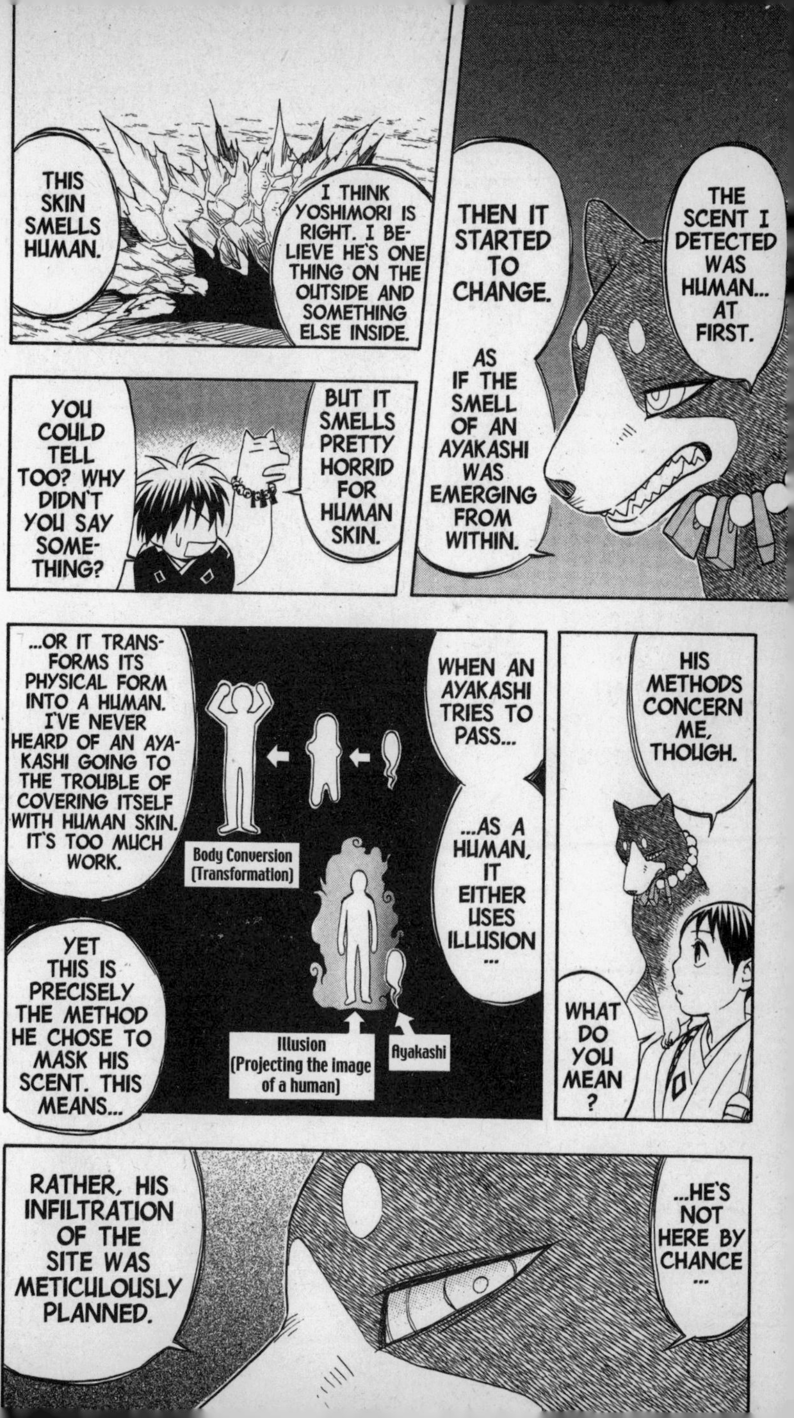
THE SCENT I DETECTED WAS HUMAN... AT FIRST.
THEN IT STARTED TO CHANGE.
AS IF THE SMELL OF AN AYAKASHI WAS EMERGING FROM WITHIN.
I THINK YOSHIMORI IS RIGHT. I BELIEVE HE'S ONE THING ON THE OUTSIDE AND SOMETHING ELSE INSIDE.
THIS SKIN SMELLS HUMAN.
BUT IT SMELLS PRETTY HORRID FOR HUMAN SKIN.
YOU COULD TELL TOO? WHY DIDN'T YOU SAY SOMETHING?
HIS METHODS CONCERN ME, THOUGH.
WHAT DO YOU MEAN?
WHEN AN AYAKASHI TRIES TO PASS...
...AS A HUMAN, IT EITHER USES ILLUSION...
...OR IT TRANSFORMS ITS PHYSICAL FORM INTO A HUMAN. I'VE NEVER HEARD OF AN AYAKASHI GOING TO THE TROUBLE OF COVERING ITSELF WITH HUMAN SKIN. IT'S TOO MUCH WORK.
Body Conversion (Transformation)
Illusion (Projecting the image of a human)
Ayakashi
YET THIS IS PRECISELY THE METHOD HE CHOSE TO MASK HIS SCENT. THIS MEANS...
...HE'S NOT HERE BY CHANCE...
RATHER, HIS INFILTRATION OF THE SITE WAS METICULOUSLY PLANNED.

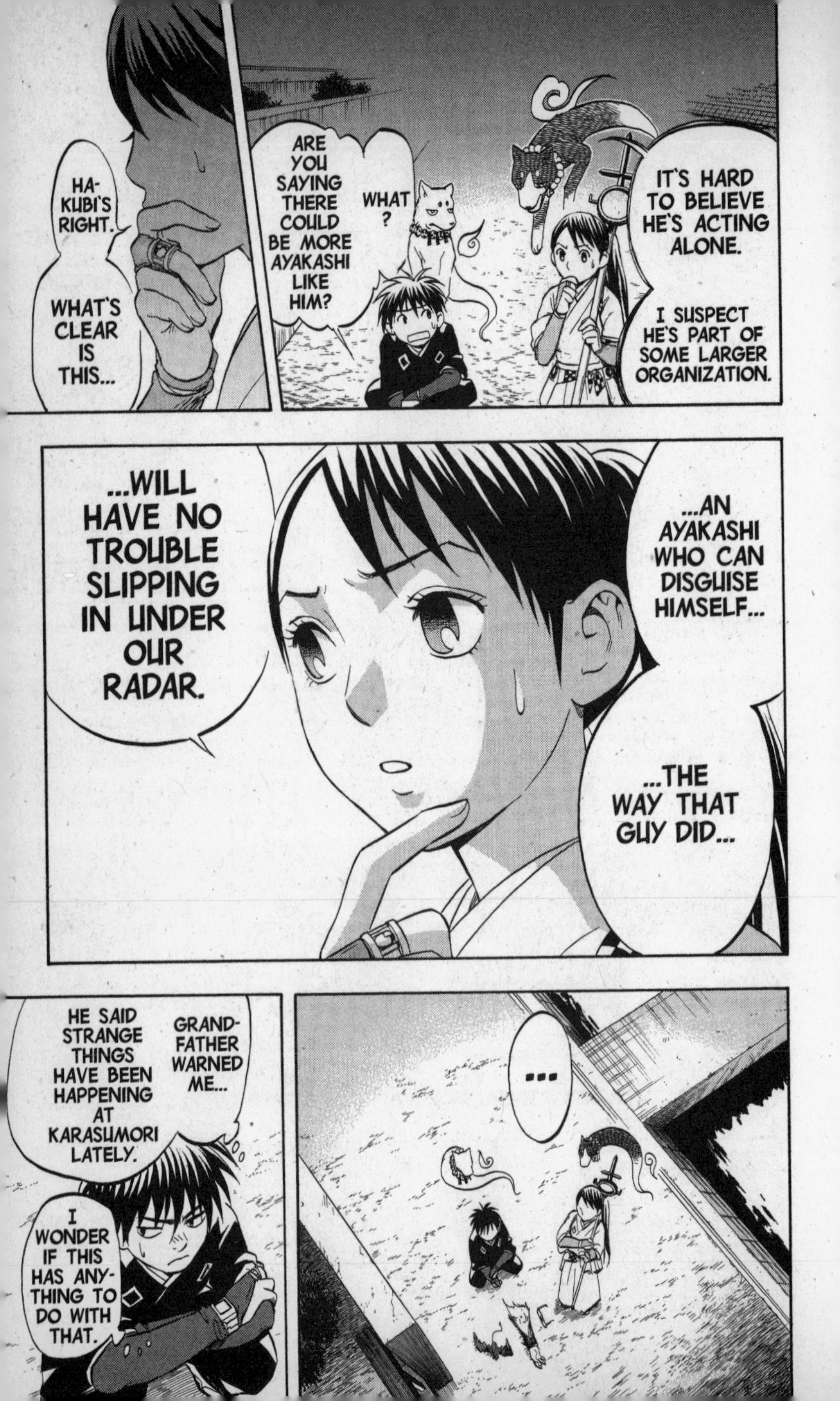
IT'S HARD TO BELIEVE HE'S ACTING ALONE.
I SUSPECT HE'S PART OF SOME LARGER ORGANIZATION.
WHAT?
ARE YOU SAYING THERE COULD BE MORE AYAKASHI LIKE HIM?
HAKUBI'S RIGHT.
WHAT'S CLEAR IS THIS...
...AN AYAKASHI WHO CAN DISGUISE HIMSELF...
...THE WAY THAT GUY DID...
...WILL HAVE NO TROUBLE SLIPPING IN UNDER OUR RADAR.
...
GRAND-FATHER WARNED ME...
HE SAID STRANGE THINGS HAVE BEEN HAPPENING AT KARASUMORI LATELY.
I WONDER IF THIS HAS ANY-THING TO DO WITH THAT.

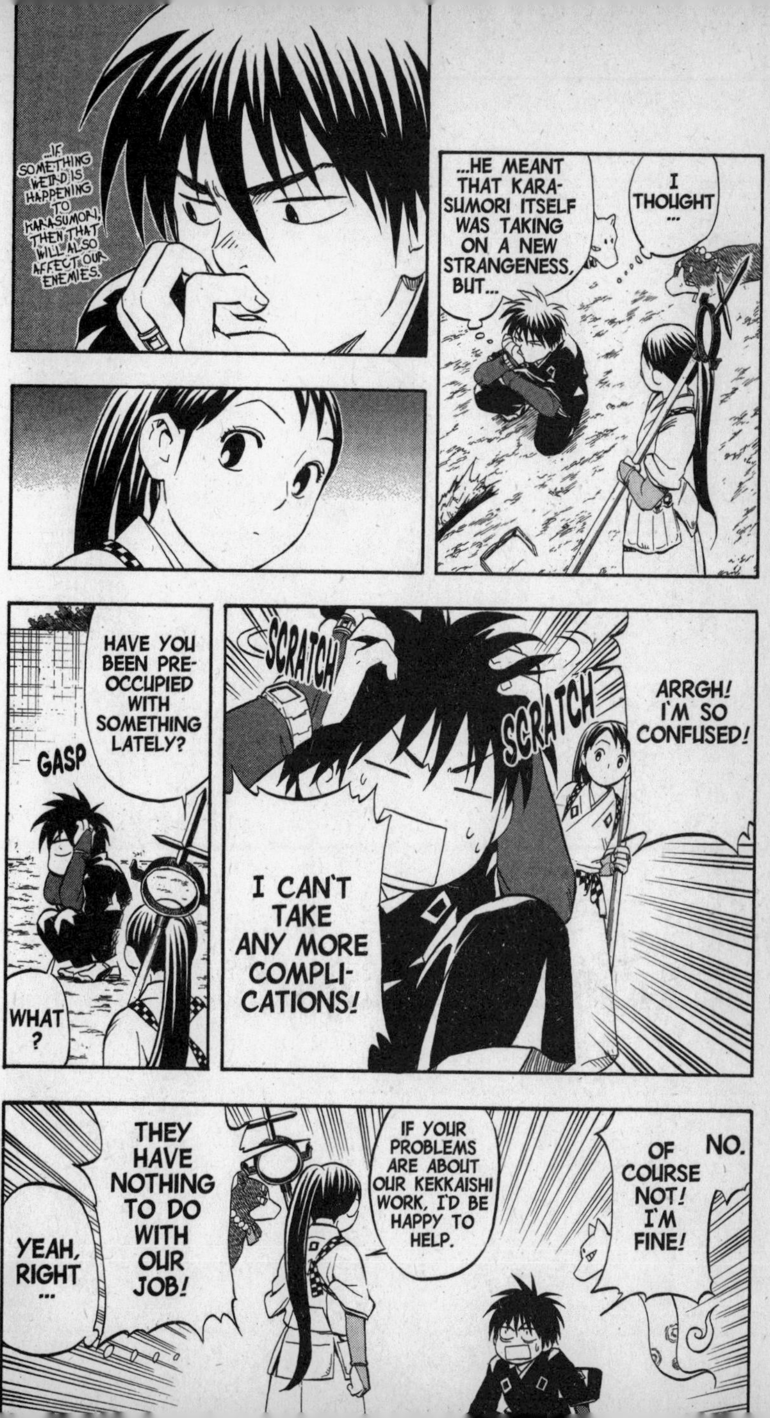
I THOUGHT...
...HE MEANT THAT KARA-SUMORI ITSELF WAS TAKING ON A NEW STRANGENESS, BUT...
...IF SOMETHING WEIRD IS HAPPENING TO KARASUMORI, THEN THAT WILL ALSO AFFECT OUR ENEMIES.
SCRATCH
SCRATCH
ARRGH! I'M SO CONFUSED!
I CAN'T TAKE ANY MORE COMPLI-CATIONS!
HAVE YOU BEEN PRE-OCCUPIED WITH SOMETHING LATELY?
GASP
WHAT?
NO.
OF COURSE NOT! I'M FINE!
IF YOUR PROBLEMS ARE ABOUT OUR KEKKAISHI WORK, I'D BE HAPPY TO HELP.
THEY HAVE NOTHING TO DO WITH OUR JOB!
YEAH, RIGHT...

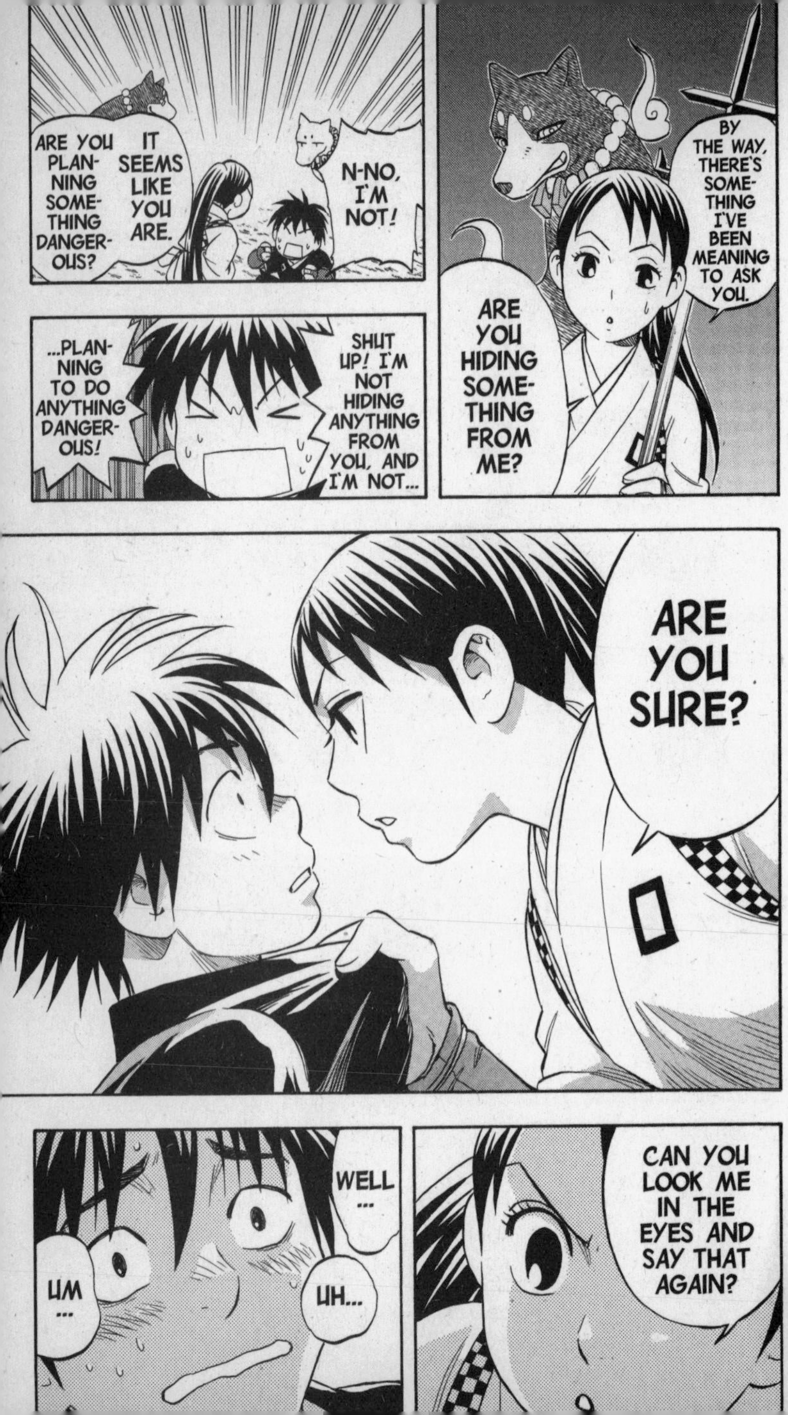
BY THE WAY, THERE'S SOMETHING I'VE BEEN MEANING TO ASK YOU.
ARE YOU HIDING SOMETHING FROM ME?
N-NO, I'M NOT!
IT SEEMS LIKE YOU ARE.
ARE YOU PLANNING SOMETHING DANGEROUS?
SHUT UP! I'M NOT HIDING ANYTHING FROM YOU, AND I'M NOT...
...PLANNING TO DO ANYTHING DANGEROUS!
ARE YOU SURE?
CAN YOU LOOK ME IN THE EYES AND SAY THAT AGAIN?
WELL...
UH...
UM...

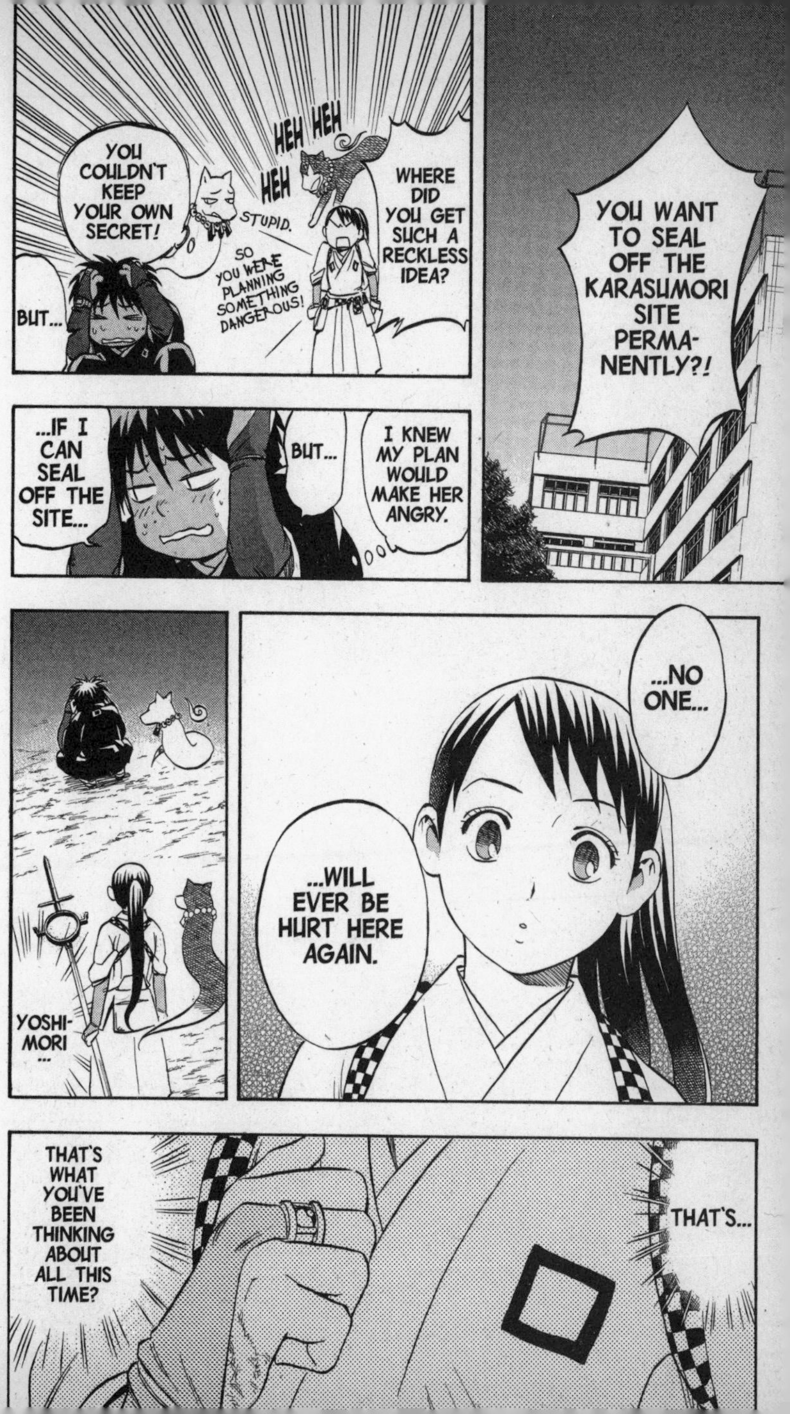
YOU WANT TO SEAL OFF THE KARASUMORI SITE PERMA-NENTLY?!
WHERE DID YOU GET SUCH A RECKLESS IDEA?
HEH HEH HEH
STUPID.
SO YOU WERE PLANNING SOMETHING DANGEROUS!
YOU COULDN'T KEEP YOUR OWN SECRET!
BUT...
I KNEW MY PLAN WOULD MAKE HER ANGRY.
BUT...
...IF I CAN SEAL OFF THE SITE...
...NO ONE...
...WILL EVER BE HURT HERE AGAIN.
YOSHI-MORI...
THAT'S...
THAT'S WHAT YOU'VE BEEN THINKING ABOUT ALL THIS TIME?

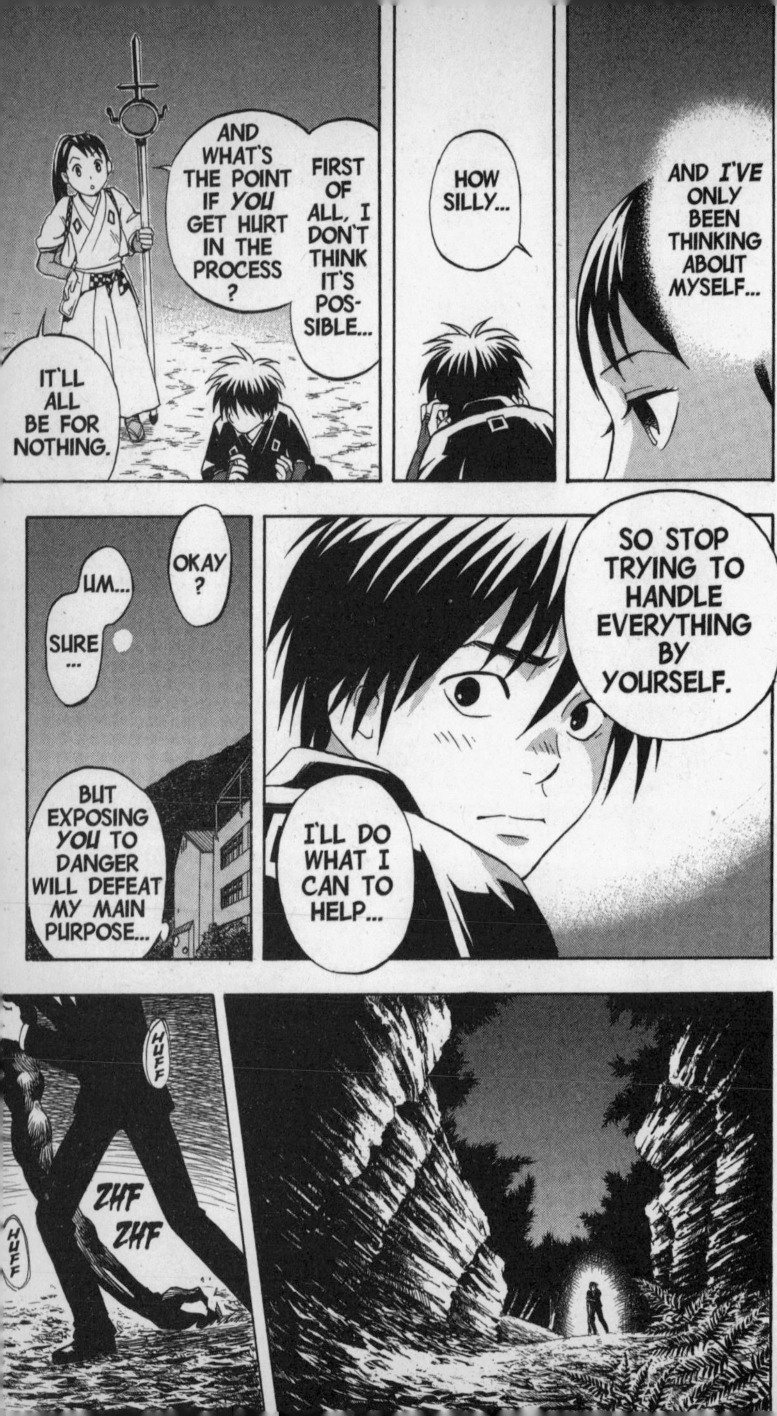
AND I'VE ONLY BEEN THINKING ABOUT MYSELF...
HOW SILLY...
FIRST OF ALL, I DON'T THINK IT'S POS-SIBLE...
AND WHAT'S THE POINT IF YOU GET HURT IN THE PROCESS ?
IT'LL ALL BE FOR NOTHING.
SO STOP TRYING TO HANDLE EVERYTHING BY YOURSELF.
I'LL DO WHAT I CAN TO HELP...
OKAY ?
UM...
SURE ...
BUT EXPOSING YOU TO DANGER WILL DEFEAT MY MAIN PURPOSE...
HUFF
ZHF ZHF
HUFF

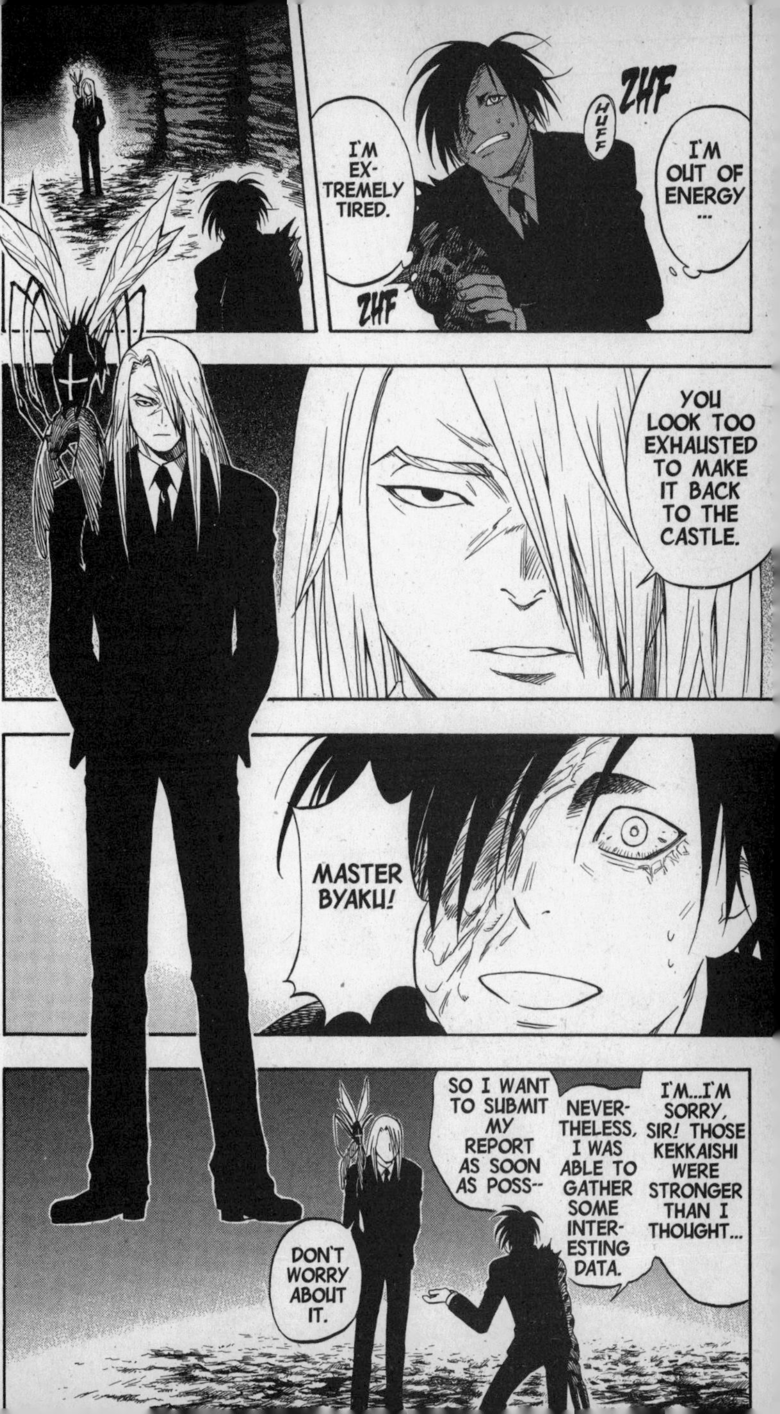
ZHF
I'M OUT OF ENERGY...
HUFF
I'M EX-TREMELY TIRED.
ZHF
YOU LOOK TOO EXHAUSTED TO MAKE IT BACK TO THE CASTLE.
MASTER BYAKU!
I'M...I'M SORRY, SIR! THOSE KEKKAISHI WERE STRONGER THAN I THOUGHT...
NEVER-THELESS, I WAS ABLE TO GATHER SOME INTER-ESTING DATA.
SO I WANT TO SUBMIT MY REPORT AS SOON AS POSS--
DON'T WORRY ABOUT IT.

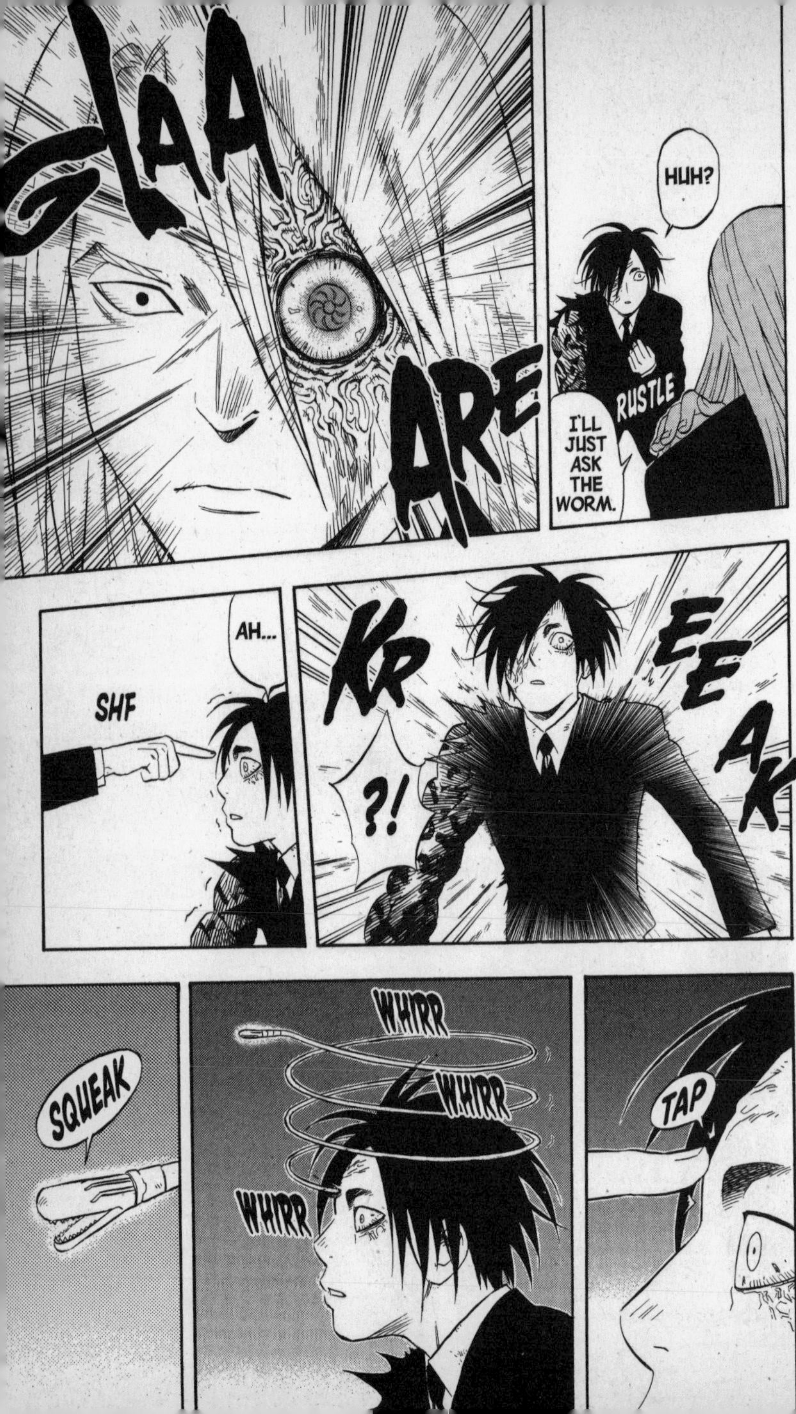

HUH?
RUSTLE
I'LL JUST ASK THE WORM.
GLAARE
KR EEEAK
?!
AH...
SHF
TAP
WHIRR
WHIRR
WHIRR
SQUEAK

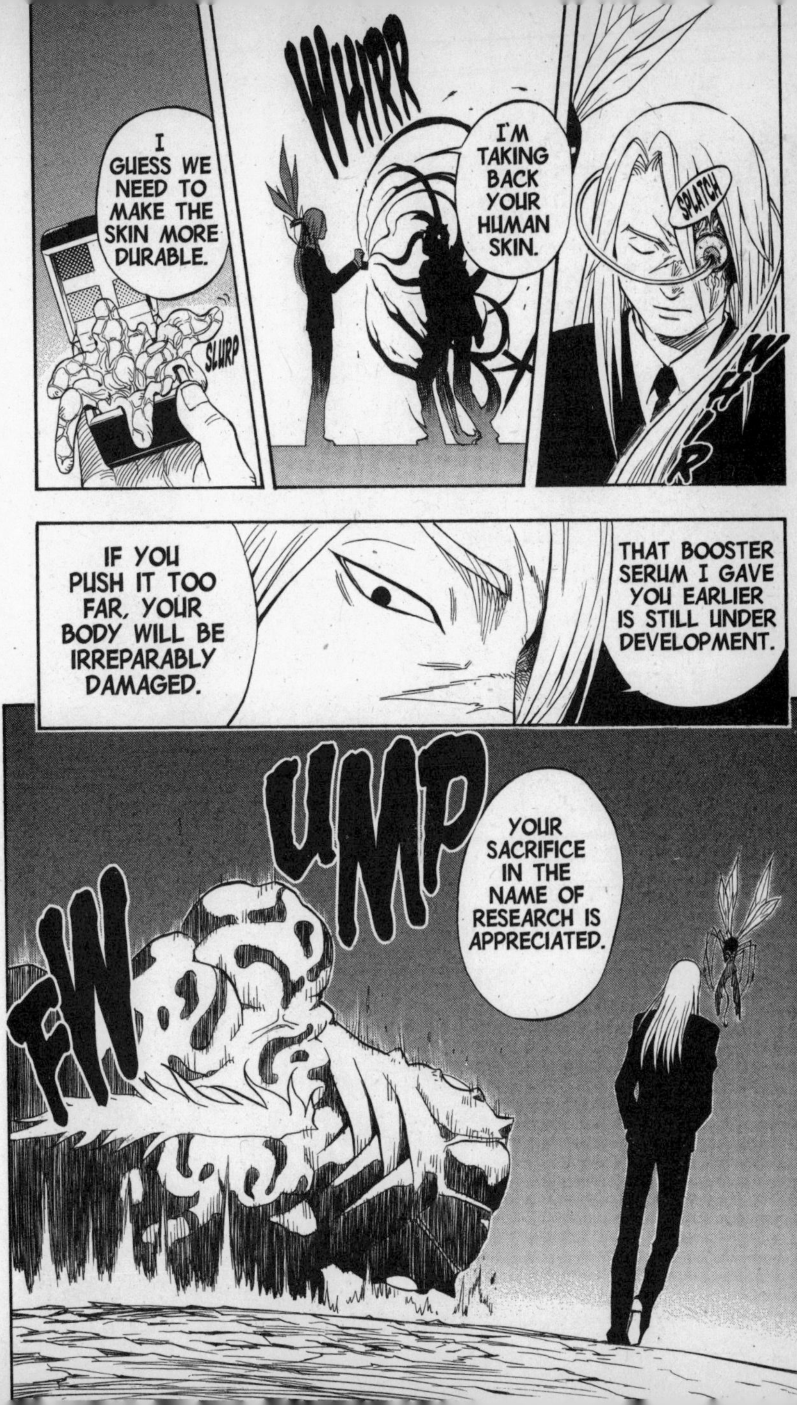
SPLATCH
WHIRR
WHIRR
I'M TAKING BACK YOUR HUMAN SKIN.
I GUESS WE NEED TO MAKE THE SKIN MORE DURABLE.
SLURP
THAT BOOSTER SERUM I GAVE YOU EARLIER IS STILL UNDER DEVELOPMENT.
IF YOU PUSH IT TOO FAR, YOUR BODY WILL BE IRREPARABLY DAMAGED.
YOUR SACRIFICE IN THE NAME OF RESEARCH IS APPRECIATED.
FWUMP

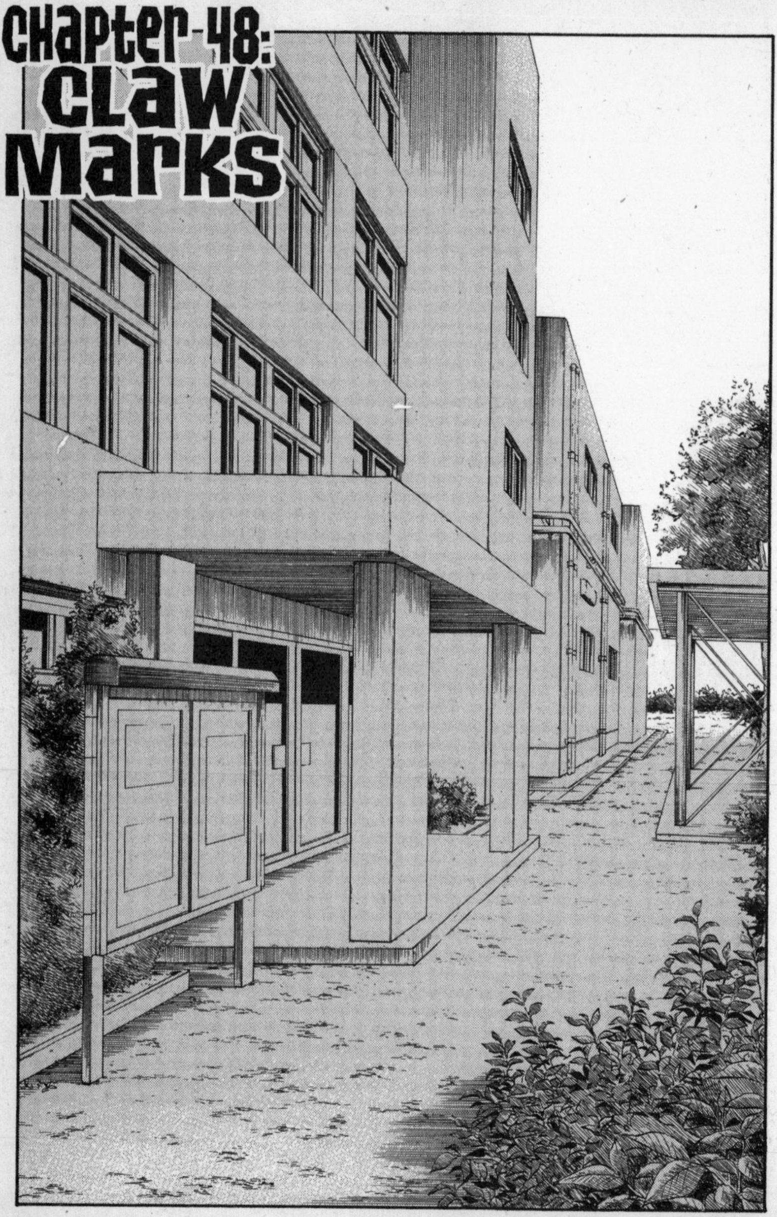
Chapter 48:
Claw Marks

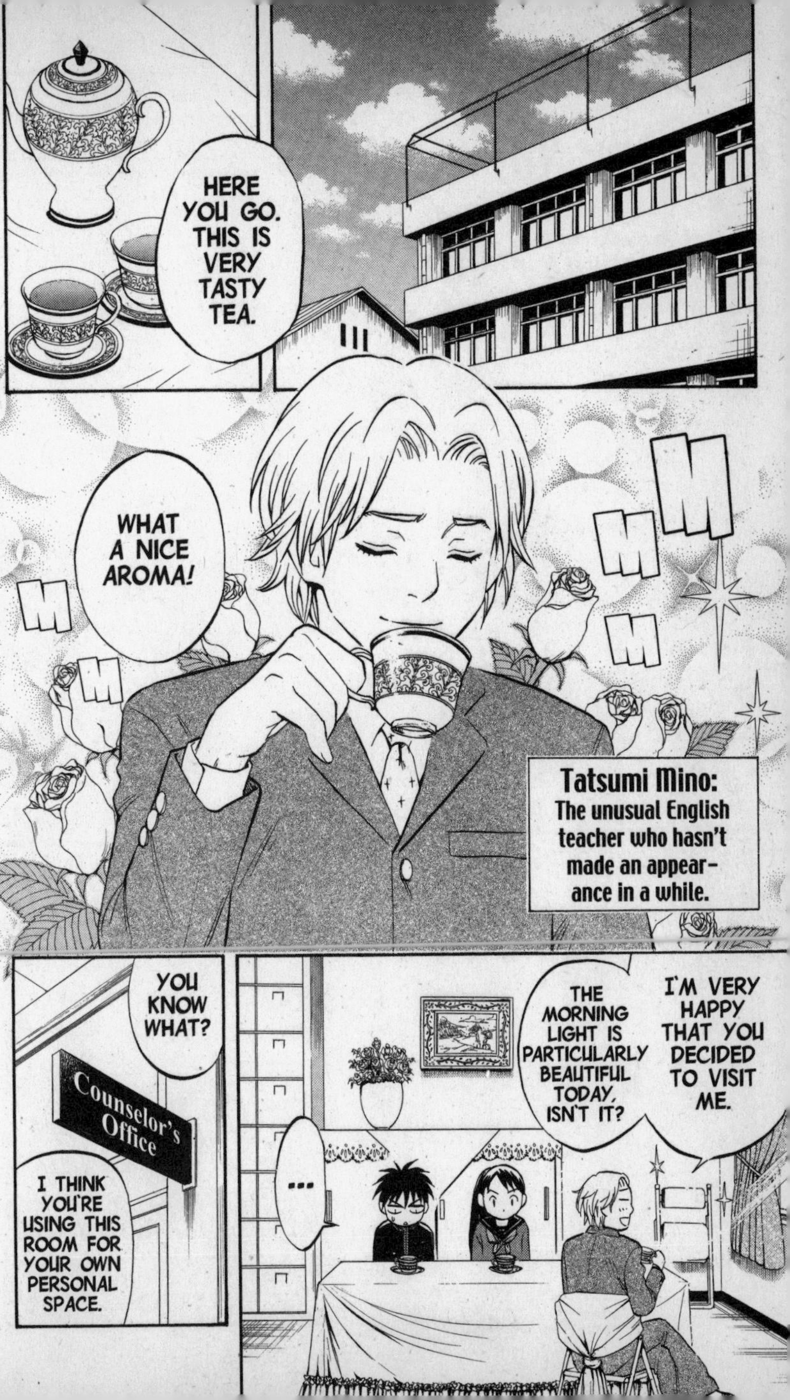

HERE YOU GO. THIS IS VERY TASTY TEA.
M M M M
Tatsumi Mino: The unusual English teacher who hasn't made an appear-ance in a while.
WHAT A NICE AROMA!
M M
I'M VERY HAPPY THAT YOU DECIDED TO VISIT ME.
THE MORNING LIGHT IS PARTICULARLY BEAUTIFUL TODAY, ISN'T IT?
...
YOU KNOW WHAT?
Counselor's Office
I THINK YOU'RE USING THIS ROOM FOR YOUR OWN PERSONAL SPACE.

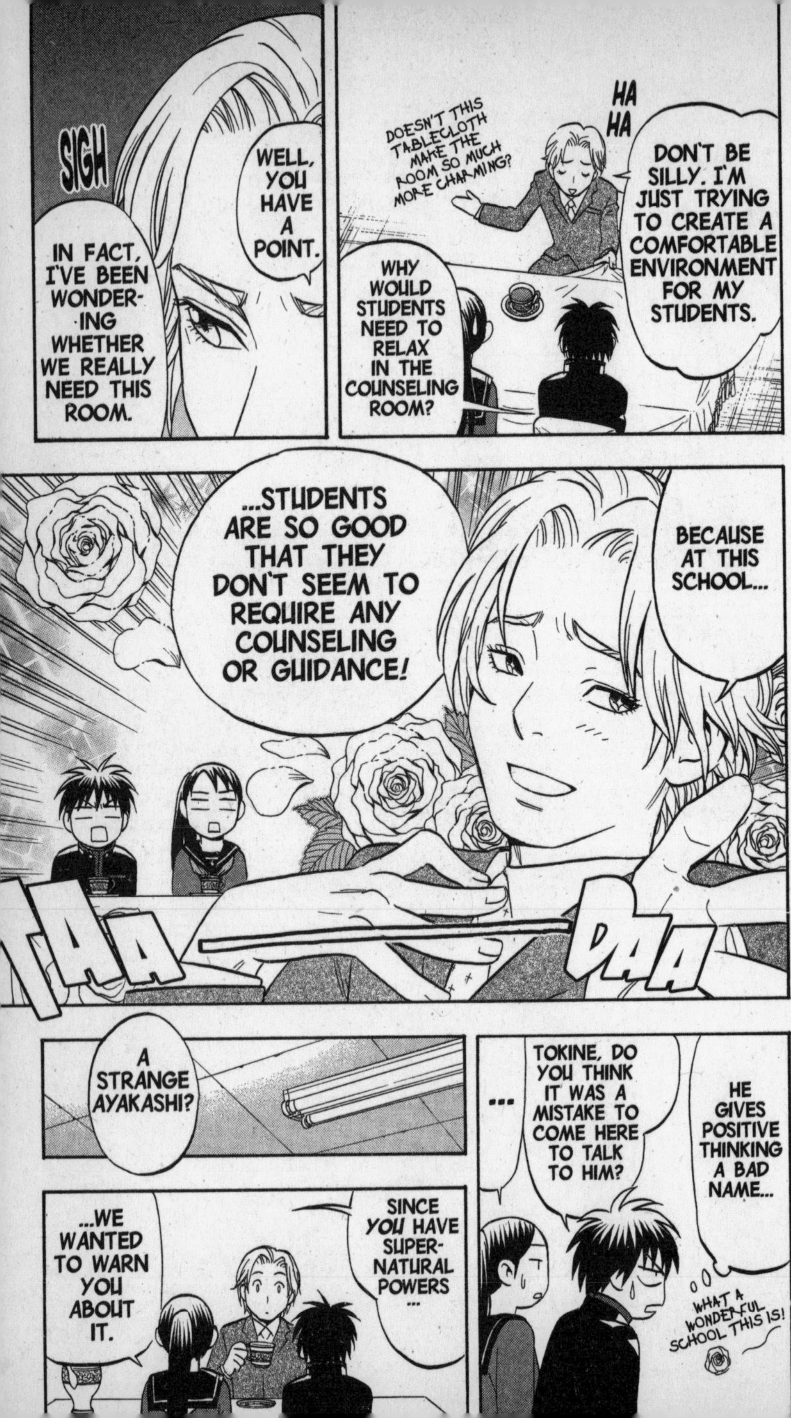
HA HA
DON'T BE SILLY. I'M JUST TRYING TO CREATE A COMFORTABLE ENVIRONMENT FOR MY STUDENTS.
DOESN'T THIS TABLECLOTH MAKE THE ROOM SO MUCH MORE CHARMING?
WHY WOULD STUDENTS NEED TO RELAX IN THE COUNSELING ROOM?
WELL, YOU HAVE A POINT.
SIGH
IN FACT, I'VE BEEN WONDER-ING WHETHER WE REALLY NEED THIS ROOM.
BECAUSE AT THIS SCHOOL...
...STUDENTS ARE SO GOOD THAT THEY DON'T SEEM TO REQUIRE ANY COUNSELING OR GUIDANCE!
DAA
TAA
HE GIVES POSITIVE THINKING A BAD NAME...
TOKINE, DO YOU THINK IT WAS A MISTAKE TO COME HERE TO TALK TO HIM?
...
WHAT A WONDERFUL SCHOOL THIS IS!
A STRANGE AYAKASHI?
SINCE YOU HAVE SUPER-NATURAL POWERS...
...WE WANTED TO WARN YOU ABOUT IT.

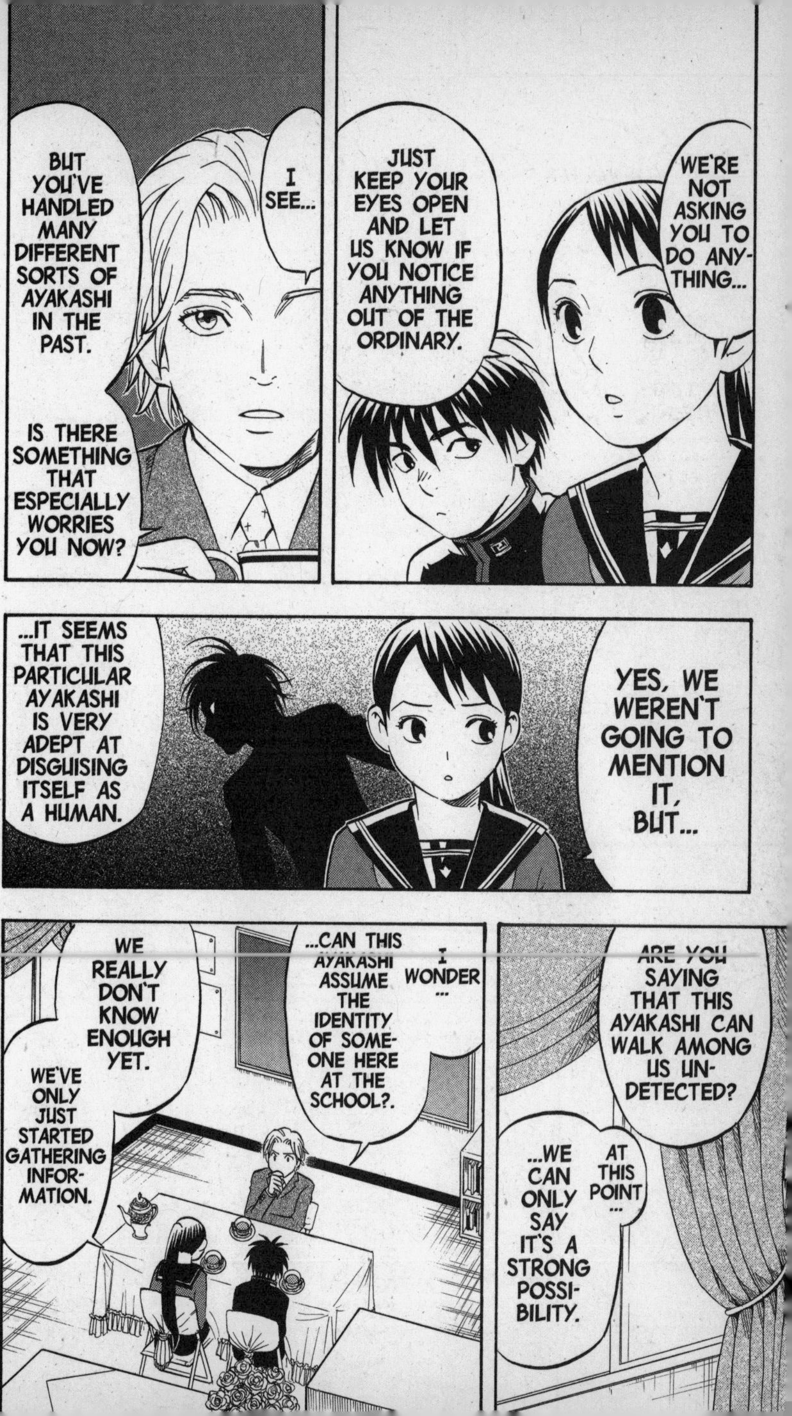
WE'RE NOT ASKING YOU TO DO ANY-THING...
JUST KEEP YOUR EYES OPEN AND LET US KNOW IF YOU NOTICE ANYTHING OUT OF THE ORDINARY.
I SEE...
BUT YOU'VE HANDLED MANY DIFFERENT SORTS OF AYAKASHI IN THE PAST.
IS THERE SOMETHING THAT ESPECIALLY WORRIES YOU NOW?
YES, WE WEREN'T GOING TO MENTION IT, BUT...
...IT SEEMS THAT THIS PARTICULAR AYAKASHI IS VERY ADEPT AT DISGUISING ITSELF AS A HUMAN.
ARE YOU SAYING THAT THIS AYAKASHI CAN WALK AMONG US UN-DETECTED?
AT THIS POINT...
...WE CAN ONLY SAY IT'S A STRONG POSSI-BILITY.
I WONDER...
...CAN THIS AYAKASHI ASSUME THE IDENTITY OF SOME-ONE HERE AT THE SCHOOL?.
WE REALLY DON'T KNOW ENOUGH YET.
WE'VE ONLY JUST STARTED GATHERING INFOR-MATION.

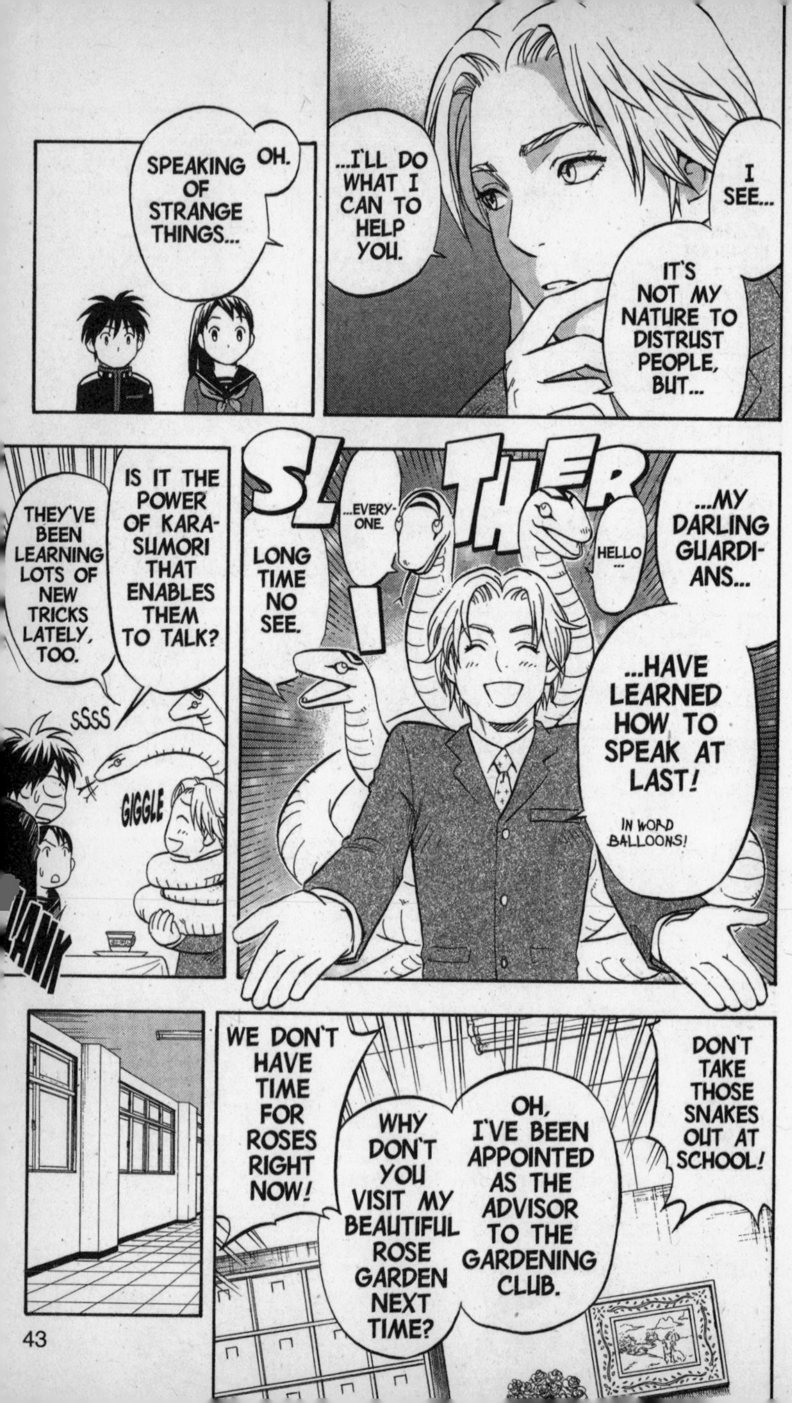
I SEE...
IT'S NOT MY NATURE TO DISTRUST PEOPLE, BUT...
...I'LL DO WHAT I CAN TO HELP YOU.
OH.
SPEAKING OF STRANGE THINGS...
SLITHER
...MY DARLING GUARDIANS...
...HAVE LEARNED HOW TO SPEAK AT LAST!
IN WORD BALLOONS!
HELLO...
...EVERYONE.
LONG TIME NO SEE.
IS IT THE POWER OF KARASUMORI THAT ENABLES THEM TO TALK?
THEY'VE BEEN LEARNING LOTS OF NEW TRICKS LATELY, TOO.
SSSS
GIGGLE
DON'T TAKE THOSE SNAKES OUT AT SCHOOL!
OH, I'VE BEEN APPOINTED AS THE ADVISOR TO THE GARDENING CLUB.
WHY DON'T YOU VISIT MY BEAUTIFUL ROSE GARDEN NEXT TIME?
WE DON'T HAVE TIME FOR ROSES RIGHT NOW!

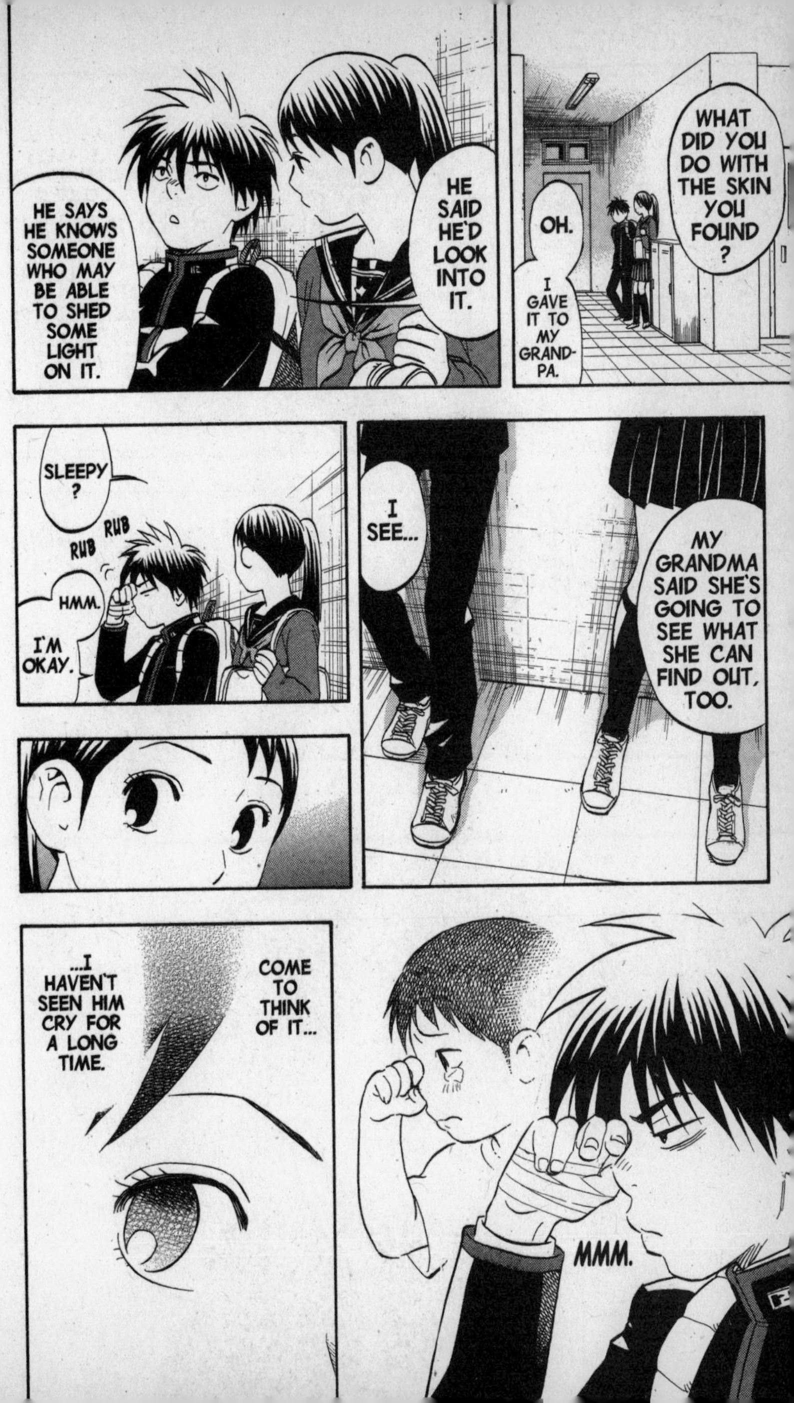
WHAT DID YOU DO WITH THE SKIN YOU FOUND?
OH.
I GAVE IT TO MY GRANDPA.
HE SAID HE'D LOOK INTO IT.
HE SAYS HE KNOWS SOMEONE WHO MAY BE ABLE TO SHED SOME LIGHT ON IT.
MY GRANDMA SAID SHE'S GOING TO SEE WHAT SHE CAN FIND OUT, TOO.
I SEE...
SLEEPY?
RUB RUB
HMM.
I'M OKAY.
COME TO THINK OF IT...
...I HAVEN'T SEEN HIM CRY FOR A LONG TIME.
MMM.

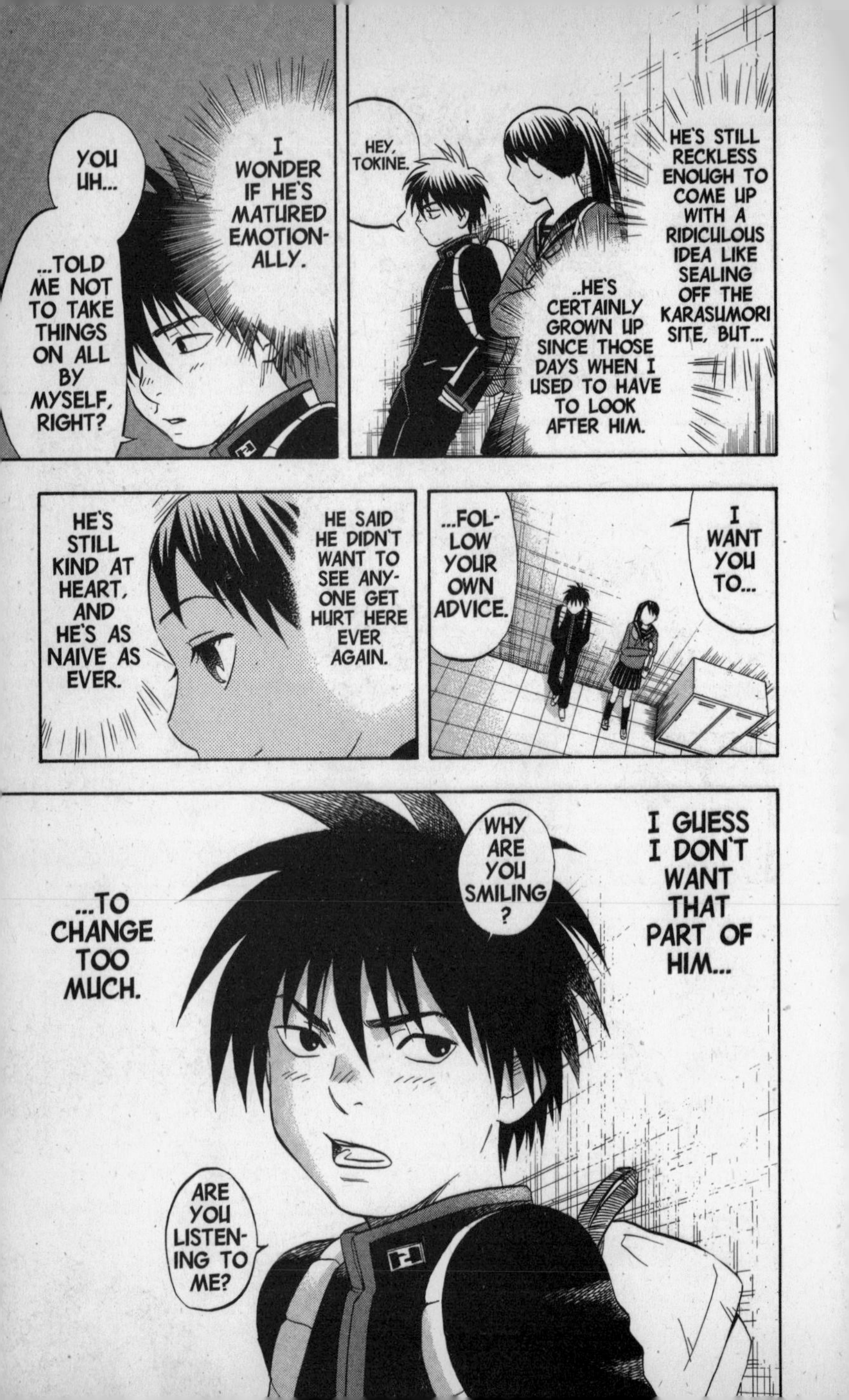
HE'S STILL RECKLESS ENOUGH TO COME UP WITH A RIDICULOUS IDEA LIKE SEALING OFF THE KARASUMORI SITE, BUT...
..HE'S CERTAINLY GROWN UP SINCE THOSE DAYS WHEN I USED TO HAVE TO LOOK AFTER HIM.
HEY, TOKINE.
I WONDER IF HE'S MATURED EMOTION-ALLY.
YOU UH...
...TOLD ME NOT TO TAKE THINGS ON ALL BY MYSELF, RIGHT?
I WANT YOU TO...
...FOL-LOW YOUR OWN ADVICE.
HE SAID HE DIDN'T WANT TO SEE ANY-ONE GET HURT HERE EVER AGAIN.
HE'S STILL KIND AT HEART, AND HE'S AS NAIVE AS EVER.
I GUESS I DON'T WANT THAT PART OF HIM...
WHY ARE YOU SMILING?
...TO CHANGE TOO MUCH.
ARE YOU LISTEN-ING TO ME?

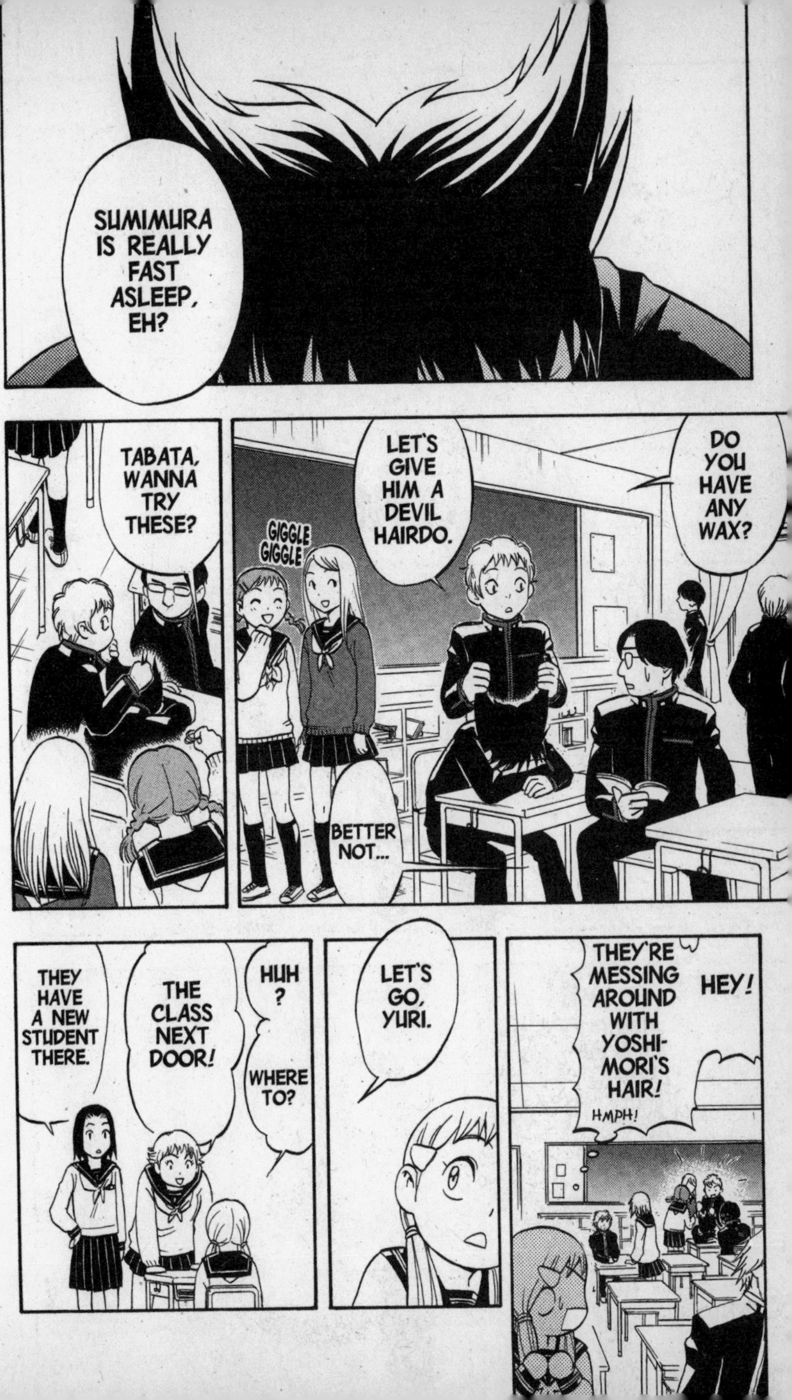
SUMIMURA IS REALLY FAST ASLEEP, EH?
DO YOU HAVE ANY WAX?
LET'S GIVE HIM A DEVIL HAIRDO.
GIGGLE GIGGLE
BETTER NOT...
TABATA, WANNA TRY THESE?
HEY!
THEY'RE MESSING AROUND WITH YOSHI-MORI'S HAIR!
HMPH!
LET'S GO, YURI.
HUH?
WHERE TO?
THE CLASS NEXT DOOR!
THEY HAVE A NEW STUDENT THERE.

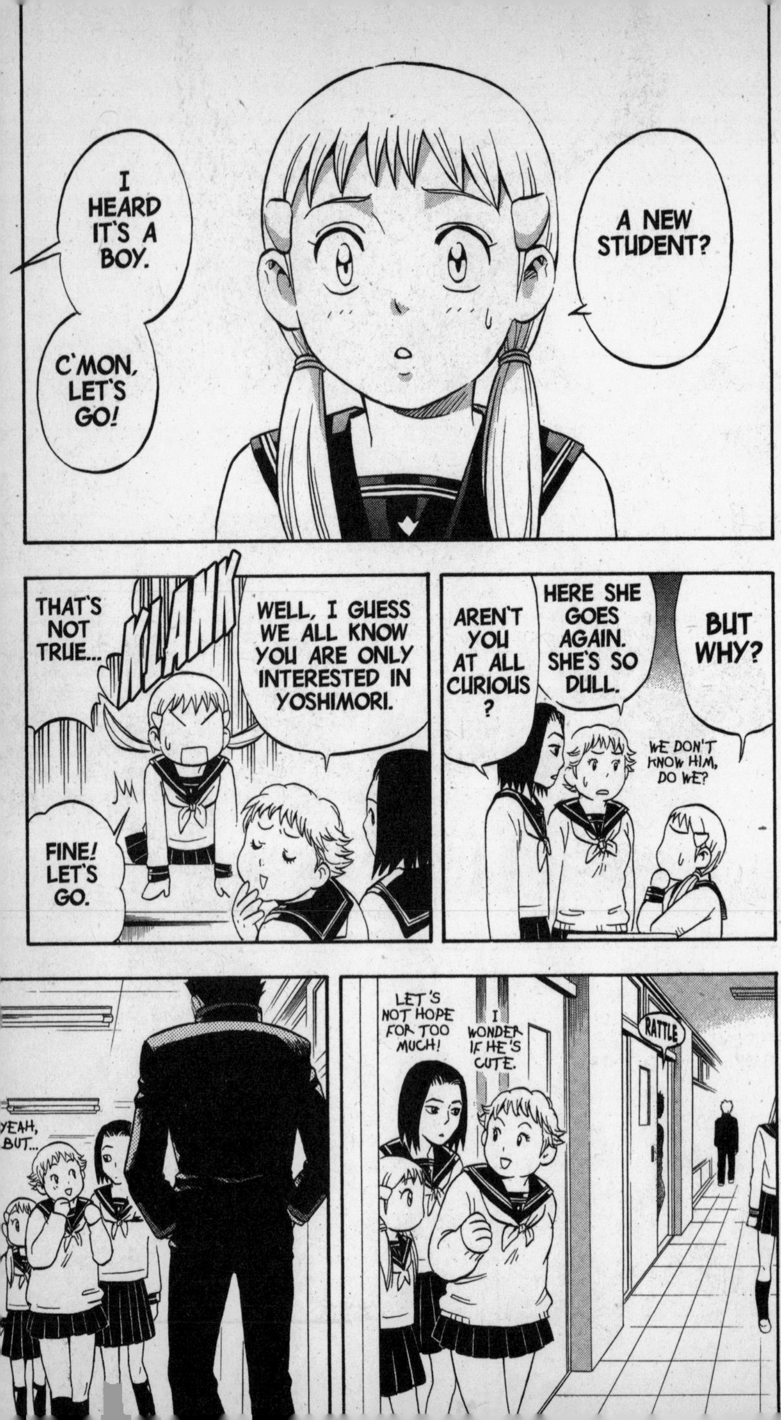
A NEW STUDENT?
I HEARD IT'S A BOY.
C'MON, LET'S GO!
BUT WHY?
WE DON'T KNOW HIM, DO WE?
HERE SHE GOES AGAIN. SHE'S SO DULL.
AREN'T YOU AT ALL CURIOUS?
WELL, I GUESS WE ALL KNOW YOU ARE ONLY INTERESTED IN YOSHIMORI.
KLANK
THAT'S NOT TRUE...
FINE! LET'S GO.
RATTLE
I WONDER IF HE'S CUTE.
LET'S NOT HOPE FOR TOO MUCH!
YEAH, BUT...

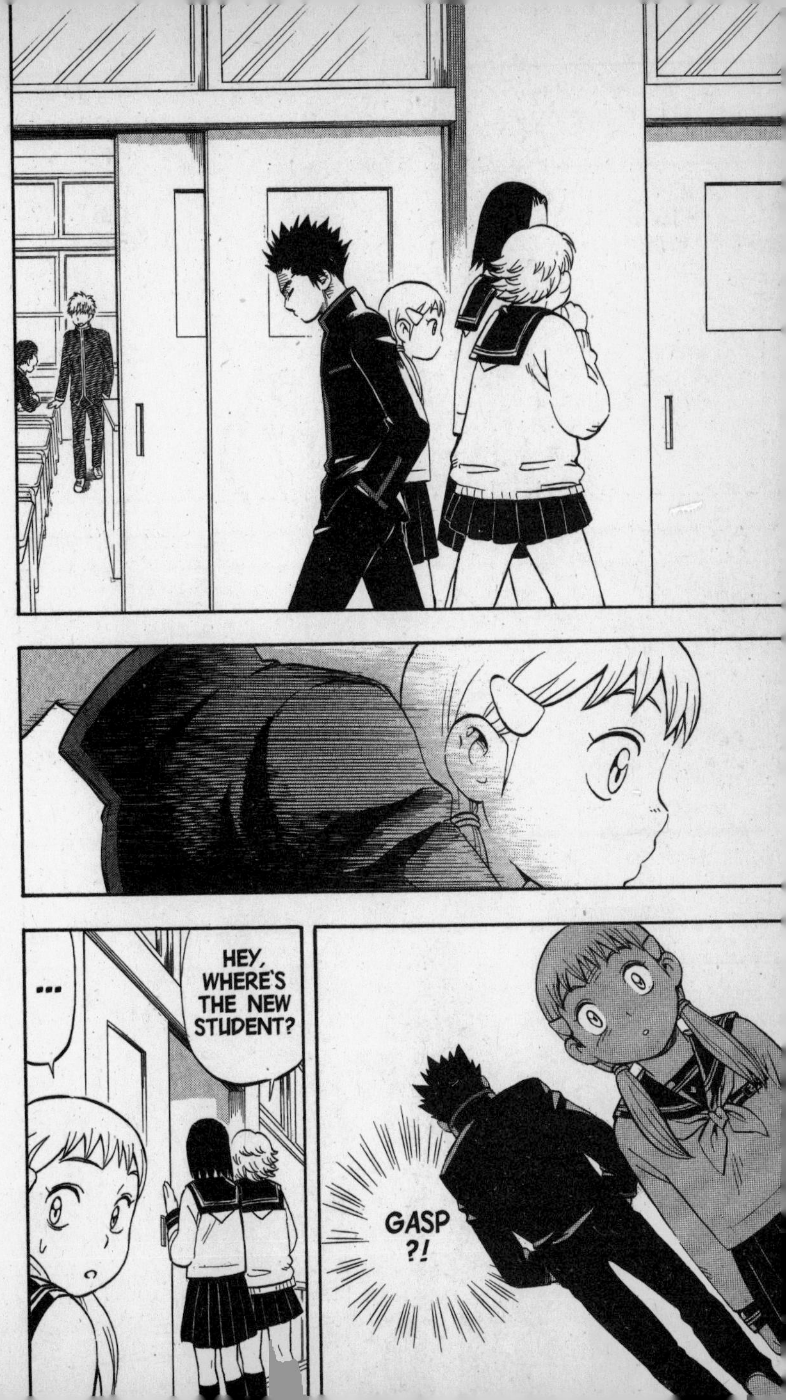
GASP ?!
HEY, WHERE'S THE NEW STUDENT?
...

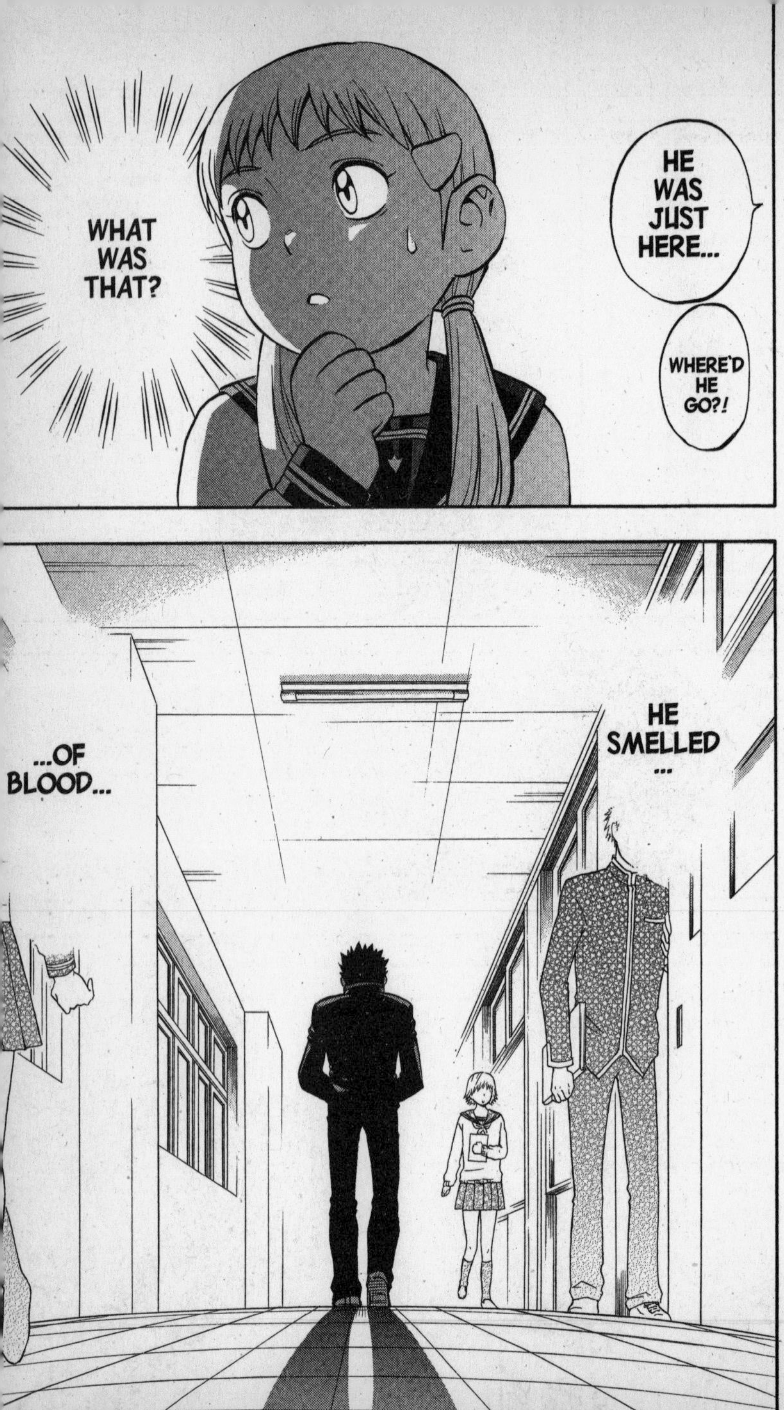
HE WAS JUST HERE...
WHERE'D HE GO?!
WHAT WAS THAT?
HE SMELLED ...
...OF BLOOD...

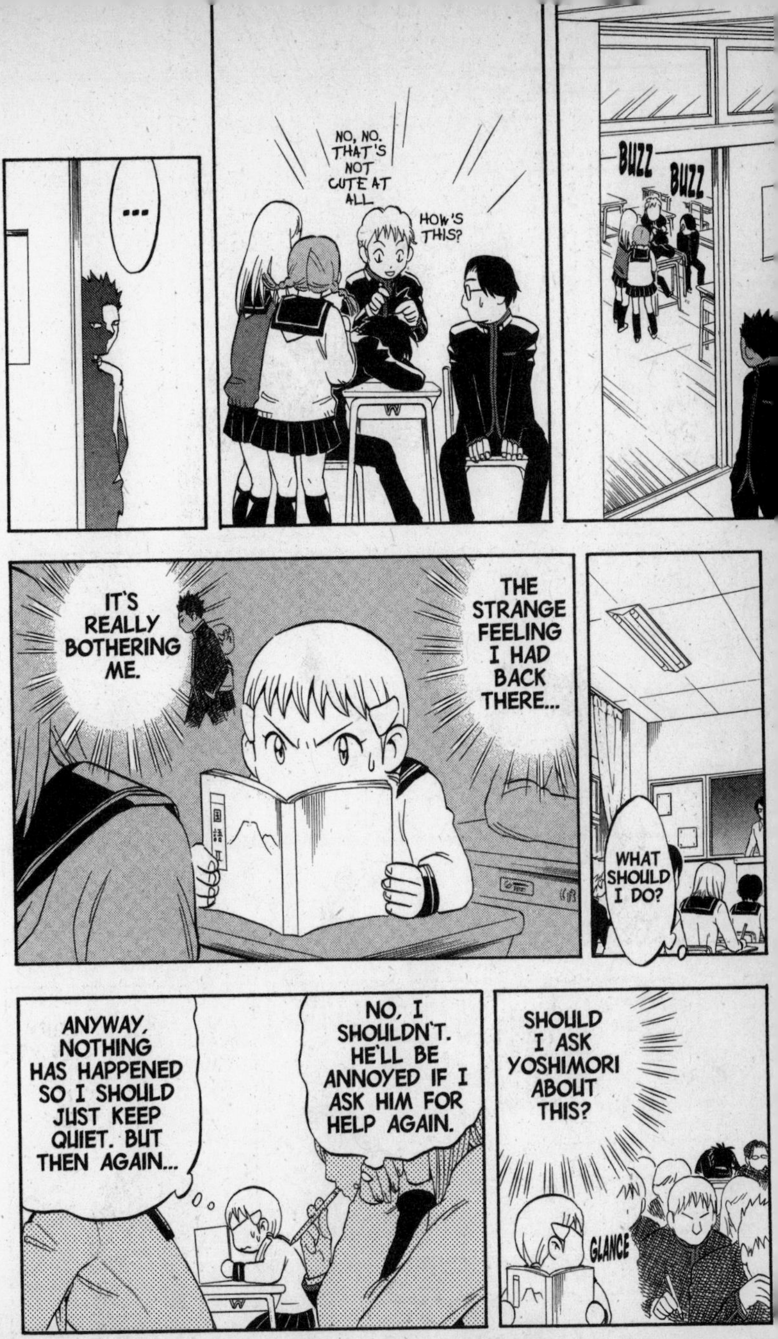
BUZZ
BUZZ
HOW'S THIS?
NO, NO. THAT'S NOT CUTE AT ALL
...
WHAT SHOULD I DO?
THE STRANGE FEELING I HAD BACK THERE...
IT'S REALLY BOTHERING ME.
SHOULD I ASK YOSHIMORI ABOUT THIS?
GLANCE
NO, I SHOULDN'T. HE'LL BE ANNOYED IF I ASK HIM FOR HELP AGAIN.
ANYWAY, NOTHING HAS HAPPENED SO I SHOULD JUST KEEP QUIET. BUT THEN AGAIN...

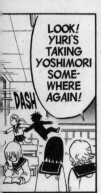

LOOK! YURI'S TAKING YOSHIMORI SOMEWHERE AGAIN!

DASH

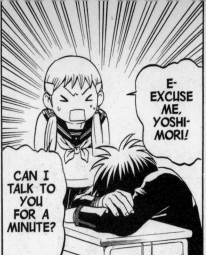

E-EXCUSE ME, YOSHIMORI!

CAN I TALK TO YOU FOR A MINUTE?

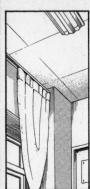

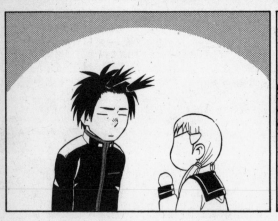

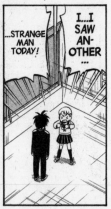

...STRANGE MAN TODAY!

I...I SAW ANOTHER...

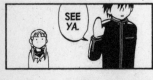

SEE YA.

HMM?

YOU'D BETTER TAKE THESE OFF, THOUGH.

YANK

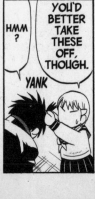

OH... I'M SORRY.

I'M SORRY, BUT CAN WE DISCUSS THIS LATER?

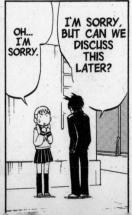

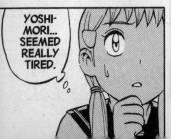

YOSHIMORI... SEEMED REALLY TIRED.

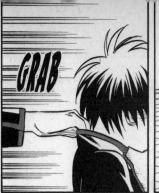
GRAB

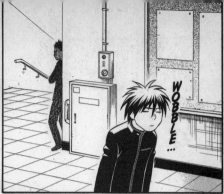
WOBBLE...

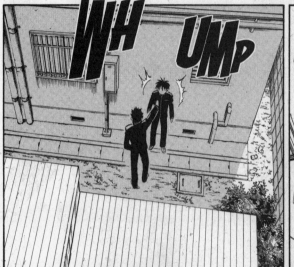
WH UMP

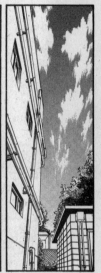

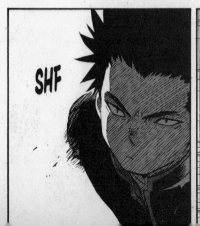
SHF

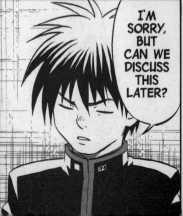
I'M SORRY, BUT CAN WE DISCUSS THIS LATER?

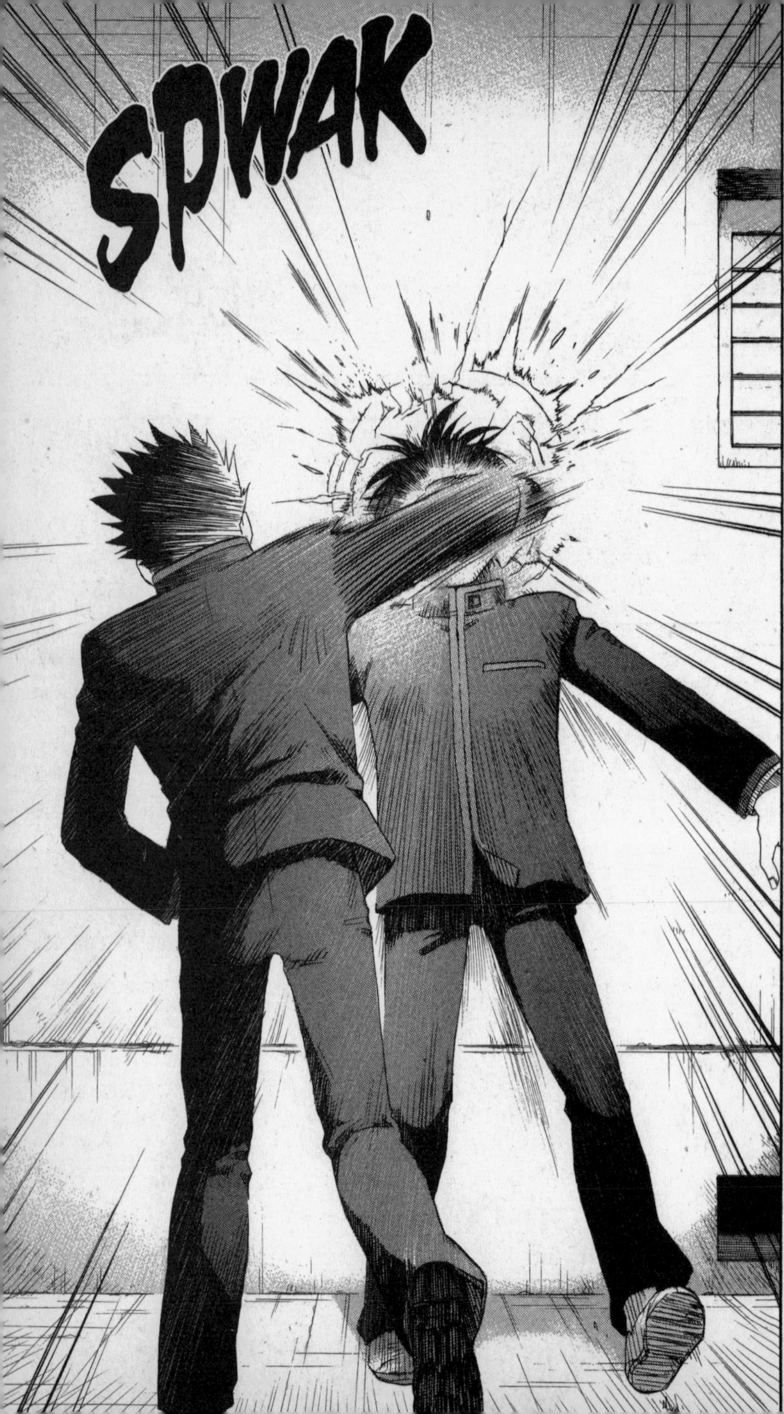
SPWAK

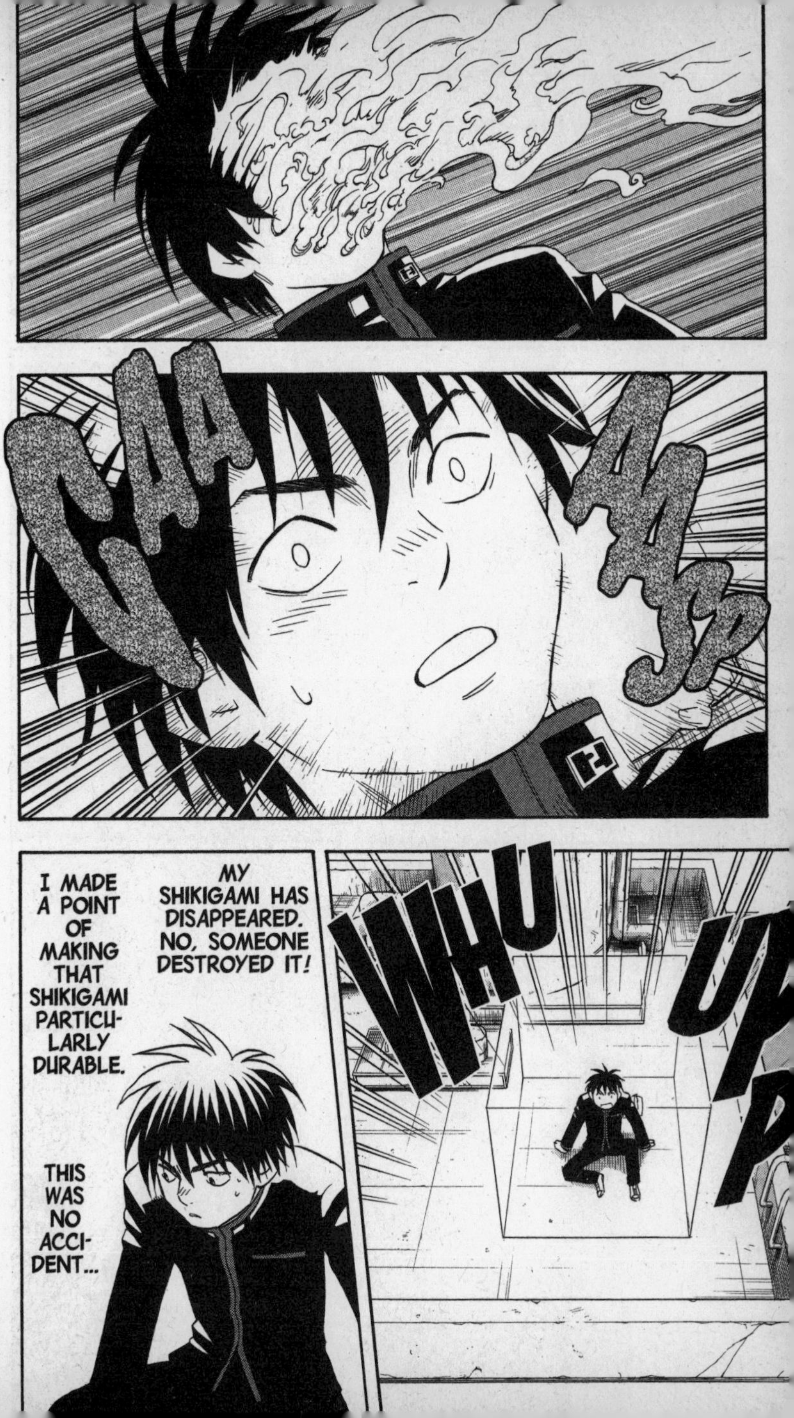
GAAAASP
WHU
MY SHIKIGAMI HAS DISAPPEARED. NO, SOMEONE DESTROYED IT!
I MADE A POINT OF MAKING THAT SHIKIGAMI PARTICULARLY DURABLE.
THIS WAS NO ACCIDENT...

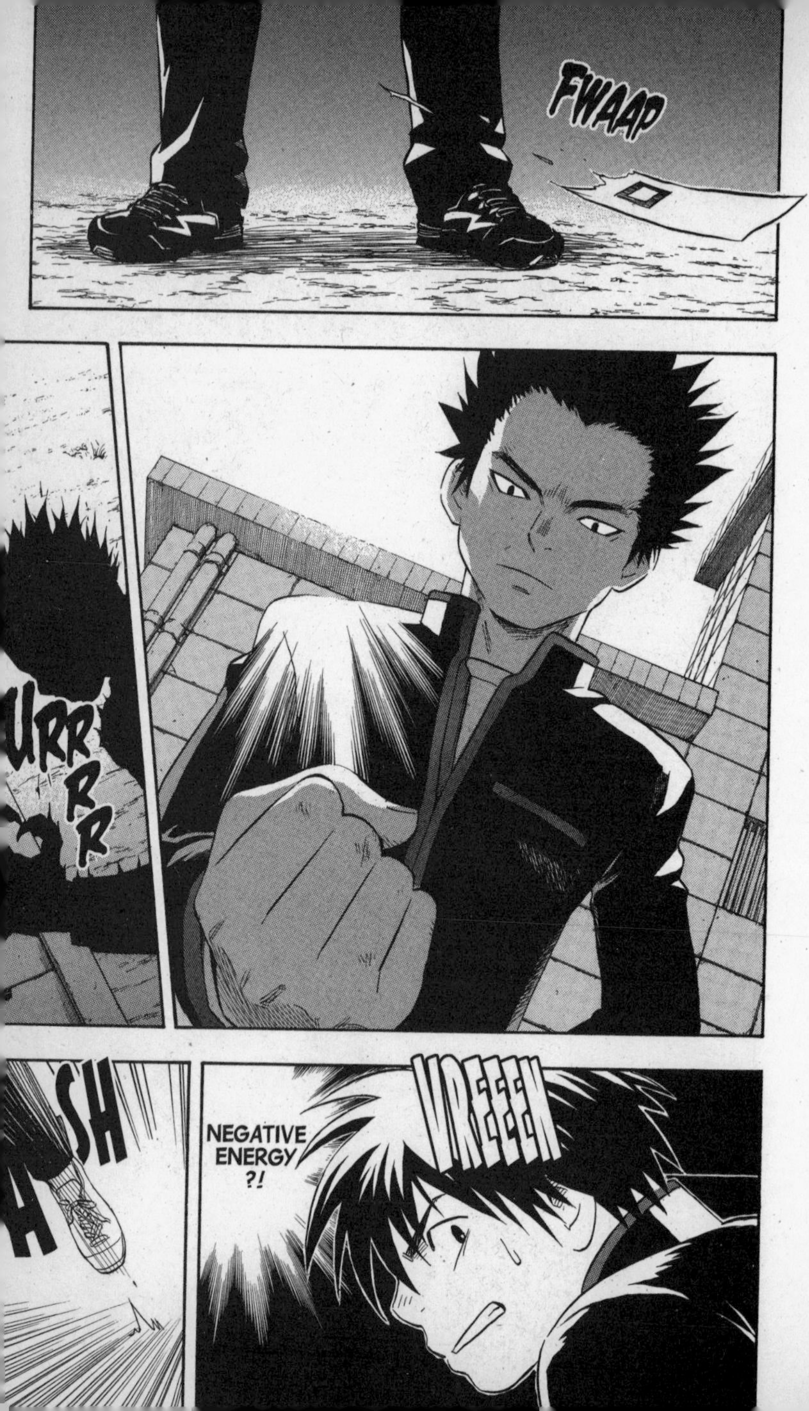
FWAAP
URRRR
VREEEN
NEGATIVE ENERGY ?!
SH

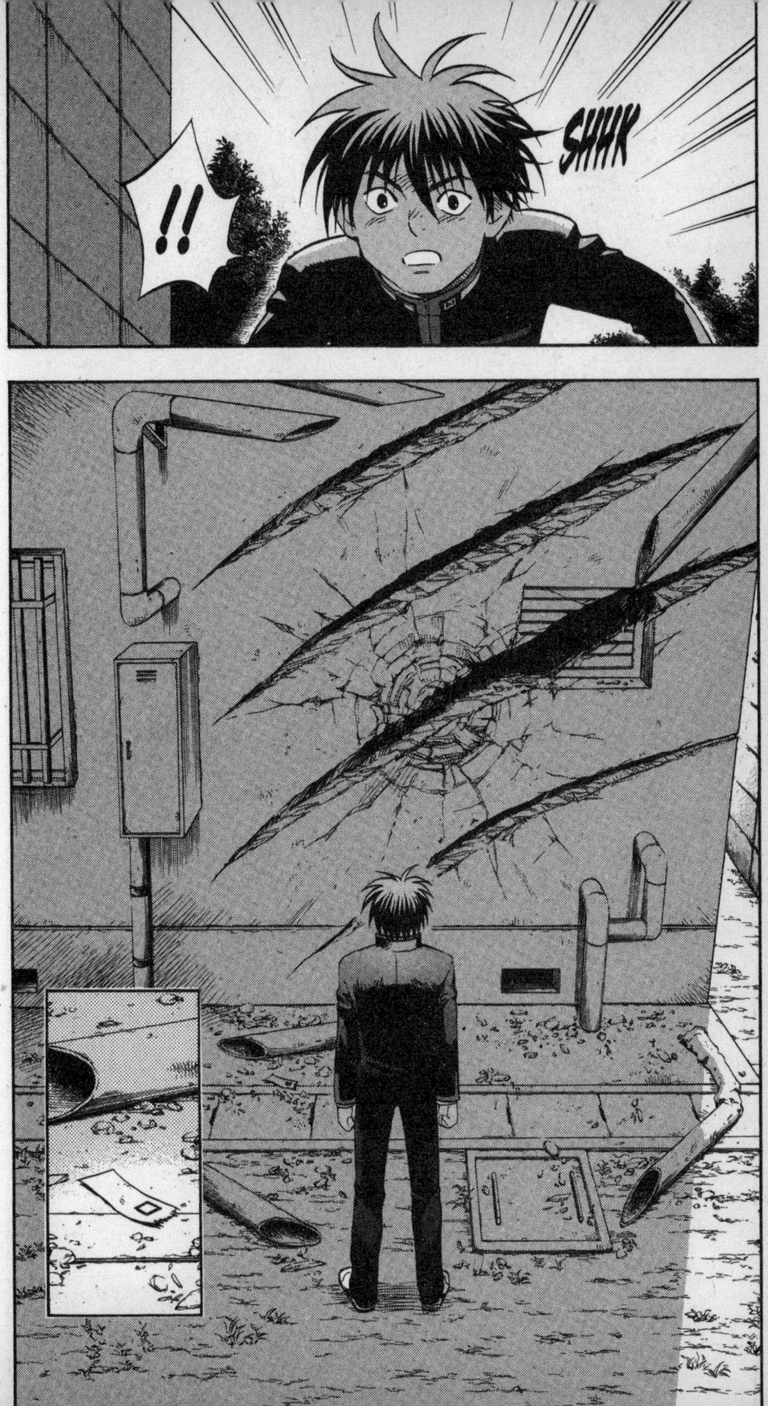
SHHK
!!

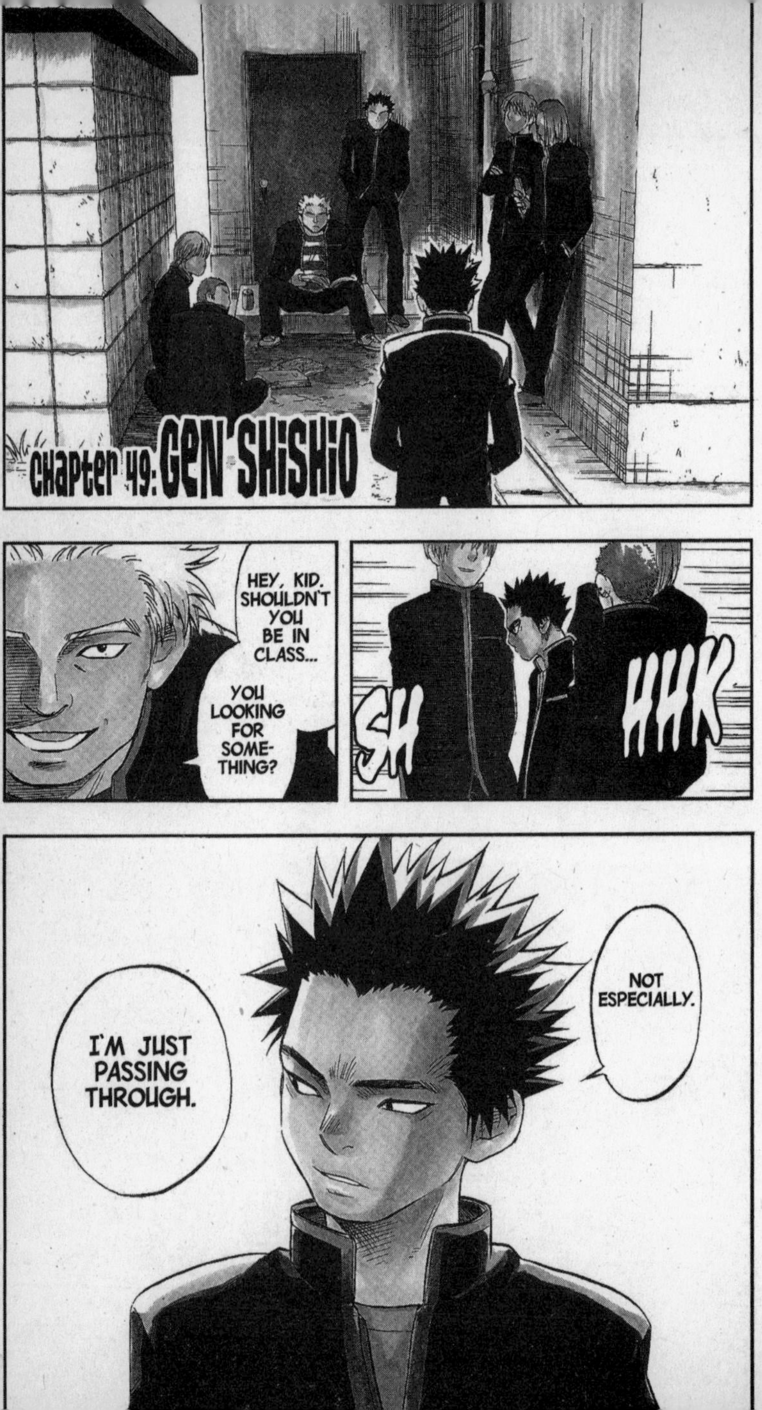
Chapter 49: Gen Shishio
HHK
SH
HEY, KID. SHOULDN'T YOU BE IN CLASS...
YOU LOOKING FOR SOME-THING?
NOT ESPECIALLY.
I'M JUST PASSING THROUGH.

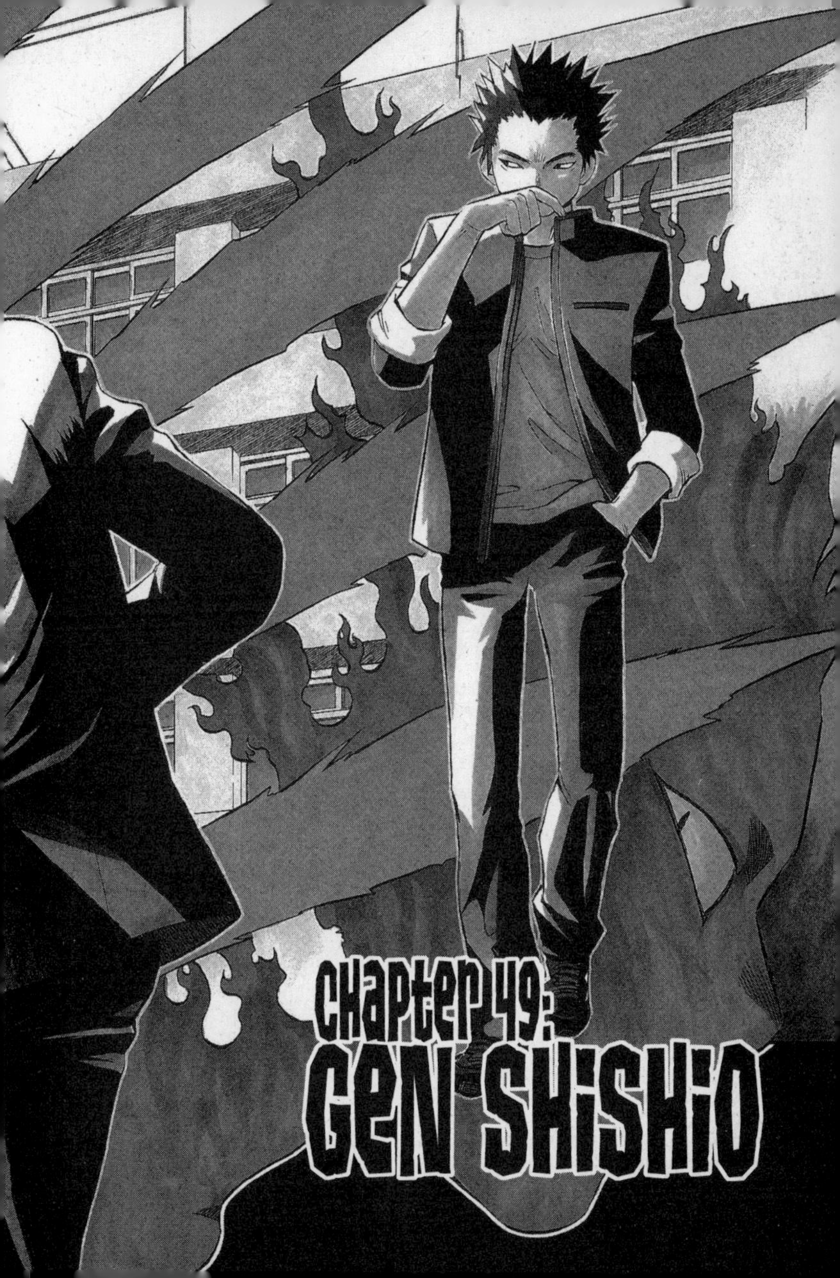
CHAPTER 49:
GEN SHISHIO

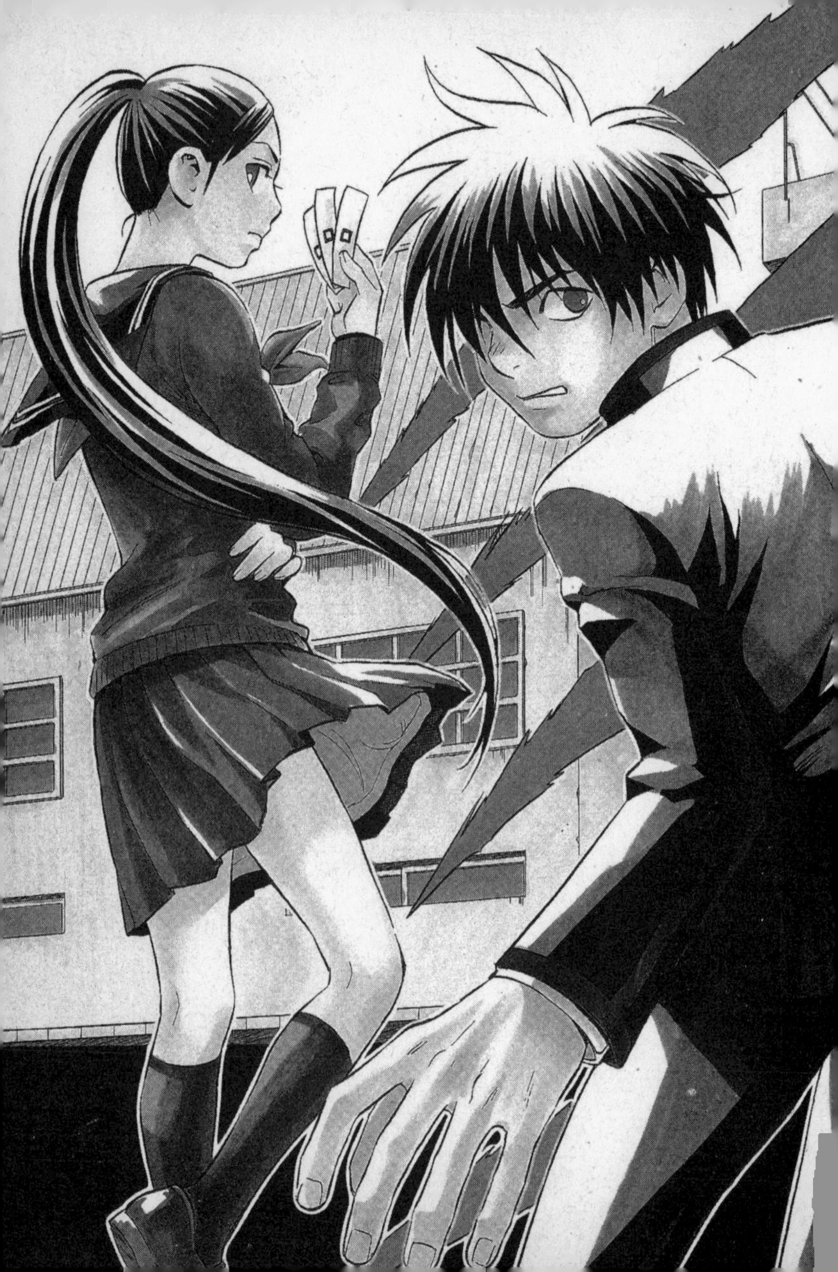

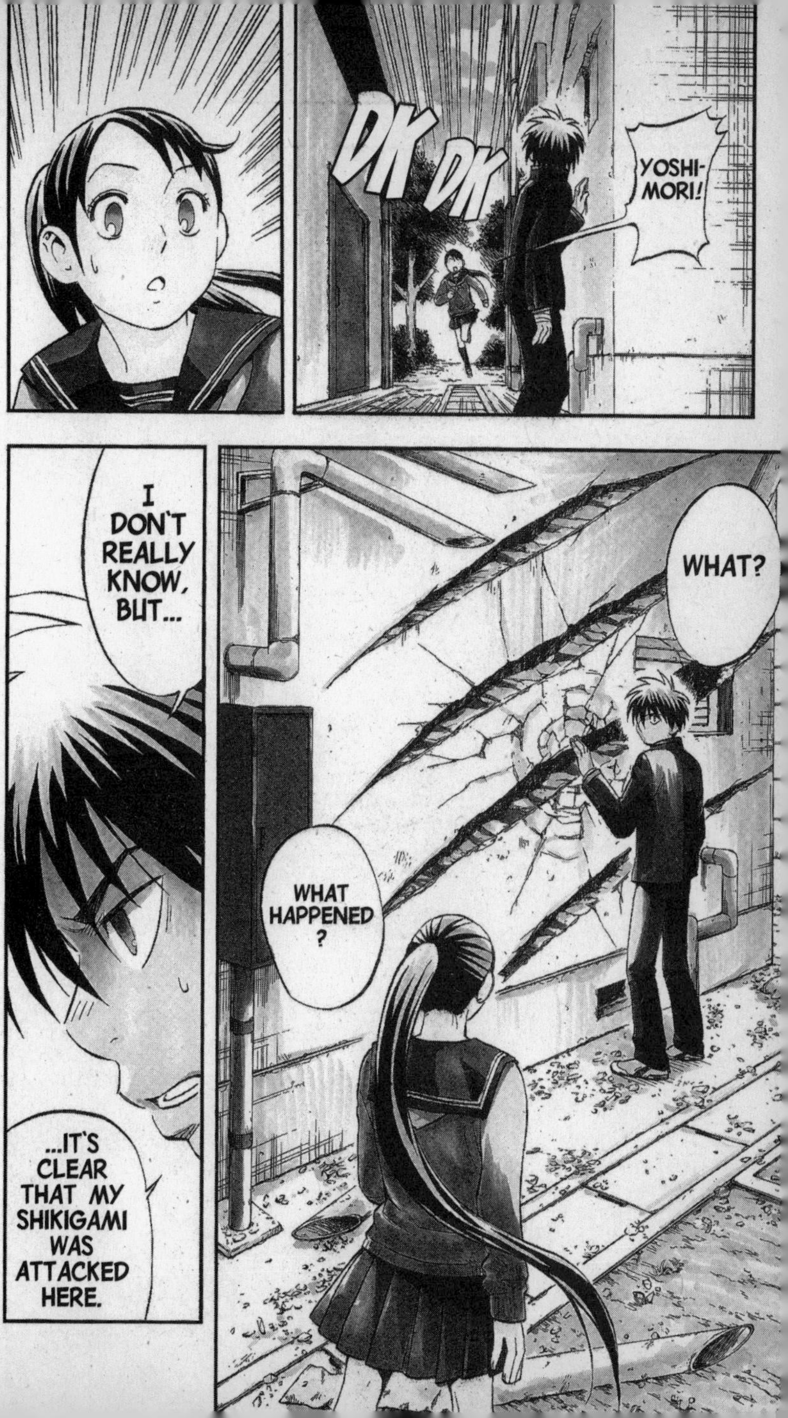
YOSHI-MORI!
DK DK
WHAT?
WHAT HAPPENED?
I DON'T REALLY KNOW, BUT...
...IT'S CLEAR THAT MY SHIKIGAMI WAS ATTACKED HERE.

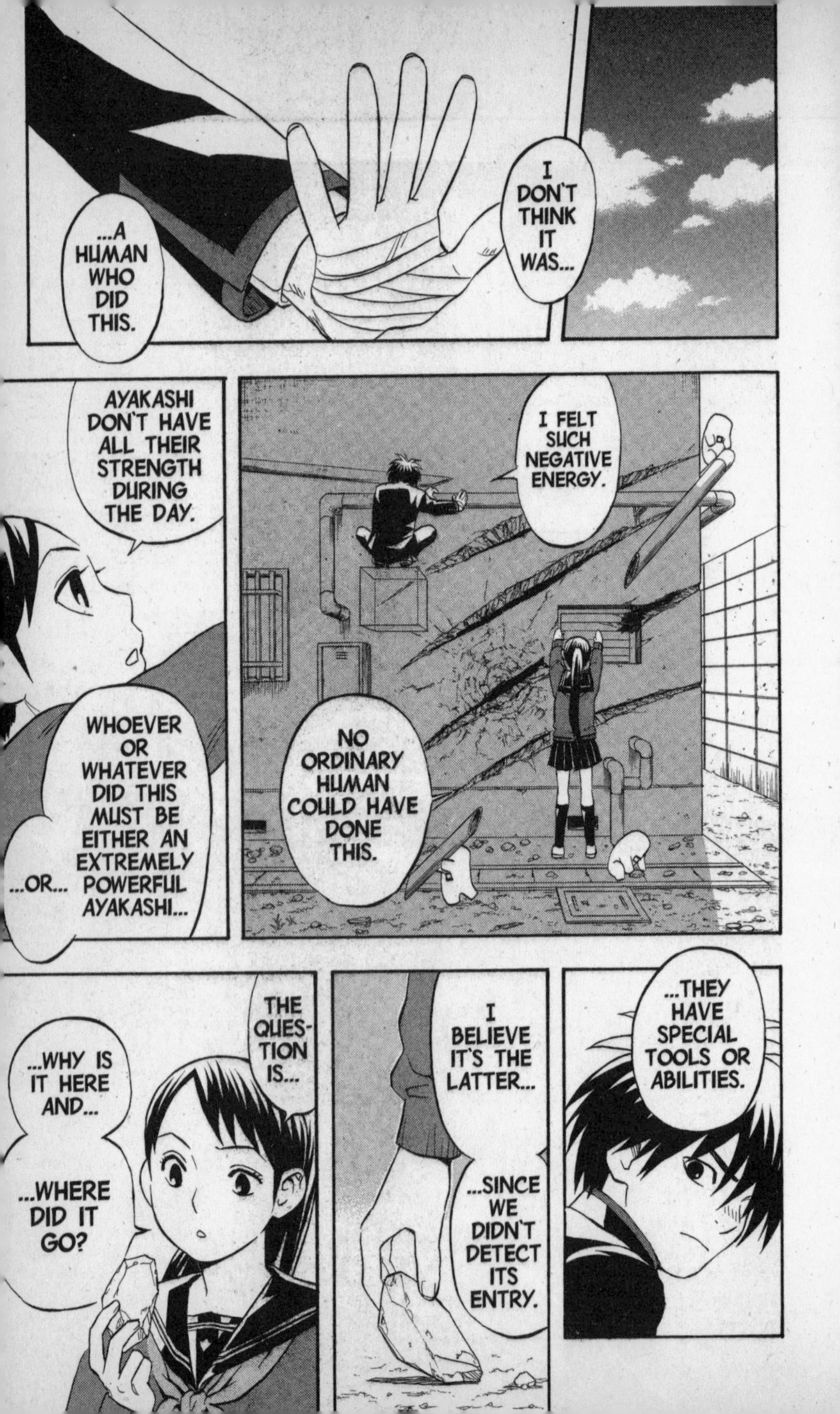
I DON'T THINK IT WAS...
...A HUMAN WHO DID THIS.
I FELT SUCH NEGATIVE ENERGY.
NO ORDINARY HUMAN COULD HAVE DONE THIS.
AYAKASHI DON'T HAVE ALL THEIR STRENGTH DURING THE DAY.
WHOEVER OR WHATEVER DID THIS MUST BE EITHER AN EXTREMELY POWERFUL AYAKASHI...
...OR...
...THEY HAVE SPECIAL TOOLS OR ABILITIES.
I BELIEVE IT'S THE LATTER...
...SINCE WE DIDN'T DETECT ITS ENTRY.
THE QUES-TION IS...
...WHY IS IT HERE AND...
...WHERE DID IT GO?

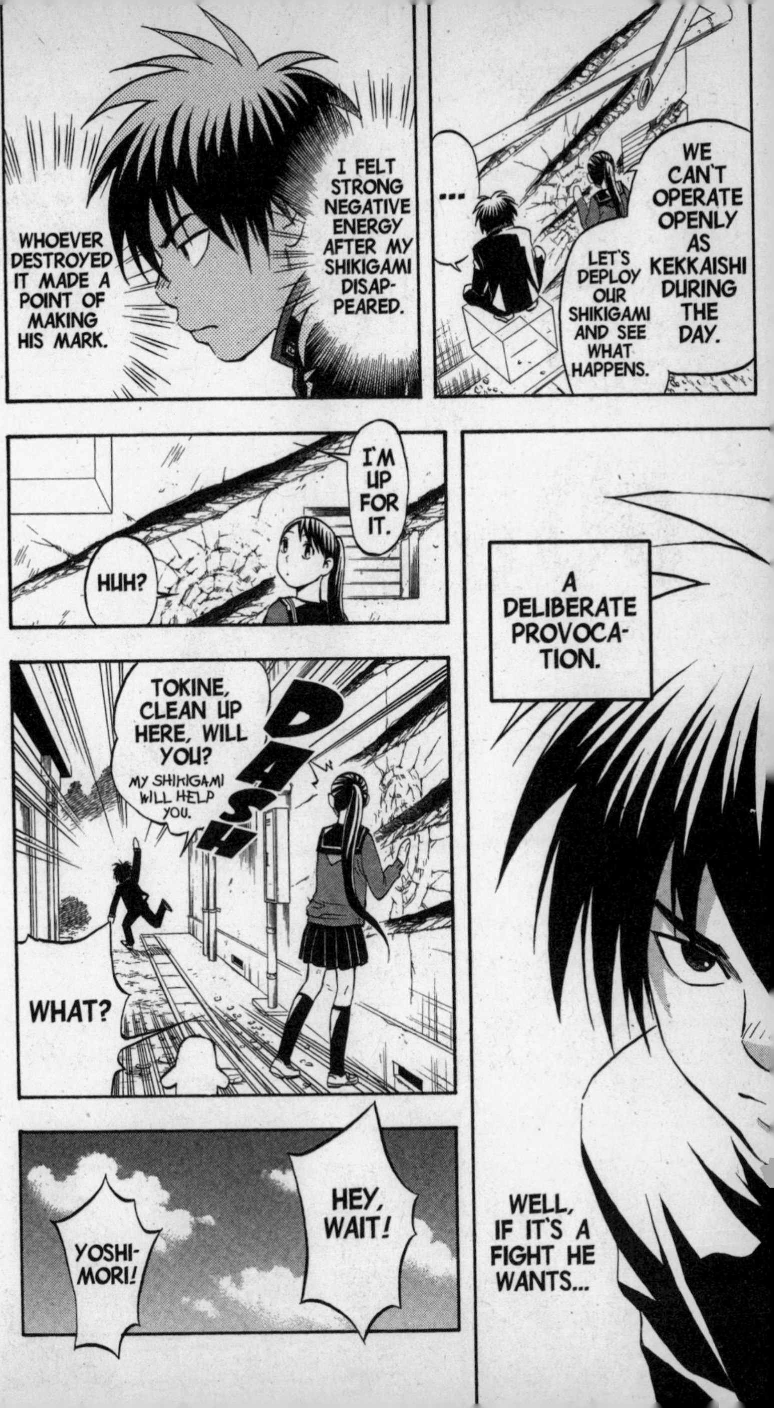
WE CAN'T OPERATE OPENLY AS KEKKAISHI DURING THE DAY.
LET'S DEPLOY OUR SHIKIGAMI AND SEE WHAT HAPPENS.
...
I FELT STRONG NEGATIVE ENERGY AFTER MY SHIKIGAMI DISAP-PEARED.
WHOEVER DESTROYED IT MADE A POINT OF MAKING HIS MARK.
A DELIBERATE PROVOCA-TION.
WELL, IF IT'S A FIGHT HE WANTS...
I'M UP FOR IT.
HUH?
TOKINE, CLEAN UP HERE, WILL YOU?
MY SHIKIGAMI WILL HELP YOU.
DASH
WHAT?
HEY, WAIT!
YOSHI-MORI!

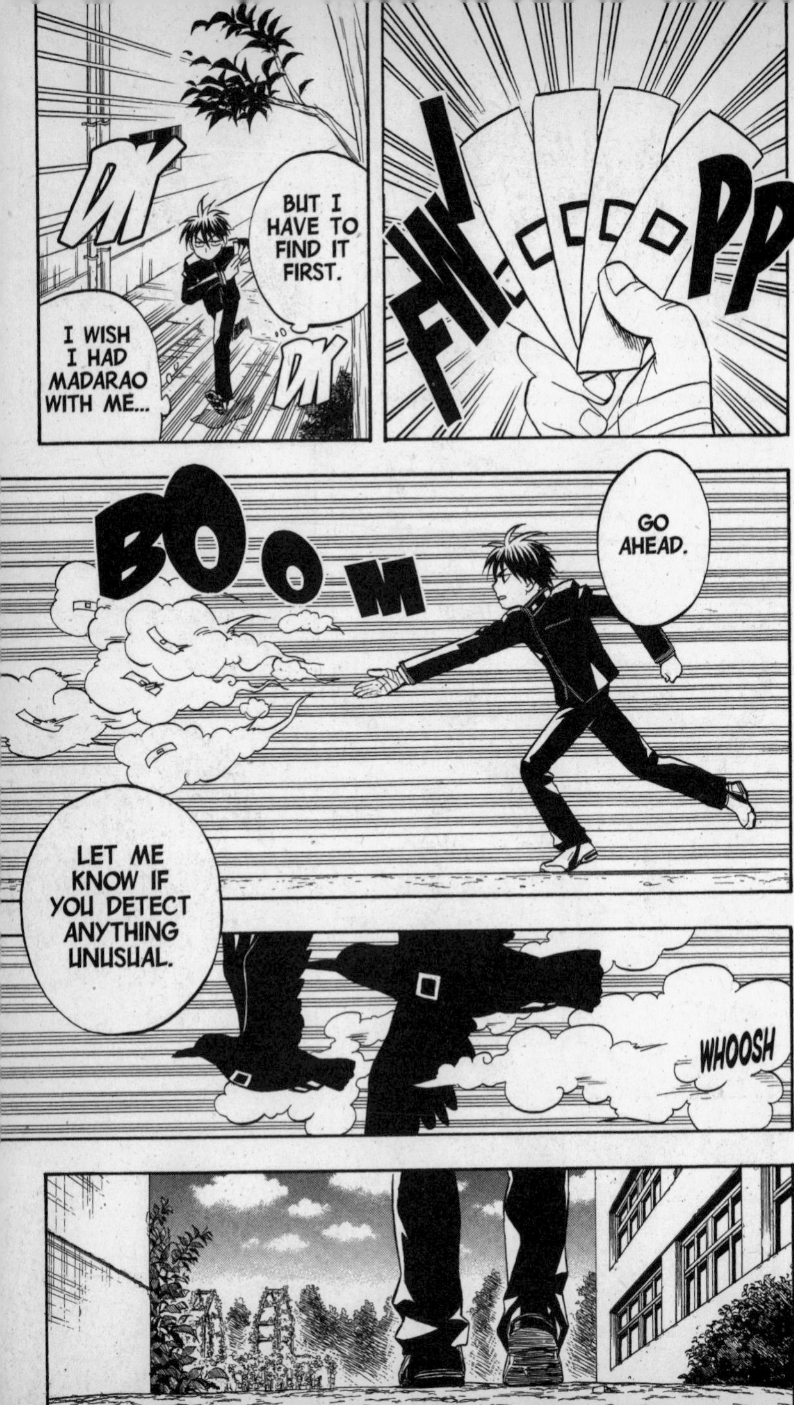
FWOOOOPP
DK
BUT I HAVE TO FIND IT FIRST.
I WISH I HAD MADARAO WITH ME...
DK
GO AHEAD.
BOOM
LET ME KNOW IF YOU DETECT ANYTHING UNUSUAL.
WHOOSH

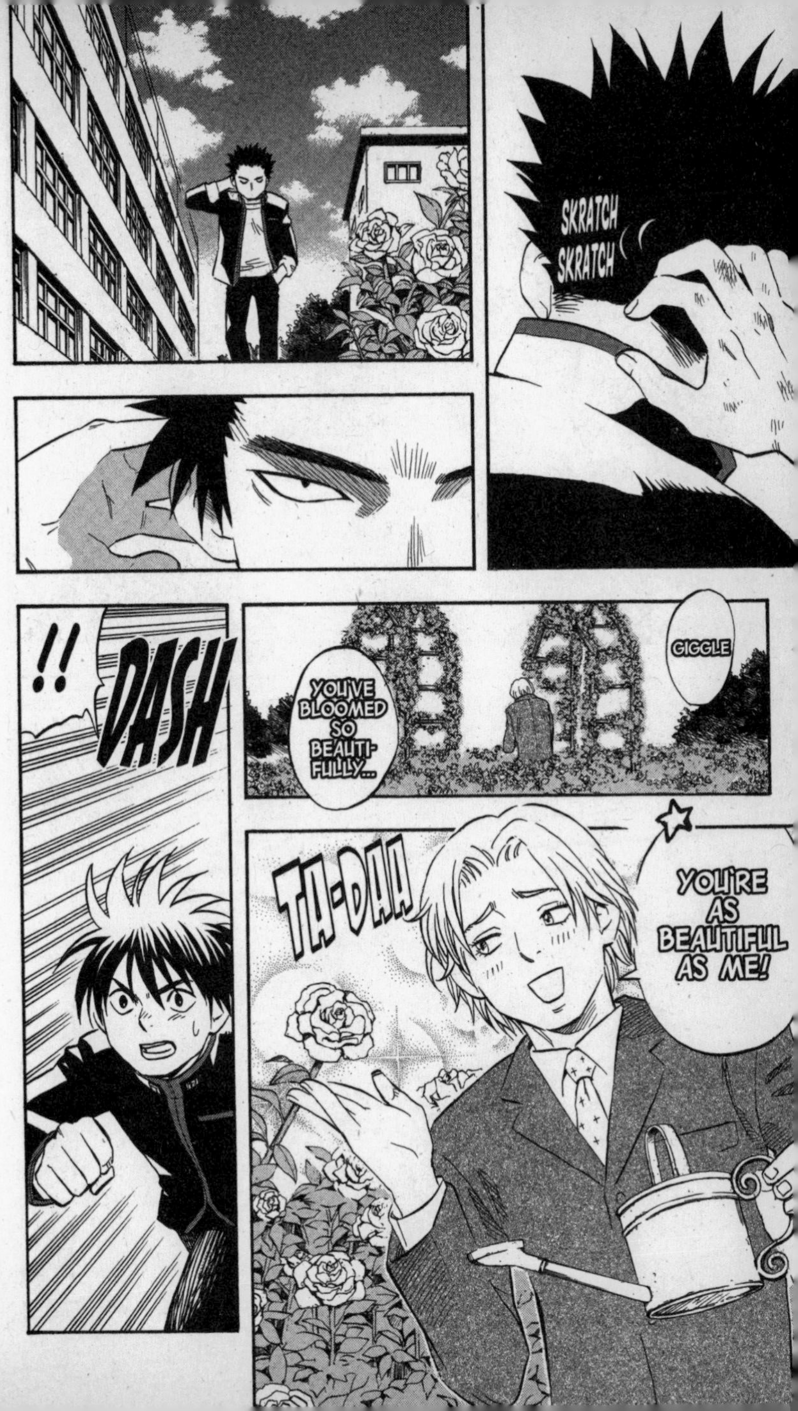
SKRATCH SKRATCH
GIGGLE
YOU'VE BLOOMED SO BEAUTI-FULLY...
TA-DAA
YOU'RE AS BEAUTIFUL AS ME!
!!
DASH

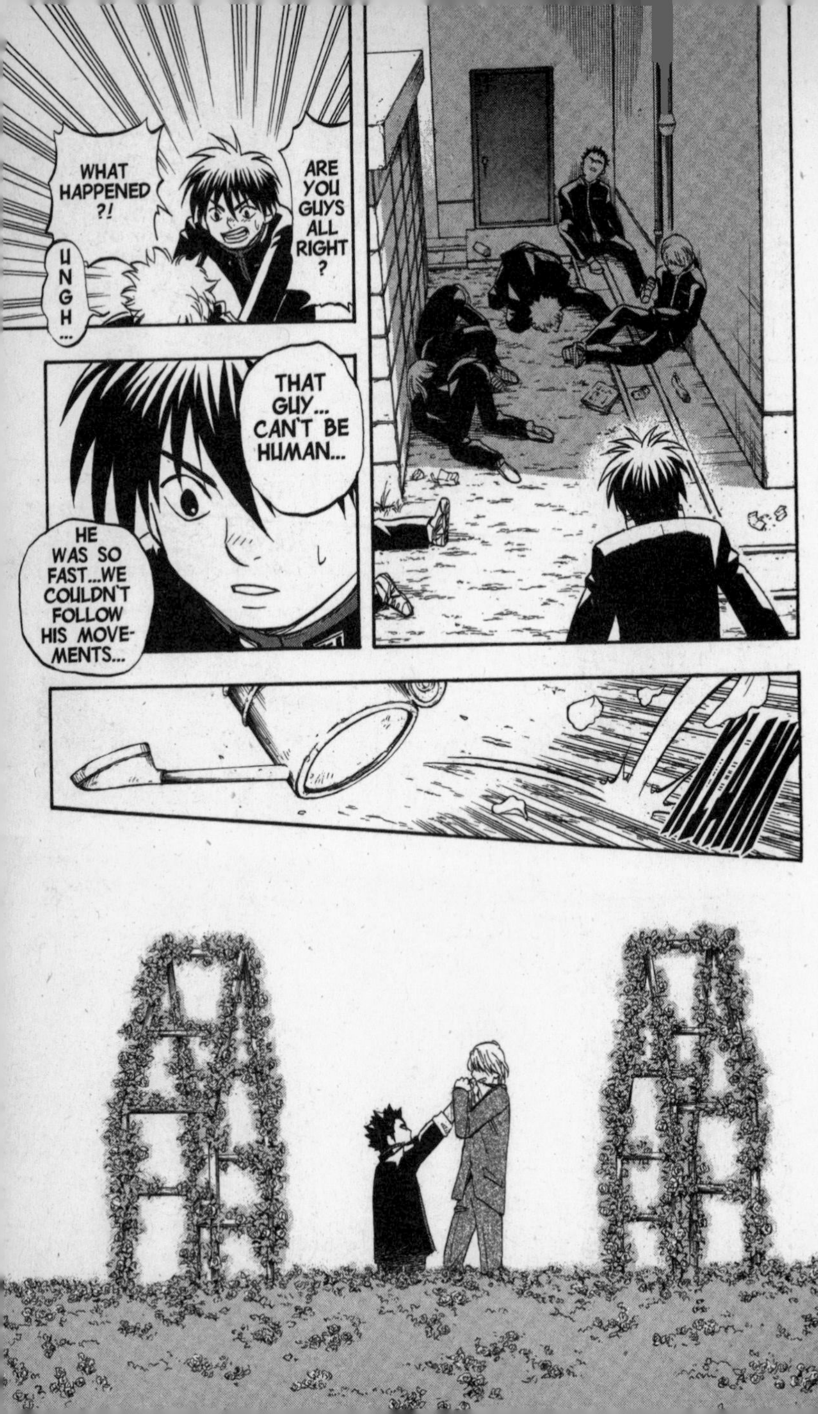
ARE YOU GUYS ALL RIGHT?
WHAT HAPPENED?!
UNGH...
THAT GUY... CAN'T BE HUMAN...
HE WAS SO FAST...WE COULDN'T FOLLOW HIS MOVEMENTS...

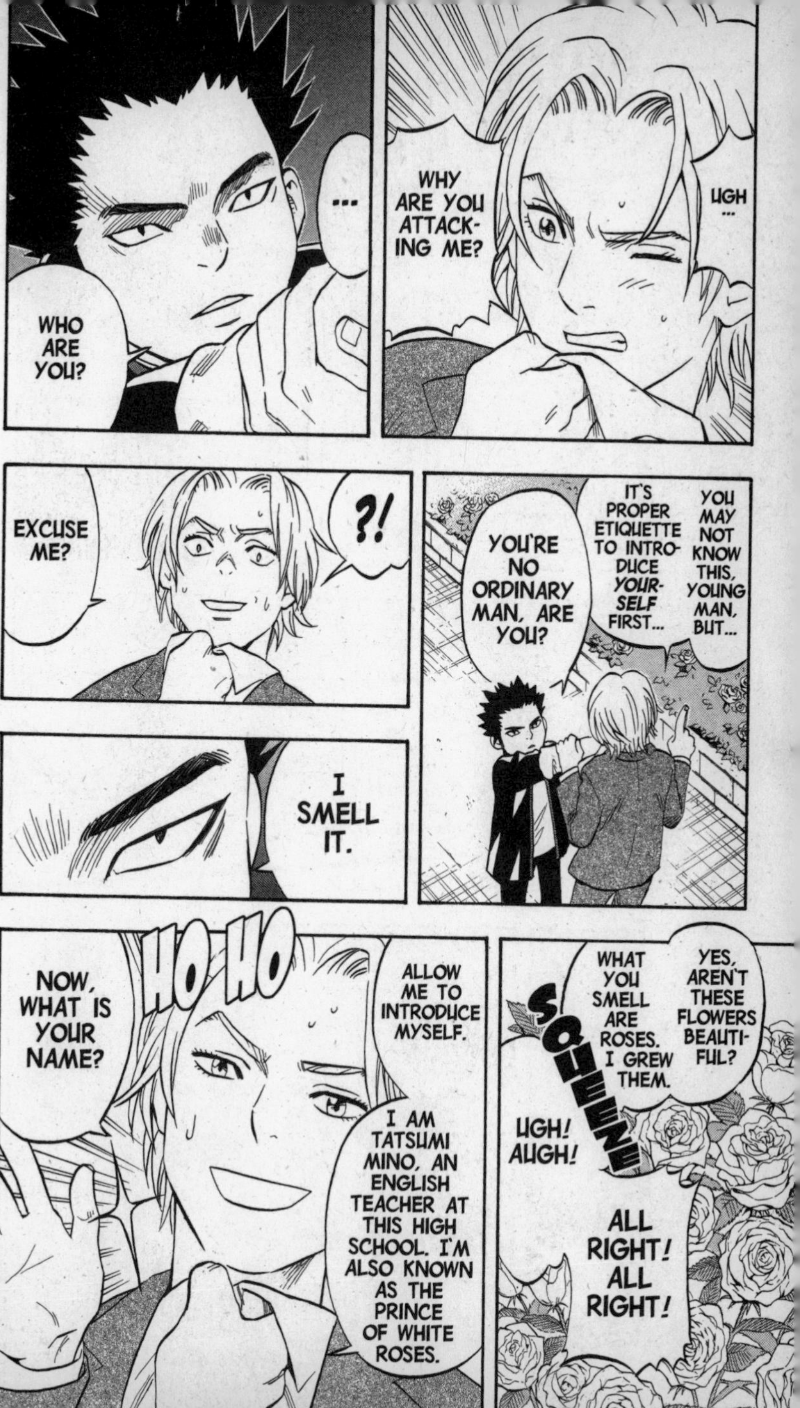
UGH ...
WHY ARE YOU ATTACKING ME?
...
WHO ARE YOU?
YOU MAY NOT KNOW THIS, YOUNG MAN, BUT...
IT'S PROPER ETIQUETTE TO INTRODUCE *YOURSELF* FIRST...
YOU'RE NO ORDINARY MAN, ARE YOU?
?!
EXCUSE ME?
I SMELL IT.
YES, AREN'T THESE FLOWERS BEAUTIFUL?
WHAT YOU SMELL ARE ROSES. I GREW THEM.
SQUEEZE
UGH! AUGH!
ALL RIGHT! ALL RIGHT!
ALLOW ME TO INTRODUCE MYSELF.
HO HO
I AM TATSUMI MINO, AN ENGLISH TEACHER AT THIS HIGH SCHOOL. I'M ALSO KNOWN AS THE PRINCE OF WHITE ROSES.
NOW, WHAT IS YOUR NAME?

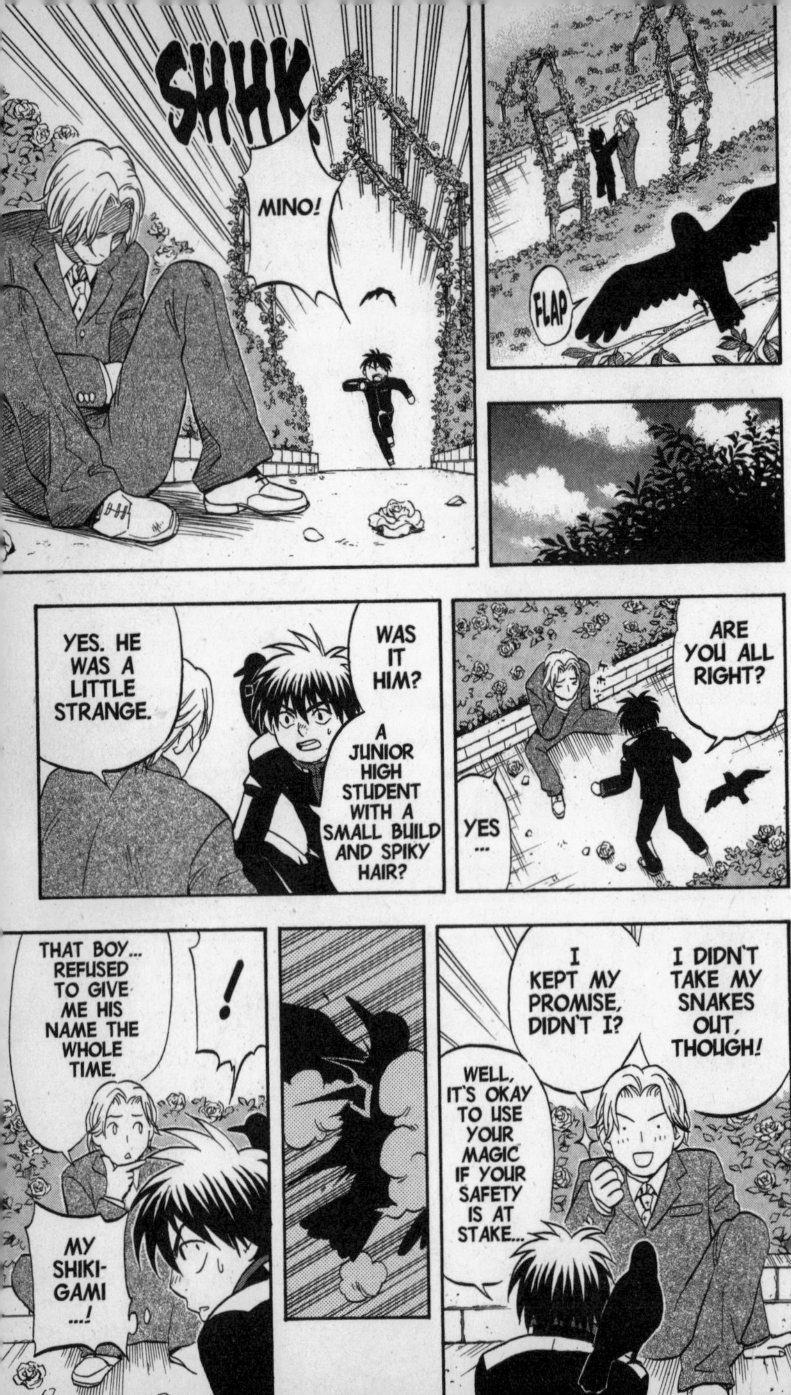
FLAP
SHHK
MINO!
ARE YOU ALL RIGHT?
YES...
WAS IT HIM?
A JUNIOR HIGH STUDENT WITH A SMALL BUILD AND SPIKY HAIR?
YES. HE WAS A LITTLE STRANGE.
I DIDN'T TAKE MY SNAKES OUT, THOUGH!
I KEPT MY PROMISE, DIDN'T I?
WELL, IT'S OKAY TO USE YOUR MAGIC IF YOUR SAFETY IS AT STAKE...
!
THAT BOY... REFUSED TO GIVE ME HIS NAME THE WHOLE TIME.
MY SHIKI-GAMI...!

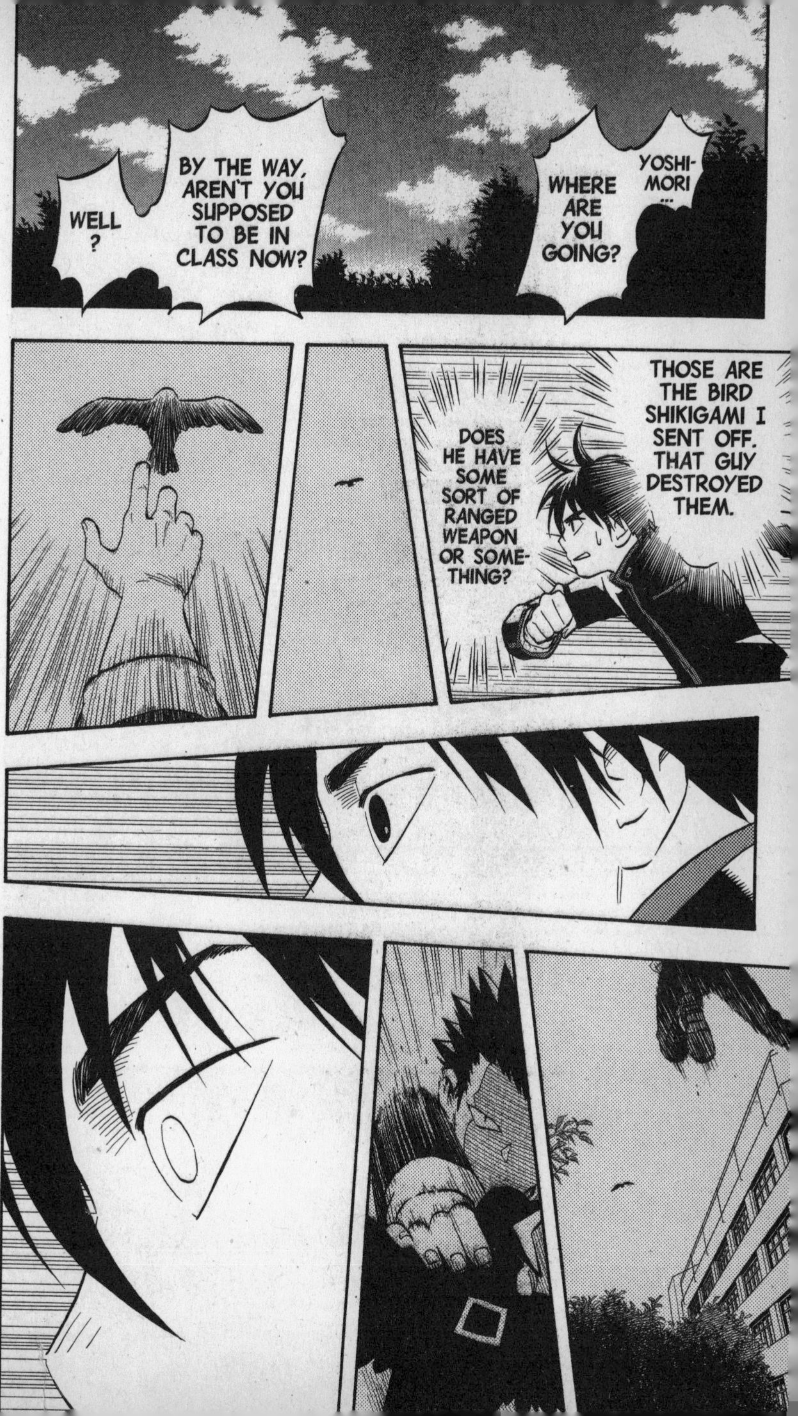
YOSHIMORI...
WHERE ARE YOU GOING?
BY THE WAY, AREN'T YOU SUPPOSED TO BE IN CLASS NOW?
WELL?
THOSE ARE THE BIRD SHIKIGAMI I SENT OFF. THAT GUY DESTROYED THEM.
DOES HE HAVE SOME SORT OF RANGED WEAPON OR SOMETHING?

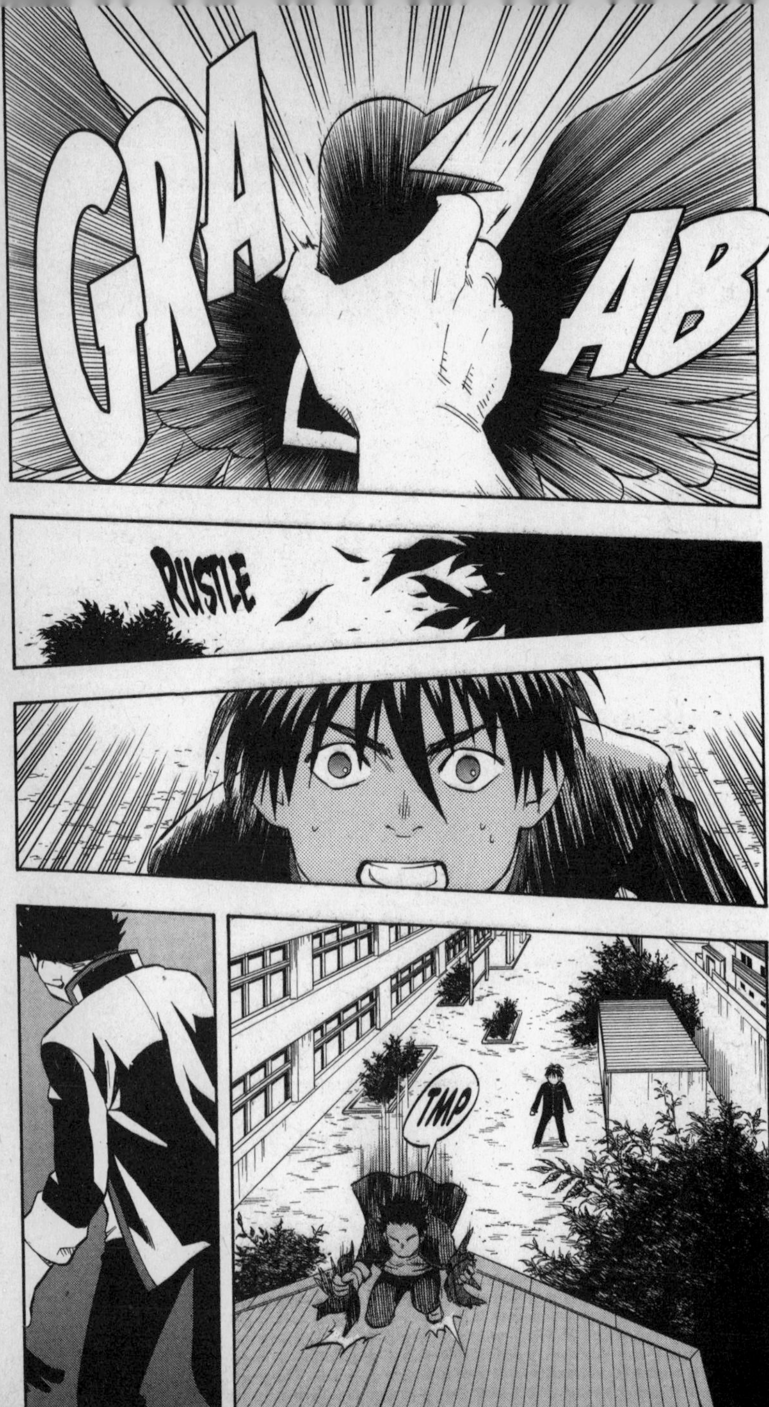
GRAB
RUSTLE
TMP

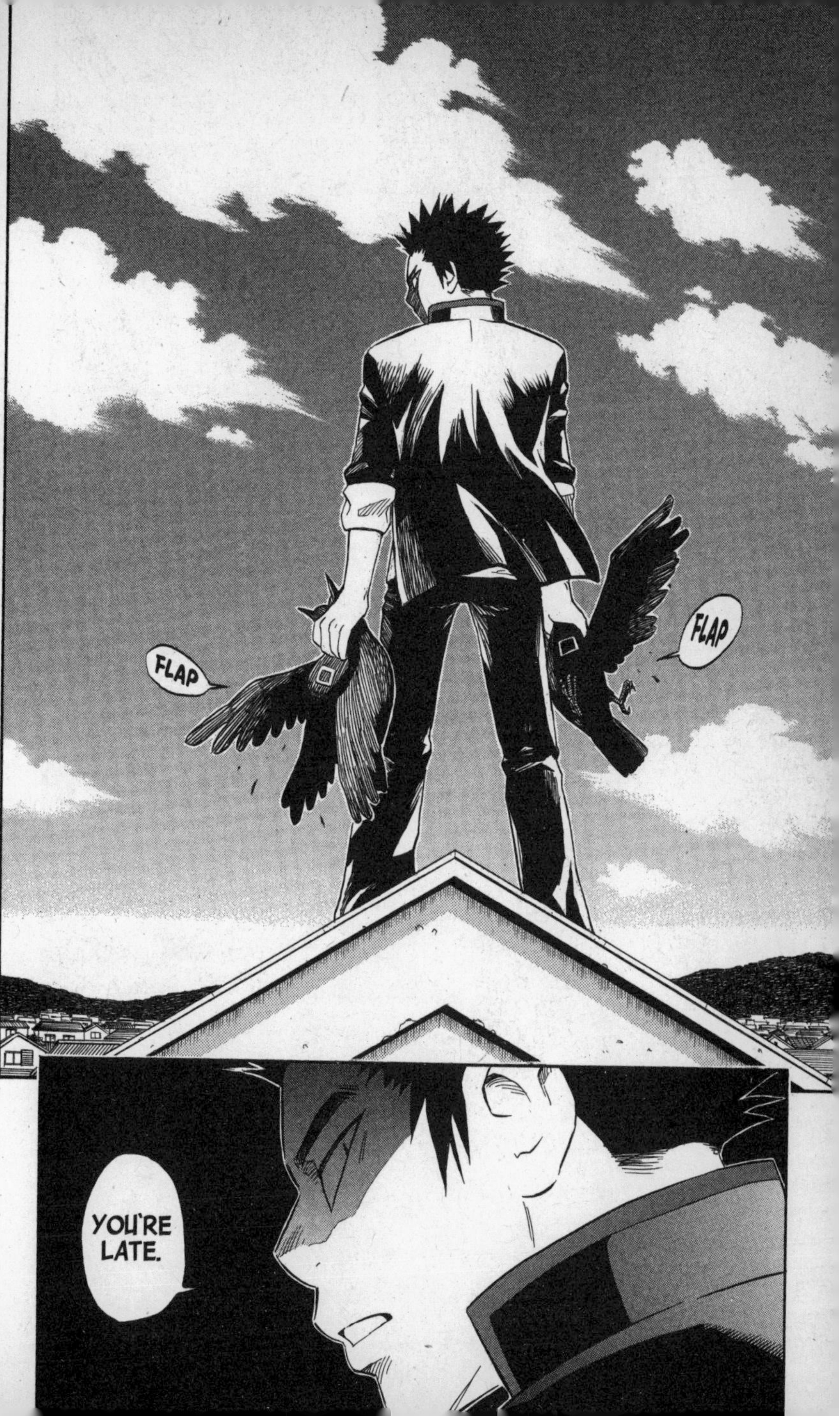
FLAP
FLAP
YOU'RE LATE.

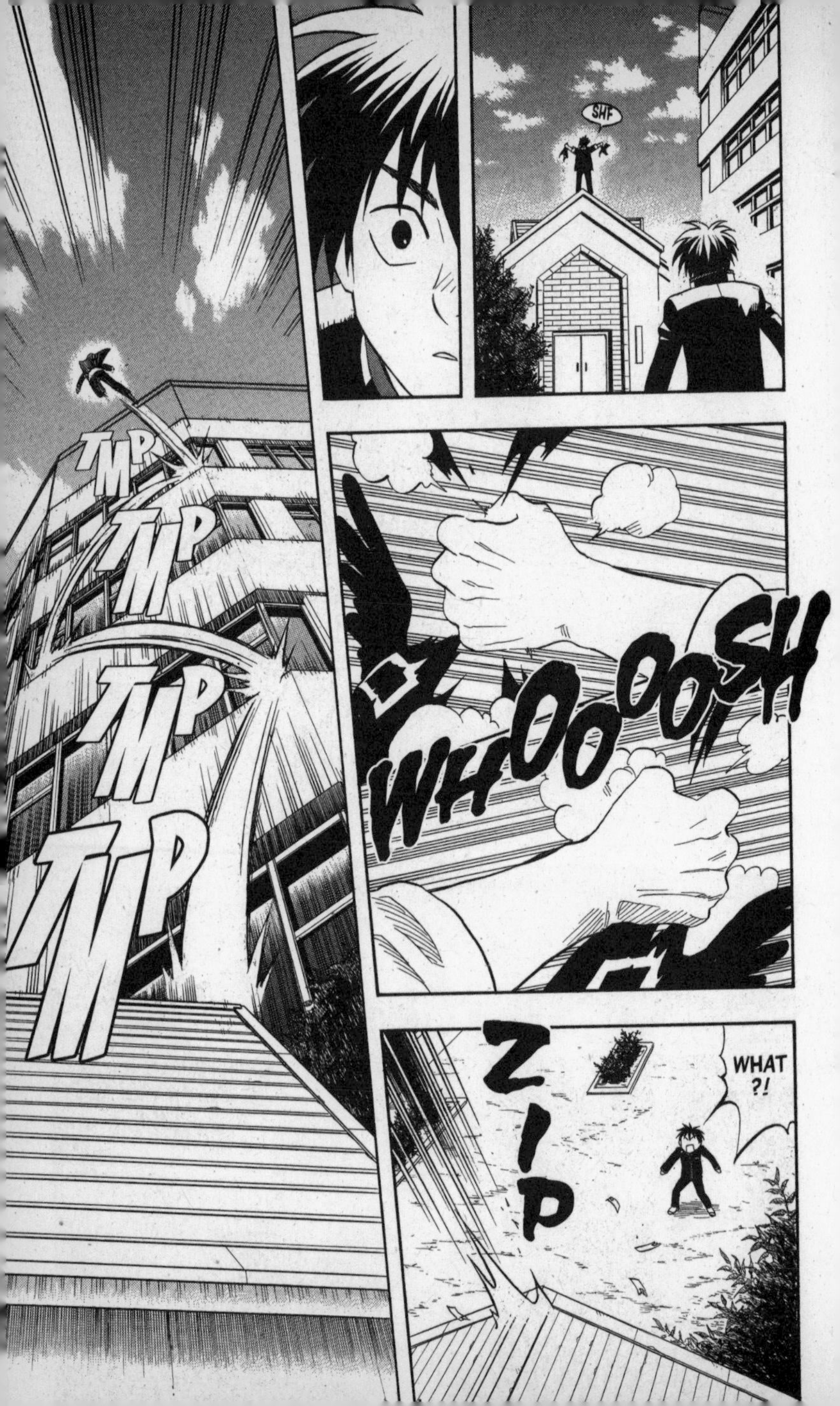
SHF
WHOOOOSH
WHAT ?!
ZIP
TMP
TMP
TMP
TMP

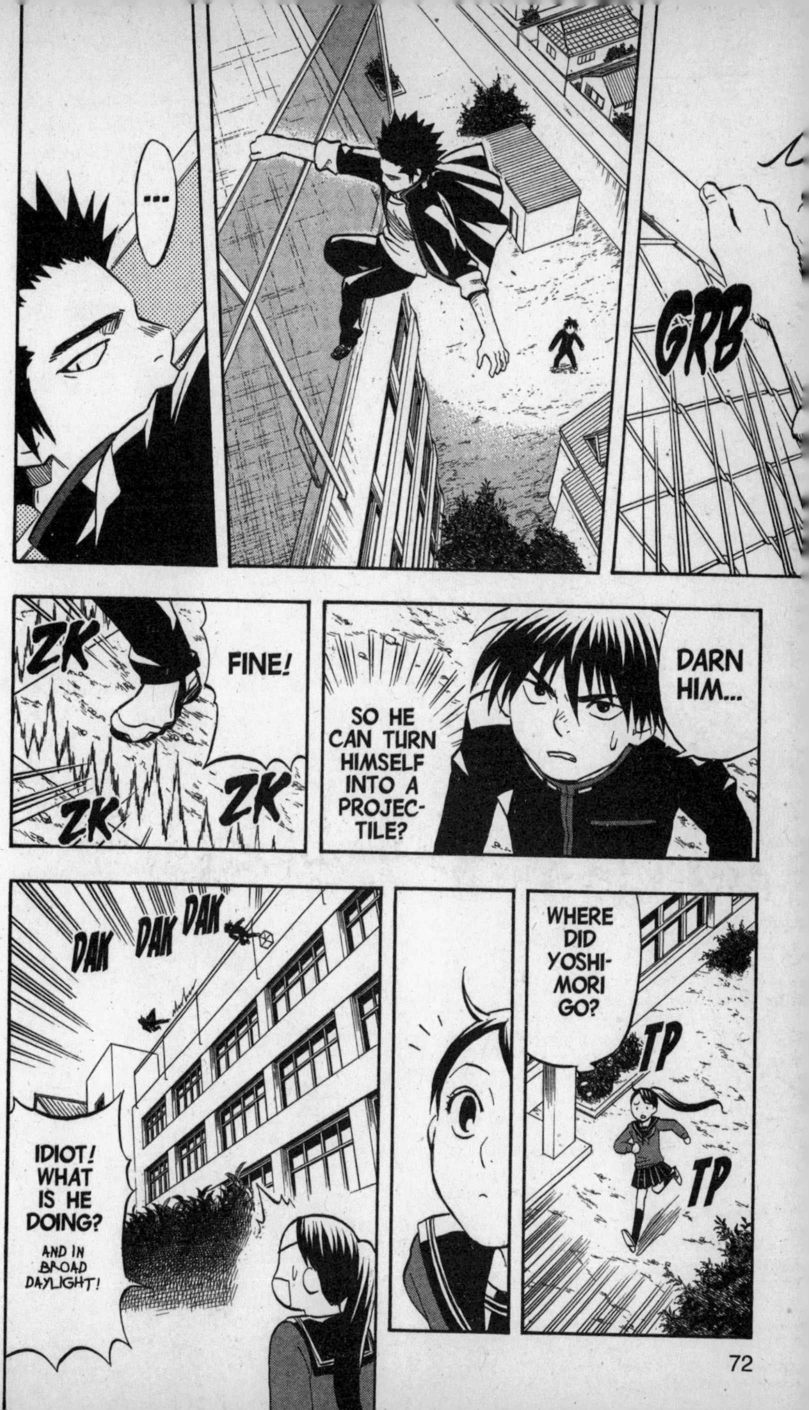
GRB
...
DARN HIM...
SO HE CAN TURN HIMSELF INTO A PROJECTILE?
ZK
FINE!
ZK
ZK
WHERE DID YOSHIMORI GO?
TP
TP
DAK DAK DAK
IDIOT! WHAT IS HE DOING?
AND IN BROAD DAYLIGHT!

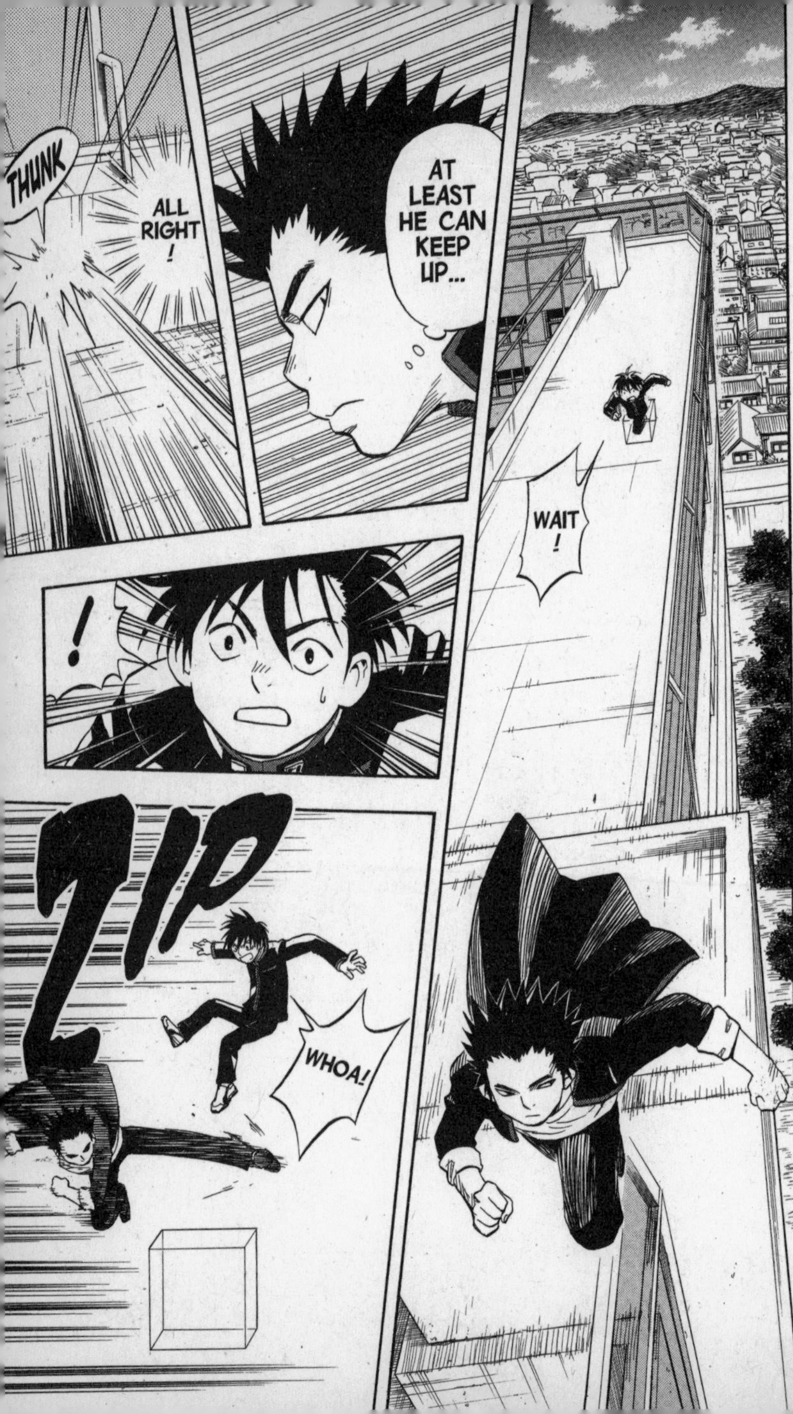
WAIT!
AT LEAST HE CAN KEEP UP...
THUNK
ALL RIGHT!
!
ZIP
WHOA!

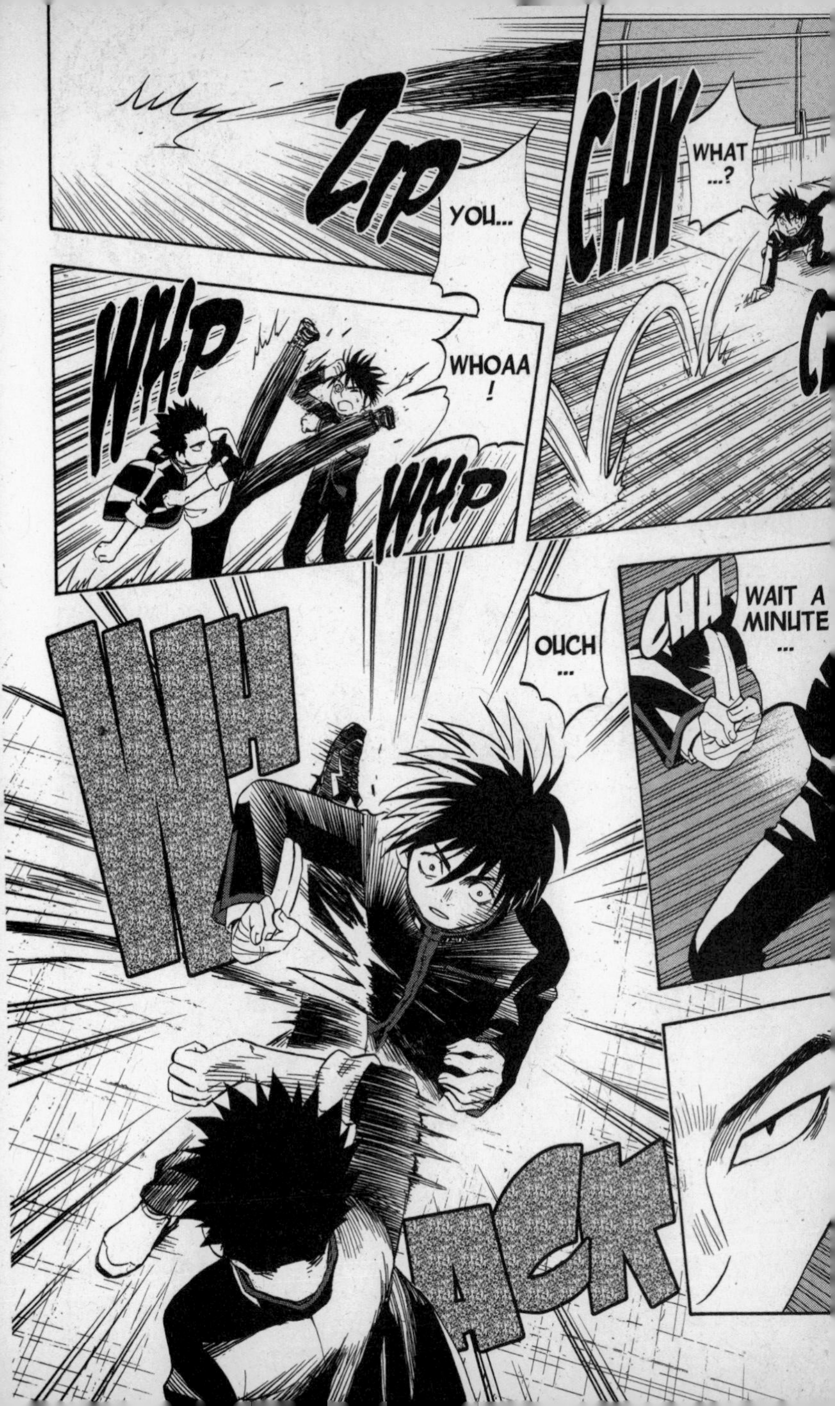
CHK
WHAT ...?
ZIP
YOU...
WHP
WHOAA !
WHP
CHA
WAIT A MINUTE ...
OUCH ...
WH
ACK

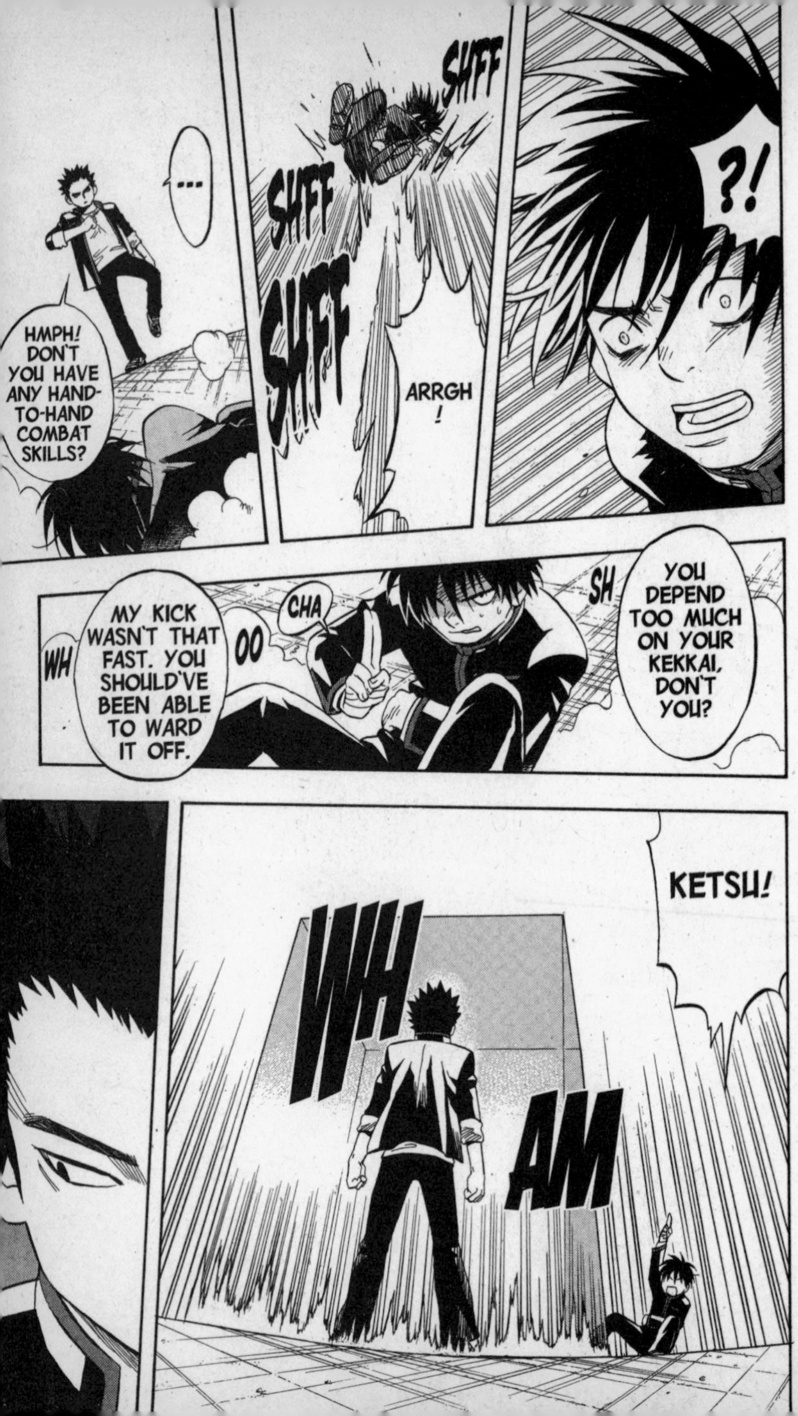
?!
SHFF
SHFF
SHFF
ARRGH!
...
HMPH! DON'T YOU HAVE ANY HAND-TO-HAND COMBAT SKILLS?
YOU DEPEND TOO MUCH ON YOUR KEKKAI, DON'T YOU?
SH
CHA
OO
WH
MY KICK WASN'T THAT FAST. YOU SHOULD'VE BEEN ABLE TO WARD IT OFF.
KETSU!
WH
AM

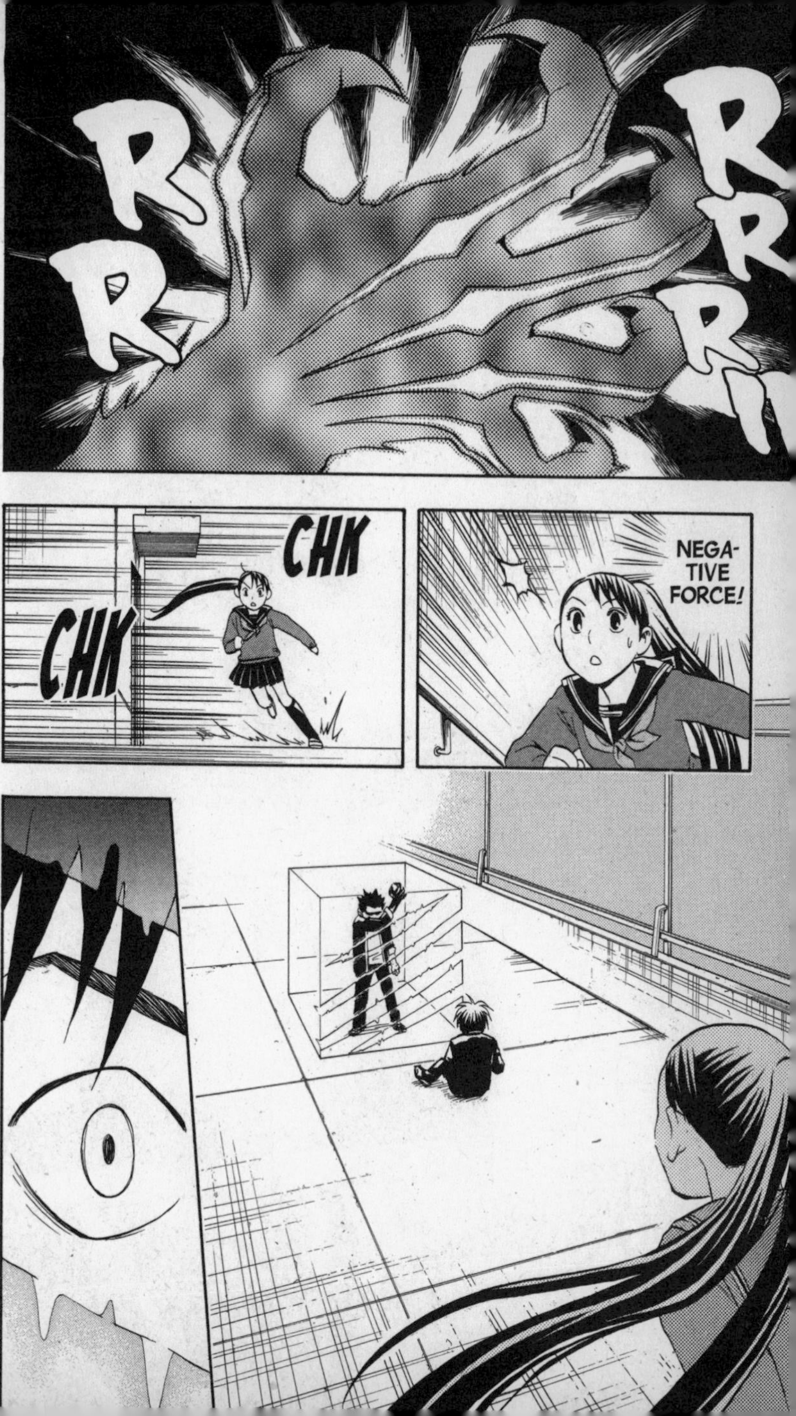
RRRR
RR
NEGA-
TIVE
FORCE!
CHK
CHK

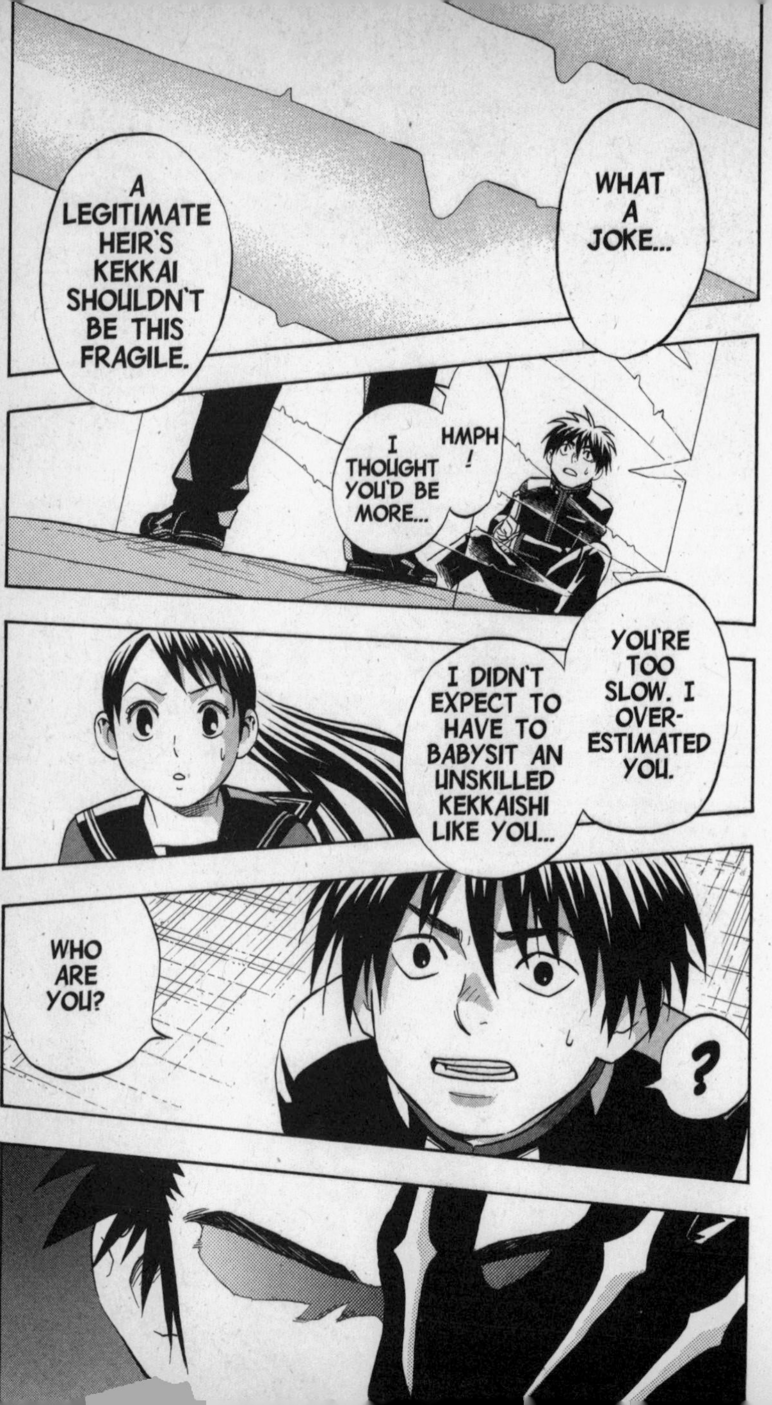
WHAT A JOKE...
A LEGITIMATE HEIR'S KEKKAI SHOULDN'T BE THIS FRAGILE.
HMPH!
I THOUGHT YOU'D BE MORE...
YOU'RE TOO SLOW. I OVER-ESTIMATED YOU.
I DIDN'T EXPECT TO HAVE TO BABYSIT AN UNSKILLED KEKKAISHI LIKE YOU...
?
WHO ARE YOU?

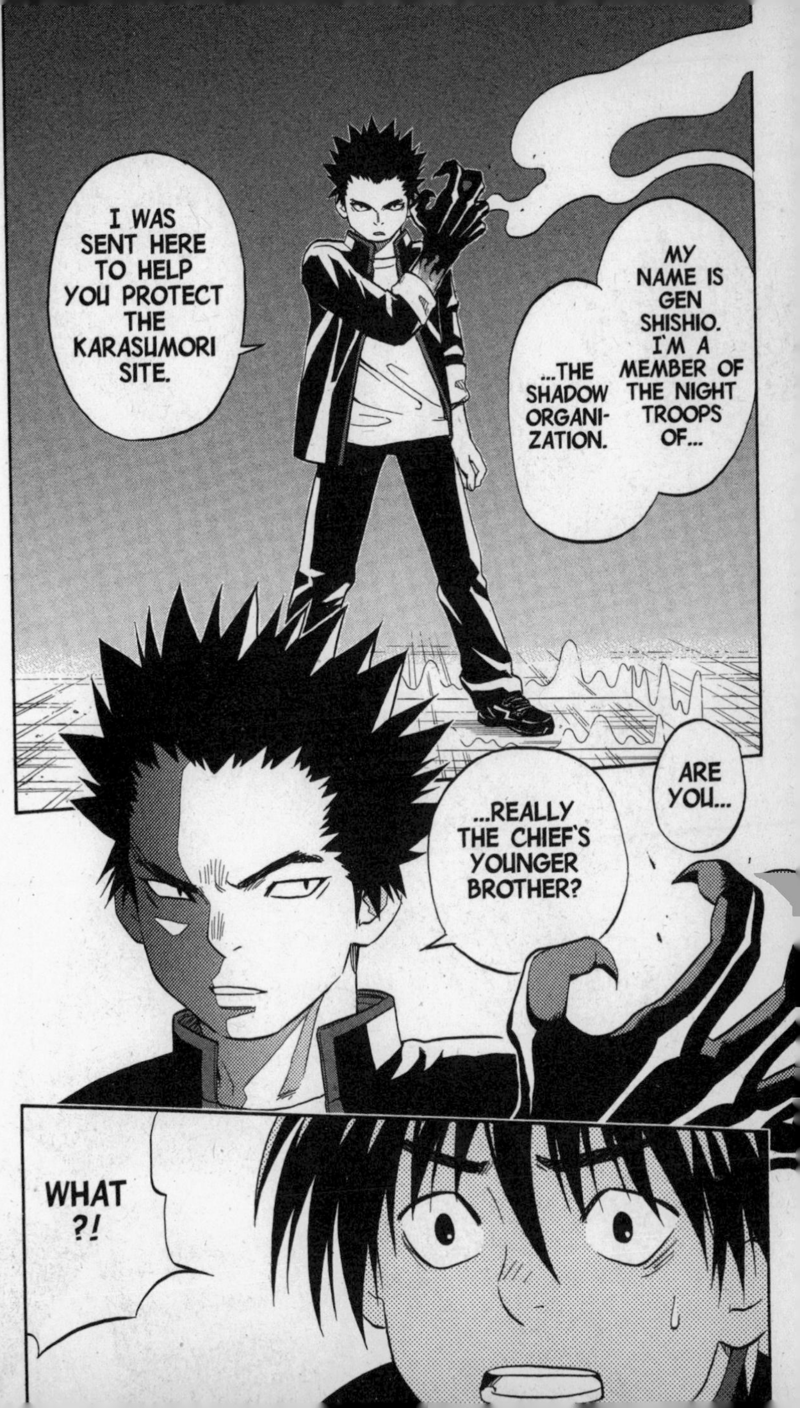
MY NAME IS GEN SHISHIO. I'M A MEMBER OF THE NIGHT TROOPS OF...
...THE SHADOW ORGANI-ZATION.
I WAS SENT HERE TO HELP YOU PROTECT THE KARASUMORI SITE.
ARE YOU...
...REALLY THE CHIEF'S YOUNGER BROTHER?
WHAT ?!

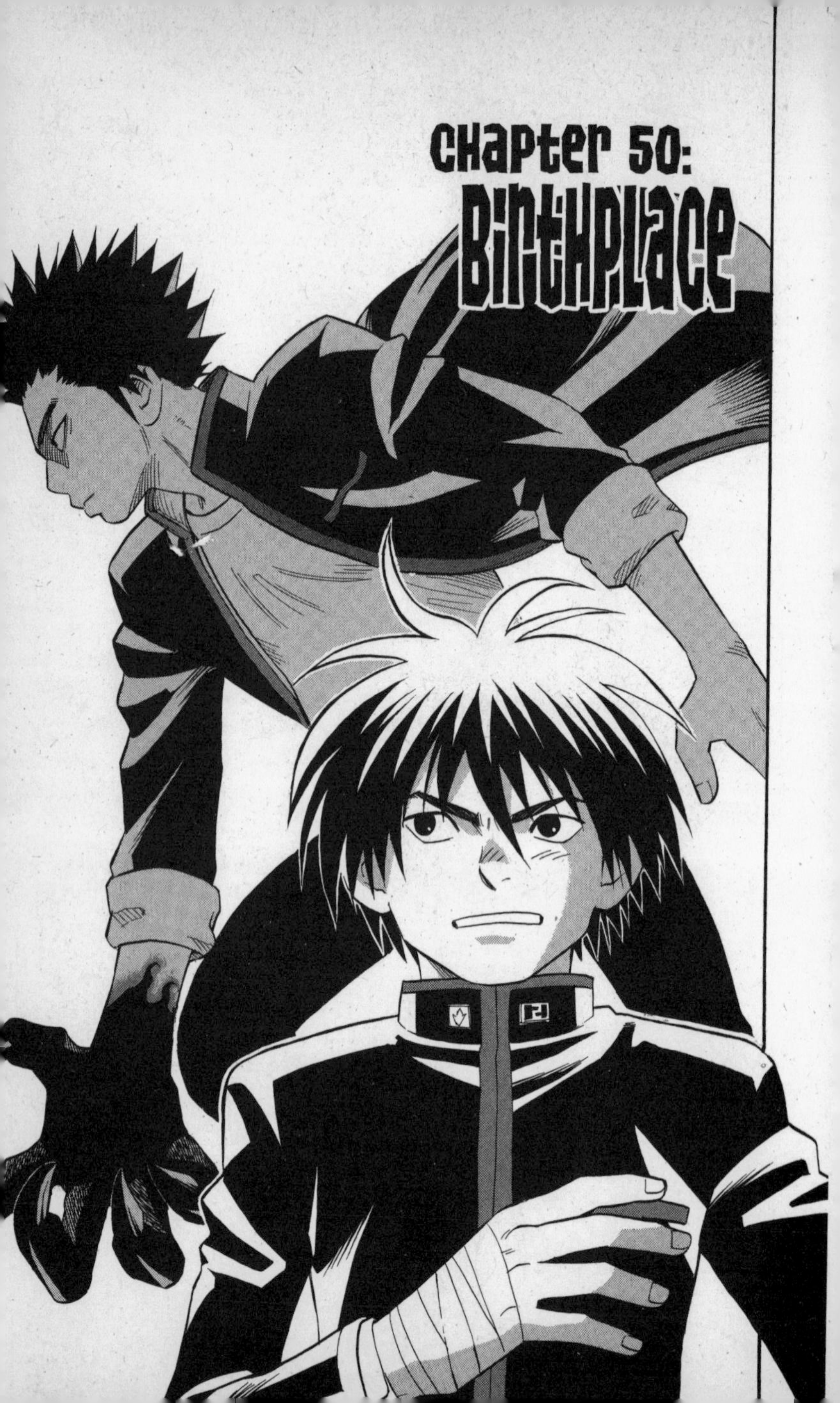
Chapter 50:
Birthplace

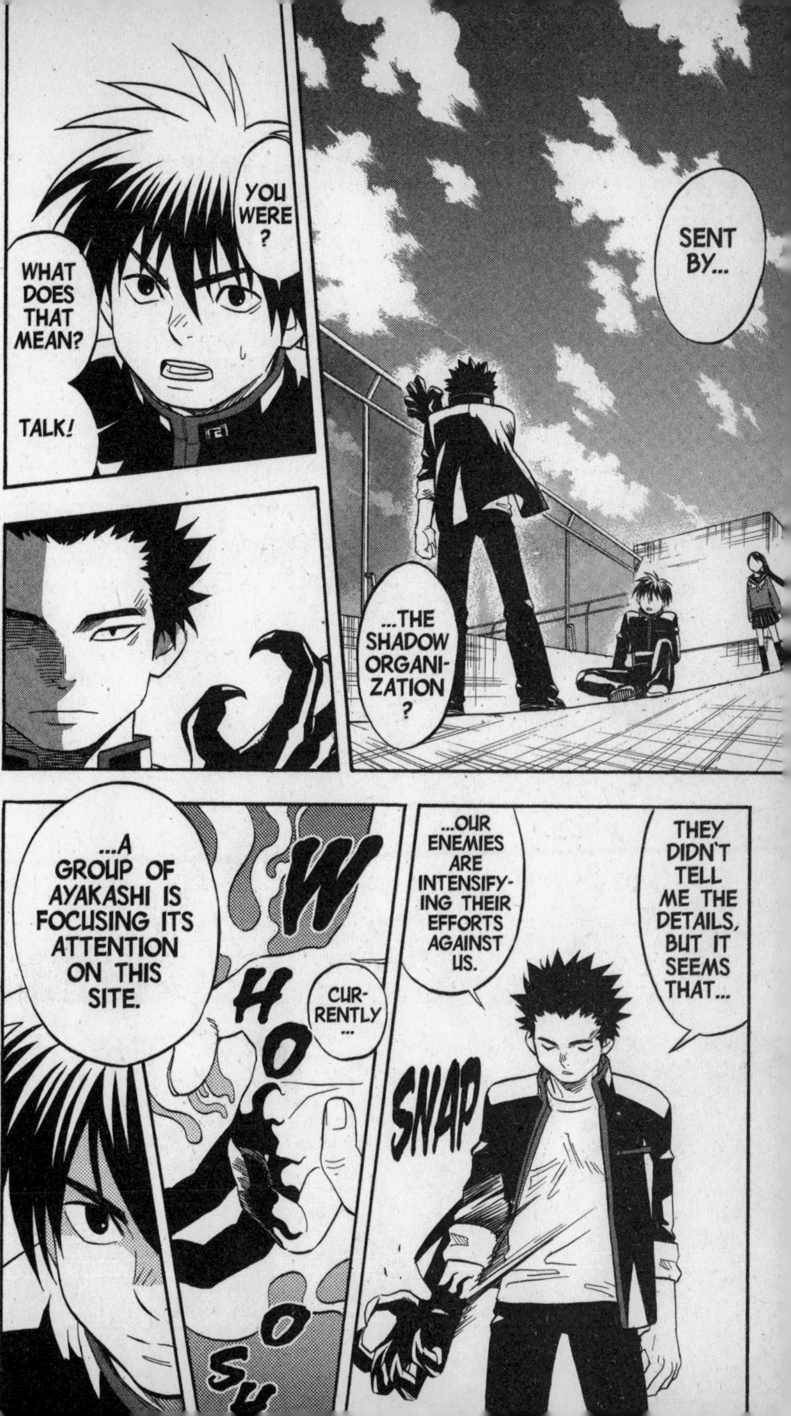
SENT BY...
...THE SHADOW ORGANIZATION?
YOU WERE?
WHAT DOES THAT MEAN?
TALK!
THEY DIDN'T TELL ME THE DETAILS, BUT IT SEEMS THAT...
...OUR ENEMIES ARE INTENSIFYING THEIR EFFORTS AGAINST US.
SNAP
CURRENTLY...
...A GROUP OF AYAKASHI IS FOCUSING ITS ATTENTION ON THIS SITE.

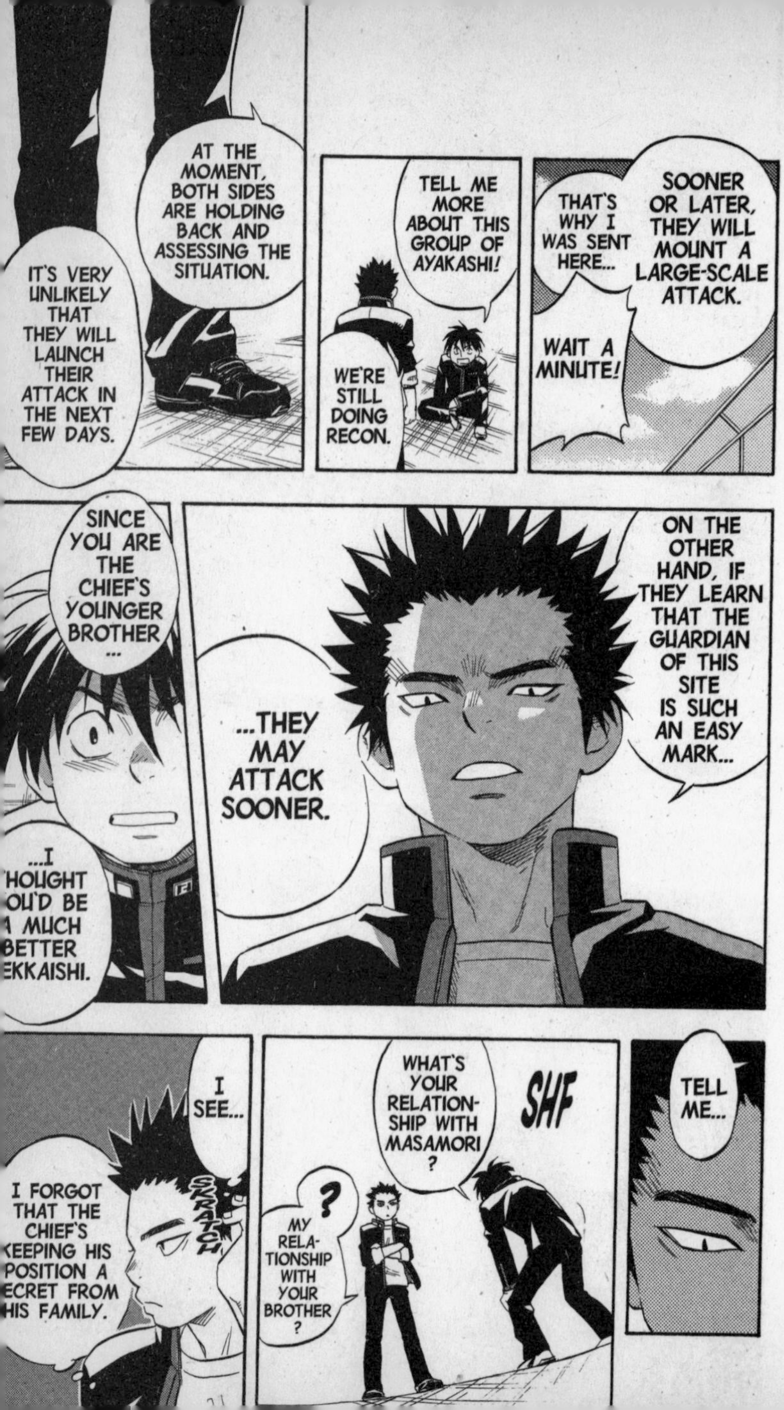
SOONER OR LATER, THEY WILL MOUNT A LARGE-SCALE ATTACK.
THAT'S WHY I WAS SENT HERE...
WAIT A MINUTE!
TELL ME MORE ABOUT THIS GROUP OF AYAKASHI!
WE'RE STILL DOING RECON.
AT THE MOMENT, BOTH SIDES ARE HOLDING BACK AND ASSESSING THE SITUATION.
IT'S VERY UNLIKELY THAT THEY WILL LAUNCH THEIR ATTACK IN THE NEXT FEW DAYS.
ON THE OTHER HAND, IF THEY LEARN THAT THE GUARDIAN OF THIS SITE IS SUCH AN EASY MARK...
...THEY MAY ATTACK SOONER.
SINCE YOU ARE THE CHIEF'S YOUNGER BROTHER...
...I HOUGHT OU'D BE MUCH BETTER EKKAISHI.
TELL ME...
SHF
WHAT'S YOUR RELATIONSHIP WITH MASAMORI?
?
MY RELATIONSHIP WITH YOUR BROTHER?
I SEE...
SKRATCH
I FORGOT THAT THE CHIEF'S EEPING HIS POSITION A ECRET FROM HIS FAMILY.

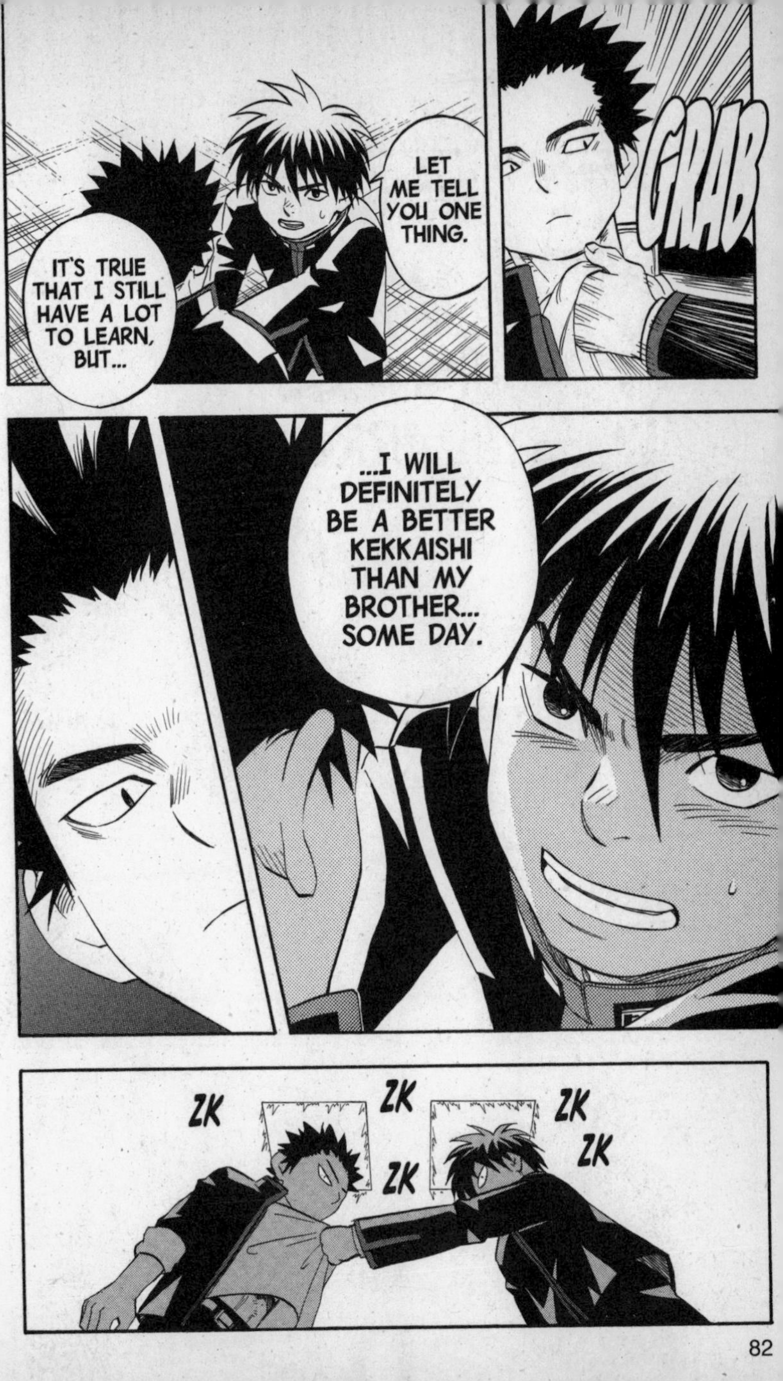
GRAB
LET ME TELL YOU ONE THING.
IT'S TRUE THAT I STILL HAVE A LOT TO LEARN, BUT...
...I WILL DEFINITELY BE A BETTER KEKKAISHI THAN MY BROTHER... SOME DAY.
ZK
ZK
ZK
ZK
ZK

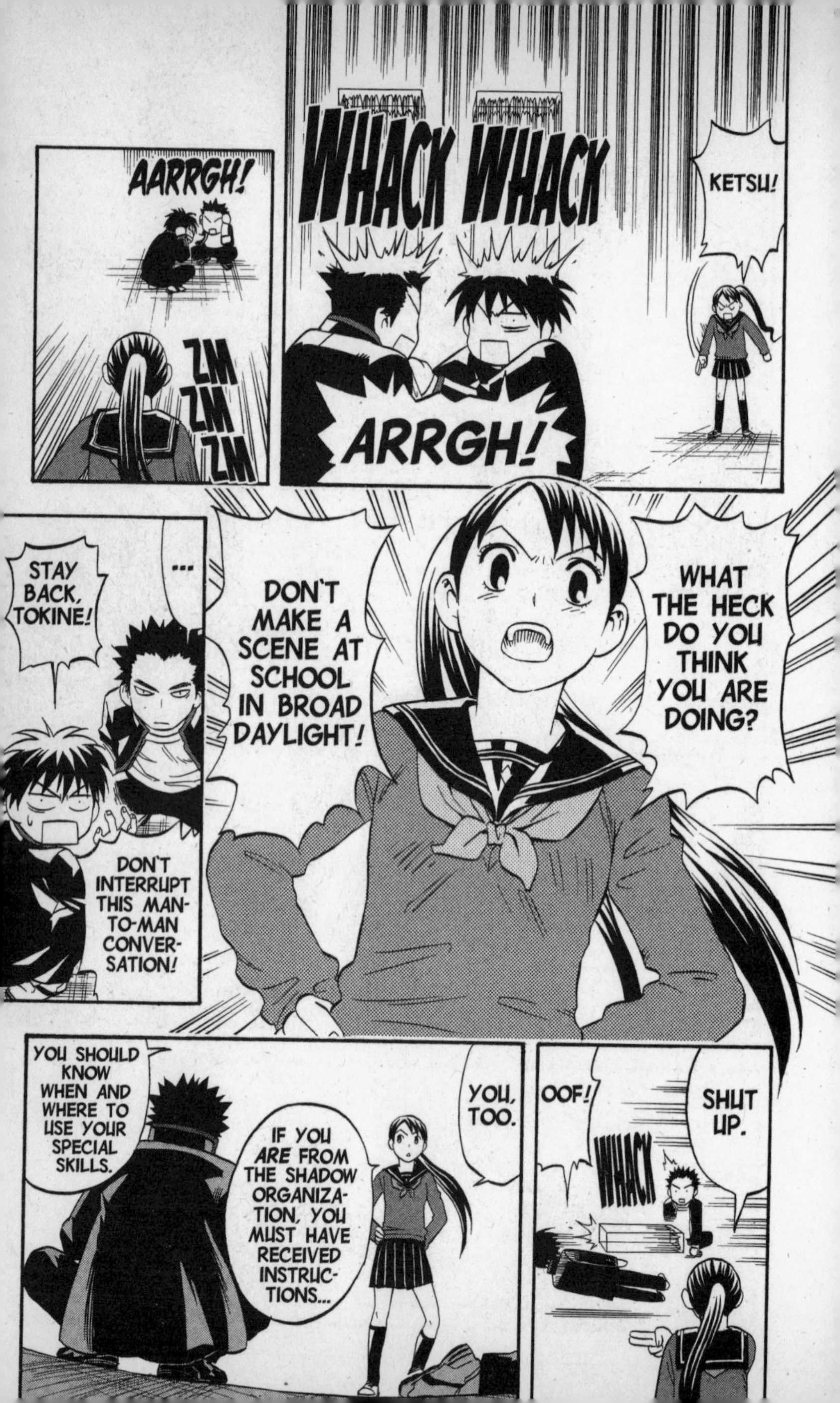
KETSU!
WHACK WHACK
ARRGH!
AARRGH!
ZM ZM ZM
WHAT THE HECK DO YOU THINK YOU ARE DOING?
DON'T MAKE A SCENE AT SCHOOL IN BROAD DAYLIGHT!
...
STAY BACK, TOKINE!
DON'T INTERRUPT THIS MAN-TO-MAN CONVER-SATION!
SHUT UP.
OOF!
WHACK
YOU, TOO.
IF YOU *ARE* FROM THE SHADOW ORGANIZA-TION, YOU MUST HAVE RECEIVED INSTRUC-TIONS...
YOU SHOULD KNOW WHEN AND WHERE TO USE YOUR SPECIAL SKILLS.

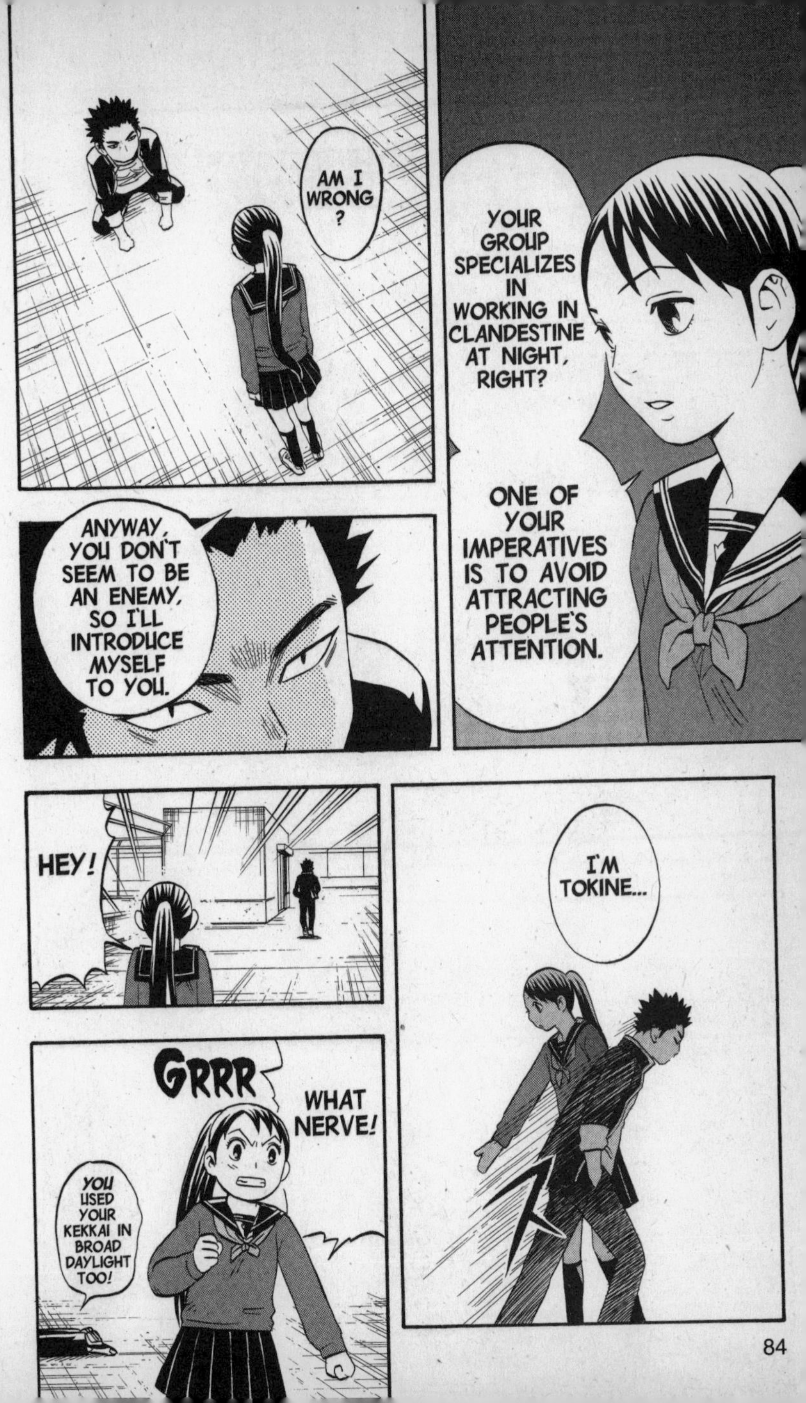
YOUR GROUP SPECIALIZES IN WORKING IN CLANDESTINE AT NIGHT, RIGHT?
ONE OF YOUR IMPERATIVES IS TO AVOID ATTRACTING PEOPLE'S ATTENTION.
AM I WRONG?
ANYWAY, YOU DON'T SEEM TO BE AN ENEMY, SO I'LL INTRODUCE MYSELF TO YOU.
I'M TOKINE...
HEY!
GRRR
WHAT NERVE!
YOU USED YOUR KEKKAI IN BROAD DAYLIGHT TOO!

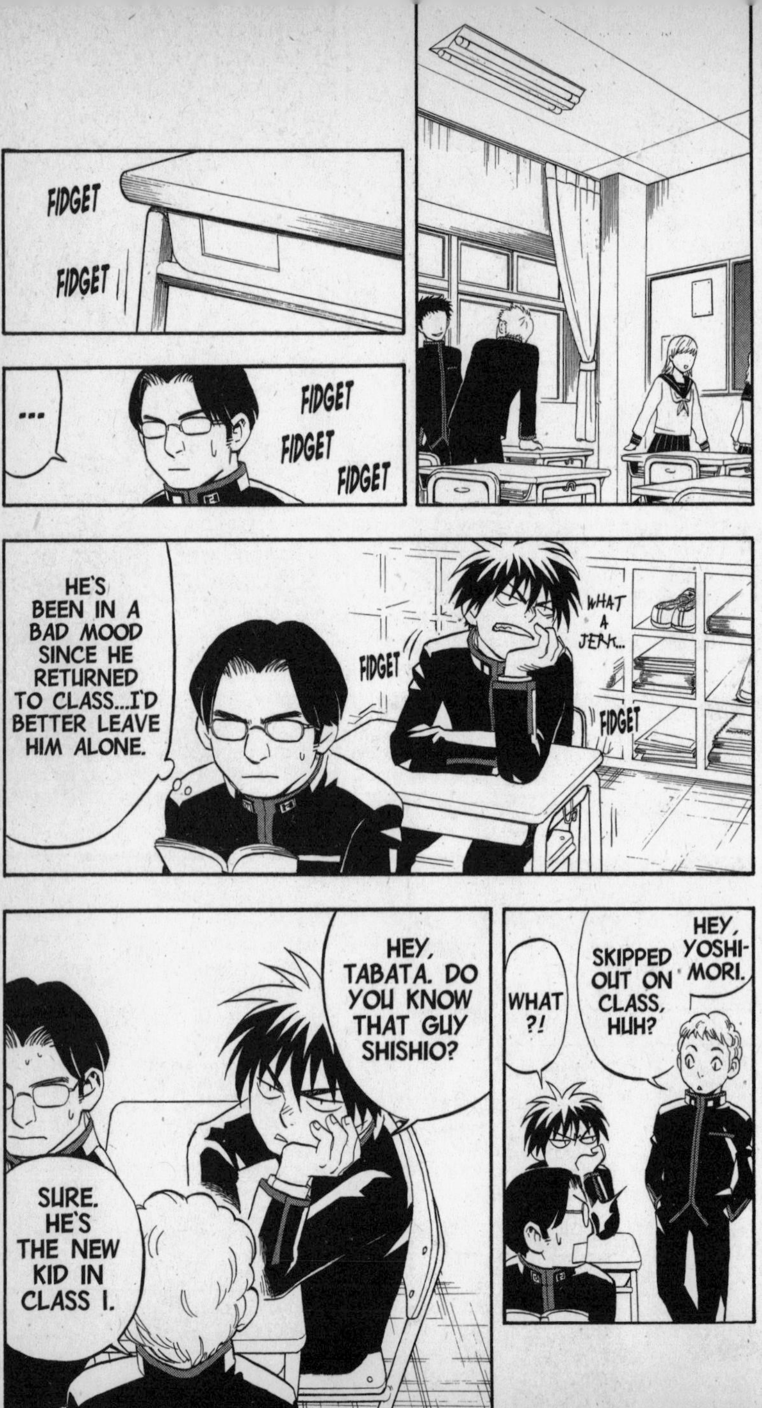
FIDGET
FIDGET
...
FIDGET
FIDGET
FIDGET
WHAT A JERK...
HE'S BEEN IN A BAD MOOD SINCE HE RETURNED TO CLASS...I'D BETTER LEAVE HIM ALONE.
FIDGET
FIDGET
HEY, YOSHI-MORI.
SKIPPED OUT ON CLASS, HUH?
WHAT?!
HEY, TABATA. DO YOU KNOW THAT GUY SHISHIO?
SURE. HE'S THE NEW KID IN CLASS I.

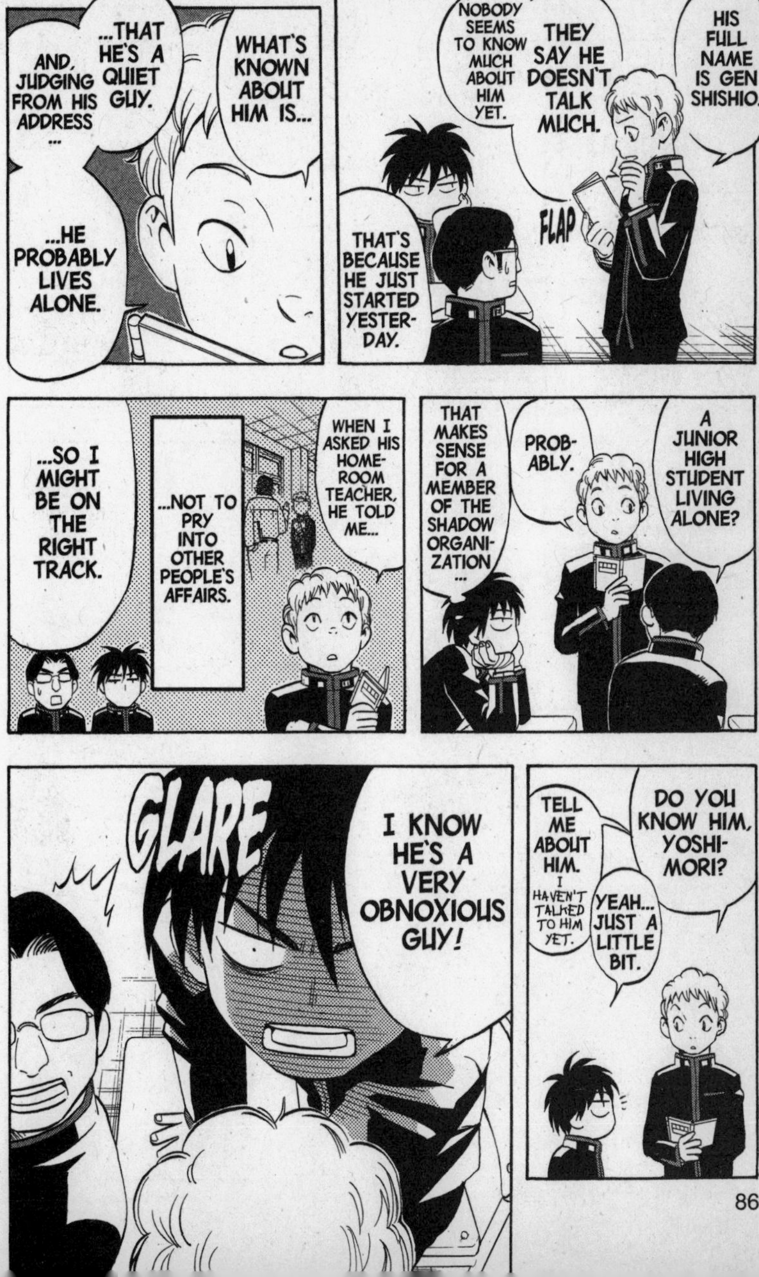
HIS FULL NAME IS GEN SHISHIO.
THEY SAY HE DOESN'T TALK MUCH.
NOBODY SEEMS TO KNOW MUCH ABOUT HIM YET.
FLAP
THAT'S BECAUSE HE JUST STARTED YESTER-DAY.
WHAT'S KNOWN ABOUT HIM IS...
...THAT HE'S A QUIET GUY.
AND, JUDGING FROM HIS ADDRESS...
...HE PROBABLY LIVES ALONE.
A JUNIOR HIGH STUDENT LIVING ALONE?
PROB-ABLY.
THAT MAKES SENSE FOR A MEMBER OF THE SHADOW ORGANI-ZATION...
WHEN I ASKED HIS HOME-ROOM TEACHER, HE TOLD ME...
...NOT TO PRY INTO OTHER PEOPLE'S AFFAIRS.
...SO I MIGHT BE ON THE RIGHT TRACK.
DO YOU KNOW HIM, YOSHI-MORI?
TELL ME ABOUT HIM.
YEAH... JUST A LITTLE BIT.
I HAVEN'T TALKED TO HIM YET.
GLARE
I KNOW HE'S A VERY OBNOXIOUS GUY!

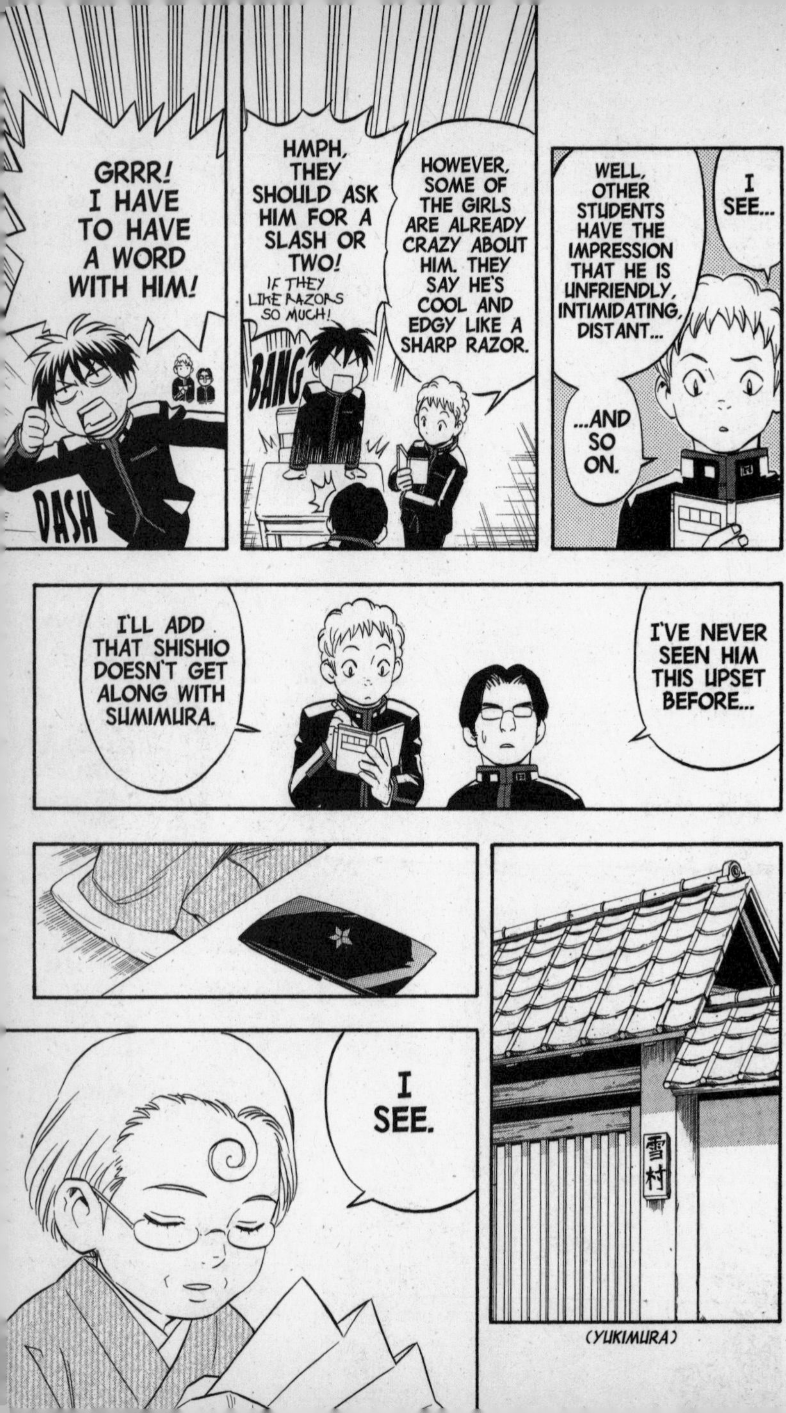

I SEE...
WELL, OTHER STUDENTS HAVE THE IMPRESSION THAT HE IS UNFRIENDLY, INTIMIDATING, DISTANT...
...AND SO ON.
HOWEVER, SOME OF THE GIRLS ARE ALREADY CRAZY ABOUT HIM. THEY SAY HE'S COOL AND EDGY LIKE A SHARP RAZOR.
HMPH, THEY SHOULD ASK HIM FOR A SLASH OR TWO!
IF THEY LIKE RAZORS SO MUCH!
BANG
GRRR! I HAVE TO HAVE A WORD WITH HIM!
DASH
I'VE NEVER SEEN HIM THIS UPSET BEFORE...
I'LL ADD THAT SHISHIO DOESN'T GET ALONG WITH SUMIMURA.
雪村
(YUKIMURA)
I SEE.

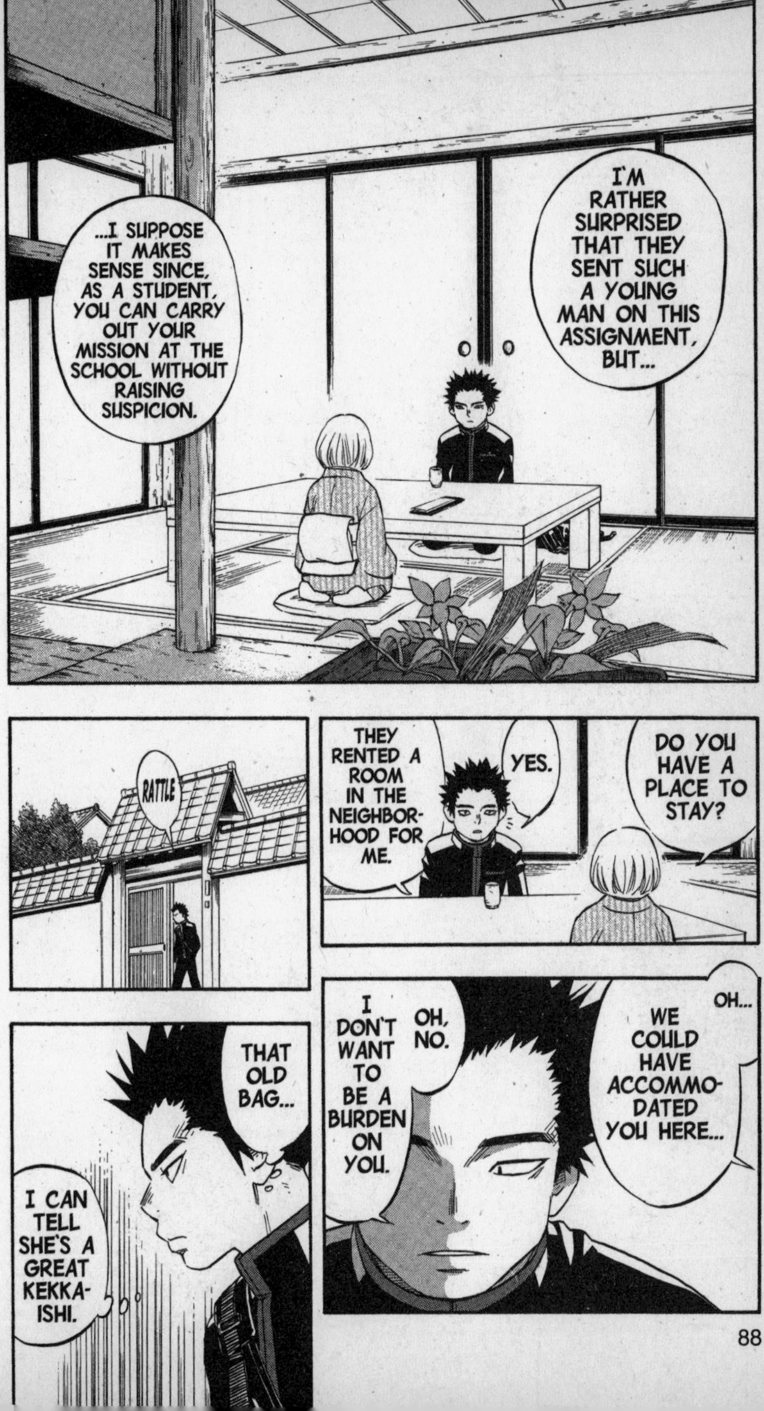
I'M RATHER SURPRISED THAT THEY SENT SUCH A YOUNG MAN ON THIS ASSIGNMENT, BUT...
...I SUPPOSE IT MAKES SENSE SINCE, AS A STUDENT, YOU CAN CARRY OUT YOUR MISSION AT THE SCHOOL WITHOUT RAISING SUSPICION.
DO YOU HAVE A PLACE TO STAY?
YES.
THEY RENTED A ROOM IN THE NEIGHBOR-HOOD FOR ME.
RATTLE
OH... WE COULD HAVE ACCOMMO-DATED YOU HERE...
OH, NO.
I DON'T WANT TO BE A BURDEN ON YOU.
THAT OLD BAG...
I CAN TELL SHE'S A GREAT KEKKA-ISHI.

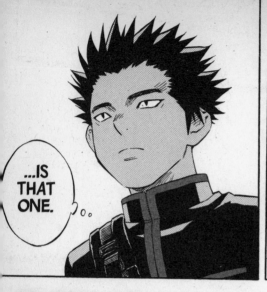

...IS THAT ONE.

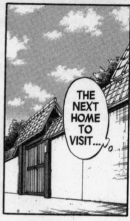

THE NEXT HOME TO VISIT....

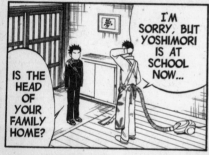

IS THE HEAD OF YOUR FAMILY HOME?

I'M SORRY, BUT YOSHIMORI IS AT SCHOOL NOW...

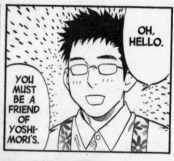

OH, HELLO.

YOU MUST BE A FRIEND OF YOSHIMORI'S.

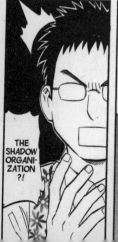

THE SHADOW ORGANIZATION?!

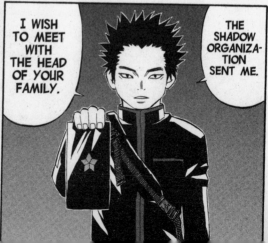

I WISH TO MEET WITH THE HEAD OF YOUR FAMILY.

THE SHADOW ORGANIZATION SENT ME.

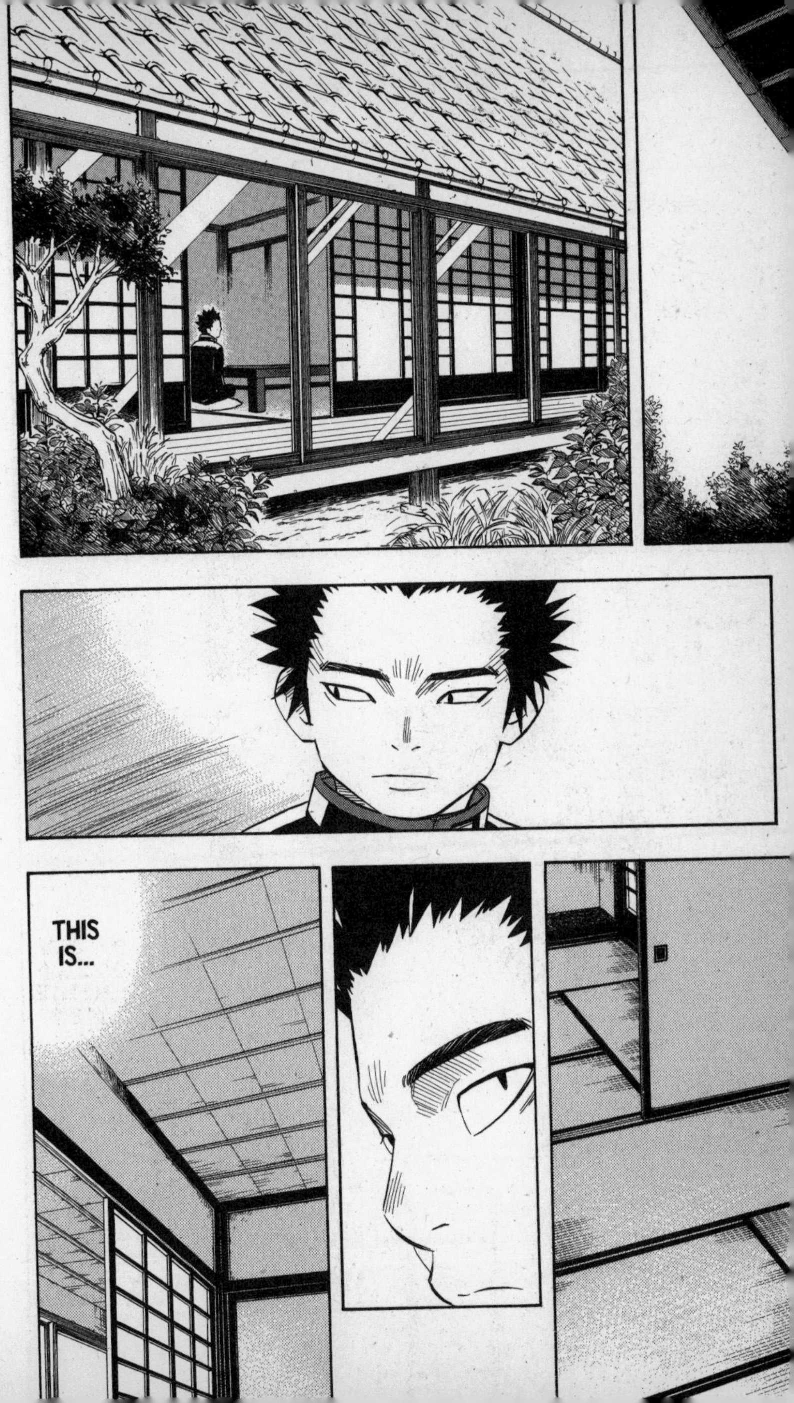
THIS IS...

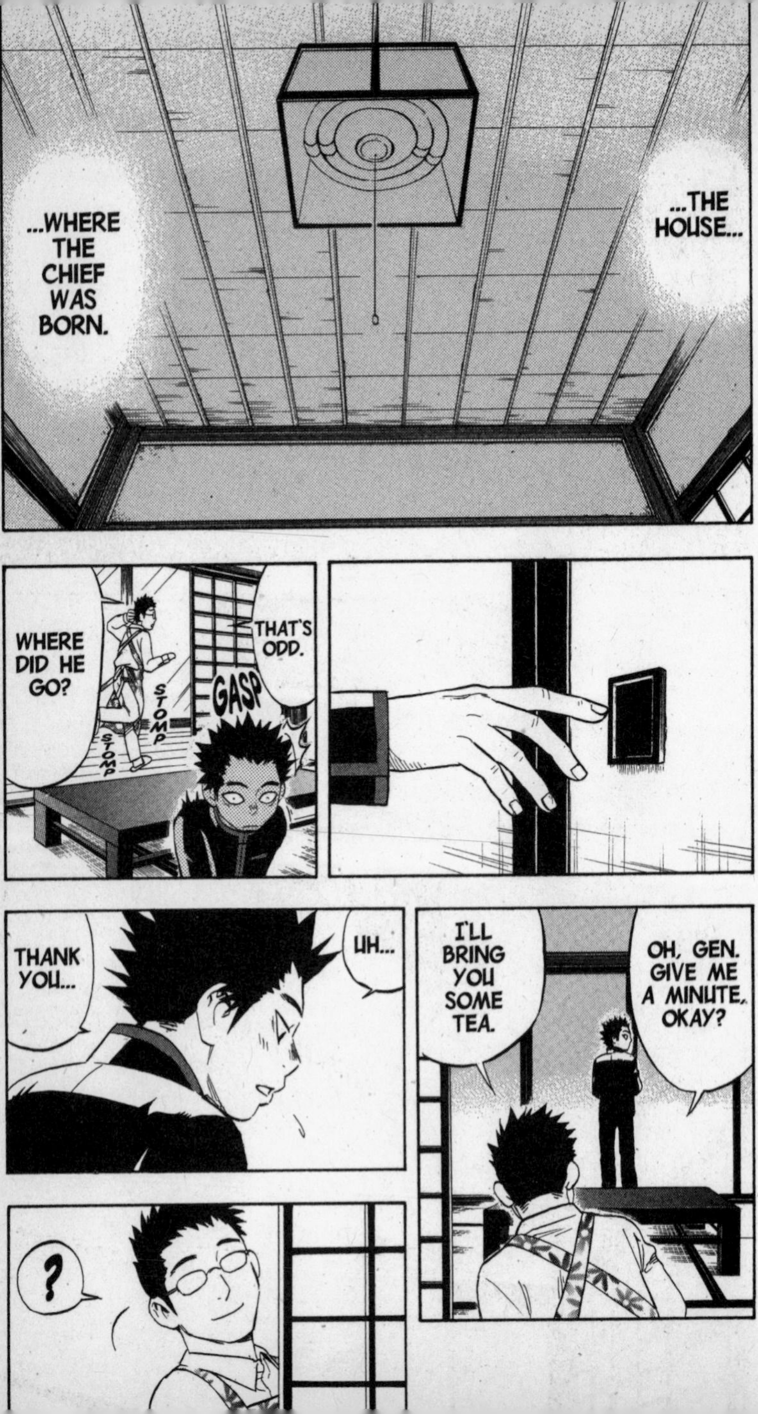
...THE HOUSE...
...WHERE THE CHIEF WAS BORN.
THAT'S ODD.
GASP
STOMP
STOMP
WHERE DID HE GO?
OH, GEN. GIVE ME A MINUTE, OKAY?
I'LL BRING YOU SOME TEA.
UH...
THANK YOU...
?

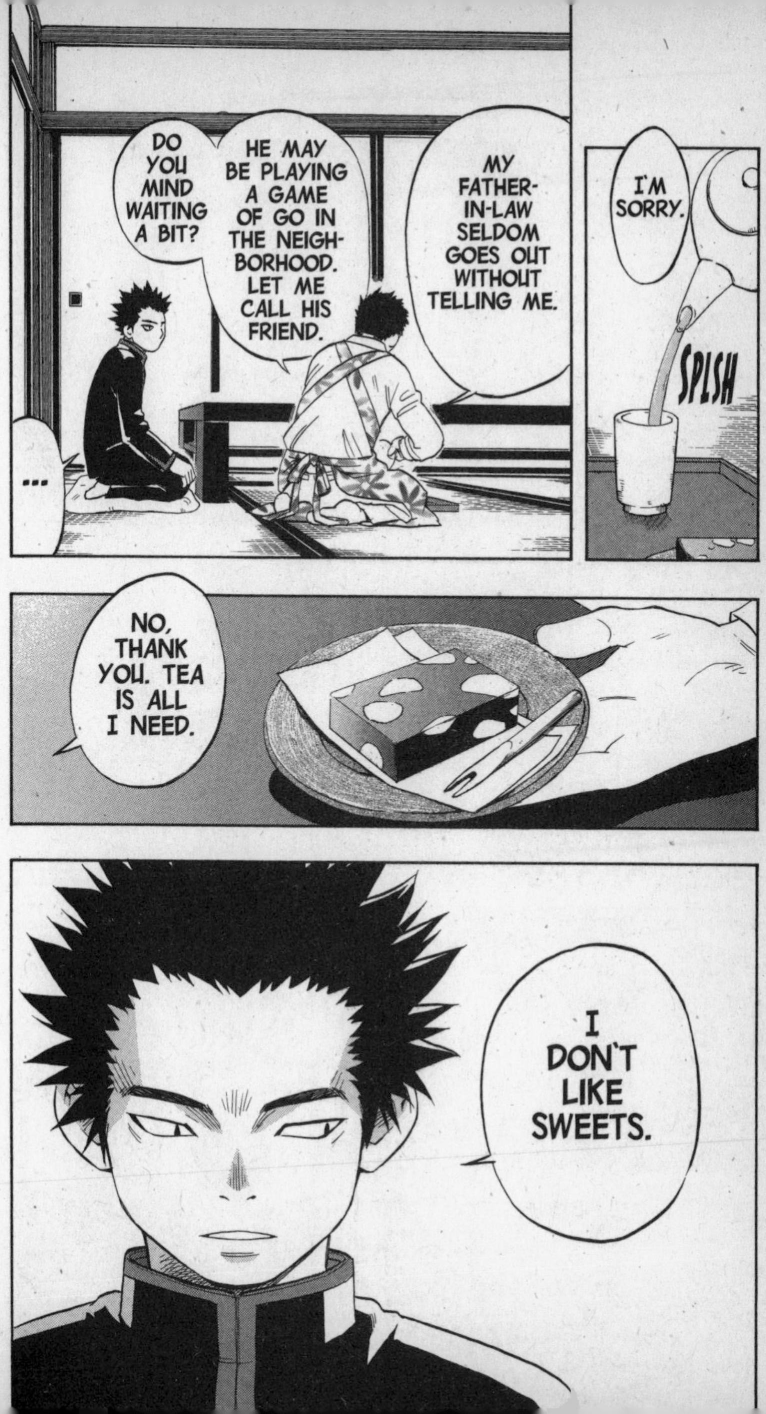
I'M SORRY.
SPLSH
MY FATHER-IN-LAW SELDOM GOES OUT WITHOUT TELLING ME.
HE MAY BE PLAYING A GAME OF GO IN THE NEIGHBORHOOD. LET ME CALL HIS FRIEND.
DO YOU MIND WAITING A BIT?
...
NO, THANK YOU. TEA IS ALL I NEED.
I DON'T LIKE SWEETS.

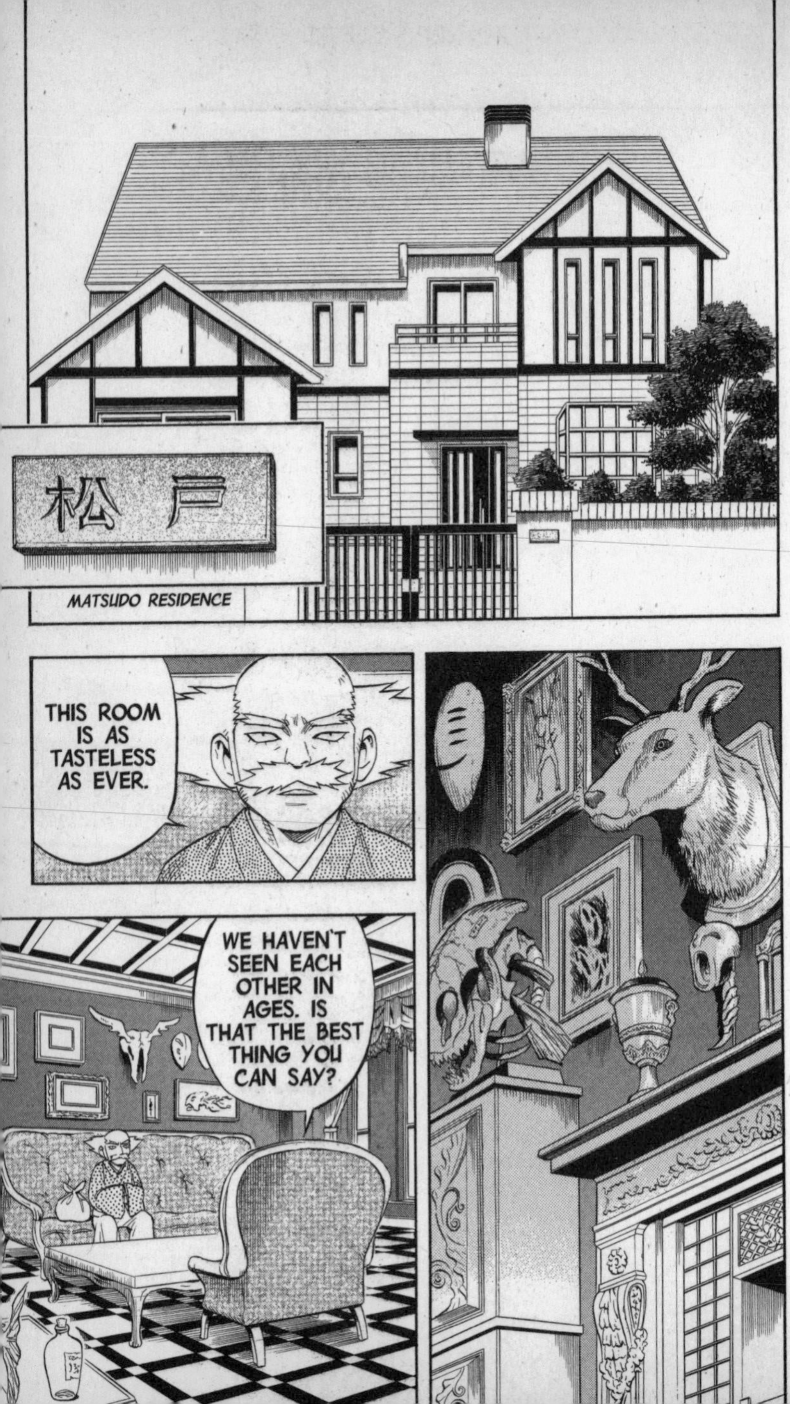
松戸
MATSUDO RESIDENCE
THIS ROOM IS AS TASTELESS AS EVER.
WE HAVEN'T SEEN EACH OTHER IN AGES. IS THAT THE BEST THING YOU CAN SAY?

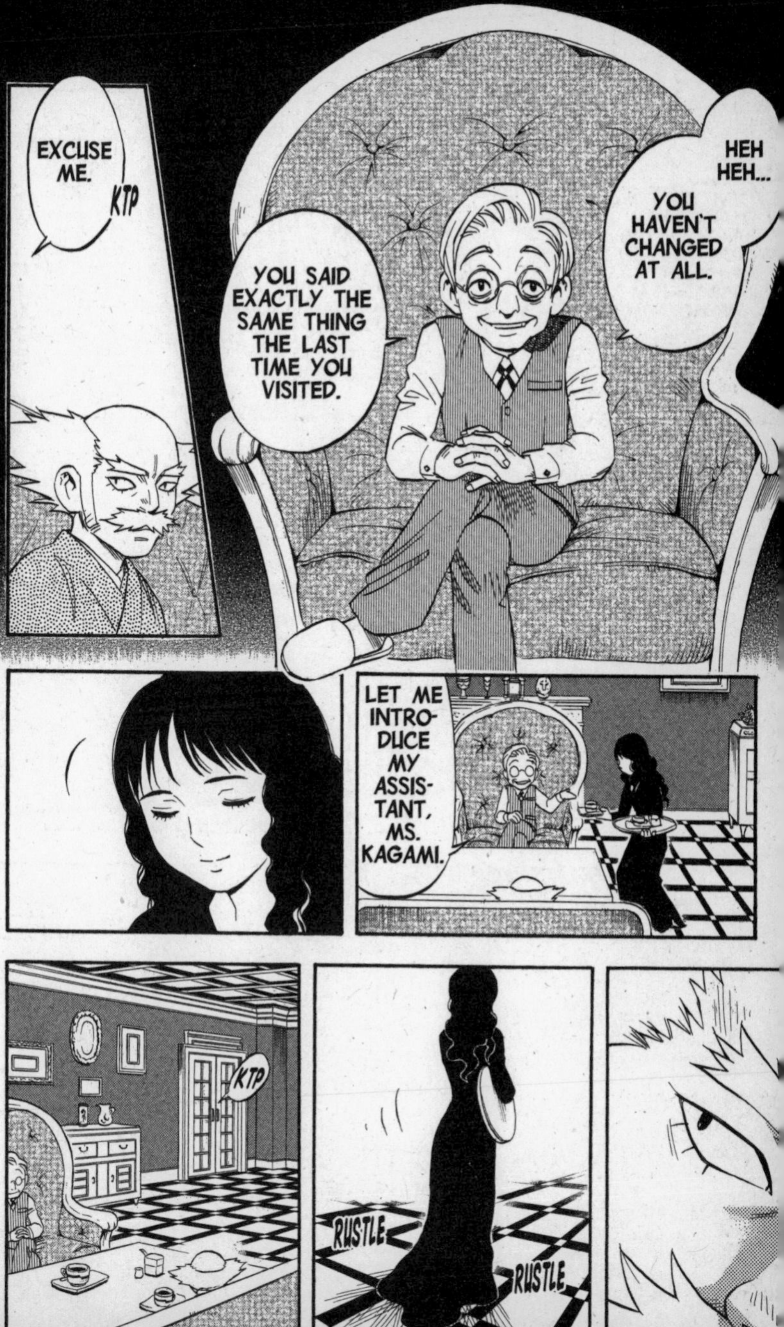
HEH HEH... YOU HAVEN'T CHANGED AT ALL.
YOU SAID EXACTLY THE SAME THING THE LAST TIME YOU VISITED.
EXCUSE ME.
KTP
LET ME INTRO-DUCE MY ASSIS-TANT, MS. KAGAMI.
RUSTLE
RUSTLE
KTP

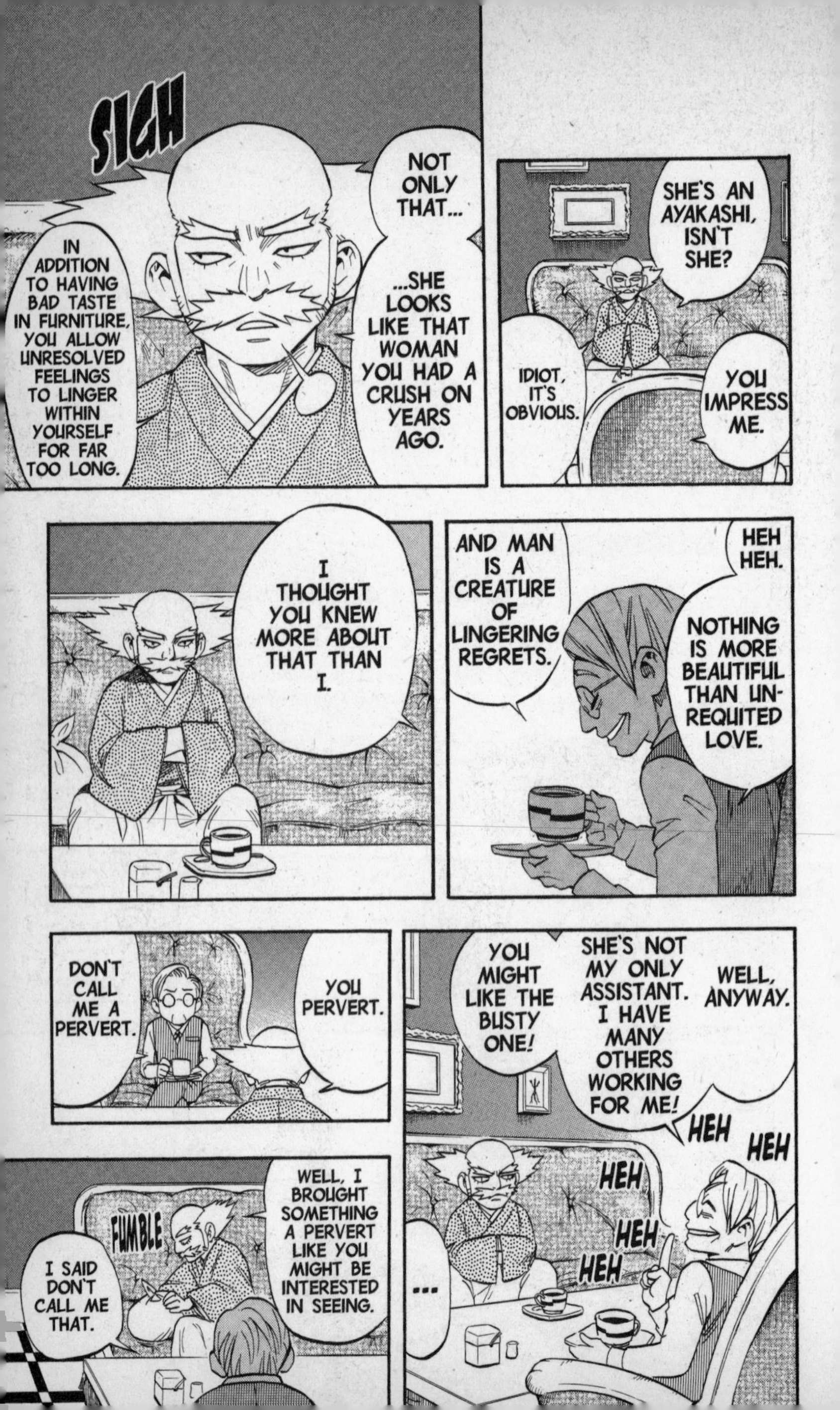
SHE'S AN AYAKASHI, ISN'T SHE?
YOU IMPRESS ME.
IDIOT, IT'S OBVIOUS.
NOT ONLY THAT...
...SHE LOOKS LIKE THAT WOMAN YOU HAD A CRUSH ON YEARS AGO.
SIGH
IN ADDITION TO HAVING BAD TASTE IN FURNITURE, YOU ALLOW UNRESOLVED FEELINGS TO LINGER WITHIN YOURSELF FOR FAR TOO LONG.
HEH HEH.
NOTHING IS MORE BEAUTIFUL THAN UNREQUITED LOVE.
AND MAN IS A CREATURE OF LINGERING REGRETS.
I THOUGHT YOU KNEW MORE ABOUT THAT THAN I.
WELL, ANYWAY.
SHE'S NOT MY ONLY ASSISTANT. I HAVE MANY OTHERS WORKING FOR ME!
YOU MIGHT LIKE THE BUSTY ONE!
HEH
HEH
HEH
HEH
HEH
...
YOU PERVERT.
DON'T CALL ME A PERVERT.
WELL, I BROUGHT SOMETHING A PERVERT LIKE YOU MIGHT BE INTERESTED IN SEEING.
FUMBLE
I SAID DON'T CALL ME THAT.

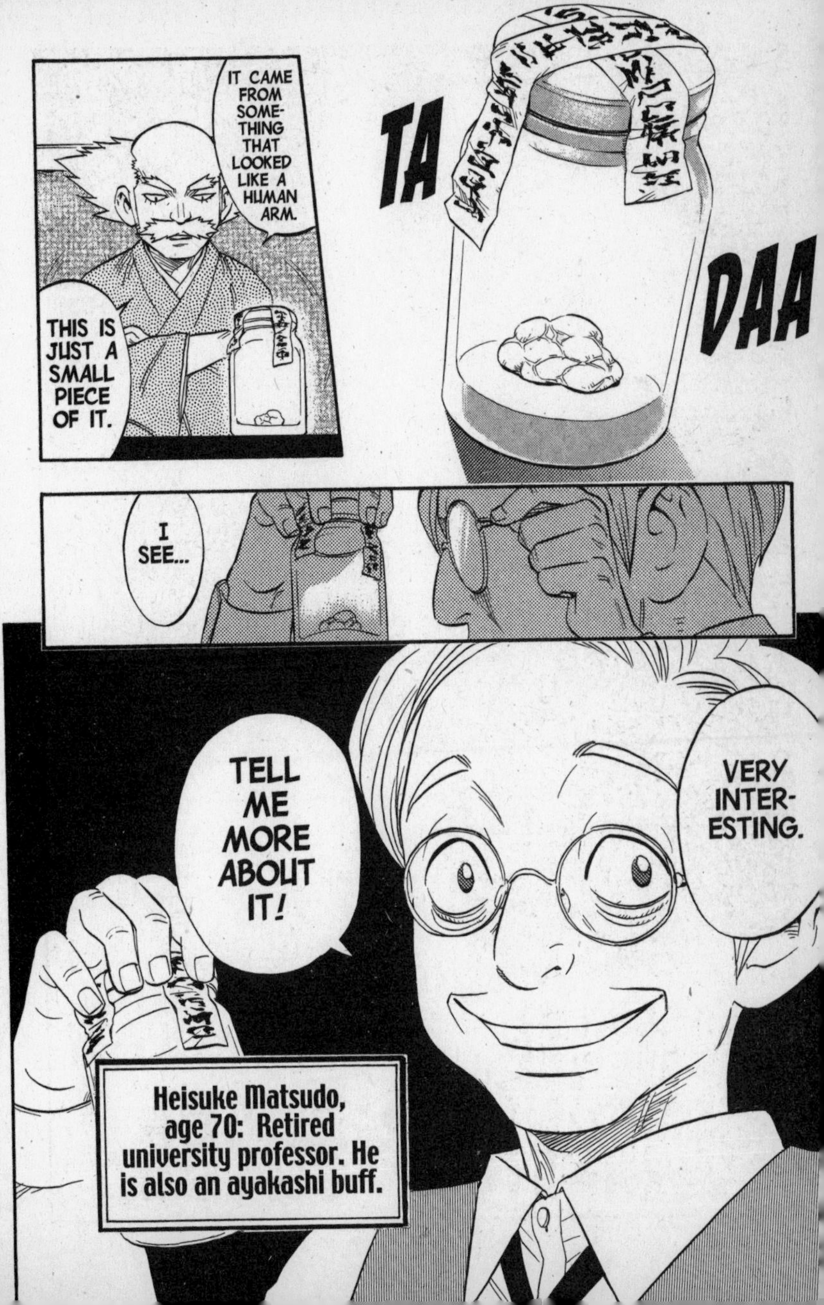
TA
DAA
IT CAME FROM SOME-THING THAT LOOKED LIKE A HUMAN ARM.
THIS IS JUST A SMALL PIECE OF IT.
I SEE...
VERY INTER-ESTING.
TELL ME MORE ABOUT IT!
Heisuke Matsudo, age 70: Retired university professor. He is also an ayakashi buff.

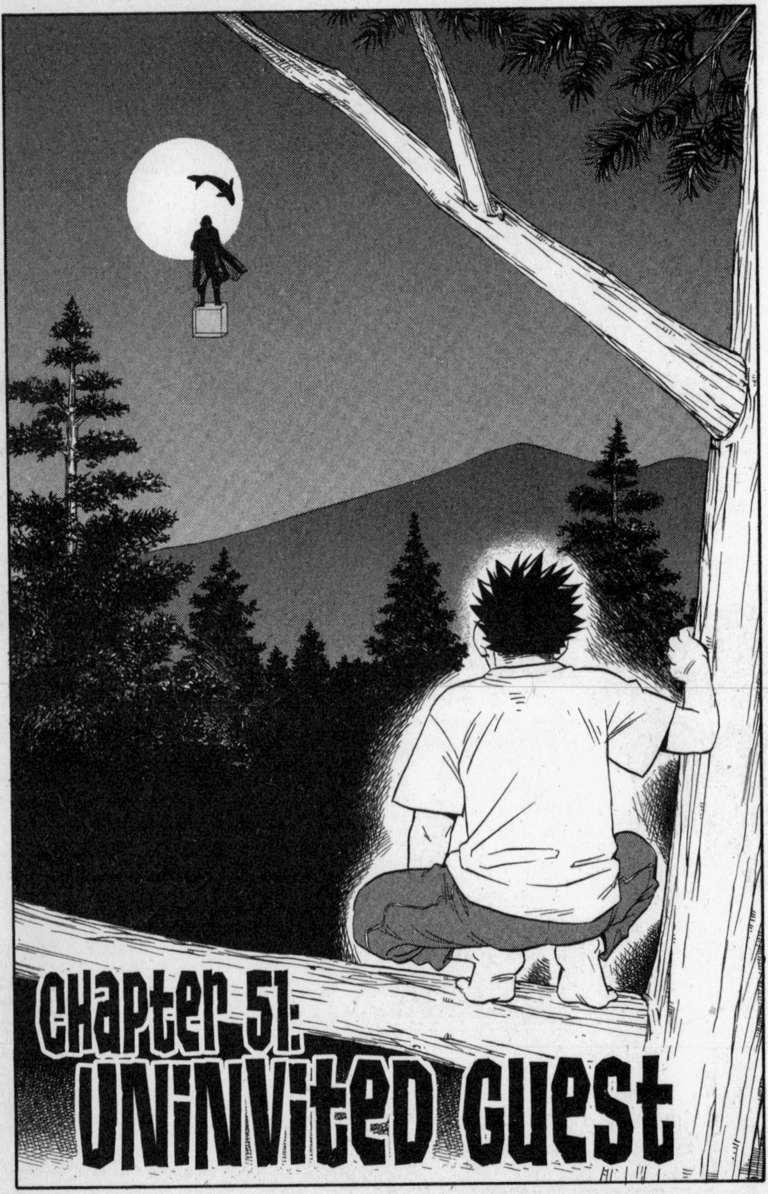
Chapter 51:
Uninvited Guest

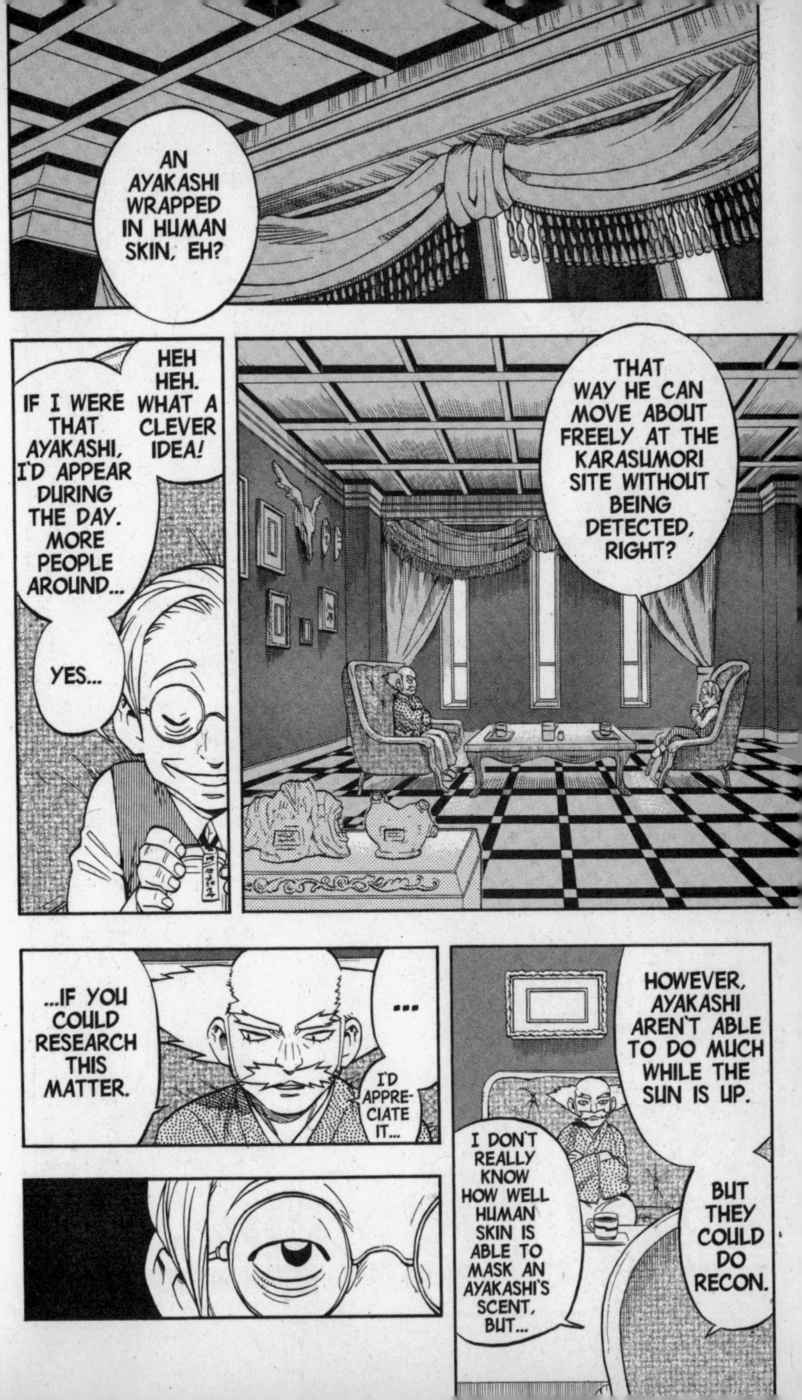
AN AYAKASHI WRAPPED IN HUMAN SKIN, EH?
THAT WAY HE CAN MOVE ABOUT FREELY AT THE KARASUMORI SITE WITHOUT BEING DETECTED, RIGHT?
HEH HEH. WHAT A CLEVER IDEA!
IF I WERE THAT AYAKASHI, I'D APPEAR DURING THE DAY. MORE PEOPLE AROUND...
YES...
HOWEVER, AYAKASHI AREN'T ABLE TO DO MUCH WHILE THE SUN IS UP.
BUT THEY COULD DO RECON.
I DON'T REALLY KNOW HOW WELL HUMAN SKIN IS ABLE TO MASK AN AYAKASHI'S SCENT, BUT...
...
I'D APPRECIATE IT...
...IF YOU COULD RESEARCH THIS MATTER.

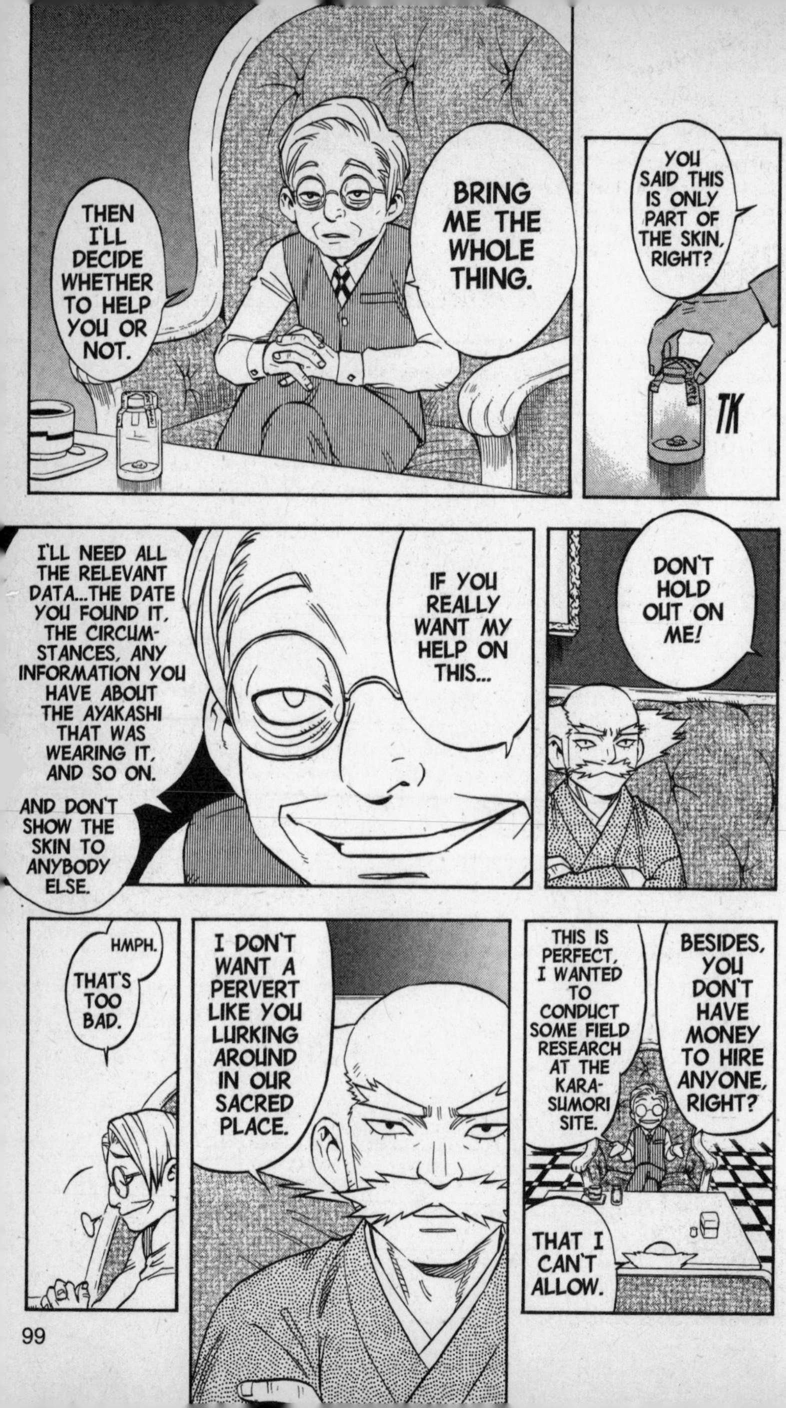
YOU SAID THIS IS ONLY PART OF THE SKIN, RIGHT?
TK
BRING ME THE WHOLE THING.
THEN I'LL DECIDE WHETHER TO HELP YOU OR NOT.
DON'T HOLD OUT ON ME!
IF YOU REALLY WANT MY HELP ON THIS...
I'LL NEED ALL THE RELEVANT DATA...THE DATE YOU FOUND IT, THE CIRCUM-STANCES, ANY INFORMATION YOU HAVE ABOUT THE AYAKASHI THAT WAS WEARING IT, AND SO ON.
AND DON'T SHOW THE SKIN TO ANYBODY ELSE.
BESIDES, YOU DON'T HAVE MONEY TO HIRE ANYONE, RIGHT?
THIS IS PERFECT, I WANTED TO CONDUCT SOME FIELD RESEARCH AT THE KARA-SUMORI SITE.
THAT I CAN'T ALLOW.
I DON'T WANT A PERVERT LIKE YOU LURKING AROUND IN OUR SACRED PLACE.
HMPH.
THAT'S TOO BAD.

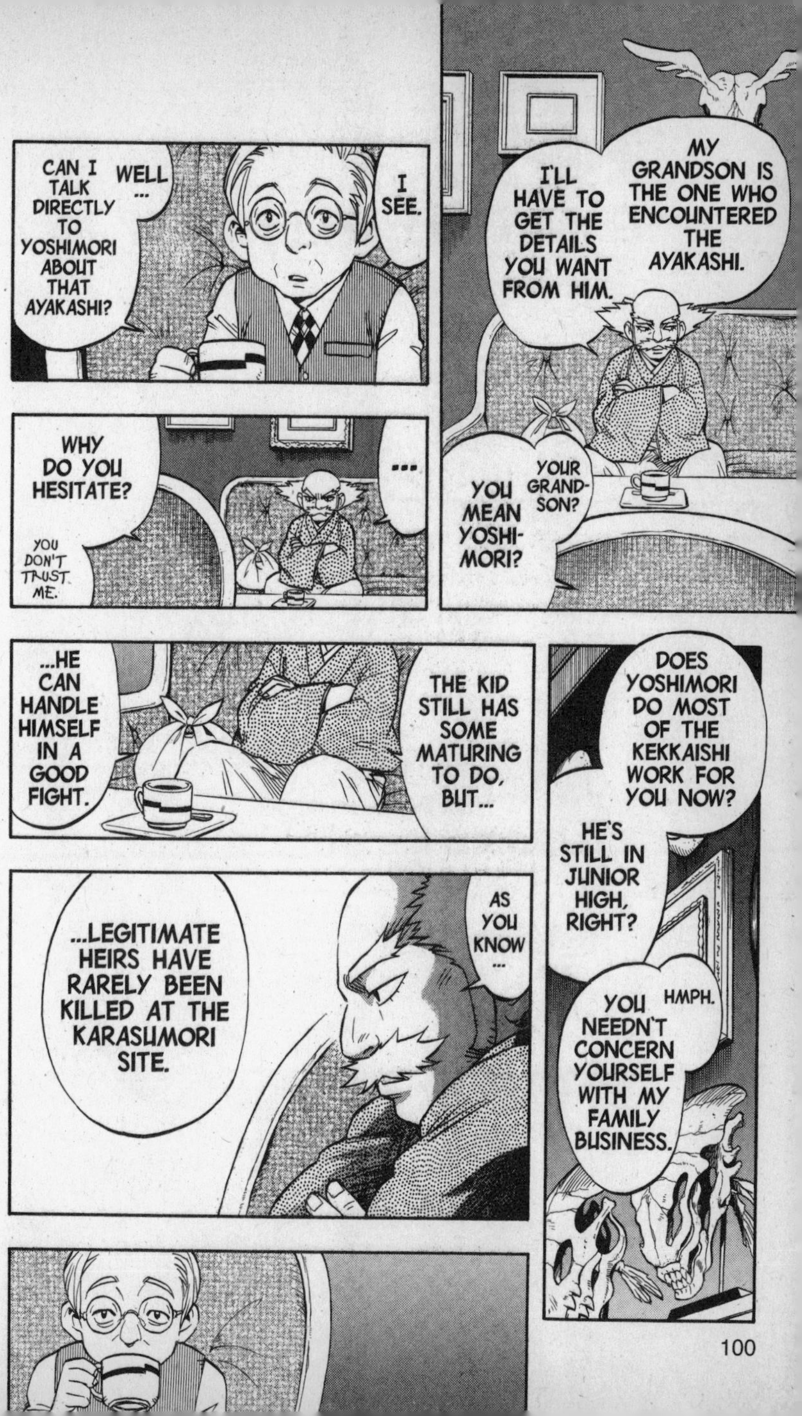
MY GRANDSON IS THE ONE WHO ENCOUNTERED THE AYAKASHI.
I'LL HAVE TO GET THE DETAILS YOU WANT FROM HIM.
YOUR GRANDSON?
YOU MEAN YOSHIMORI?
I SEE.
WELL...
CAN I TALK DIRECTLY TO YOSHIMORI ABOUT THAT AYAKASHI?
...
WHY DO YOU HESITATE?
YOU DON'T TRUST ME.
DOES YOSHIMORI DO MOST OF THE KEKKAISHI WORK FOR YOU NOW?
HE'S STILL IN JUNIOR HIGH, RIGHT?
HMPH.
YOU NEEDN'T CONCERN YOURSELF WITH MY FAMILY BUSINESS.
THE KID STILL HAS SOME MATURING TO DO, BUT...
...HE CAN HANDLE HIMSELF IN A GOOD FIGHT.
AS YOU KNOW...
...LEGITIMATE HEIRS HAVE RARELY BEEN KILLED AT THE KARASUMORI SITE.

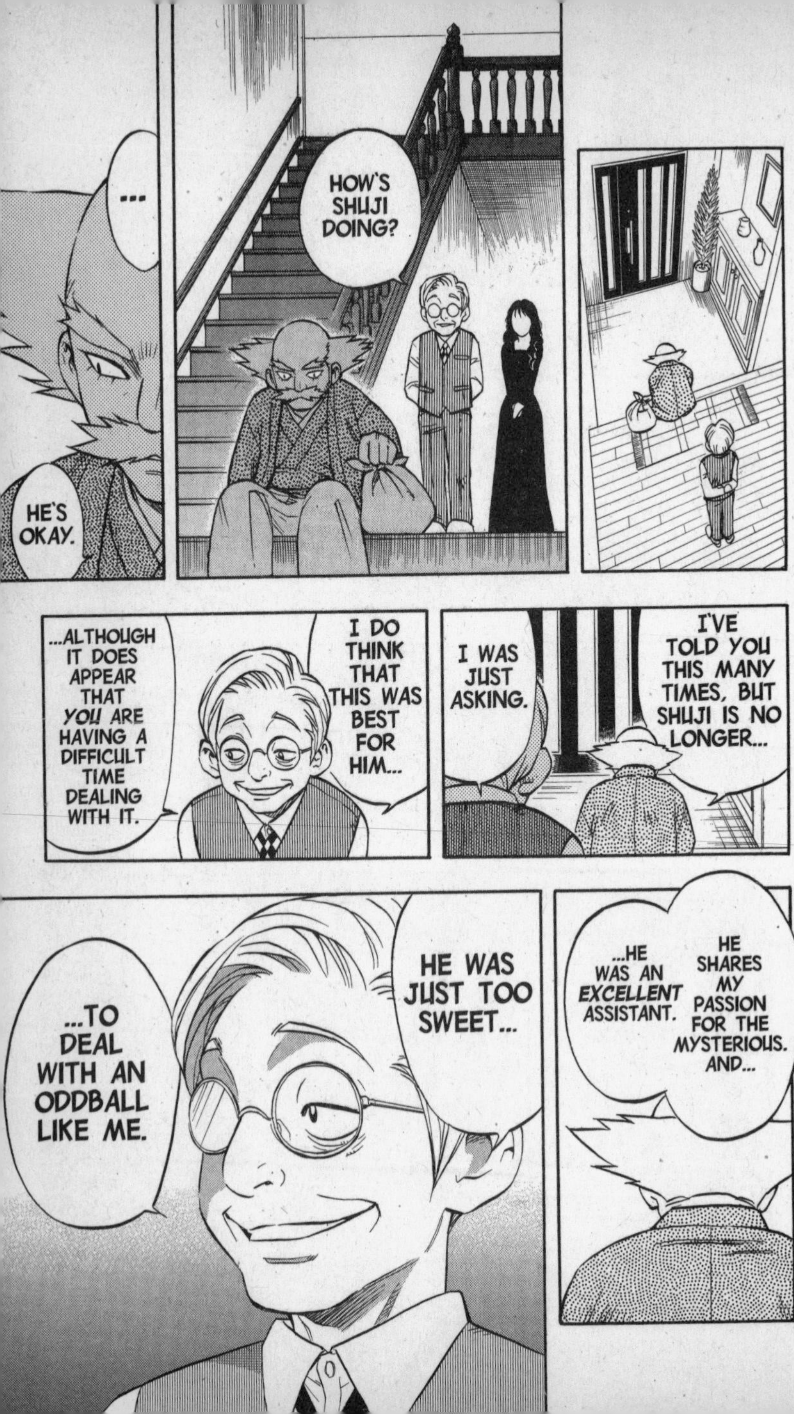
HOW'S SHUJI DOING?
...
HE'S OKAY.
I'VE TOLD YOU THIS MANY TIMES, BUT SHUJI IS NO LONGER...
I WAS JUST ASKING.
I DO THINK THAT THIS WAS BEST FOR HIM...
...ALTHOUGH IT DOES APPEAR THAT *YOU* ARE HAVING A DIFFICULT TIME DEALING WITH IT.
HE SHARES MY PASSION FOR THE MYSTERIOUS. AND...
...HE WAS AN *EXCELLENT* ASSISTANT.
HE WAS JUST TOO SWEET...
...TO DEAL WITH AN ODDBALL LIKE ME.

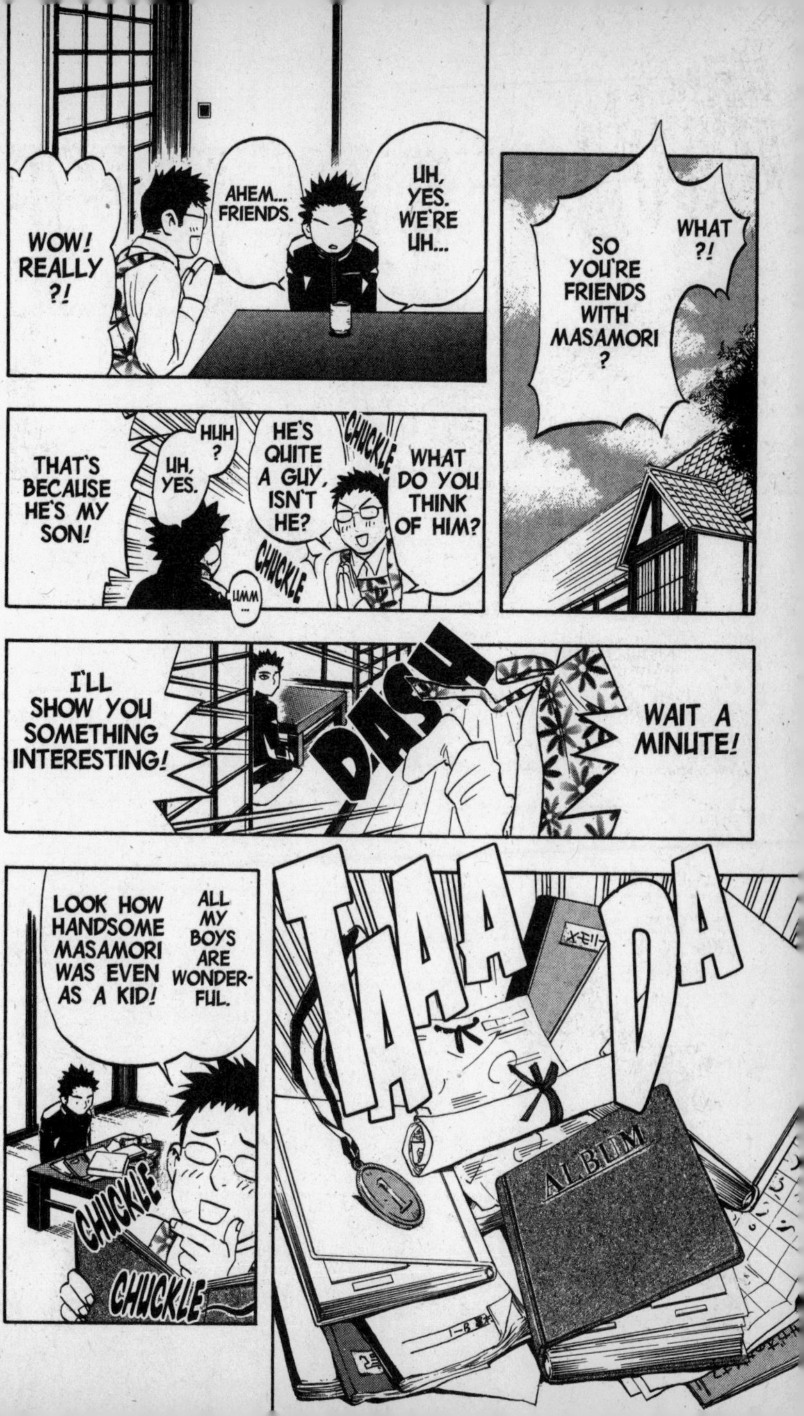
WHAT ?!
SO YOU'RE FRIENDS WITH MASAMORI ?
UH, YES. WE'RE UH...
AHEM... FRIENDS.
WOW! REALLY ?!
WHAT DO YOU THINK OF HIM?
CHUCKLE
HE'S QUITE A GUY, ISN'T HE?
HUH ?
UH, YES.
THAT'S BECAUSE HE'S MY SON!
CHUCKLE
UMM ...
WAIT A MINUTE!
DASH
I'LL SHOW YOU SOMETHING INTERESTING!
TAAA DA
ALBUM
ALL MY BOYS ARE WONDER-FUL.
LOOK HOW HANDSOME MASAMORI WAS EVEN AS A KID!
CHUCKLE
CHUCKLE

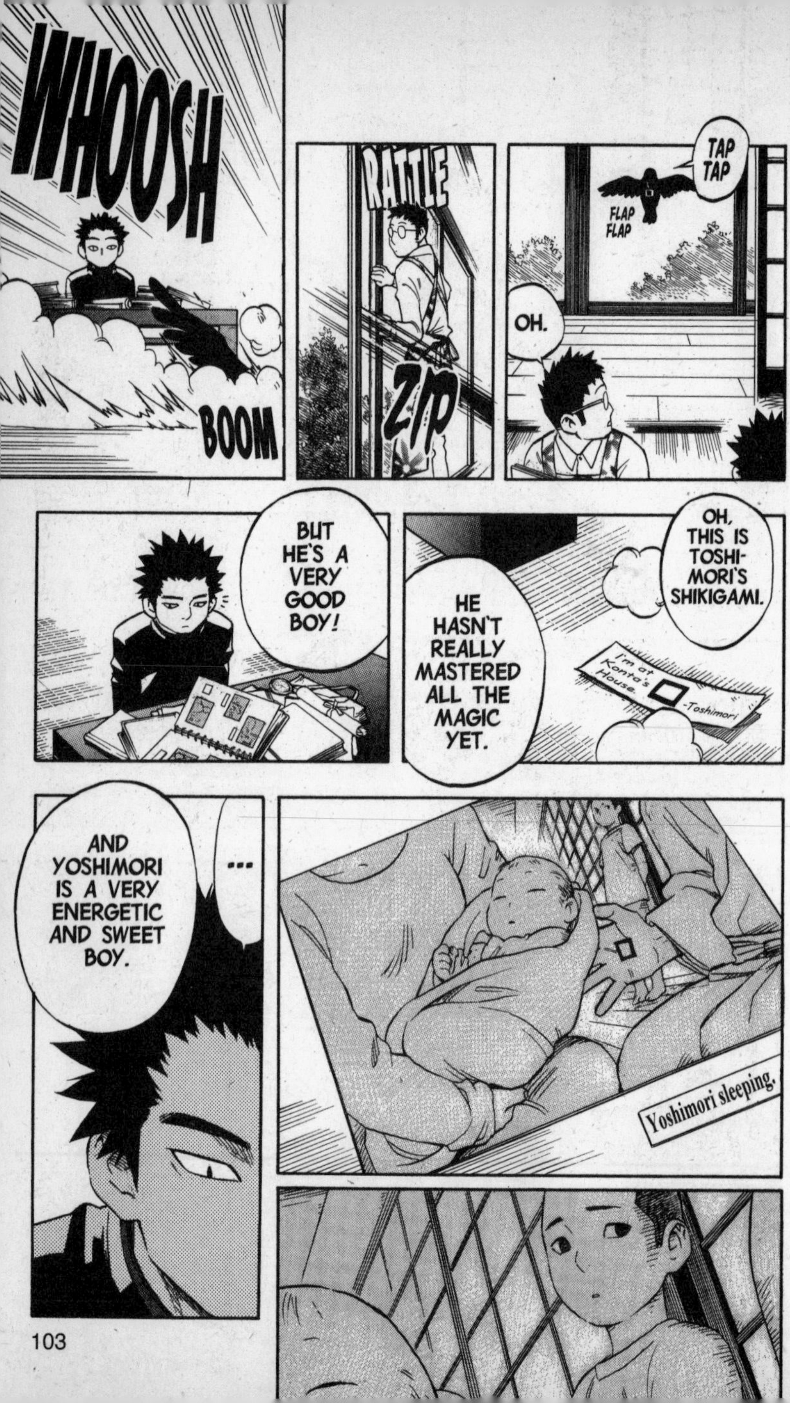
TAP TAP
FLAP FLAP
OH.
RATTLE
ZIP
WHOOSH
BOOM
OH, THIS IS TOSHIMORI'S SHIKIGAMI.
I'm at Konta's House. -Toshimori
HE HASN'T REALLY MASTERED ALL THE MAGIC YET.
BUT HE'S A VERY GOOD BOY!
Yoshimori sleeping.
...
AND YOSHIMORI IS A VERY ENERGETIC AND SWEET BOY.

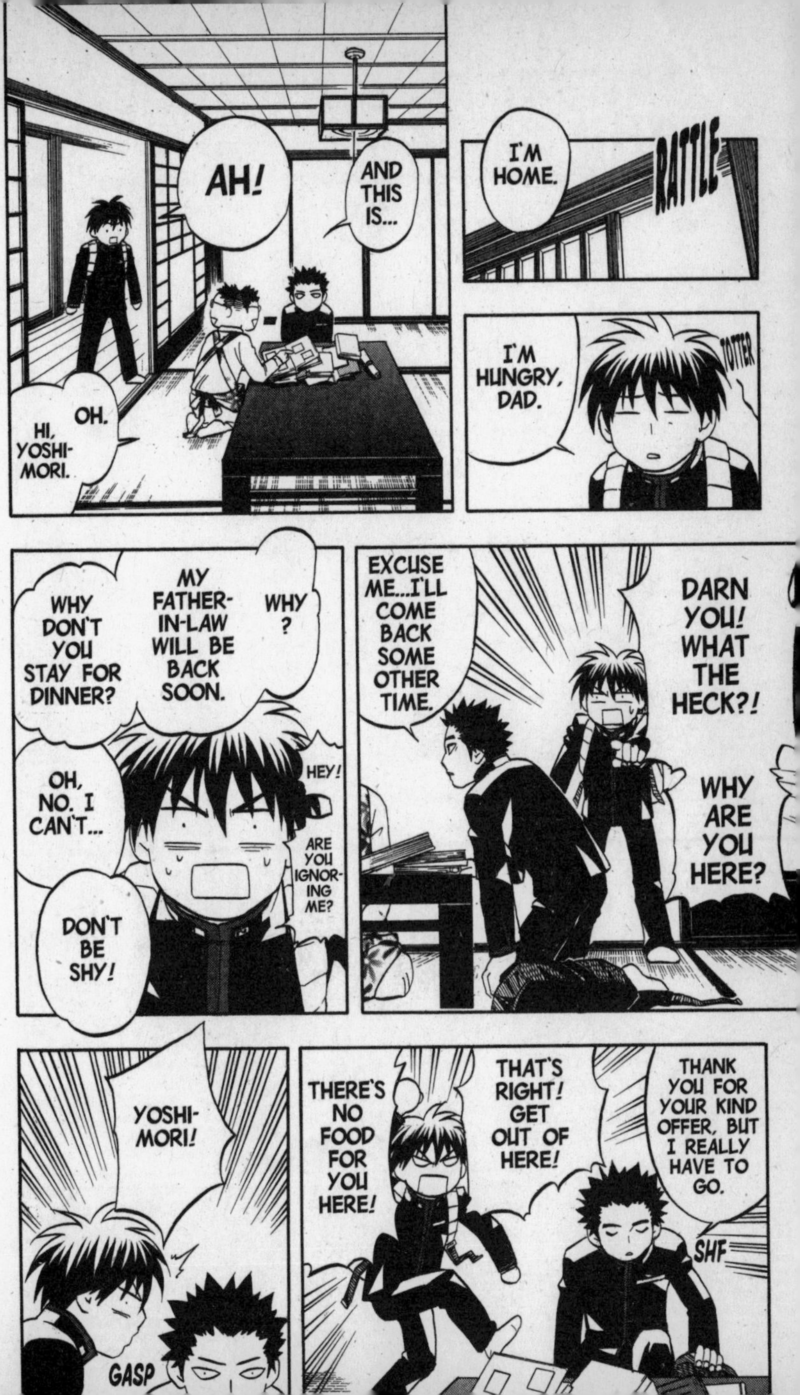
RATTLE
I'M HOME.
TOTTER
I'M HUNGRY, DAD.
AND THIS IS...
AH!
OH.
HI, YOSHI-MORI.
DARN YOU! WHAT THE HECK?!
WHY ARE YOU HERE?
EXCUSE ME...I'LL COME BACK SOME OTHER TIME.
WHY?
MY FATHER-IN-LAW WILL BE BACK SOON.
WHY DON'T YOU STAY FOR DINNER?
HEY!
ARE YOU IGNORING ME?
OH, NO. I CAN'T...
DON'T BE SHY!
THANK YOU FOR YOUR KIND OFFER, BUT I REALLY HAVE TO GO.
SHF
THAT'S RIGHT! GET OUT OF HERE!
THERE'S NO FOOD FOR YOU HERE!
YOSHI-MORI!
GASP

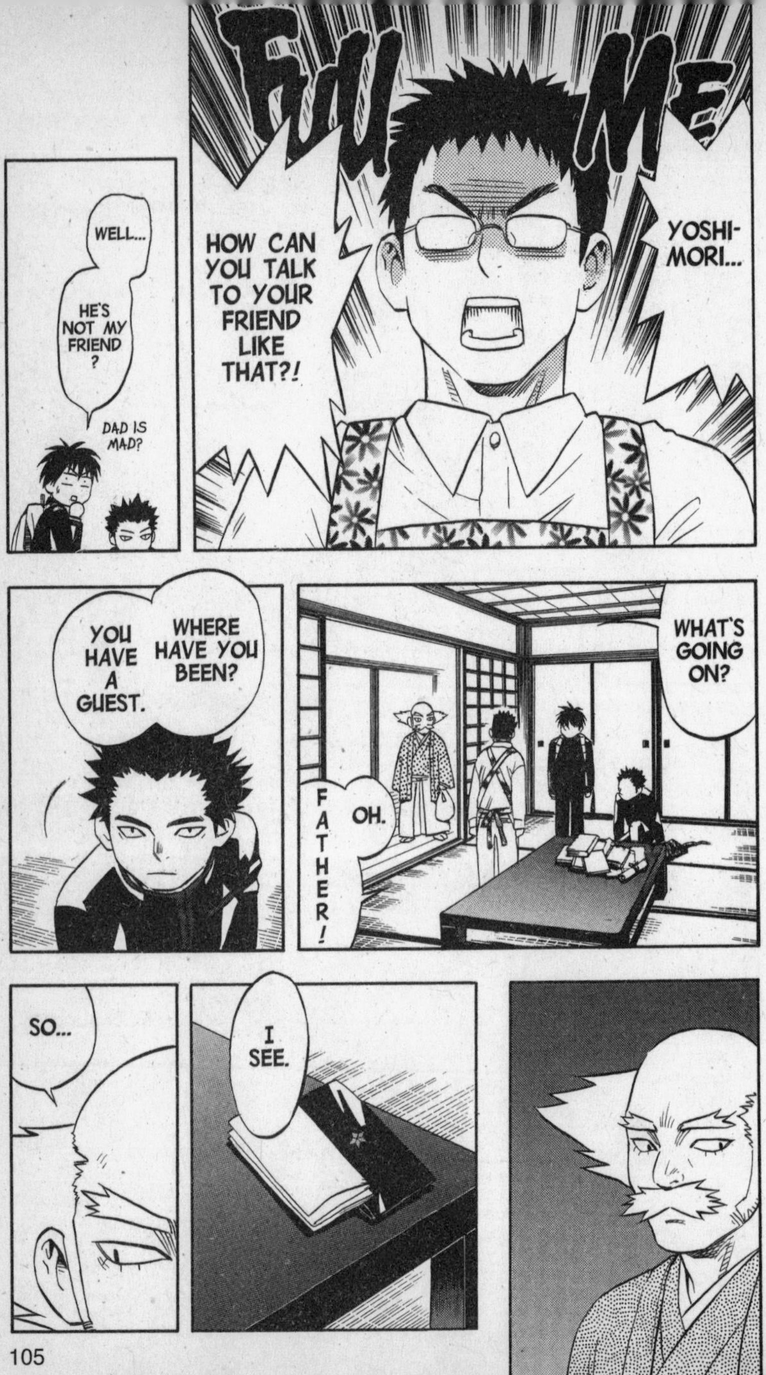
FUU ME
YOSHI-MORI...
HOW CAN YOU TALK TO YOUR FRIEND LIKE THAT?!
WELL...
HE'S NOT MY FRIEND?
DAD IS MAD?
WHAT'S GOING ON?
OH.
FATHER!
WHERE HAVE YOU BEEN?
YOU HAVE A GUEST.
I SEE.
SO...

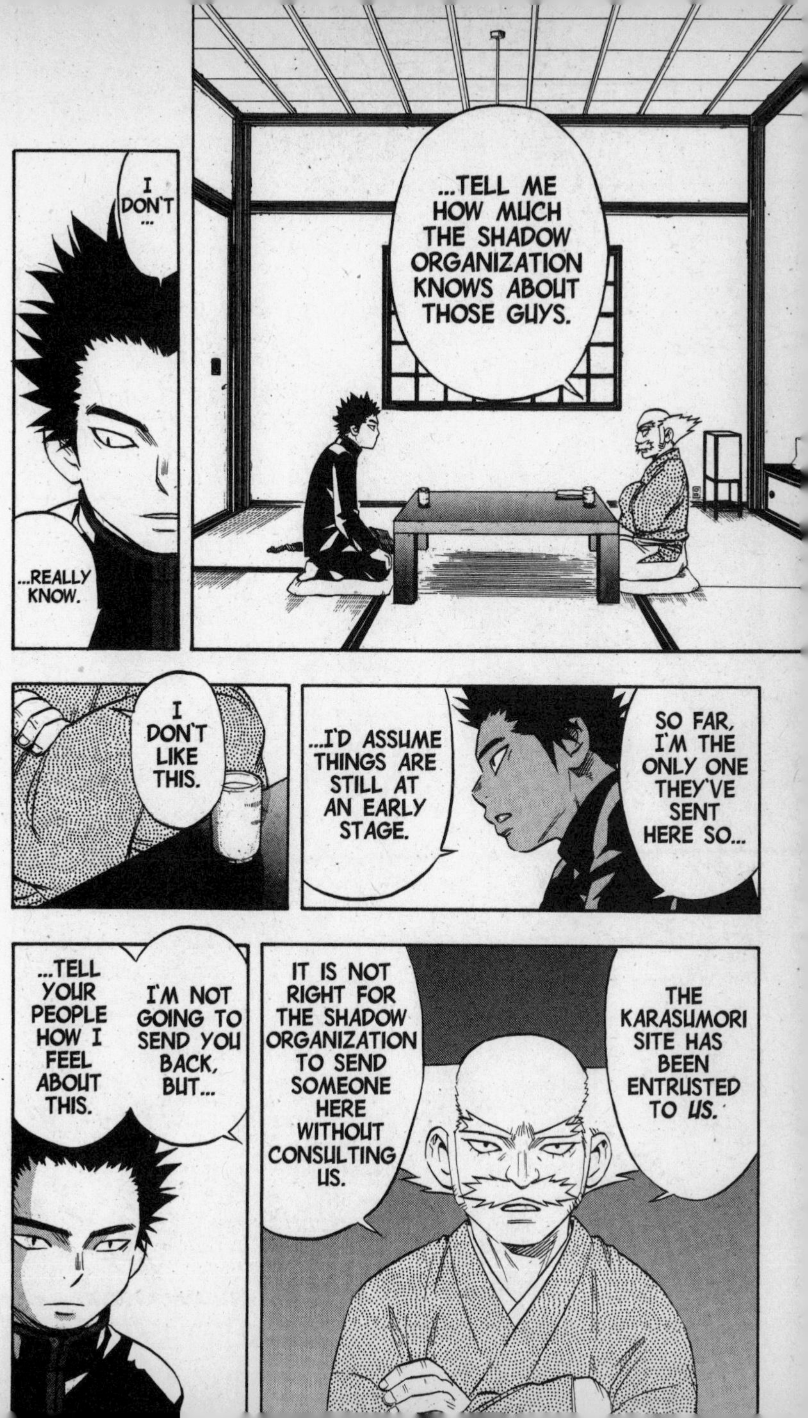
...TELL ME HOW MUCH THE SHADOW ORGANIZATION KNOWS ABOUT THOSE GUYS.
I DON'T ...
...REALLY KNOW.
SO FAR, I'M THE ONLY ONE THEY'VE SENT HERE SO...
...I'D ASSUME THINGS ARE STILL AT AN EARLY STAGE.
I DON'T LIKE THIS.
THE KARASUMORI SITE HAS BEEN ENTRUSTED TO *US.*
IT IS NOT RIGHT FOR THE SHADOW ORGANIZATION TO SEND SOMEONE HERE WITHOUT CONSULTING US.
I'M NOT GOING TO SEND YOU BACK, BUT...
...TELL YOUR PEOPLE HOW I FEEL ABOUT THIS.

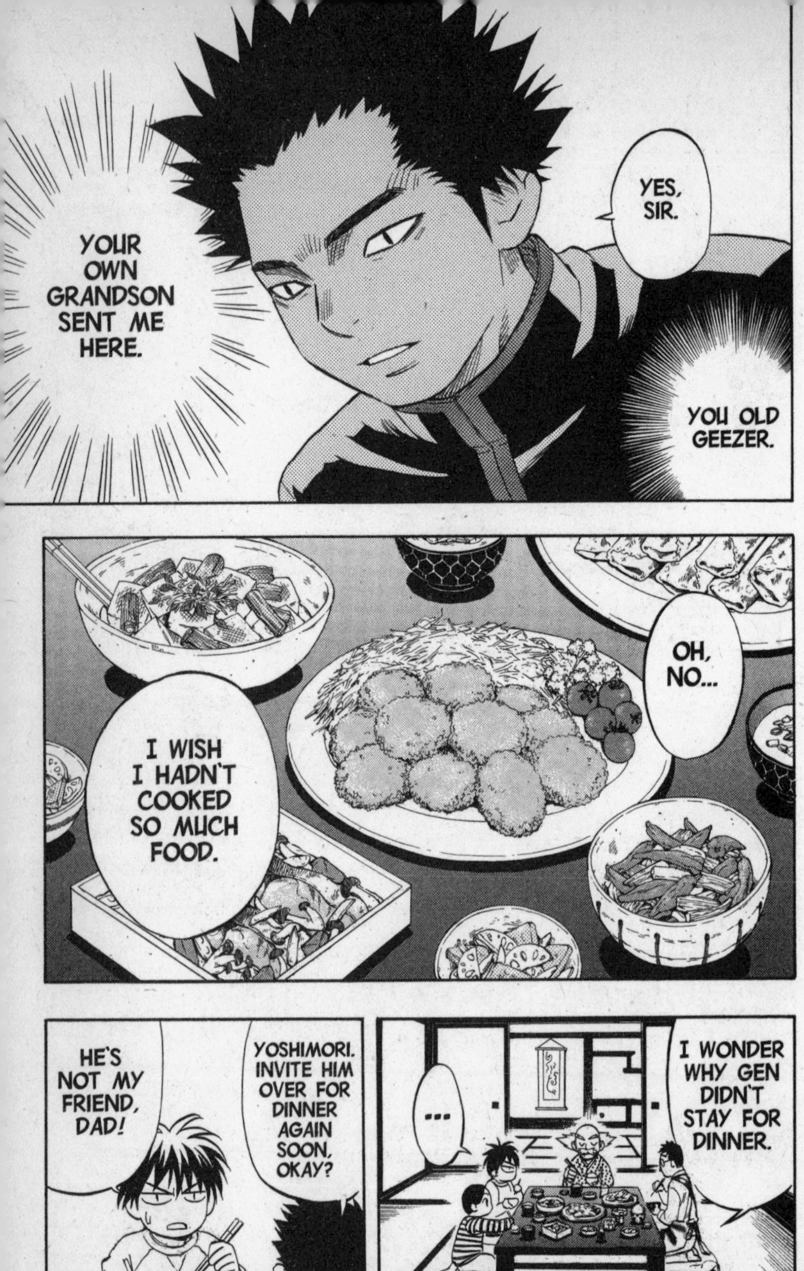
YES, SIR.
YOUR OWN GRANDSON SENT ME HERE.
YOU OLD GEEZER.
OH, NO...
I WISH I HADN'T COOKED SO MUCH FOOD.
I WONDER WHY GEN DIDN'T STAY FOR DINNER.
...
YOSHIMORI. INVITE HIM OVER FOR DINNER AGAIN SOON, OKAY?
HE'S NOT MY FRIEND, DAD!

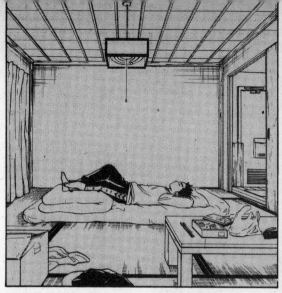
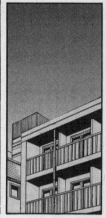
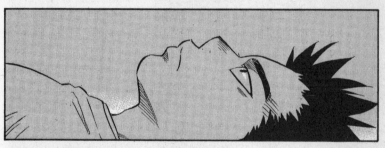
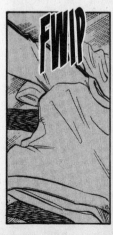

FWIP

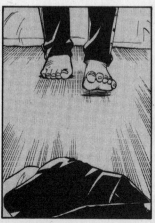
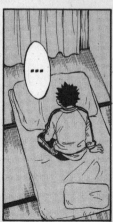

...

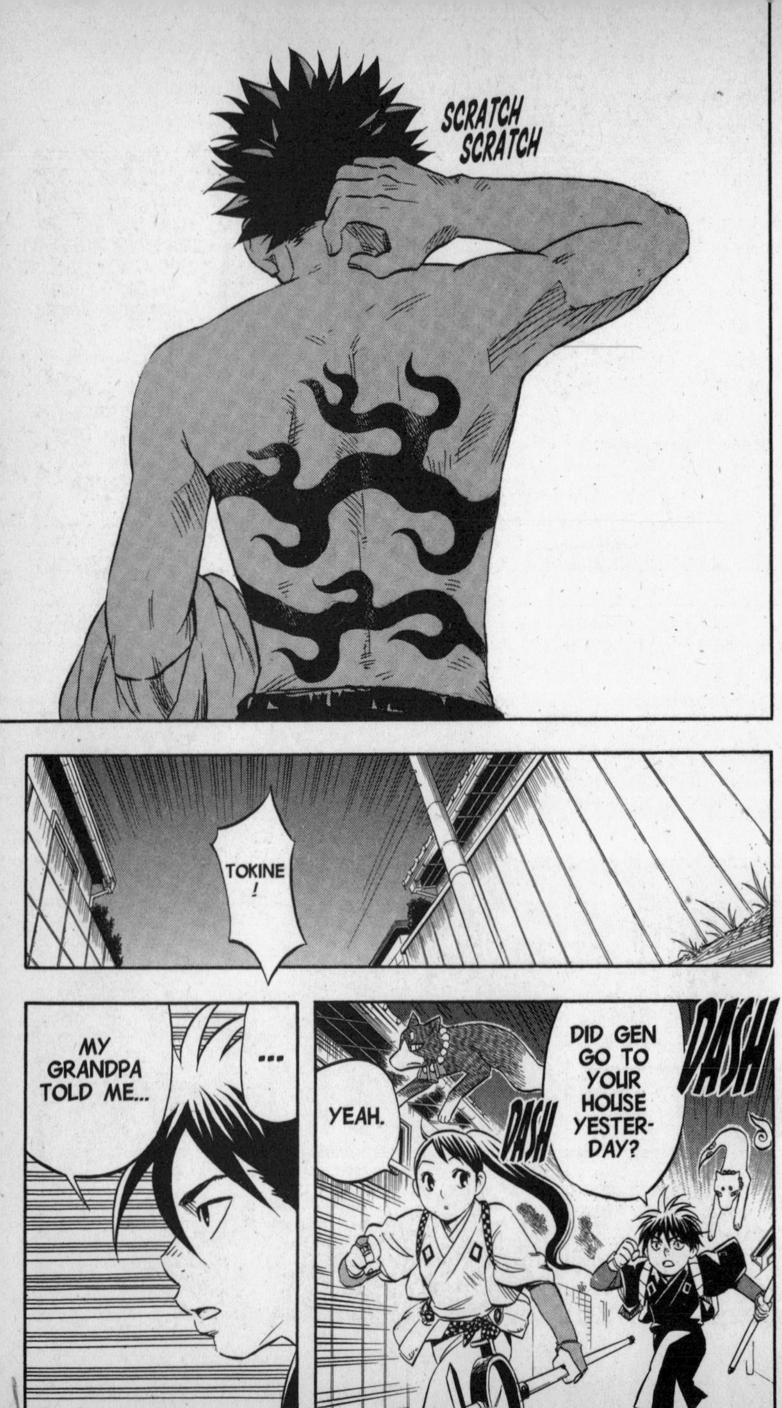
SCRATCH SCRATCH
TOKINE!
DASH
DID GEN GO TO YOUR HOUSE YESTER-DAY?
DASH
YEAH.
...
MY GRANDPA TOLD ME...

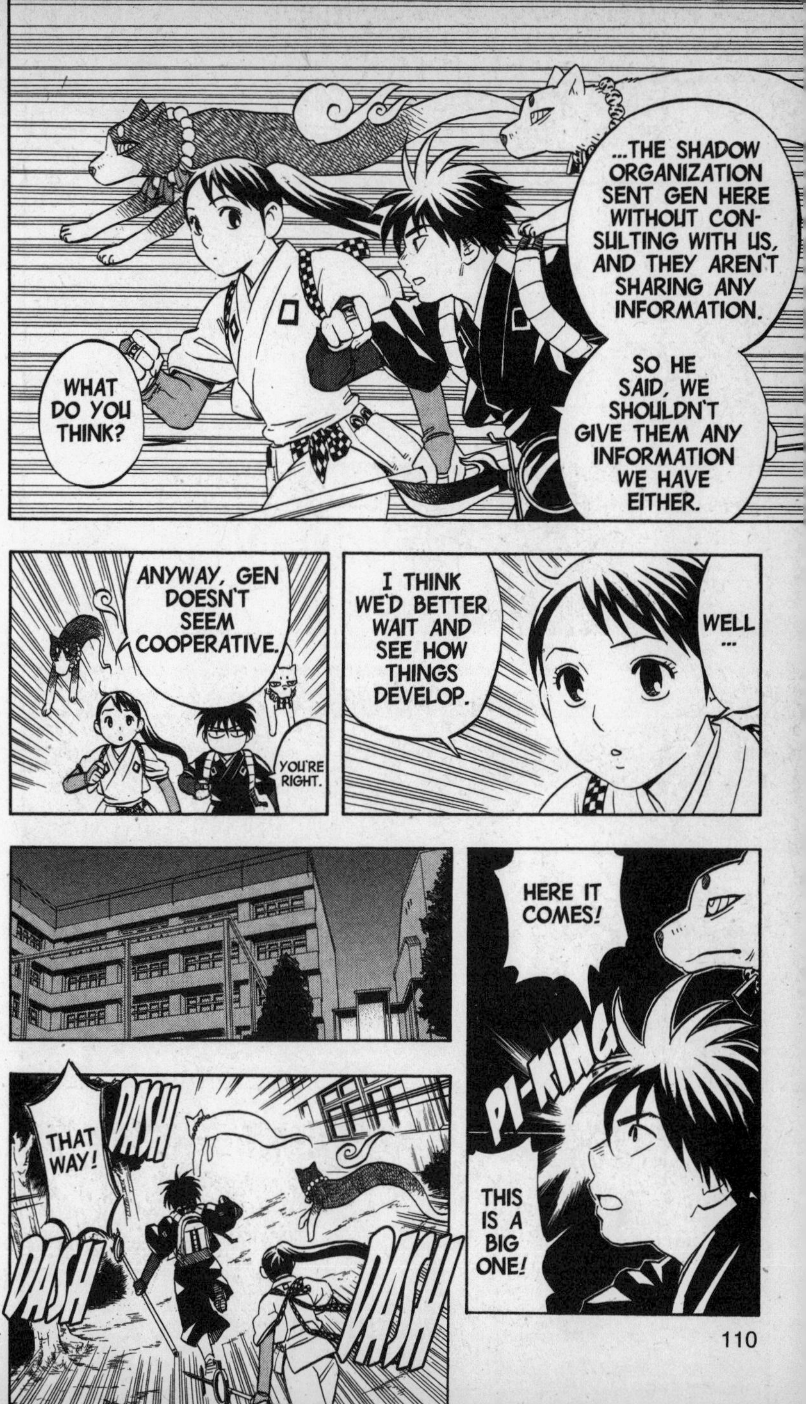
...THE SHADOW ORGANIZATION SENT GEN HERE WITHOUT CON-SULTING WITH US, AND THEY AREN'T SHARING ANY INFORMATION.
SO HE SAID, WE SHOULDN'T GIVE THEM ANY INFORMATION WE HAVE EITHER.
WHAT DO YOU THINK?
WELL ...
I THINK WE'D BETTER WAIT AND SEE HOW THINGS DEVELOP.
ANYWAY, GEN DOESN'T SEEM COOPERATIVE.
YOU'RE RIGHT.
HERE IT COMES!
PI-KING
THIS IS A BIG ONE!
THAT WAY!
DASH
DASH
DASH

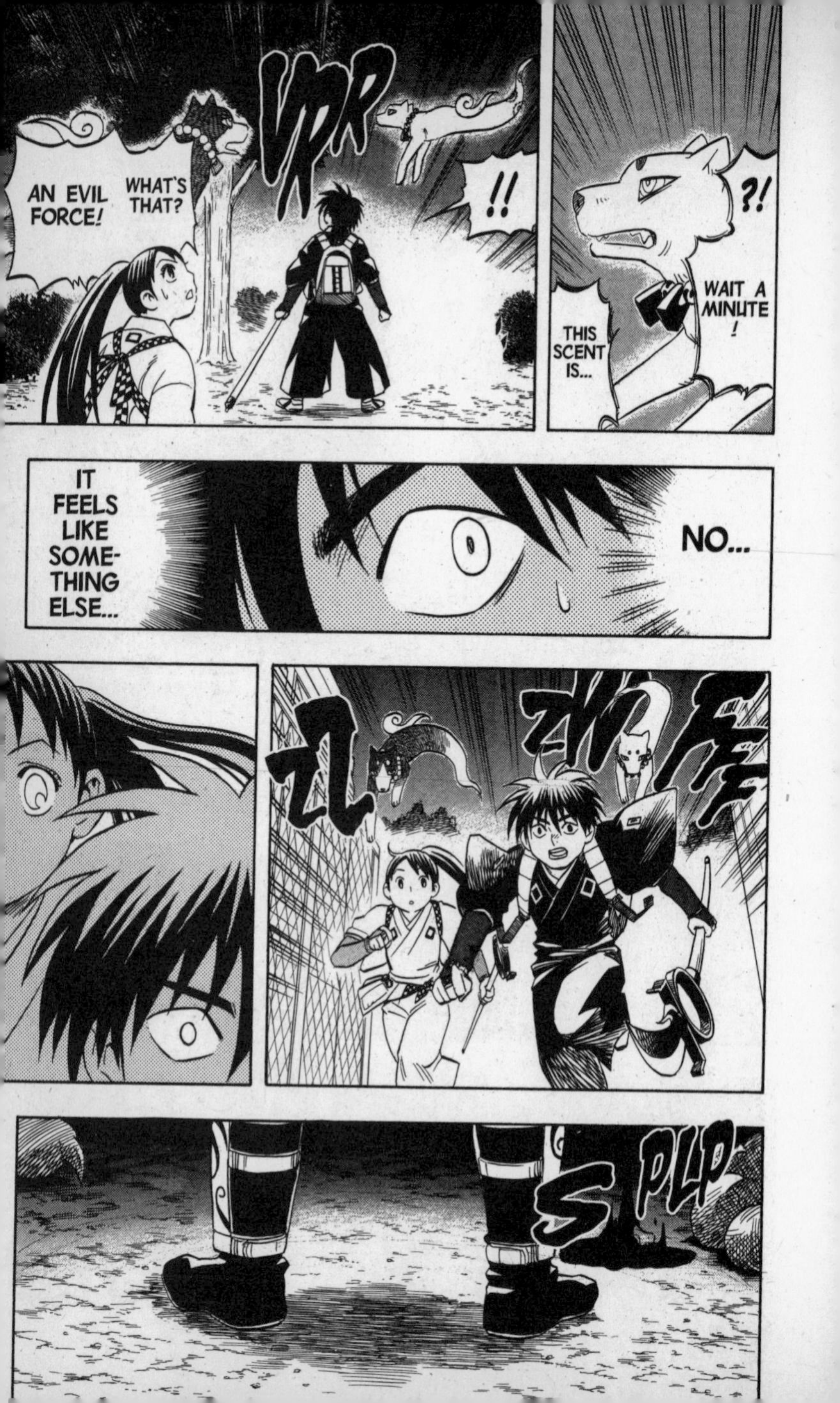
?!
WAIT A MINUTE!
THIS SCENT IS...
!!
VPR
WHAT'S THAT?
AN EVIL FORCE!
NO...
IT FEELS LIKE SOME-THING ELSE...
SPLP

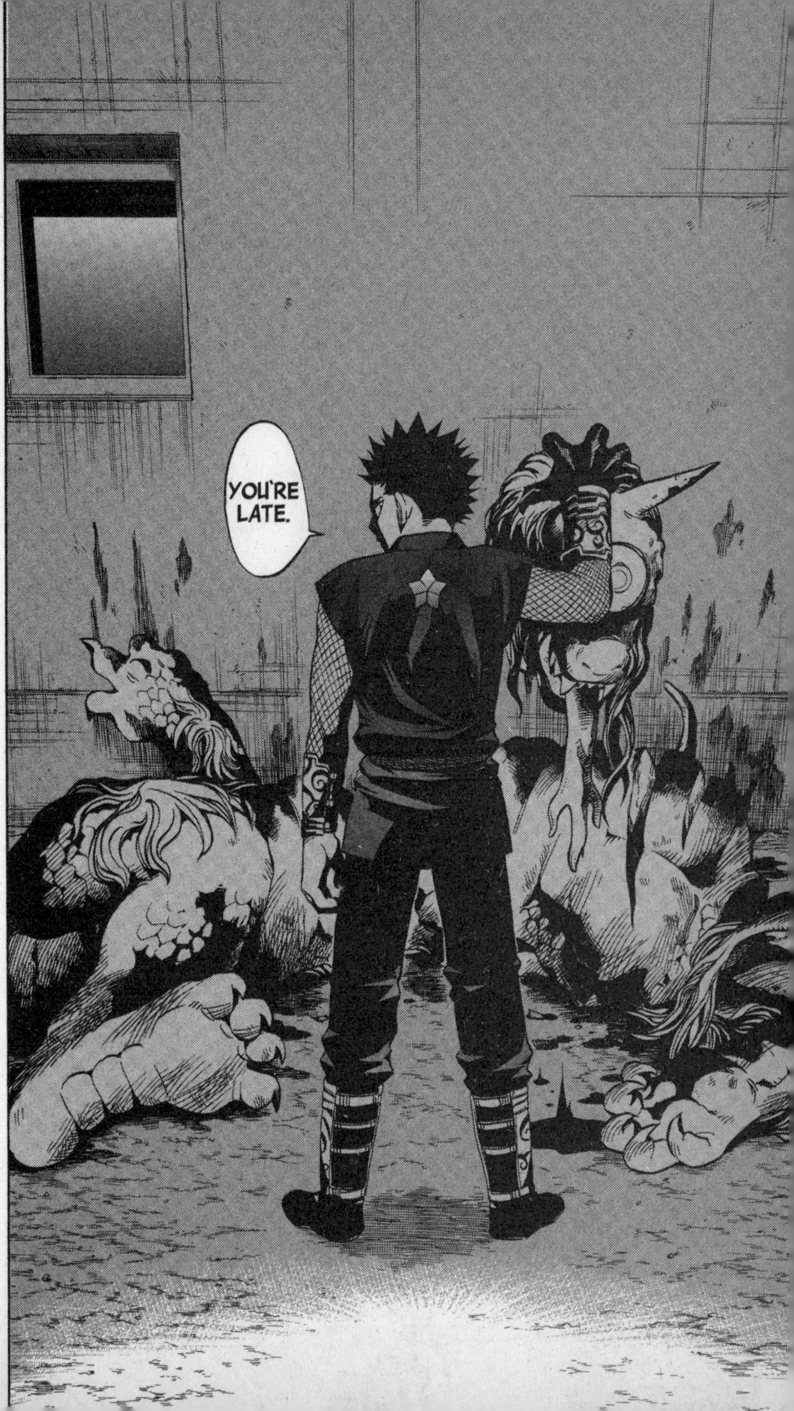
YOU'RE LATE.

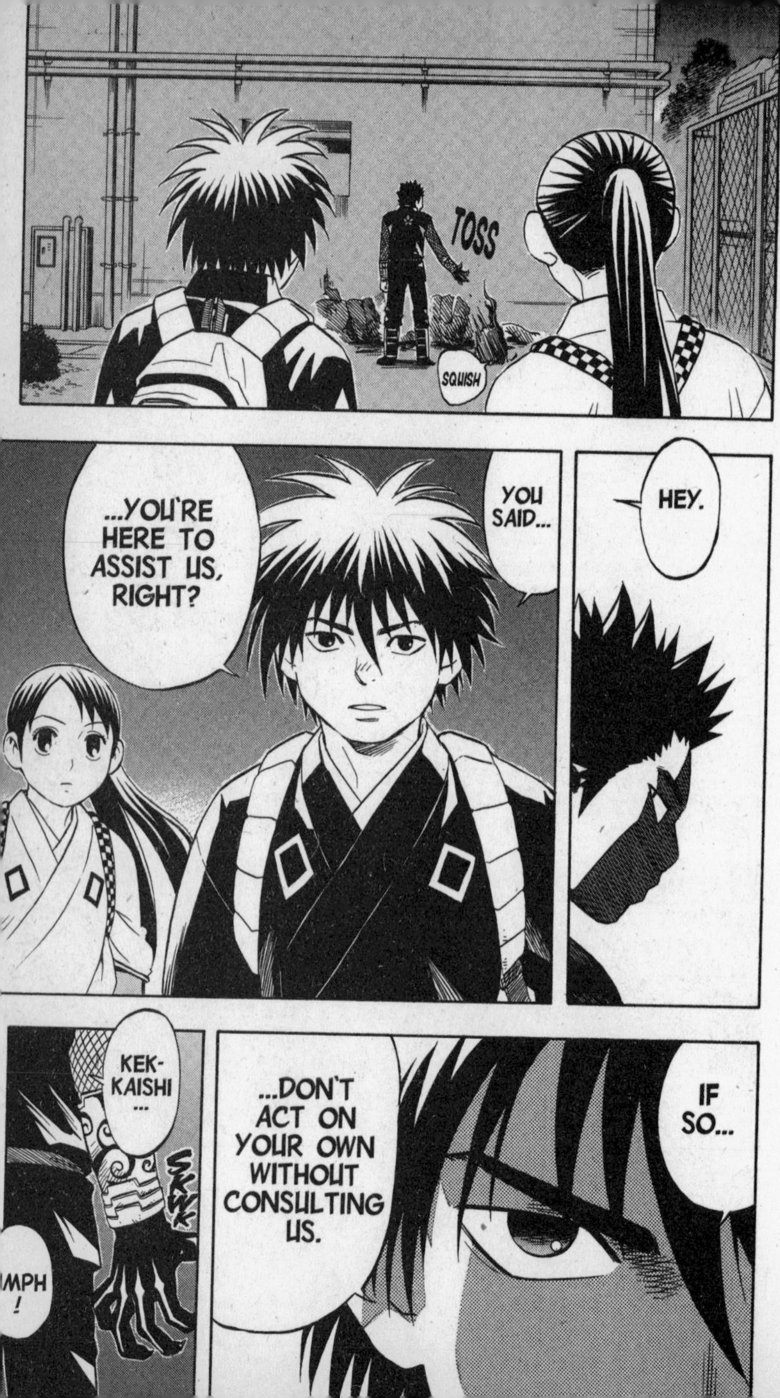
TOSS
SQUISH
HEY.
YOU SAID...
...YOU'RE HERE TO ASSIST US, RIGHT?
IF SO...
...DON'T ACT ON YOUR OWN WITHOUT CONSULTING US.
KEK-KAISHI...
MPH!

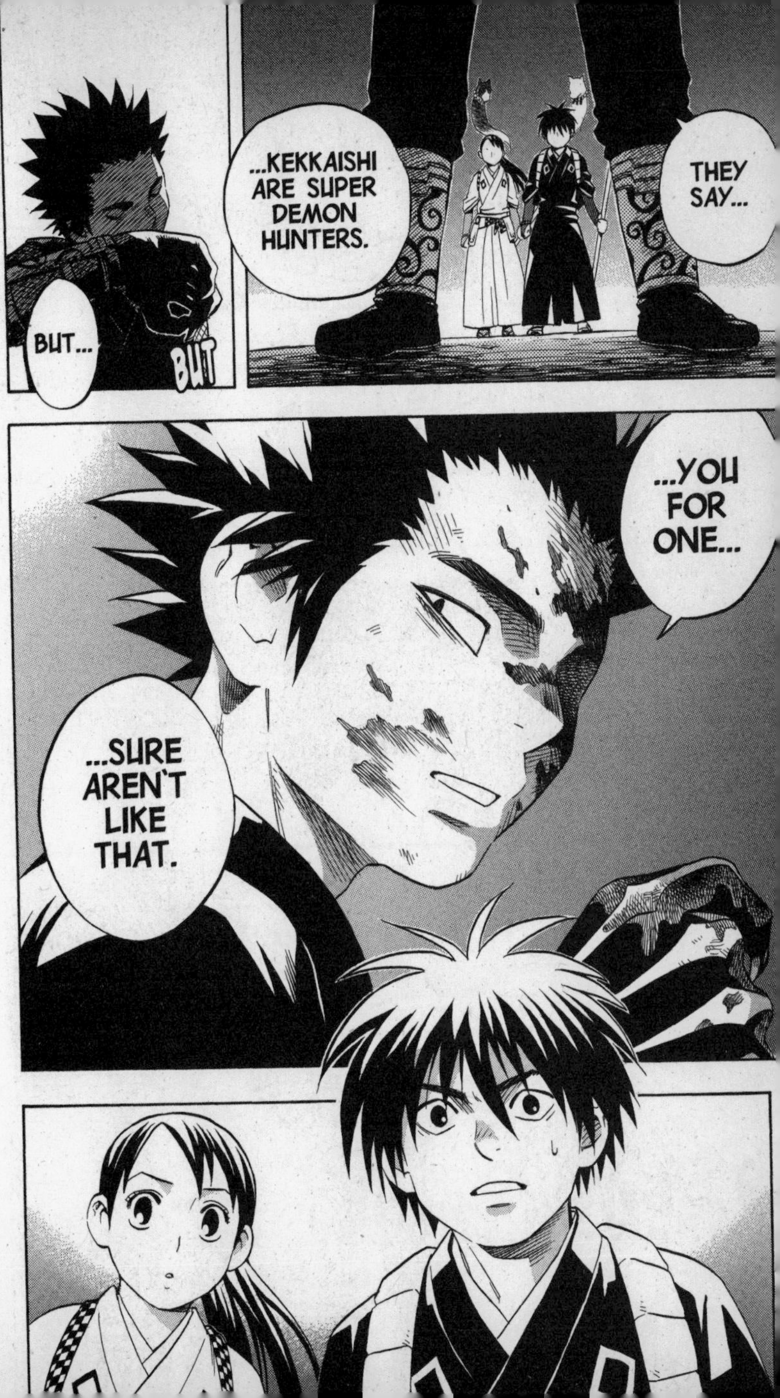
THEY SAY...
...KEKKAISHI ARE SUPER DEMON HUNTERS.
BUT...
BUT
...YOU FOR ONE...
...SURE AREN'T LIKE THAT.

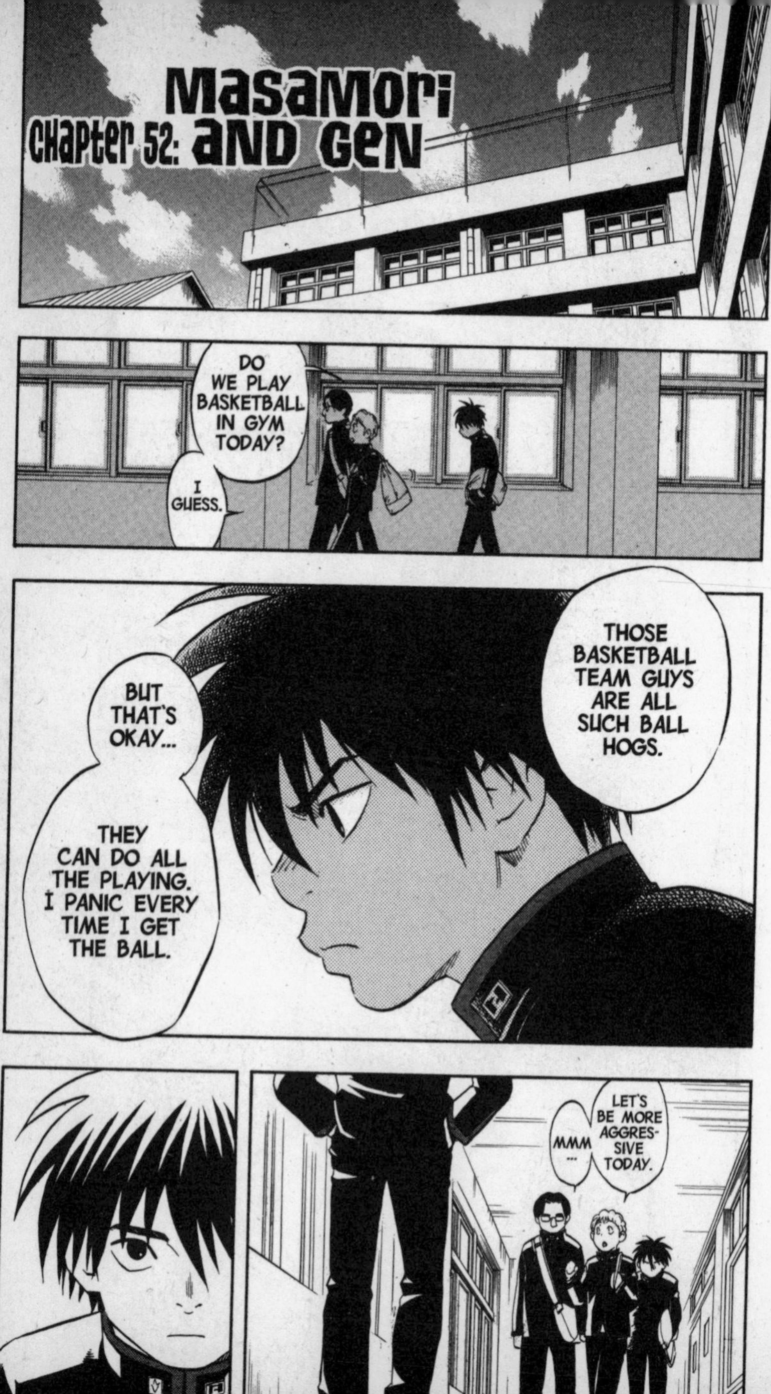
Chapter 52: Masamori and Gen
DO WE PLAY BASKETBALL IN GYM TODAY?
I GUESS.
THOSE BASKETBALL TEAM GUYS ARE ALL SUCH BALL HOGS.
BUT THAT'S OKAY...
THEY CAN DO ALL THE PLAYING. I PANIC EVERY TIME I GET THE BALL.
LET'S BE MORE AGGRES-SIVE TODAY.
MMM...

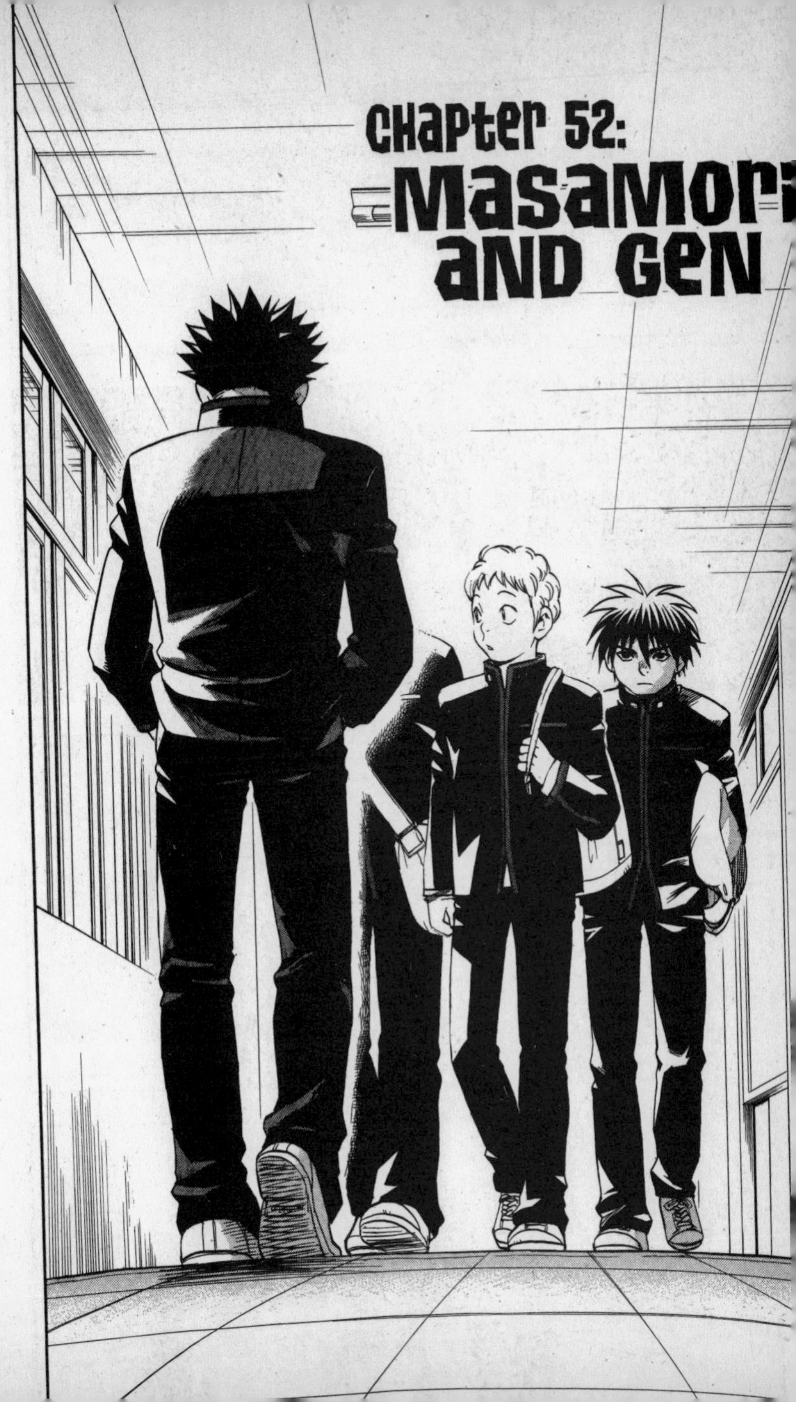
Chapter 52:
Masamori and Gen

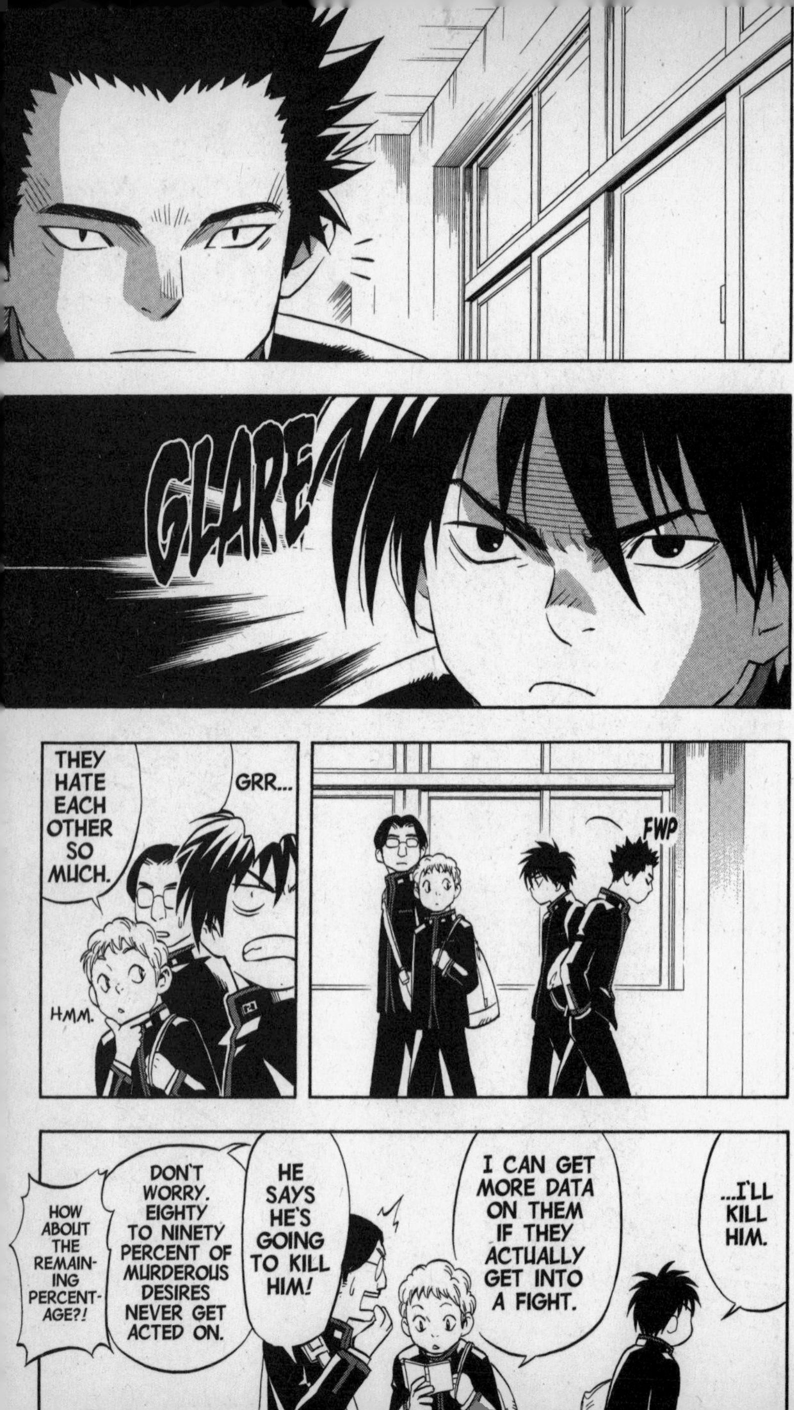
GLARE
FWP
GRR...
THEY HATE EACH OTHER SO MUCH.
HMM.
...I'LL KILL HIM.
I CAN GET MORE DATA ON THEM IF THEY ACTUALLY GET INTO A FIGHT.
HE SAYS HE'S GOING TO KILL HIM!
DON'T WORRY. EIGHTY TO NINETY PERCENT OF MURDEROUS DESIRES NEVER GET ACTED ON.
HOW ABOUT THE REMAINING PERCENTAGE?!

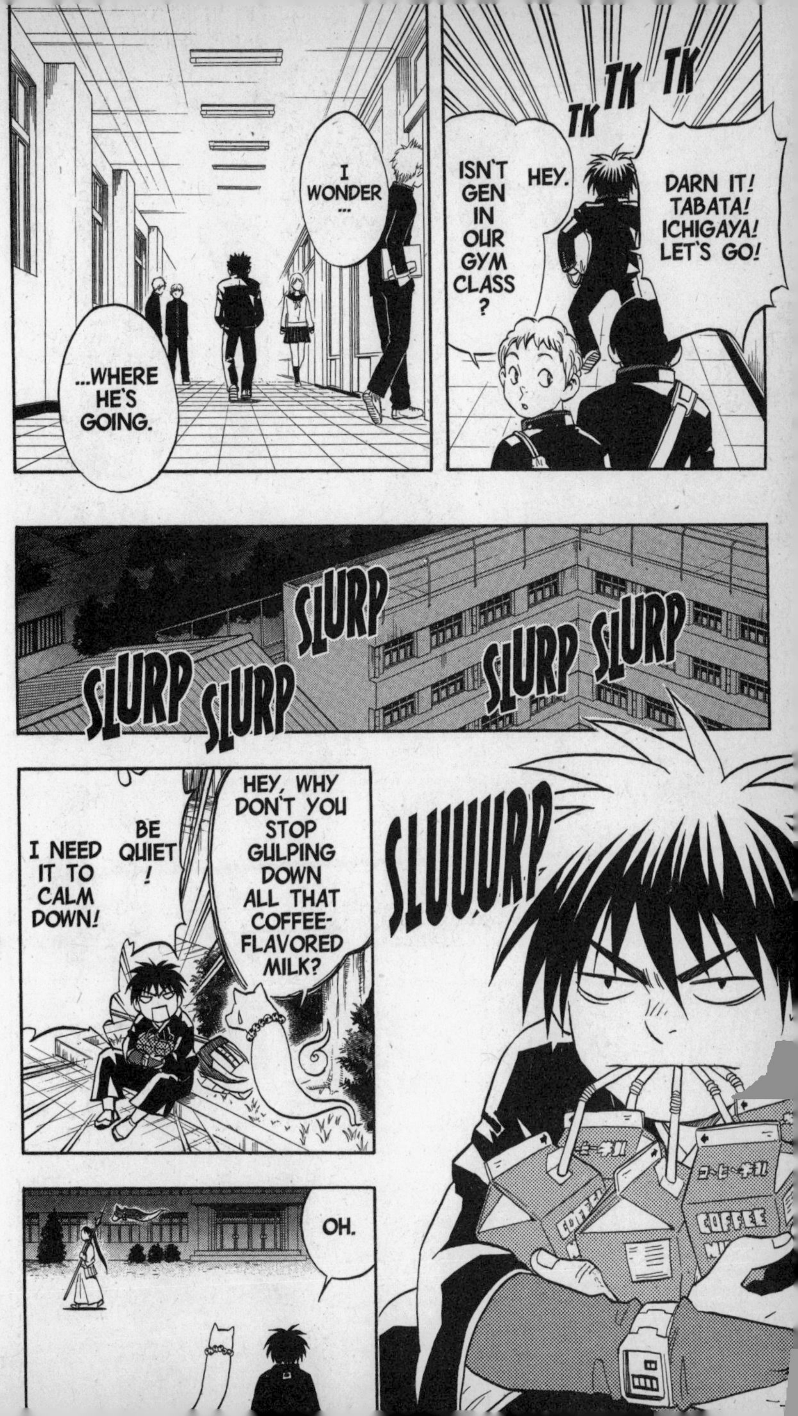
TK TK TK
DARN IT! TABATA! ICHIGAYA! LET'S GO!
HEY.
ISN'T GEN IN OUR GYM CLASS?
I WONDER...
...WHERE HE'S GOING.
SLURP SLURP
SLURP
SLURP SLURP
SLUUURP
HEY, WHY DON'T YOU STOP GULPING DOWN ALL THAT COFFEE-FLAVORED MILK?
BE QUIET!
I NEED IT TO CALM DOWN!
OH.

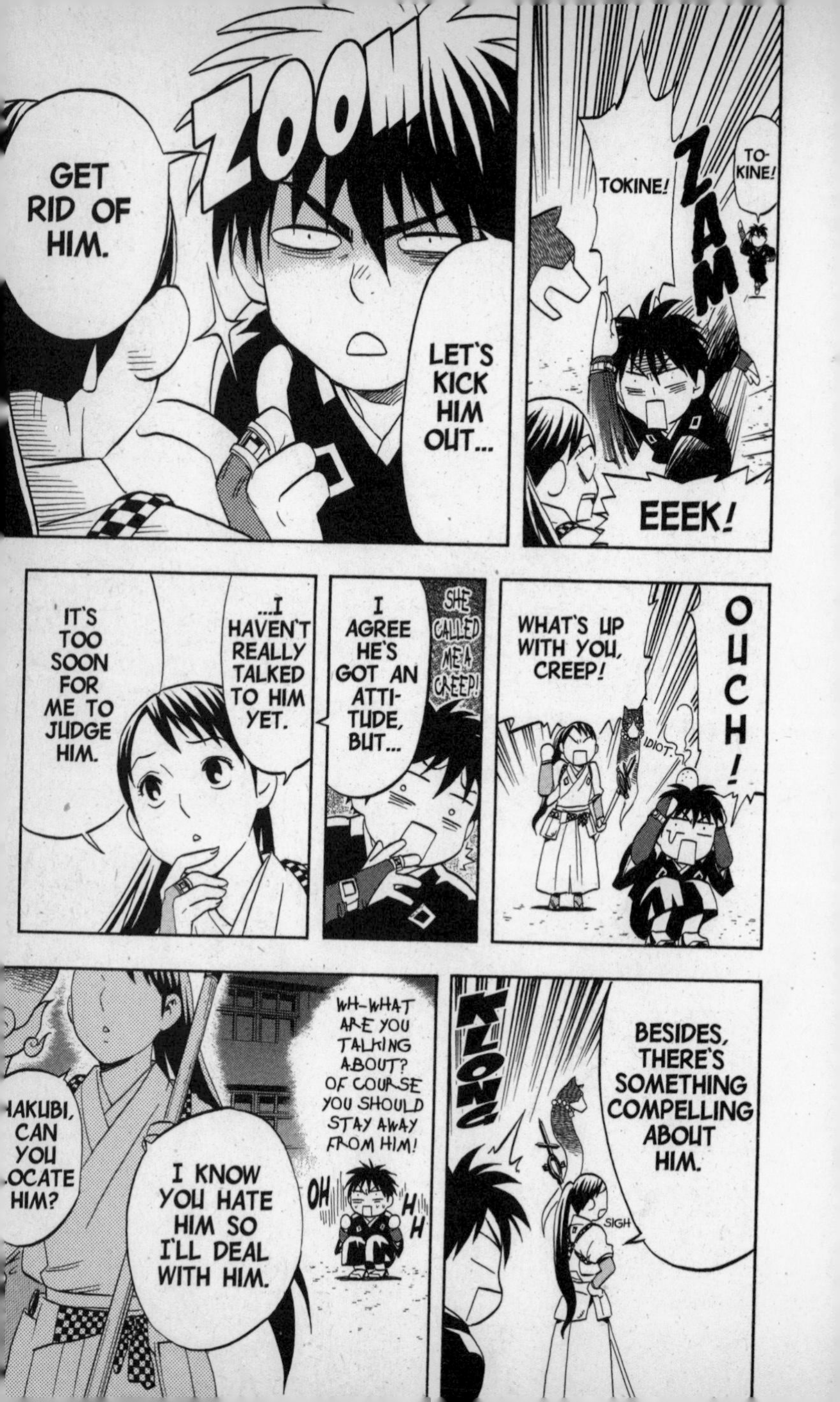
TO-KINE!
TOKINE!
ZAM
EEEK!
ZOOM
LET'S KICK HIM OUT...
GET RID OF HIM.
OUCH!
WHAT'S UP WITH YOU, CREEP!
IDIOT.
SHE CALLED ME A CREEP!
I AGREE HE'S GOT AN ATTITUDE, BUT...
...I HAVEN'T REALLY TALKED TO HIM YET.
IT'S TOO SOON FOR ME TO JUDGE HIM.
KLONG
BESIDES, THERE'S SOMETHING COMPELLING ABOUT HIM.
SIGH
WH-WHAT ARE YOU TALKING ABOUT? OF COURSE YOU SHOULD STAY AWAY FROM HIM!
OH H H
I KNOW YOU HATE HIM SO I'LL DEAL WITH HIM.
AKUBI, CAN YOU OCATE HIM?

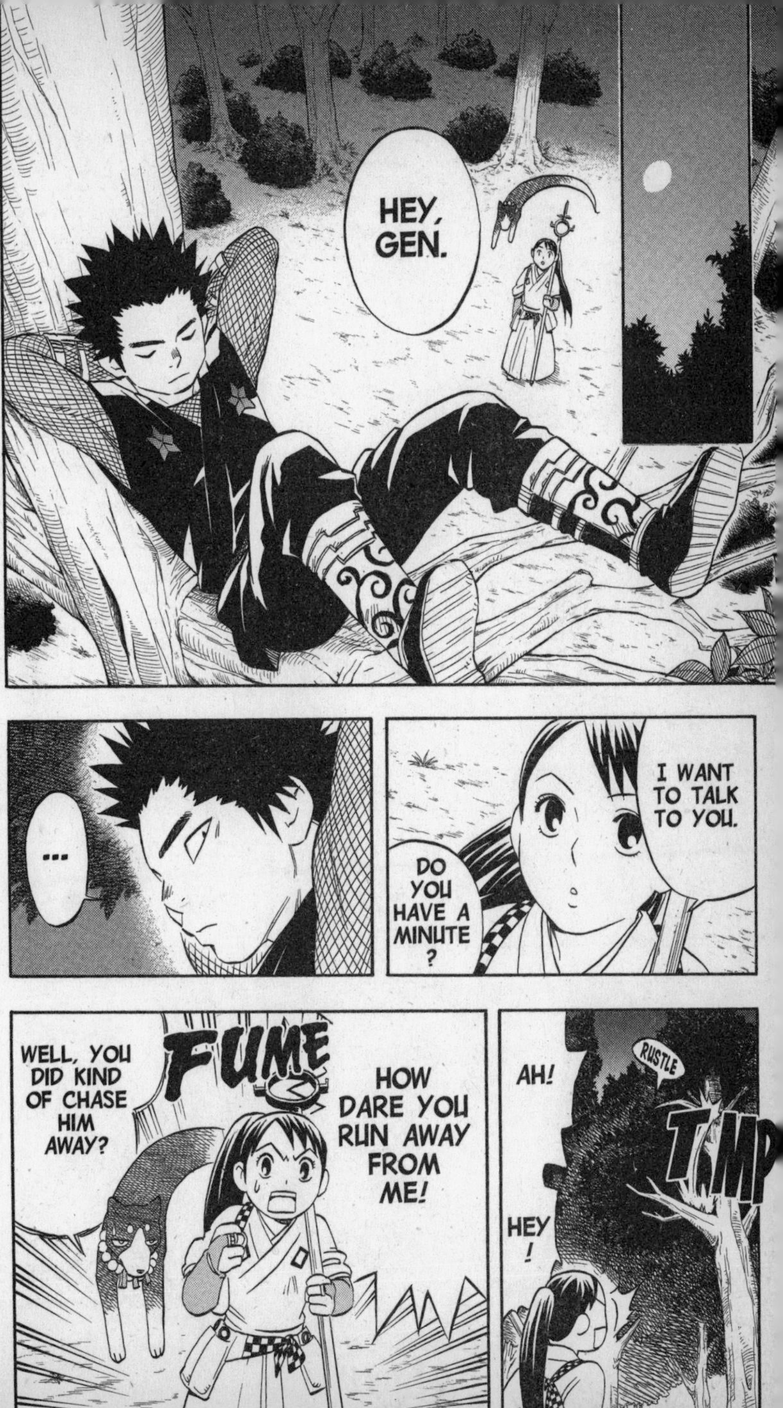
HEY, GEN.
I WANT TO TALK TO YOU.
DO YOU HAVE A MINUTE?
...
RUSTLE
AH!
TMP
HEY!
FUME
HOW DARE YOU RUN AWAY FROM ME!
WELL, YOU DID KIND OF CHASE HIM AWAY?

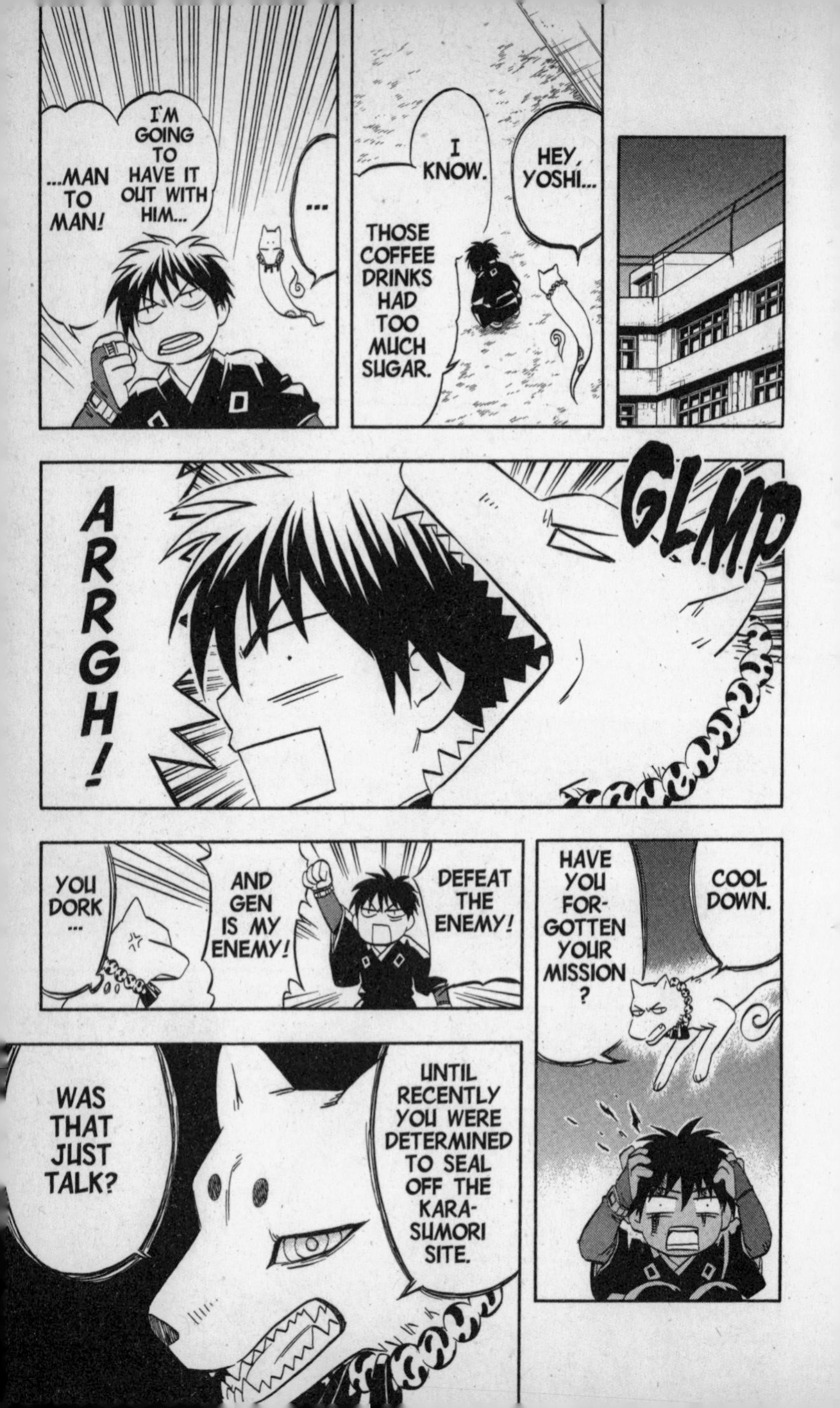
HEY, YOSHI...
I KNOW.
THOSE COFFEE DRINKS HAD TOO MUCH SUGAR.
...
I'M GOING TO HAVE IT OUT WITH HIM...
...MAN TO MAN!
GLMP
ARRGH!
COOL DOWN.
HAVE YOU FOR-GOTTEN YOUR MISSION?
DEFEAT THE ENEMY!
AND GEN IS MY ENEMY!
YOU DORK...
UNTIL RECENTLY YOU WERE DETERMINED TO SEAL OFF THE KARA-SUMORI SITE.
WAS THAT JUST TALK?

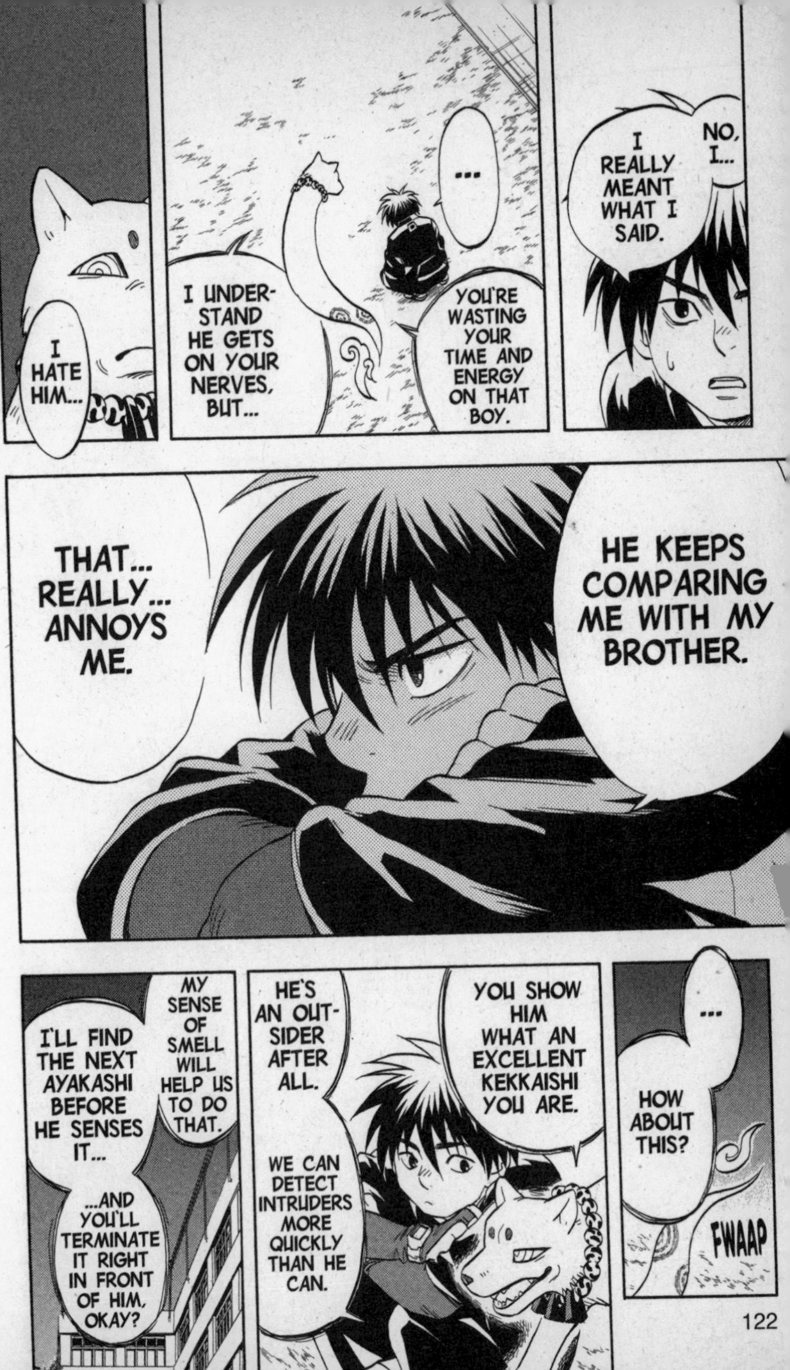

NO, I...
I REALLY MEANT WHAT I SAID.
...
YOU'RE WASTING YOUR TIME AND ENERGY ON THAT BOY.
I UNDER-STAND HE GETS ON YOUR NERVES, BUT...
I HATE HIM...
HE KEEPS COMPARING ME WITH MY BROTHER.
THAT... REALLY... ANNOYS ME.
...
HOW ABOUT THIS?
FWAAP
YOU SHOW HIM WHAT AN EXCELLENT KEKKAISHI YOU ARE.
HE'S AN OUT-SIDER AFTER ALL.
WE CAN DETECT INTRUDERS MORE QUICKLY THAN HE CAN.
MY SENSE OF SMELL WILL HELP US TO DO THAT.
I'LL FIND THE NEXT AYAKASHI BEFORE HE SENSES IT...
...AND YOU'LL TERMINATE IT RIGHT IN FRONT OF HIM, OKAY?

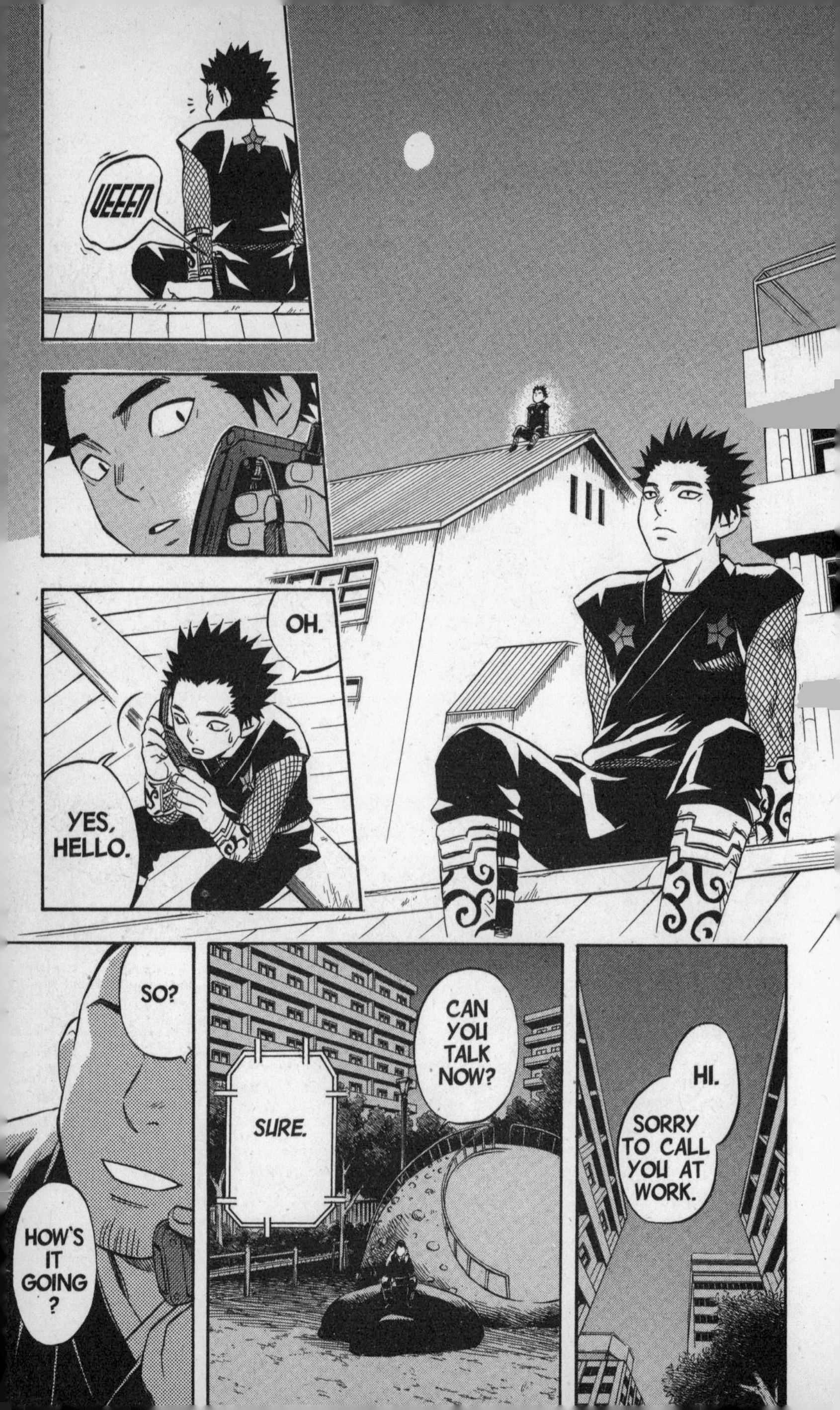
VEEEN
OH.
YES, HELLO.
HI.
SORRY TO CALL YOU AT WORK.
CAN YOU TALK NOW?
SURE.
SO?
HOW'S IT GOING?

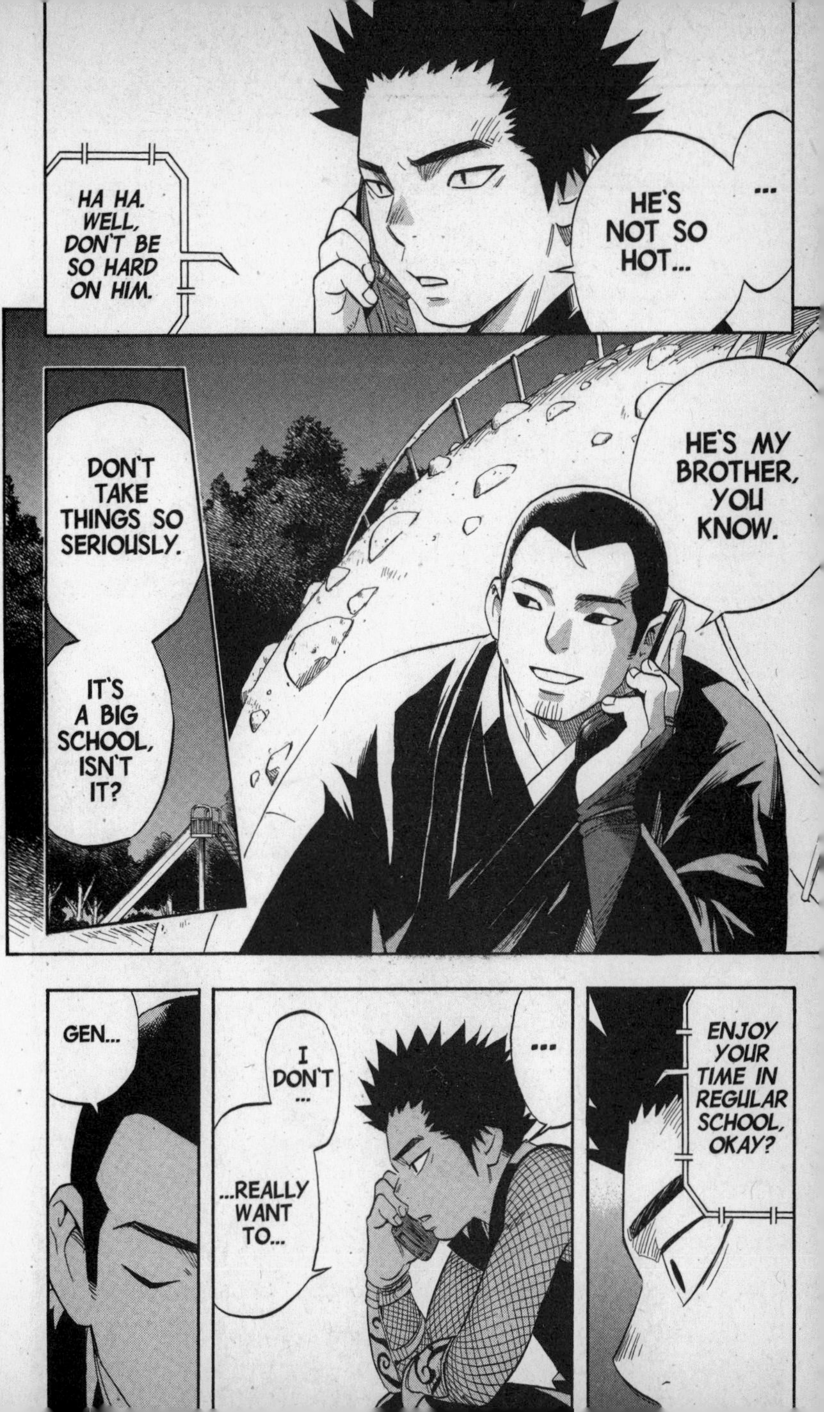
...
HE'S NOT SO HOT...
HA HA. WELL, DON'T BE SO HARD ON HIM.
HE'S MY BROTHER, YOU KNOW.
DON'T TAKE THINGS SO SERIOUSLY.
IT'S A BIG SCHOOL, ISN'T IT?
ENJOY YOUR TIME IN REGULAR SCHOOL, OKAY?
...
I DON'T ...
...REALLY WANT TO...
GEN...

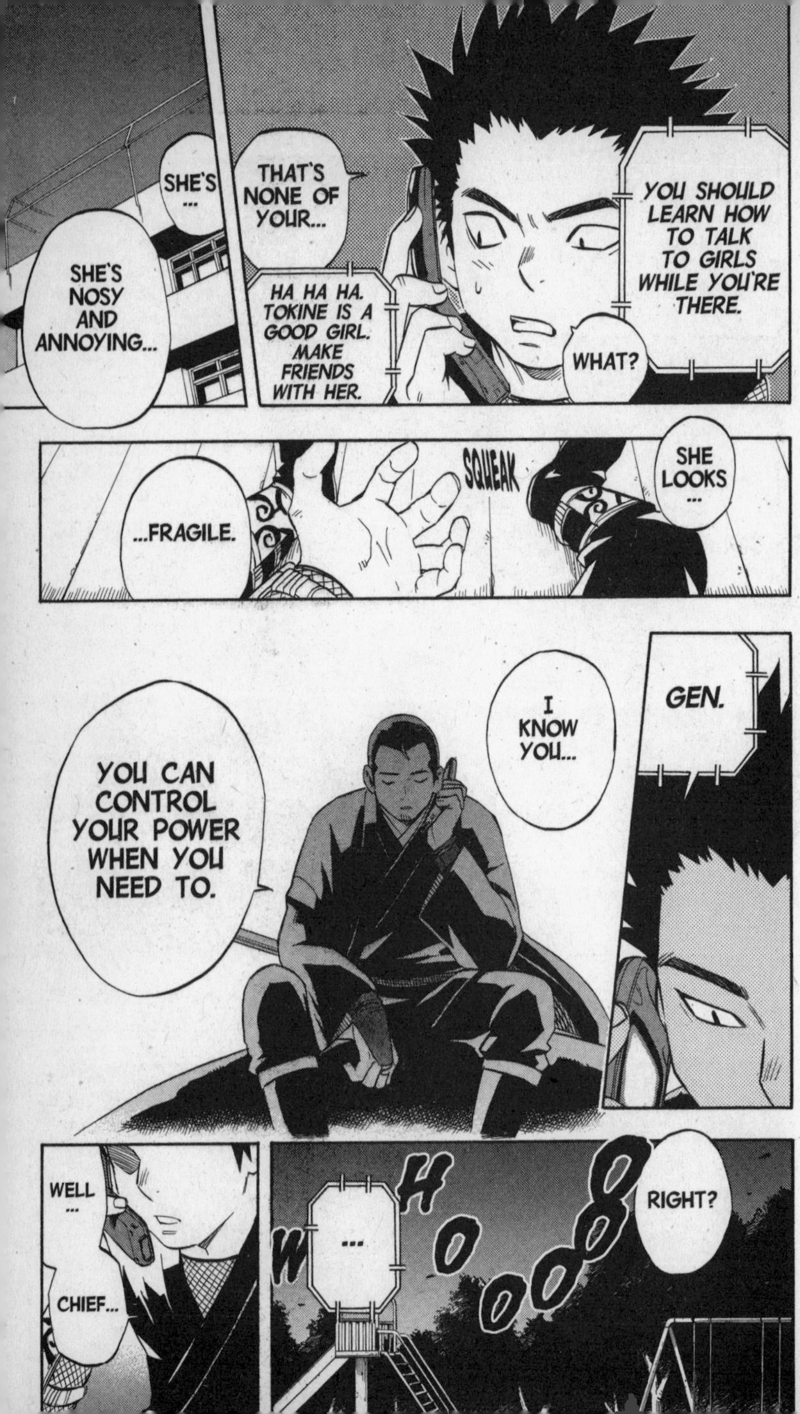
YOU SHOULD LEARN HOW TO TALK TO GIRLS WHILE YOU'RE THERE.
WHAT?
HA HA HA. TOKINE IS A GOOD GIRL. MAKE FRIENDS WITH HER.
THAT'S NONE OF YOUR...
SHE'S ...
SHE'S NOSY AND ANNOYING...
SHE LOOKS ...
SQUEAK
...FRAGILE.
GEN.
I KNOW YOU...
YOU CAN CONTROL YOUR POWER WHEN YOU NEED TO.
RIGHT?
WHOOOOO
...
WELL ...
CHIEF...

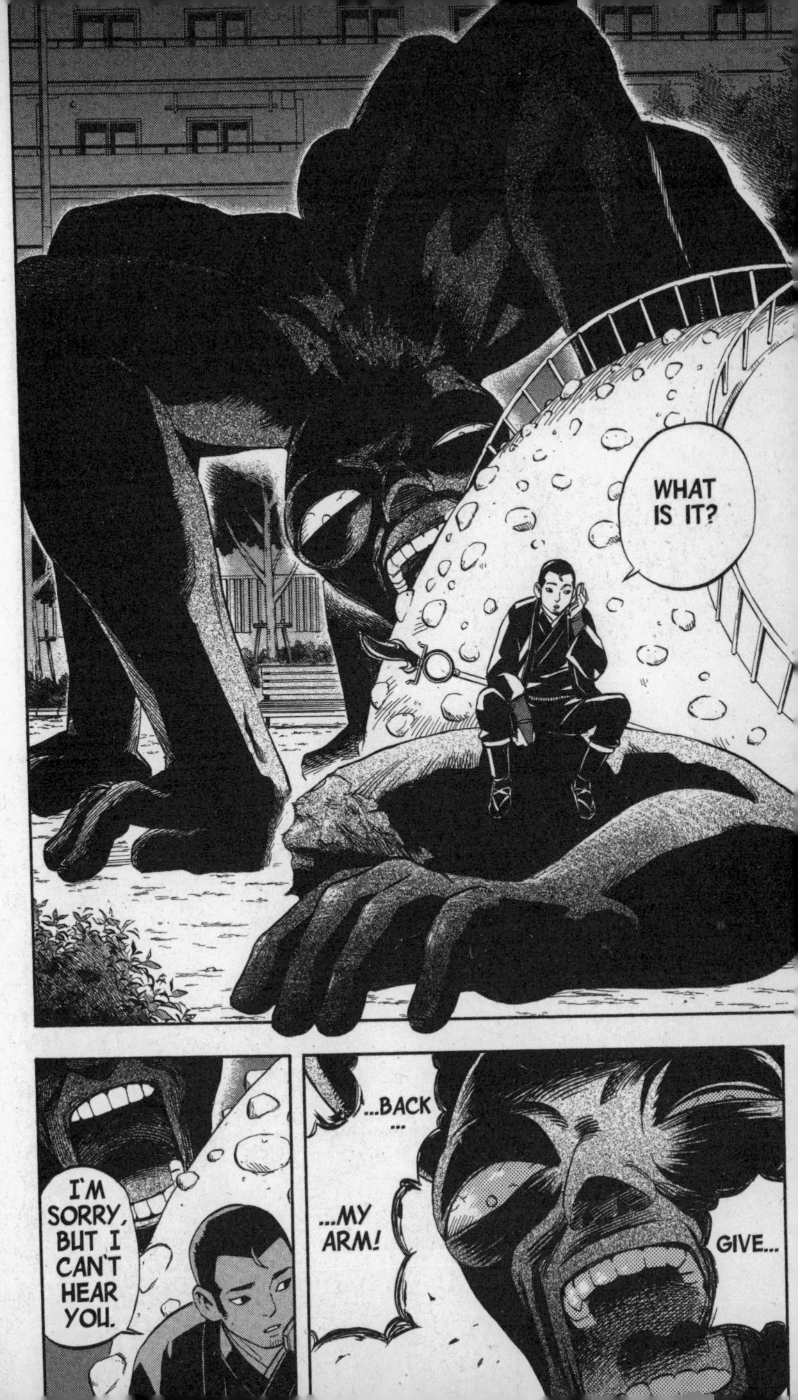
WHAT IS IT?
GIVE...
...BACK...
...MY ARM!
I'M SORRY, BUT I CAN'T HEAR YOU.

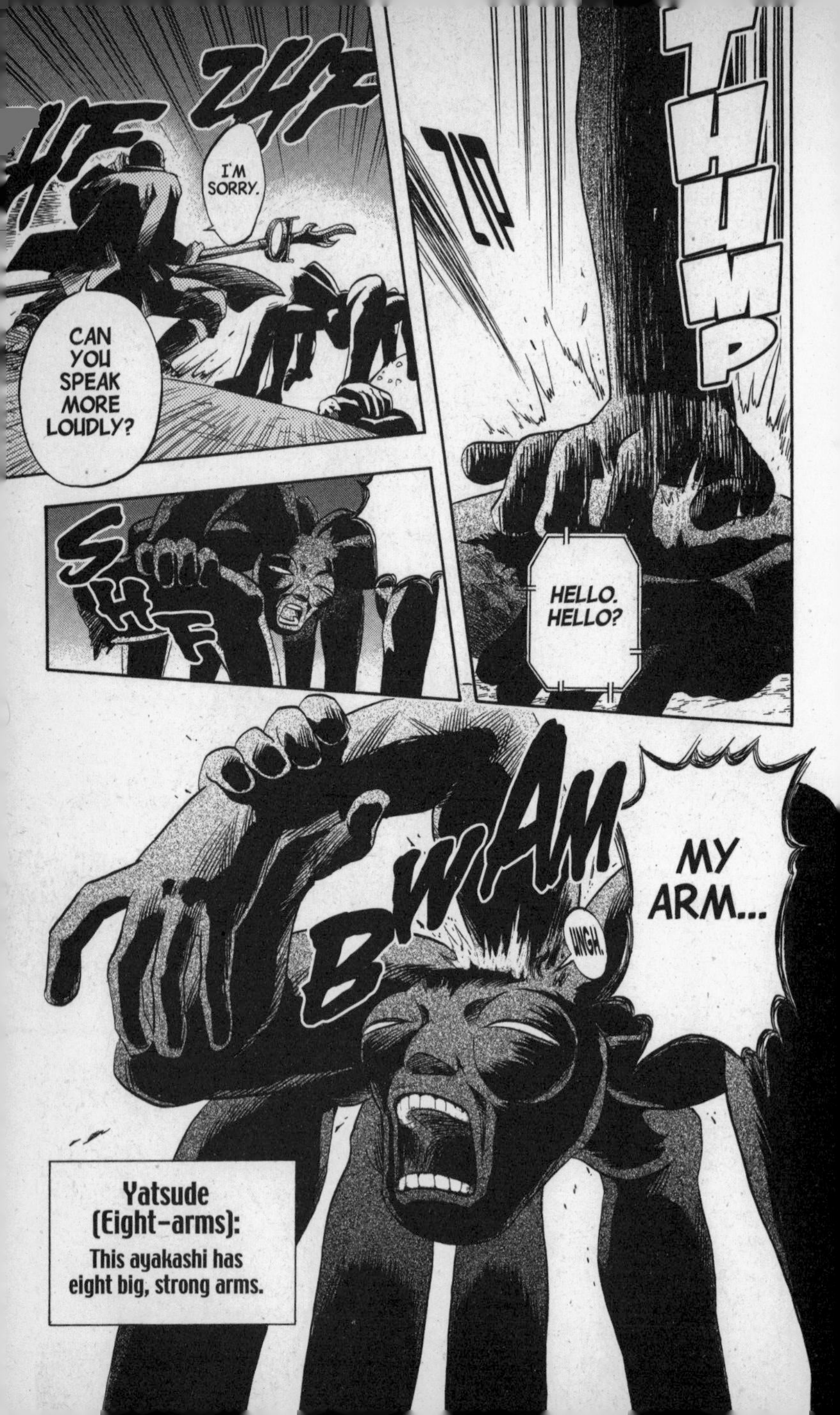
THUMP
ZIP
HELLO. HELLO?
ZAP
I'M SORRY.
SHF
CAN YOU SPEAK MORE LOUDLY?
SHF
MY ARM...
BWAM
UNGH.
Yatsude (Eight-arms): This ayakashi has eight big, strong arms.

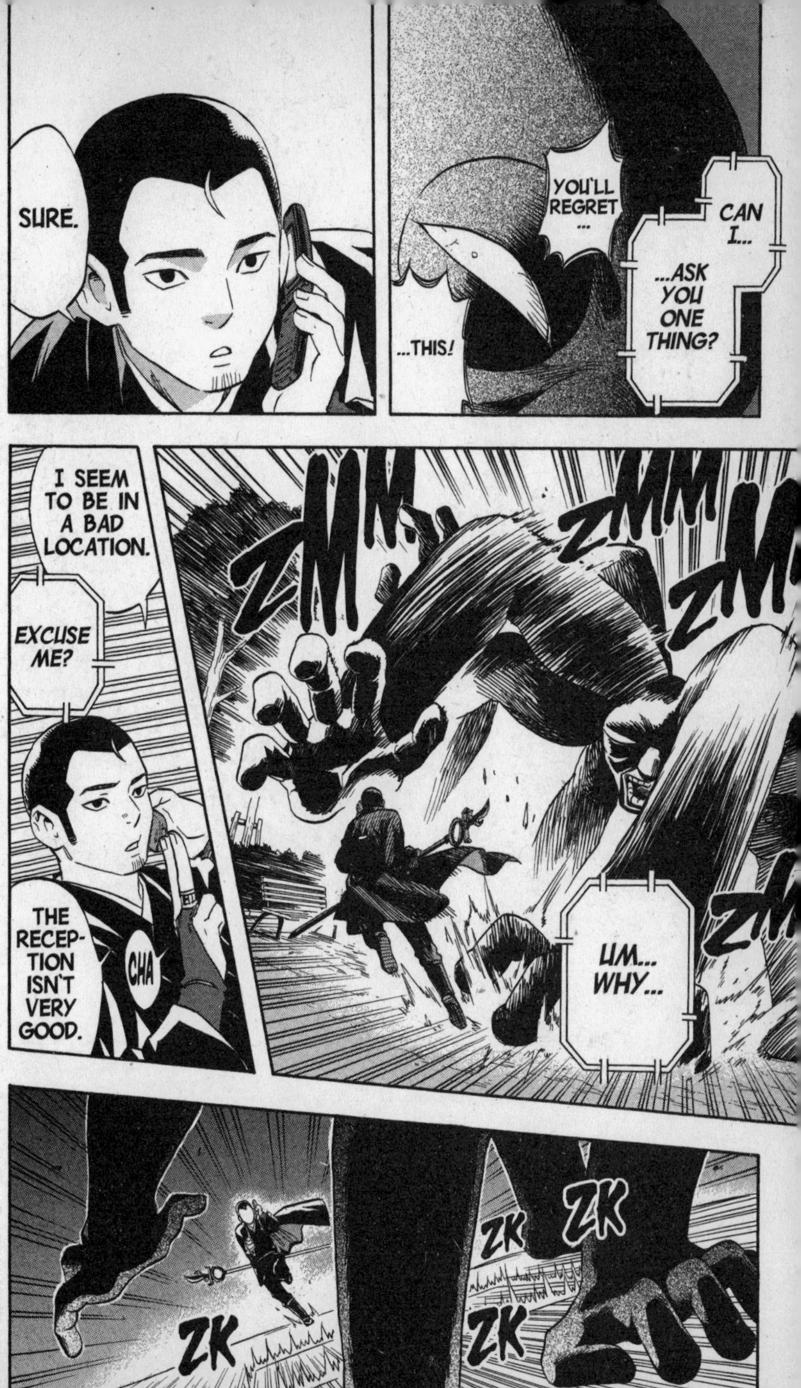
CAN I...
...ASK YOU ONE THING?
YOU'LL REGRET ...
...THIS!
SURE.
ZMM
ZMM
ZMM
ZMM
UM... WHY...
I SEEM TO BE IN A BAD LOCATION.
EXCUSE ME?
CHA
THE RECEPTION ISN'T VERY GOOD.
ZK
ZK
ZK
ZK

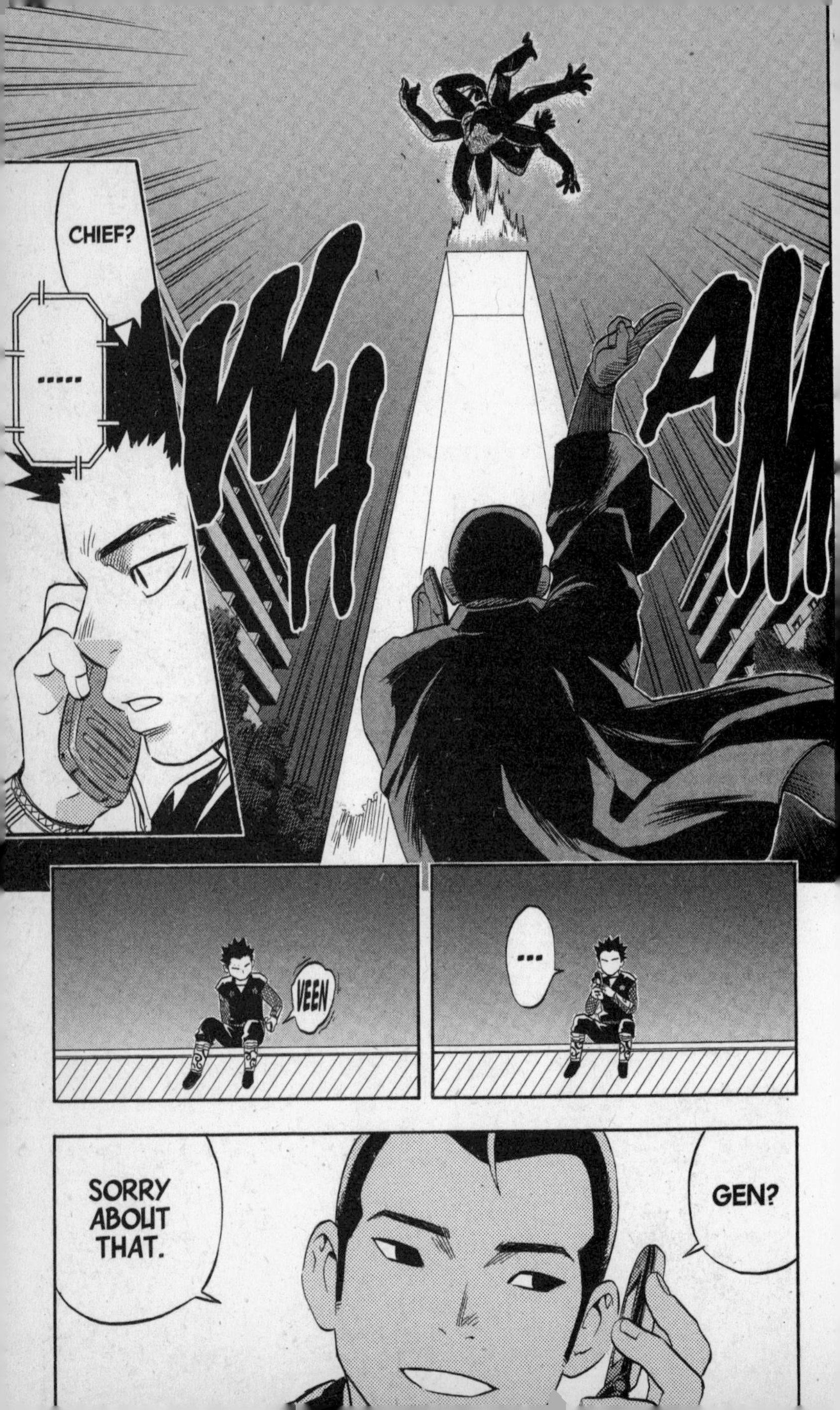
CHIEF?
.....
...
VEEN
GEN?
SORRY ABOUT THAT.

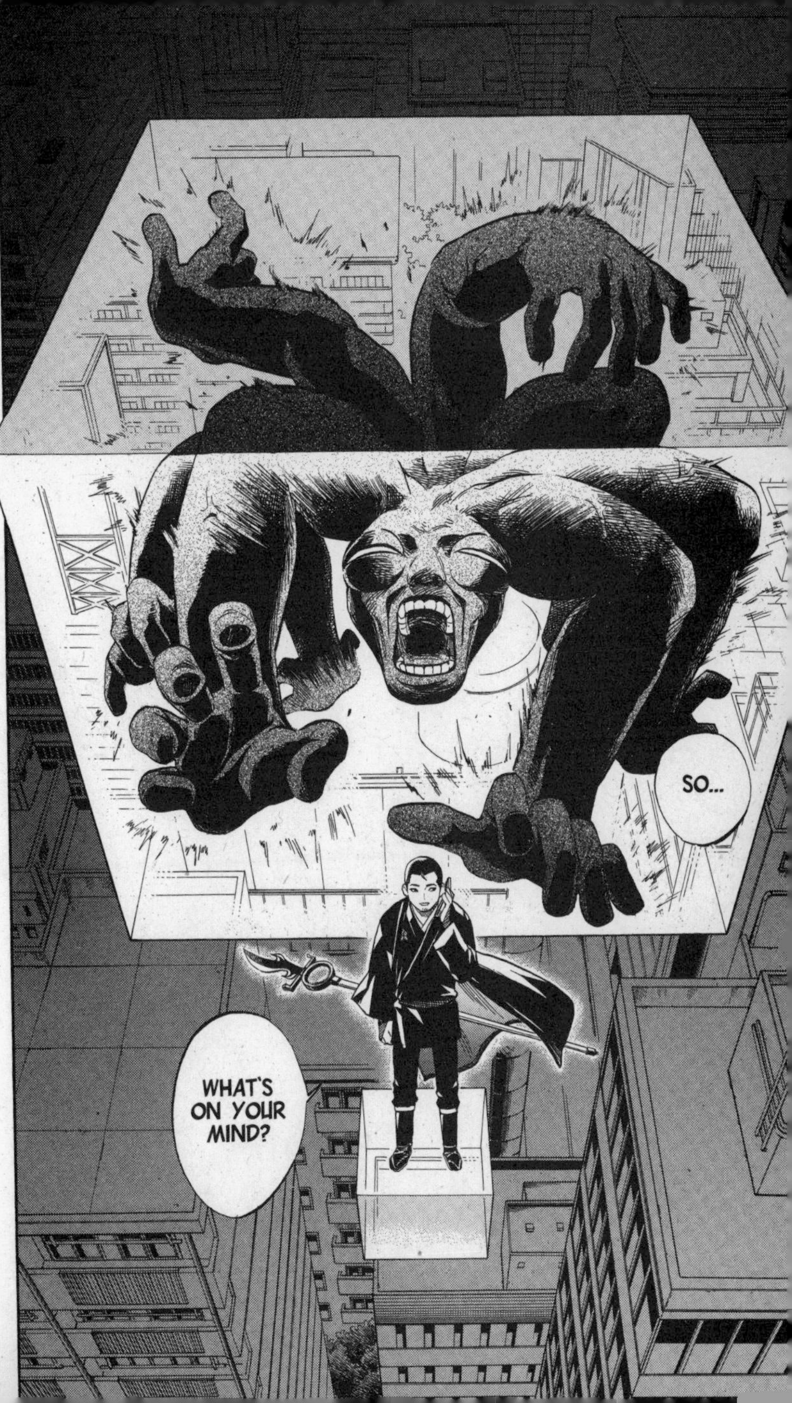
SO...
WHAT'S ON YOUR MIND?

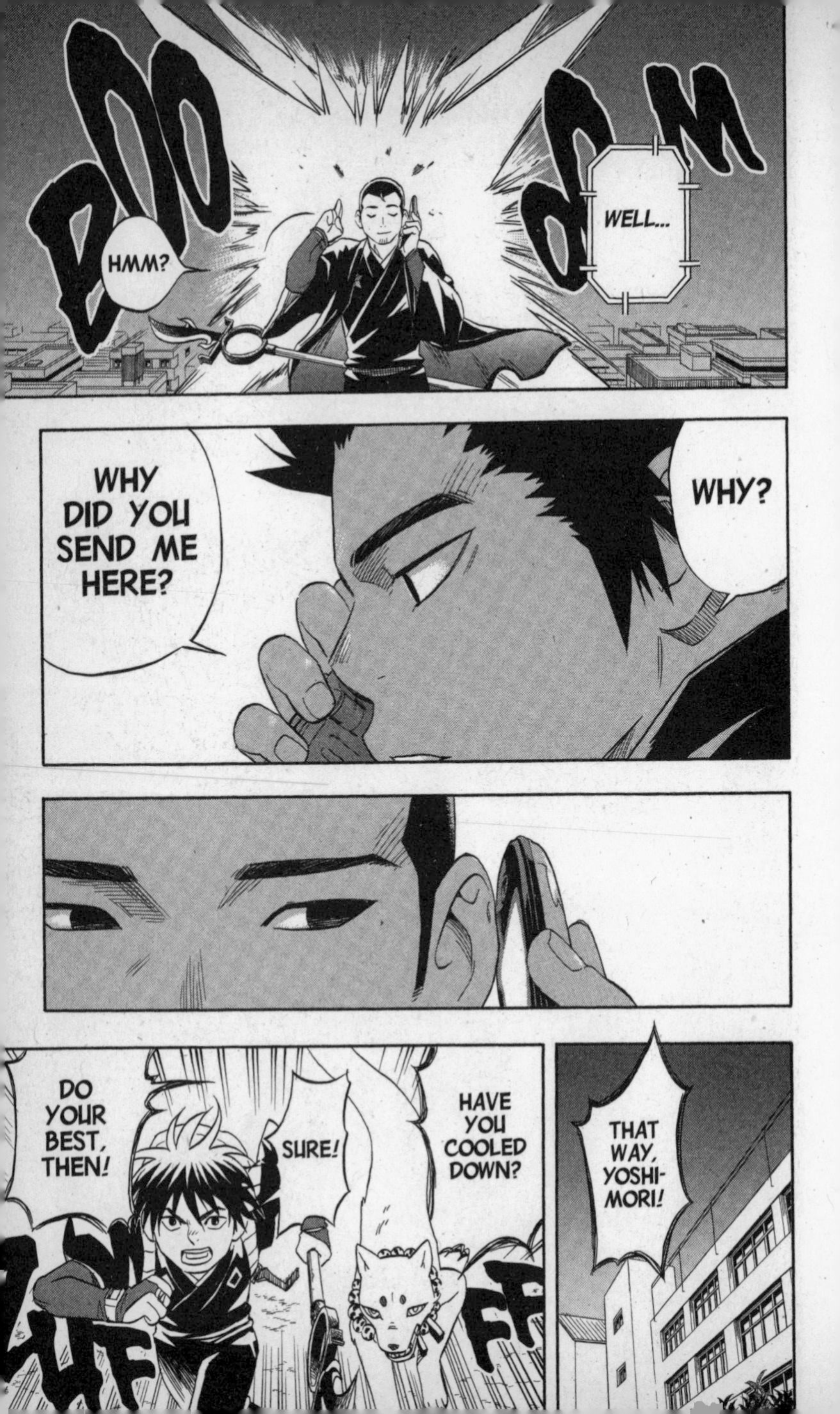
WELL...
HMM?
WHY?
WHY DID YOU SEND ME HERE?
THAT WAY, YOSHIMORI!
HAVE YOU COOLED DOWN?
SURE!
DO YOUR BEST, THEN!

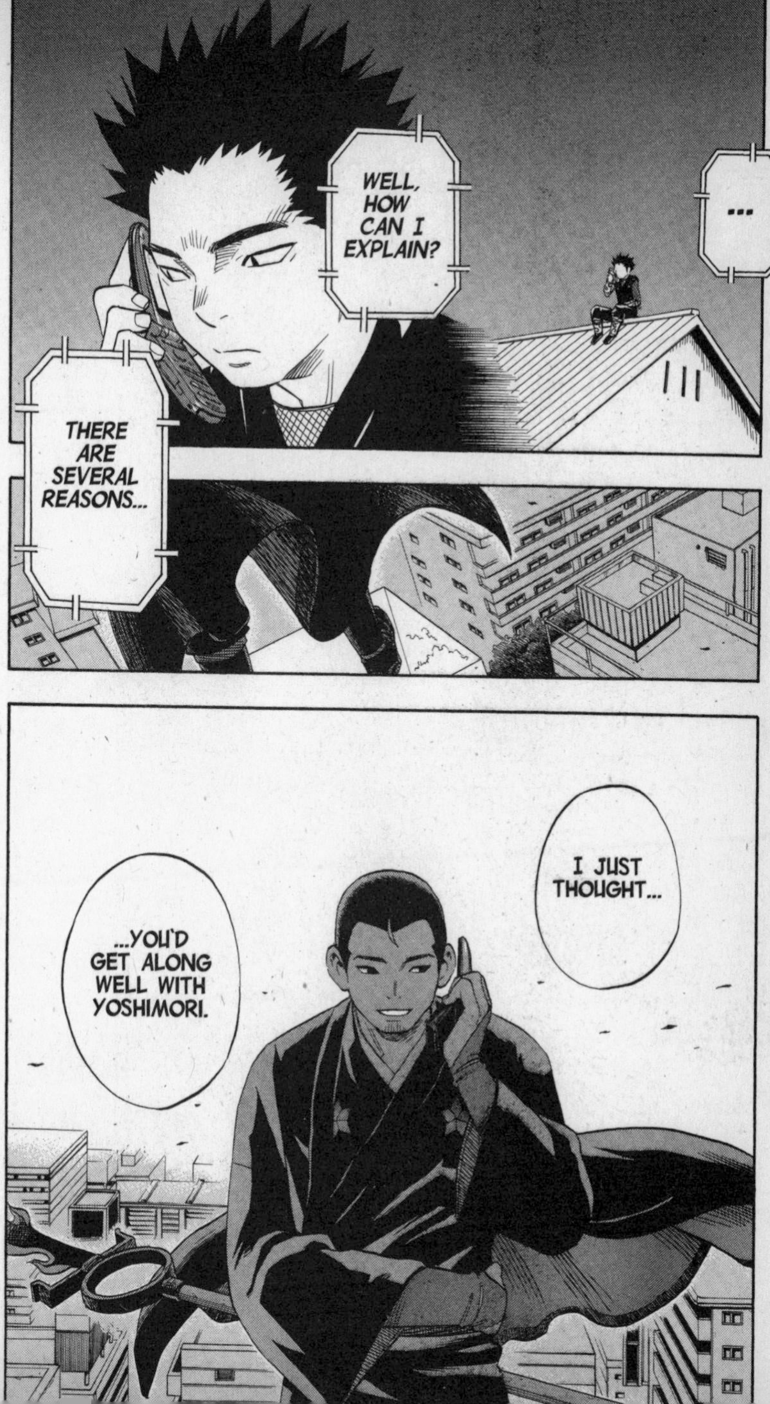
...
WELL, HOW CAN I EXPLAIN?
THERE ARE SEVERAL REASONS...
I JUST THOUGHT...
...YOU'D GET ALONG WELL WITH YOSHIMORI.

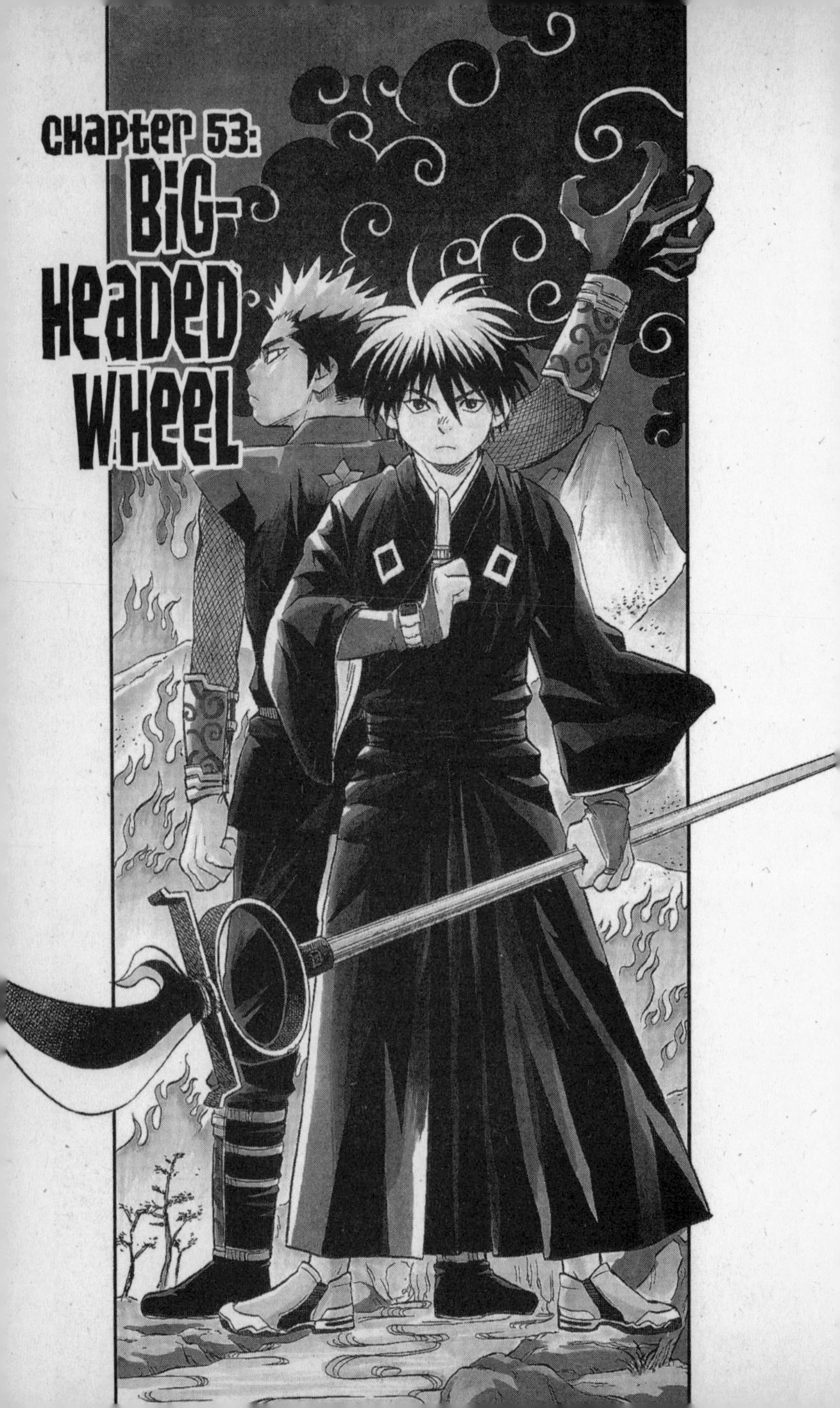
Chapter 53:
Big-
Headed
Wheel

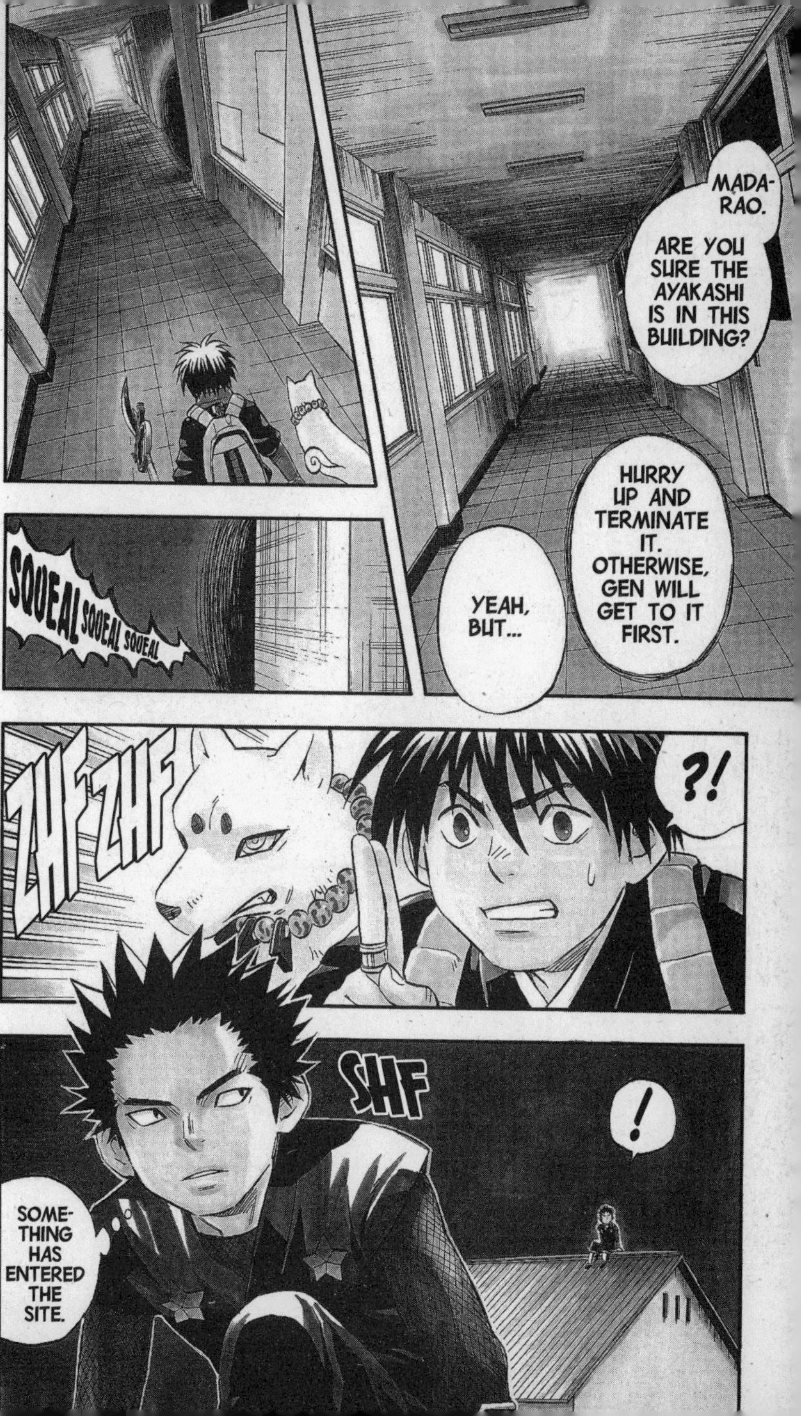
MADA-RAO.
ARE YOU SURE THE AYAKASHI IS IN THIS BUILDING?
HURRY UP AND TERMINATE IT. OTHERWISE, GEN WILL GET TO IT FIRST.
YEAH, BUT...
SQUEAL SQUEAL SQUEAL
?!
ZHF ZHF
!
SHF
SOME-THING HAS ENTERED THE SITE.

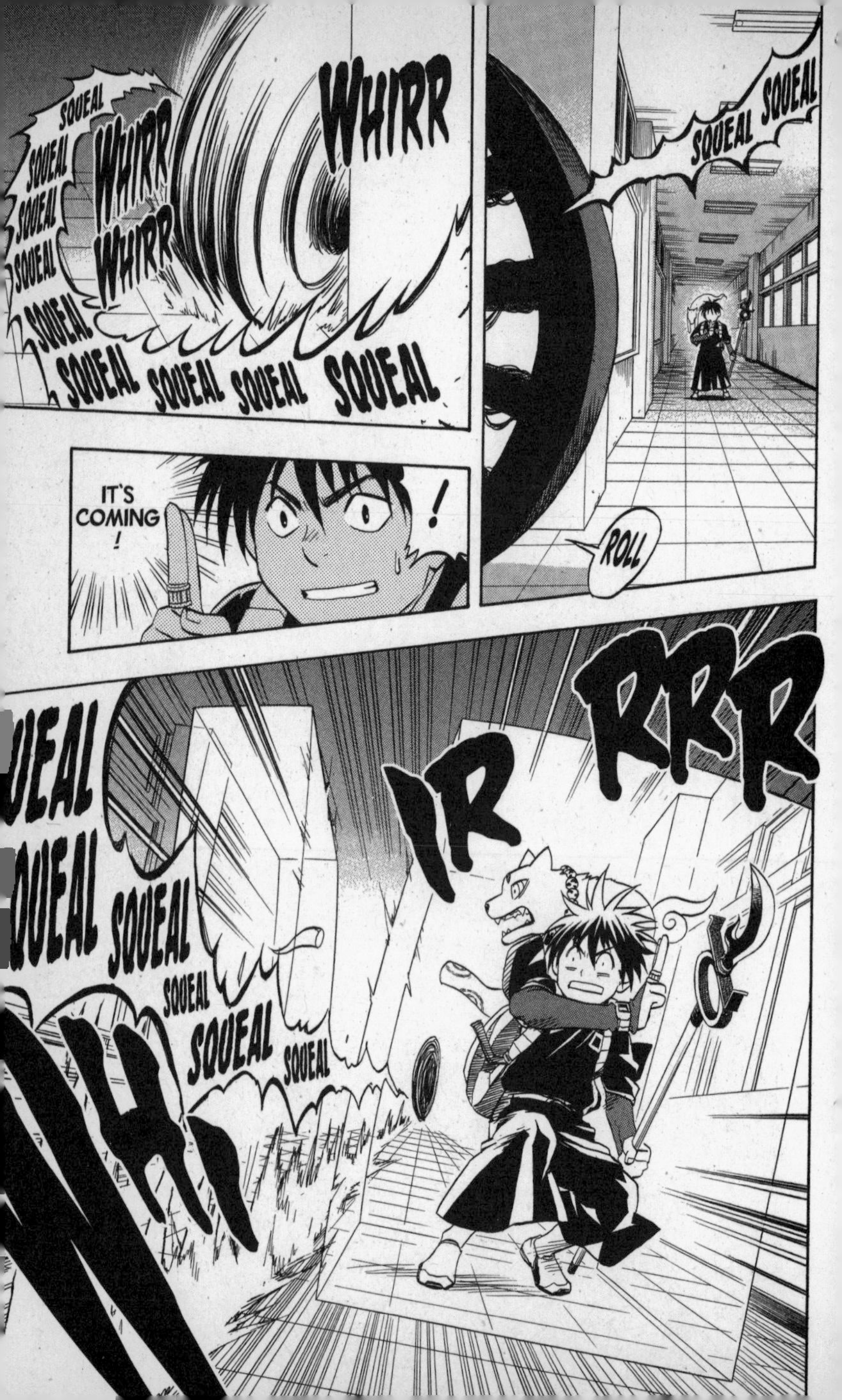
SQUEAL SQUEAL
ROLL
WHIRR
WHIRR
WHIRR
SQUEAL SQUEAL SQUEAL SQUEAL SQUEAL SQUEAL
SQUEAL SQUEAL SQUEAL SQUEAL
!
IT'S COMING!
RRR
IR
SQUEAL
SQUEAL
SQUEAL
SQUEAL
SQUEAL
SQUEAL
SQUEAL
WH

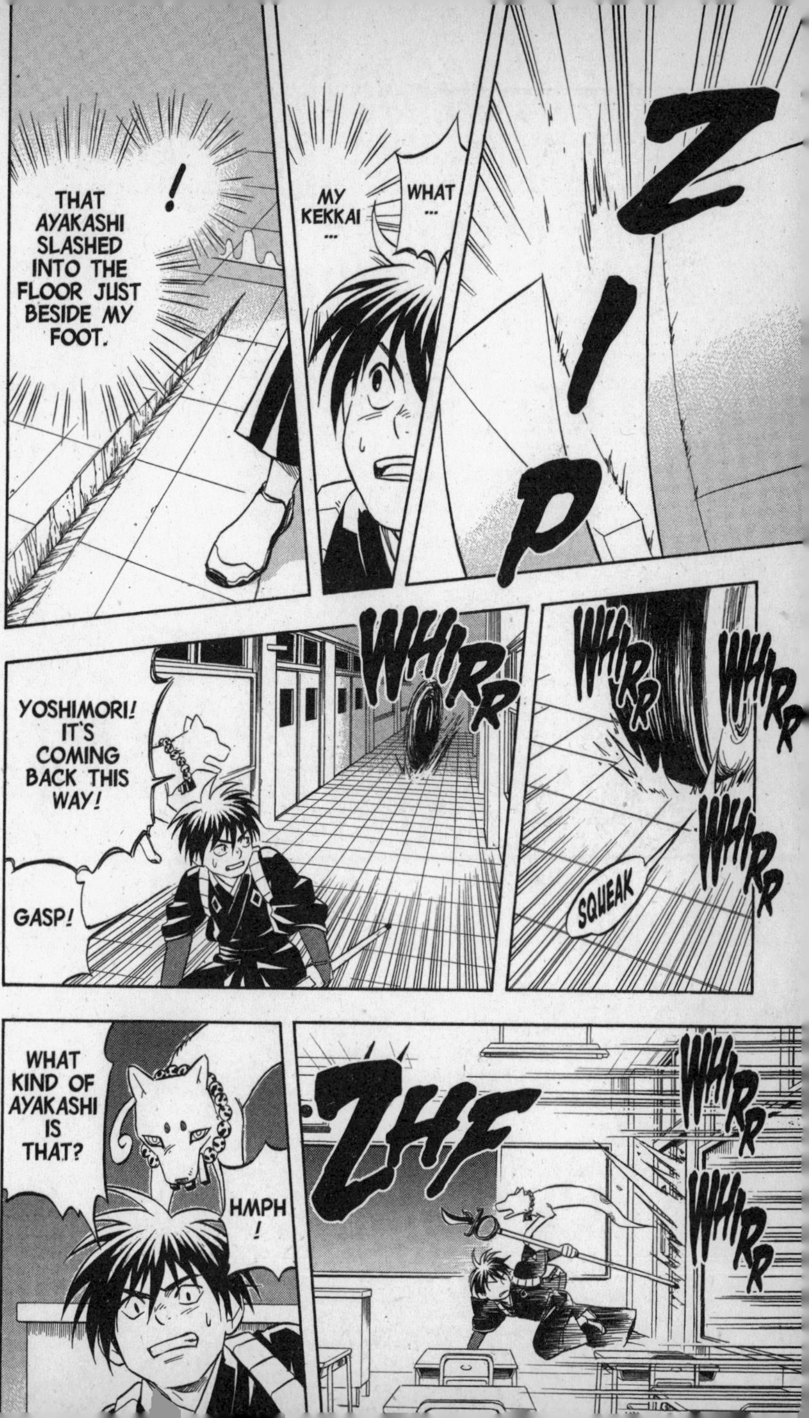
ZIP
WHAT ...
MY KEKKAI ...
!
THAT AYAKASHI SLASHED INTO THE FLOOR JUST BESIDE MY FOOT.
WHIRR
WHIRR
WHIRR
SQUEAK
WHIRR
YOSHIMORI! IT'S COMING BACK THIS WAY!
GASP!
WHIRR
WHIRR
ZHF
WHAT KIND OF AYAKASHI IS THAT?
HMPH!

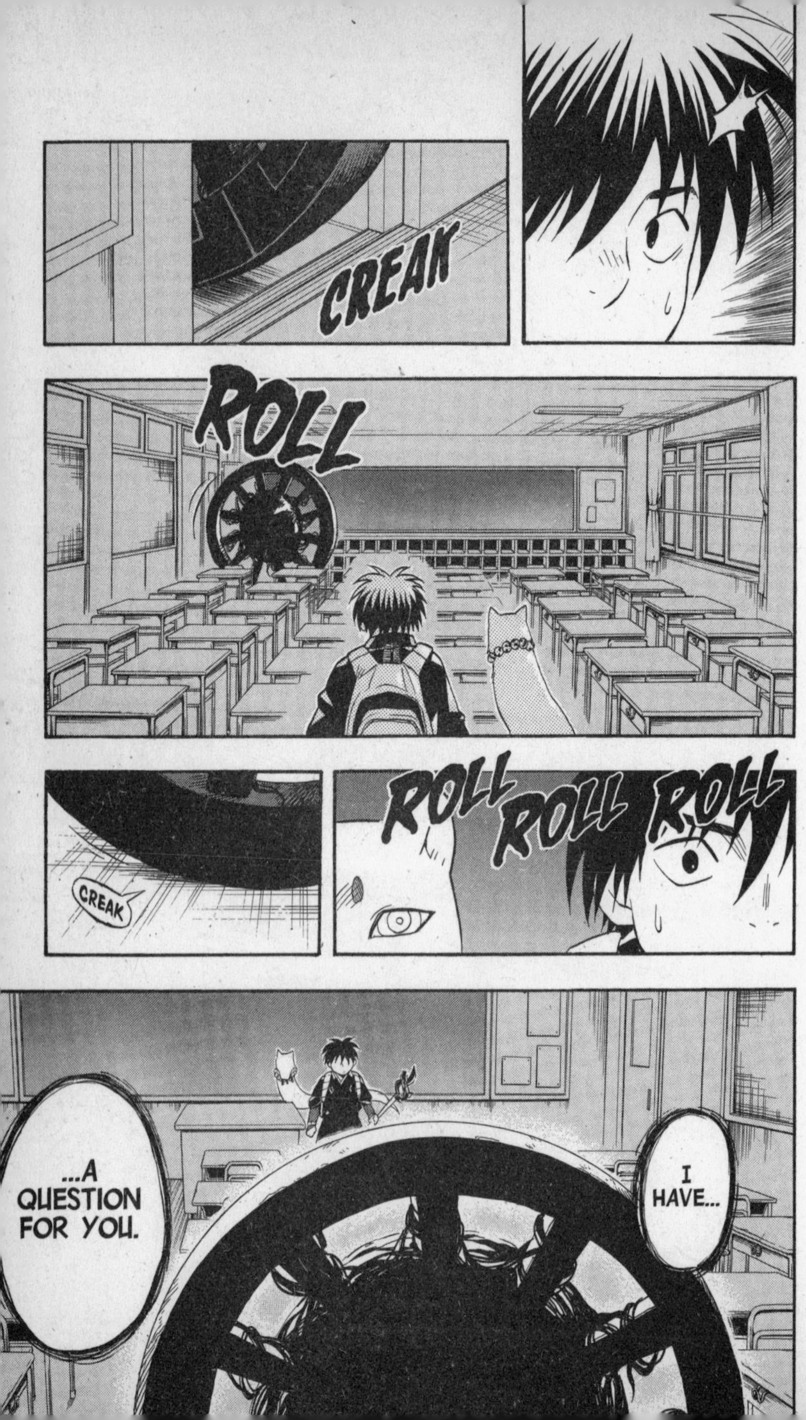
CREAK
ROLL
ROLL ROLL ROLL
CREAK
I HAVE...
...A QUESTION FOR YOU.

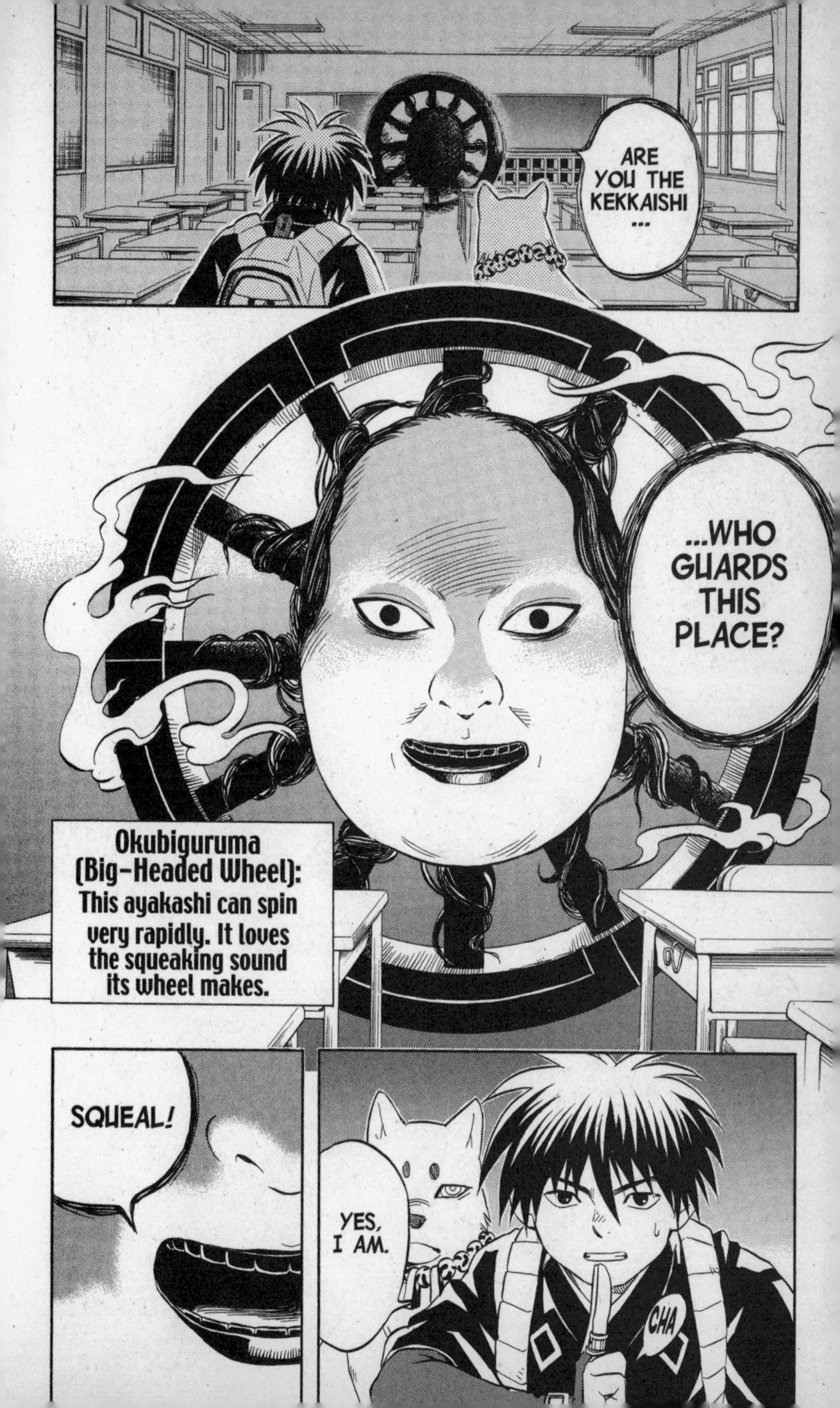
ARE YOU THE KEKKAISHI ...
...WHO GUARDS THIS PLACE?
Okubiguruma (Big-Headed Wheel): This ayakashi can spin very rapidly. It loves the squeaking sound its wheel makes.
CHA
YES, I AM.
SQUEAL!

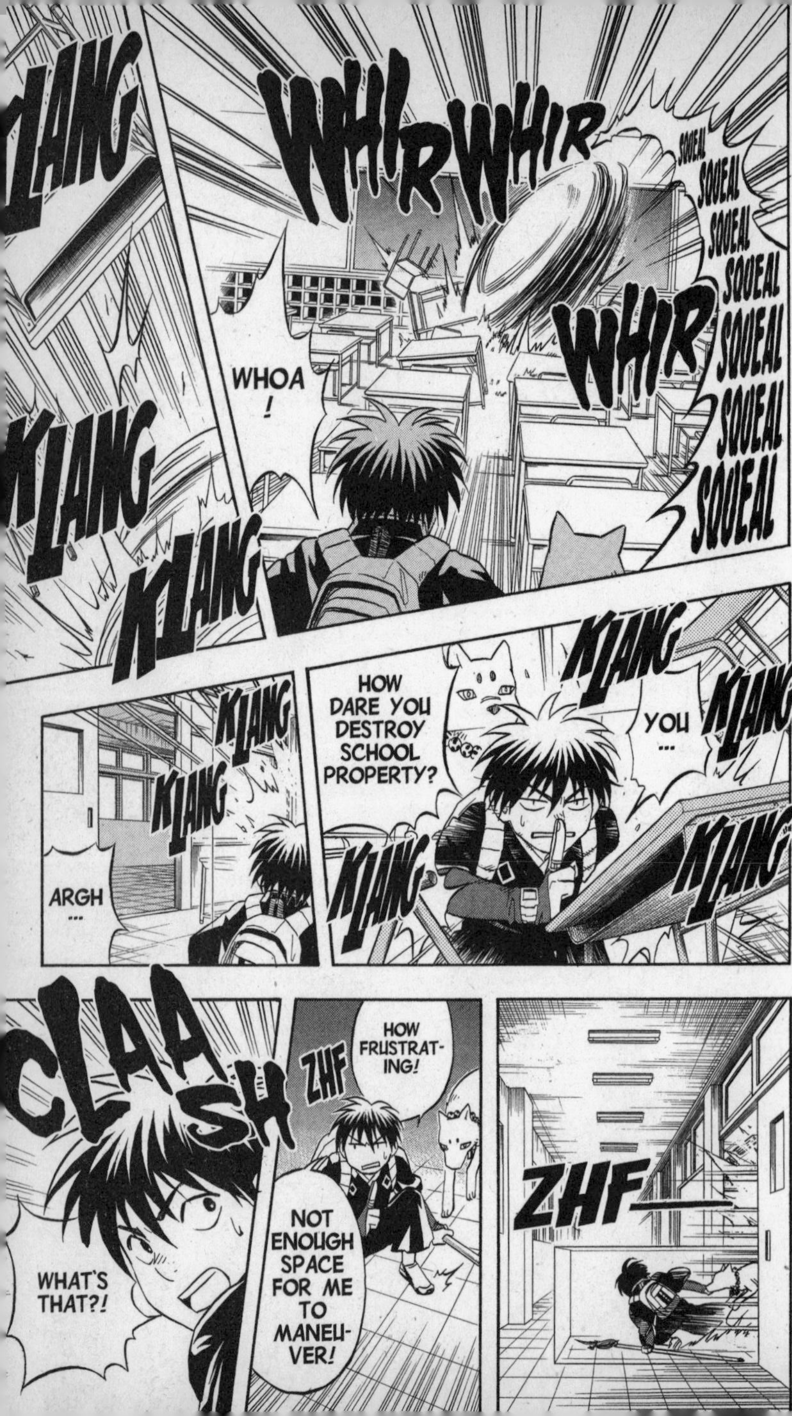
WHIR WHIR
SQUEAL
SQUEAL
SQUEAL
SQUEAL
SQUEAL
SQUEAL
SQUEAL
SQUEAL
WHIR
WHOA!
KLANG
KLANG
KLANG
KLANG
YOU ...
KLANG
HOW DARE YOU DESTROY SCHOOL PROPERTY?
KLANG
KLANG
KLANG
KLANG
ARGH ...
ZHF
HOW FRUSTRAT-ING!
ZHF
NOT ENOUGH SPACE FOR ME TO MANEU-VER!
CLAASH
WHAT'S THAT?!

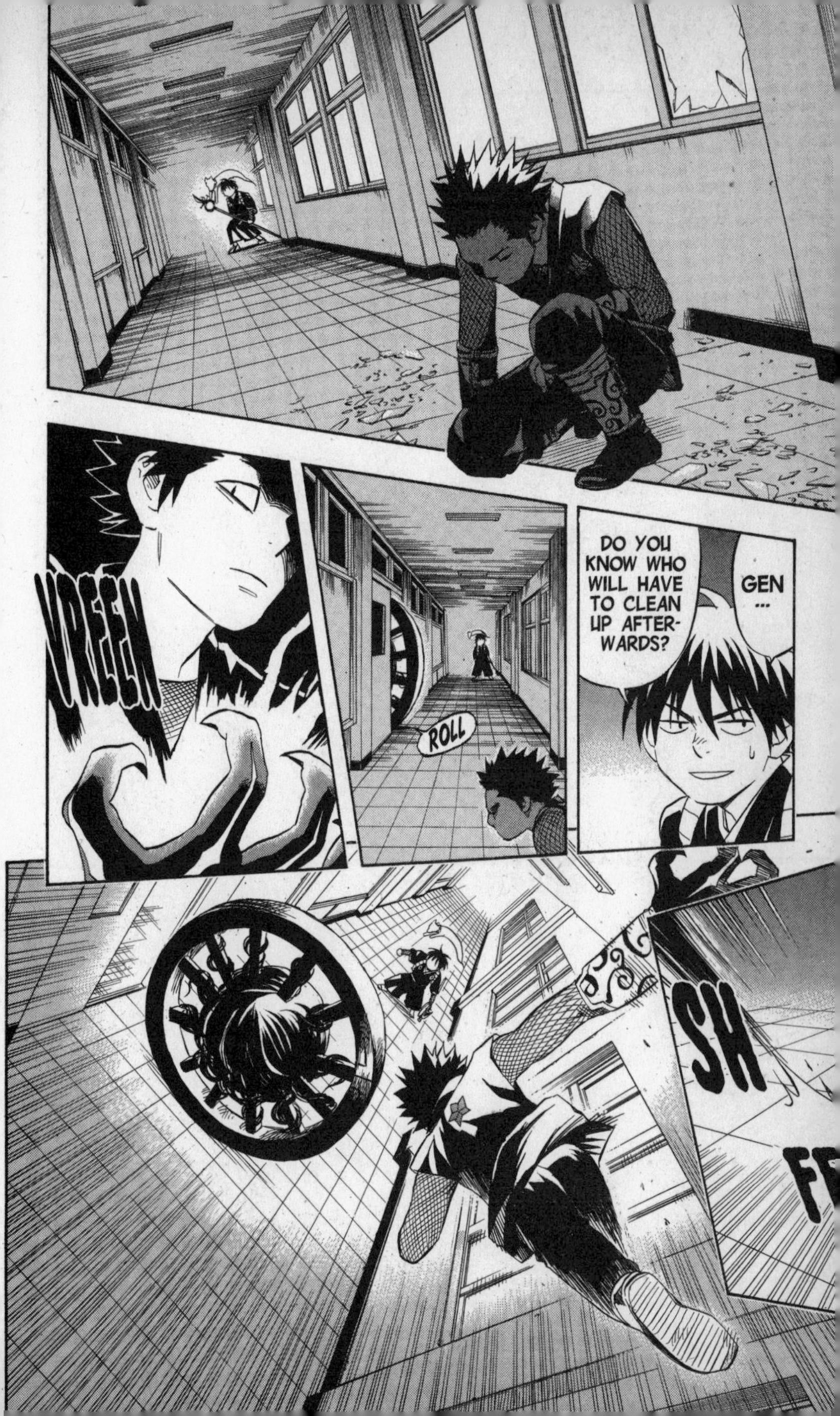
GEN ...
DO YOU KNOW WHO WILL HAVE TO CLEAN UP AFTER-WARDS?
ROLL
VREEN
SH
FF

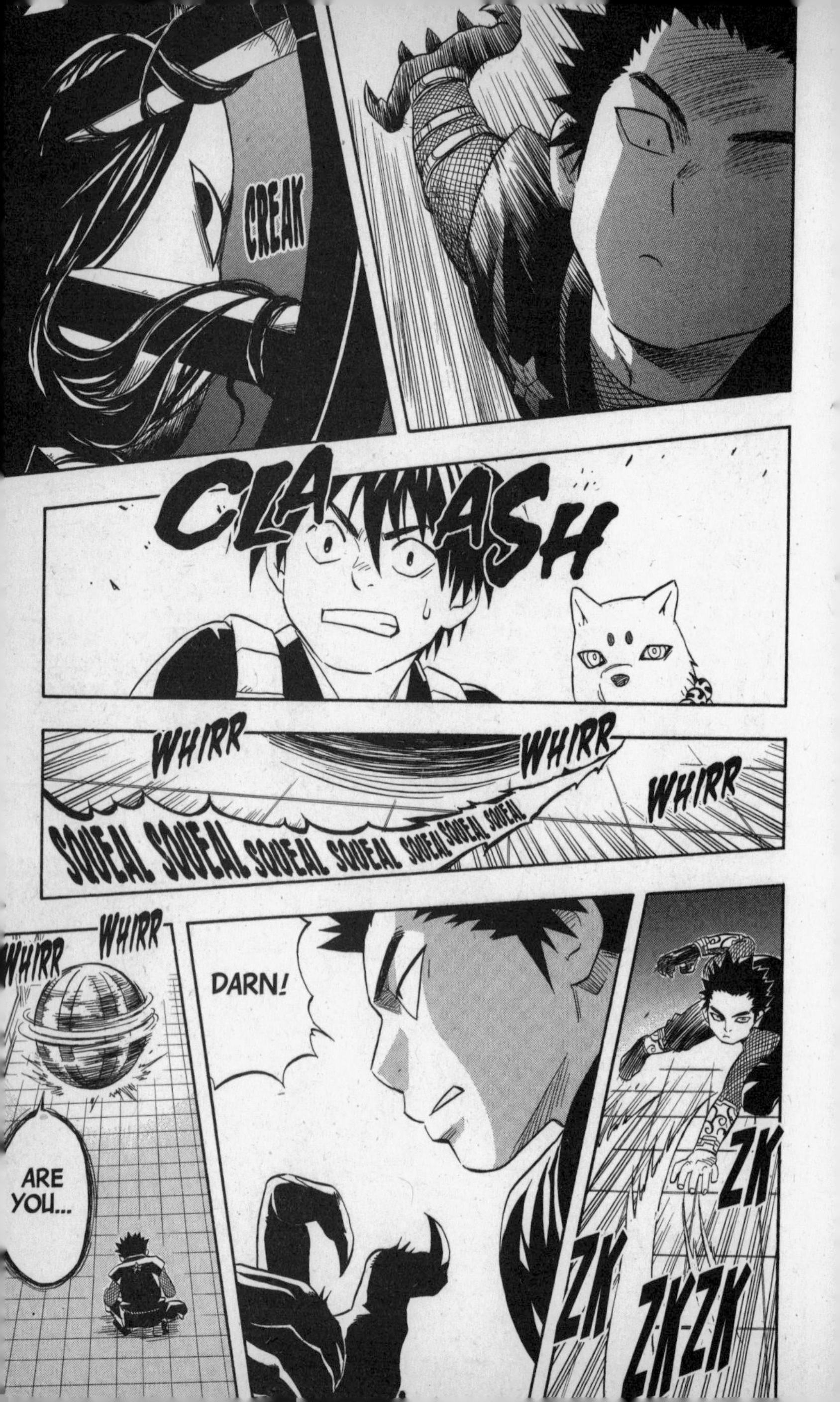

CREAK
CLAAASH
WHIRR
WHIRR
WHIRR
SQUEAL SQUEAL SQUEAL SQUEAL SQUEAL SQUEAL SQUEAL
ZK
ZK
ZK-ZK
DARN!
WHIRR
WHIRR
ARE YOU...

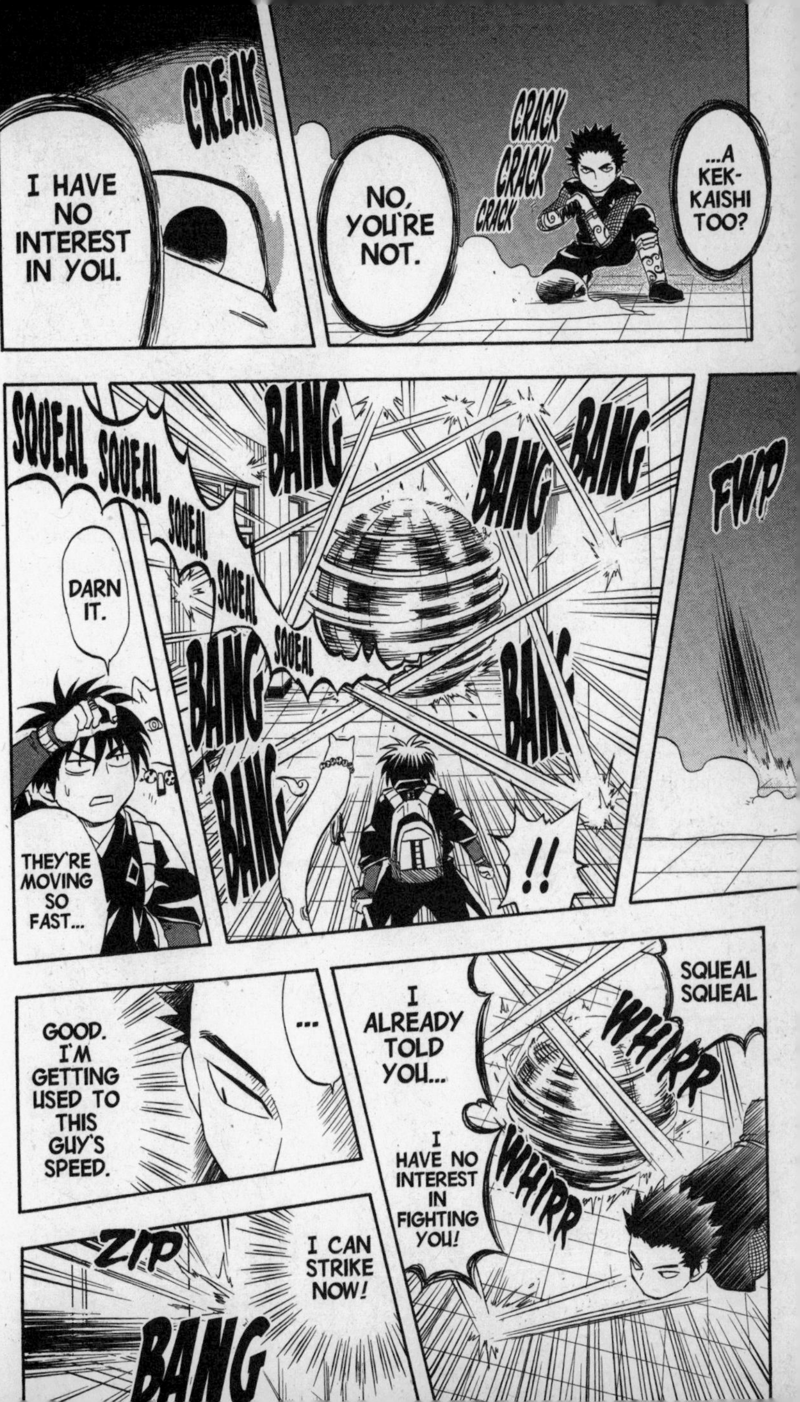
CRACK
CRACK
CRACK
...A KEK-KAISHI TOO?
NO, YOU'RE NOT.
CREAK
I HAVE NO INTEREST IN YOU.
FWP
BANG
BANG
BANG
!!
BANG
BANG
BANG
SQUEAL
SQUEAL
SQUEAL
SQUEAL
SQUEAL
DARN IT.
THEY'RE MOVING SO FAST...
SQUEAL SQUEAL
WHIRR
WHIRR
I ALREADY TOLD YOU...
I HAVE NO INTEREST IN FIGHTING YOU!
...
GOOD. I'M GETTING USED TO THIS GUY'S SPEED.
I CAN STRIKE NOW!
ZIP
BANG

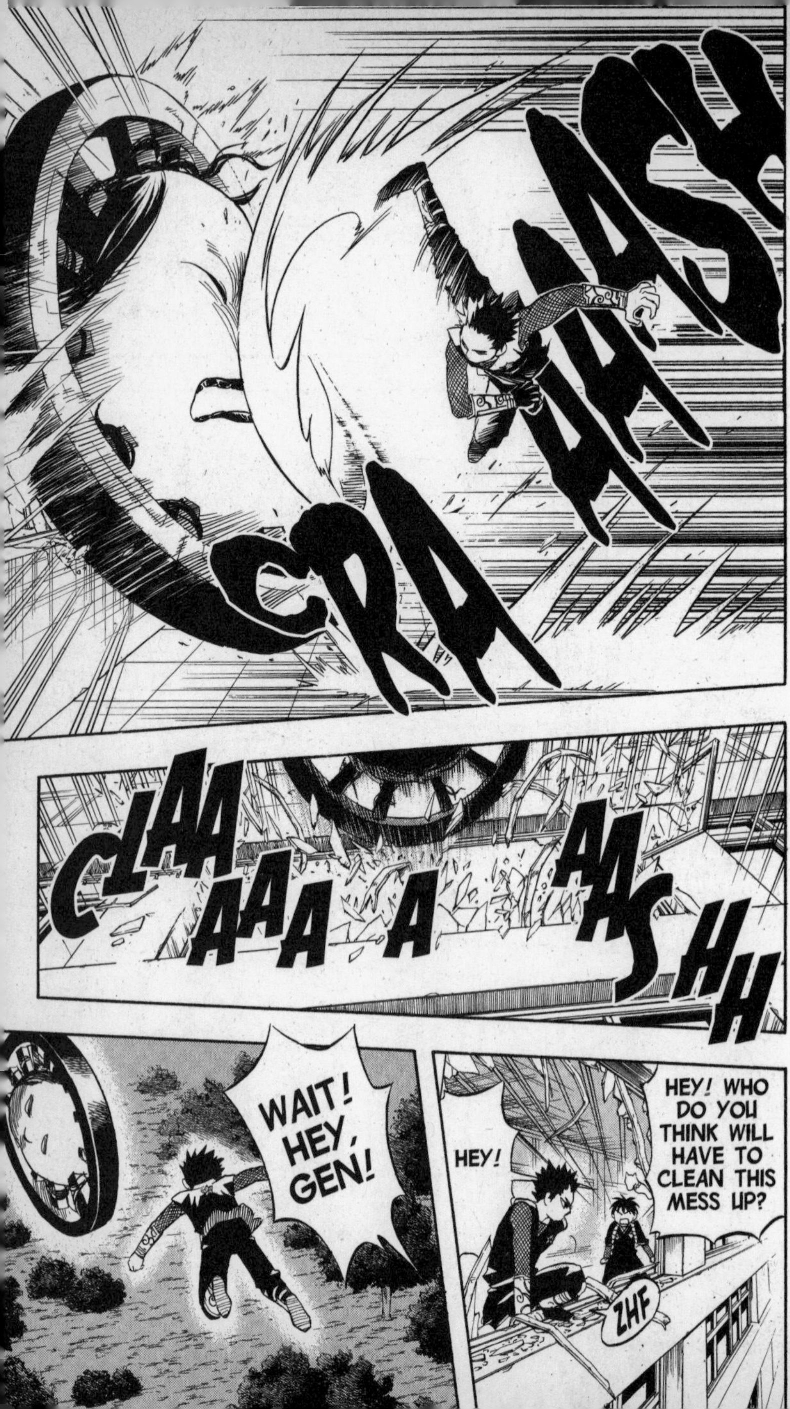
CRAAASH
CLAAAAAAAAASHH
HEY! WHO DO YOU THINK WILL HAVE TO CLEAN THIS MESS UP?
HEY!
ZHF
WAIT! HEY, GEN!

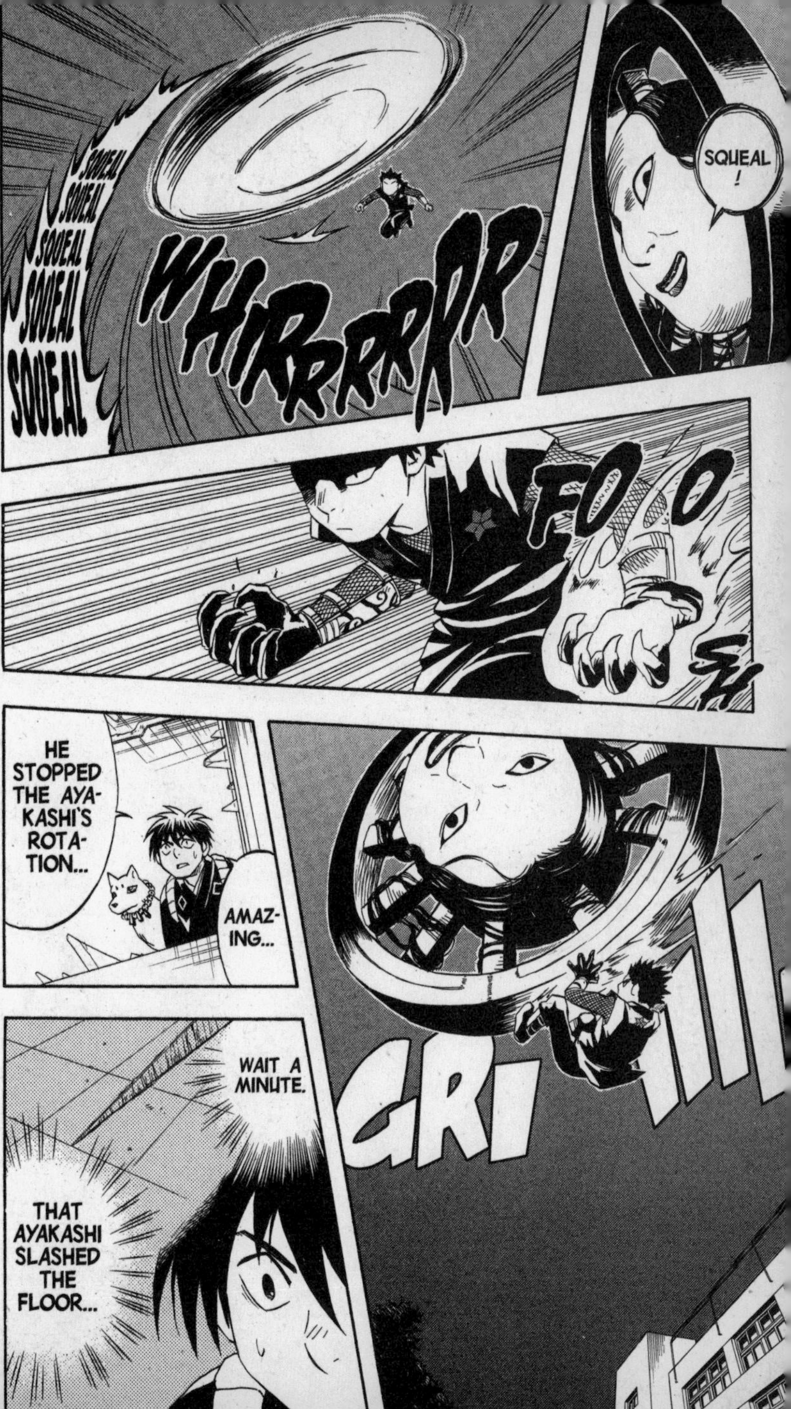
SQUEAL !
SQUEAL SQUEAL SQUEAL SQUEAL SQUEAL
WHIRRRRRR
FO O
SW
GRI
HE STOPPED THE AYA-KASHI'S ROTA-TION...
AMAZ-ING...
WAIT A MINUTE.
THAT AYAKASHI SLASHED THE FLOOR...

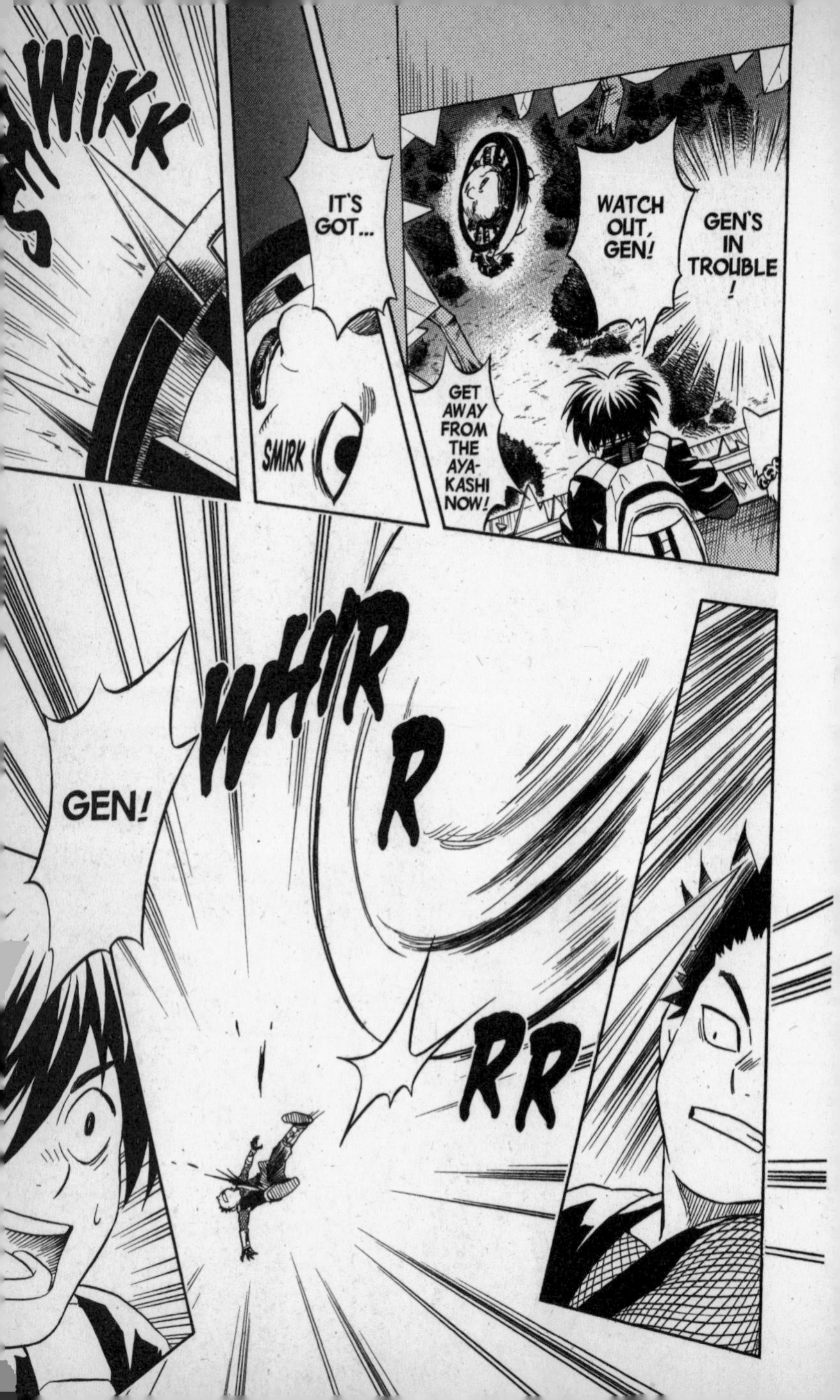

GEN'S IN TROUBLE!
WATCH OUT, GEN!
GET AWAY FROM THE AYAKASHI NOW!
IT'S GOT...
SMIRK
SWIKK
WHIRRRR
GEN!

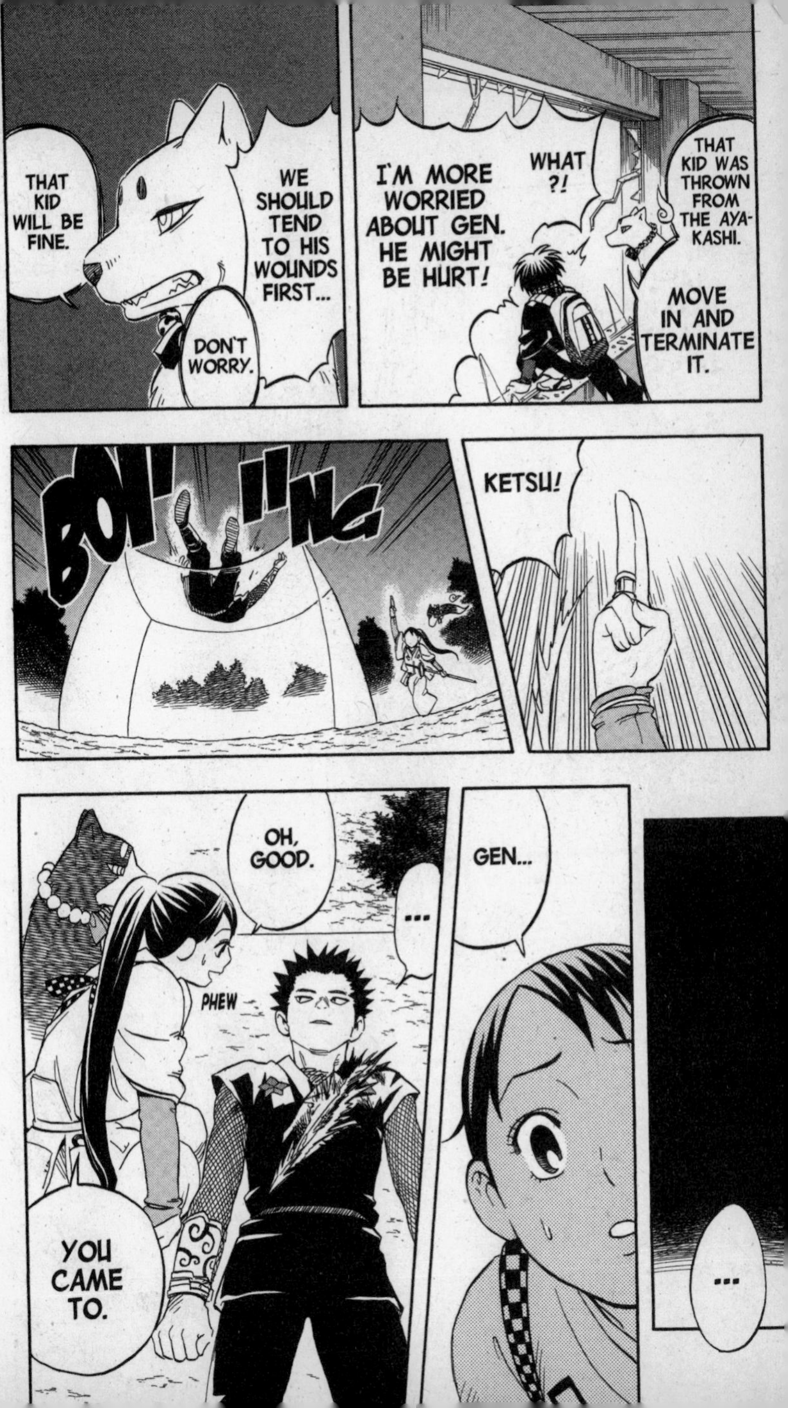
THAT KID WAS THROWN FROM THE AYA-KASHI.
MOVE IN AND TERMINATE IT.
WHAT ?!
I'M MORE WORRIED ABOUT GEN. HE MIGHT BE HURT!
WE SHOULD TEND TO HIS WOUNDS FIRST...
DON'T WORRY.
THAT KID WILL BE FINE.
KETSU!
BOI IING
...
GEN...
...
OH, GOOD.
PHEW
YOU CAME TO.

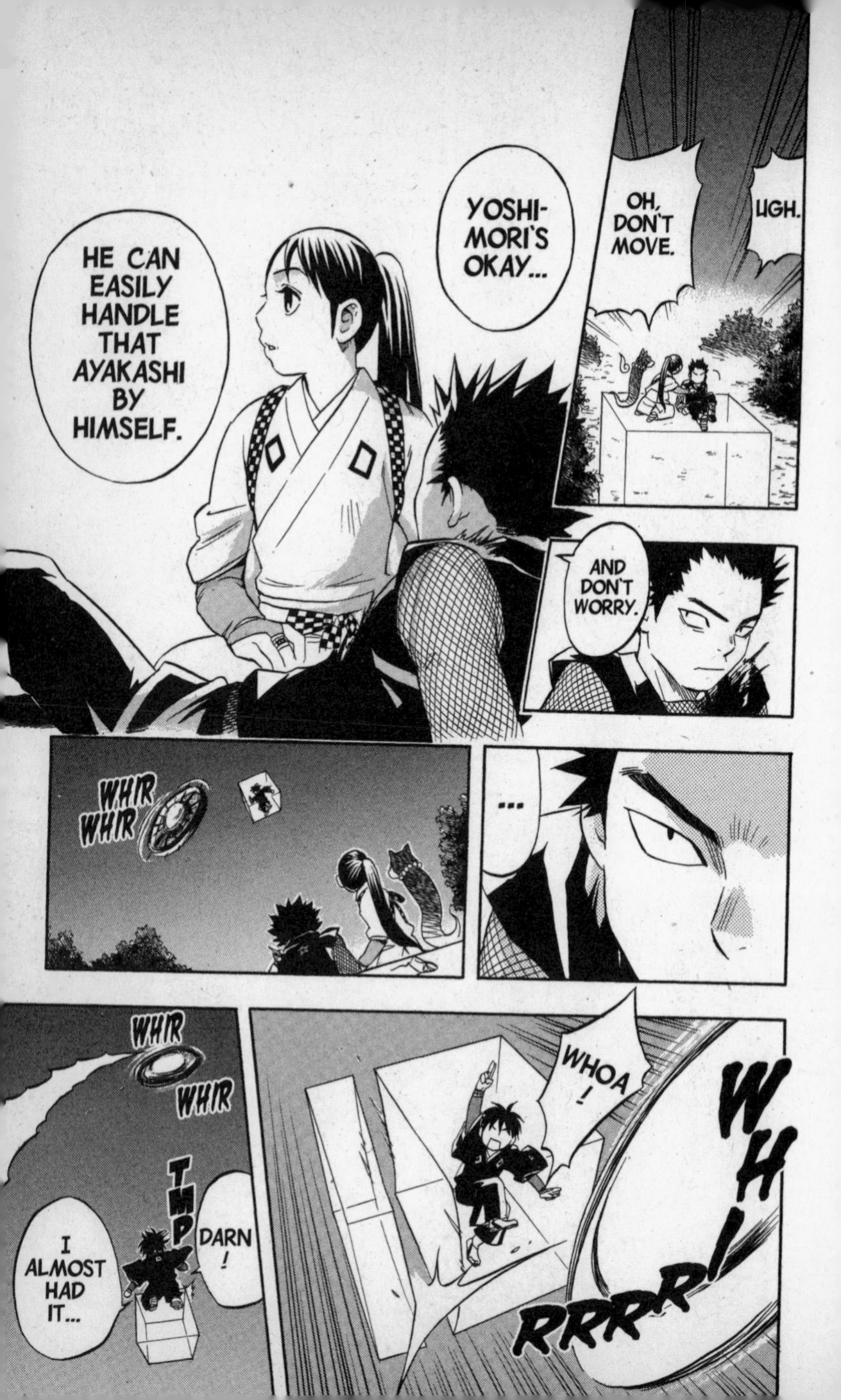
UGH.
OH, DON'T MOVE.
AND DON'T WORRY.
YOSHI-MORI'S OKAY...
HE CAN EASILY HANDLE THAT AYAKASHI BY HIMSELF.
...
WHIR WHIR
WHIRRRR!
WHOA!
WHIR
WHIR
TMP
DARN!
I ALMOST HAD IT...

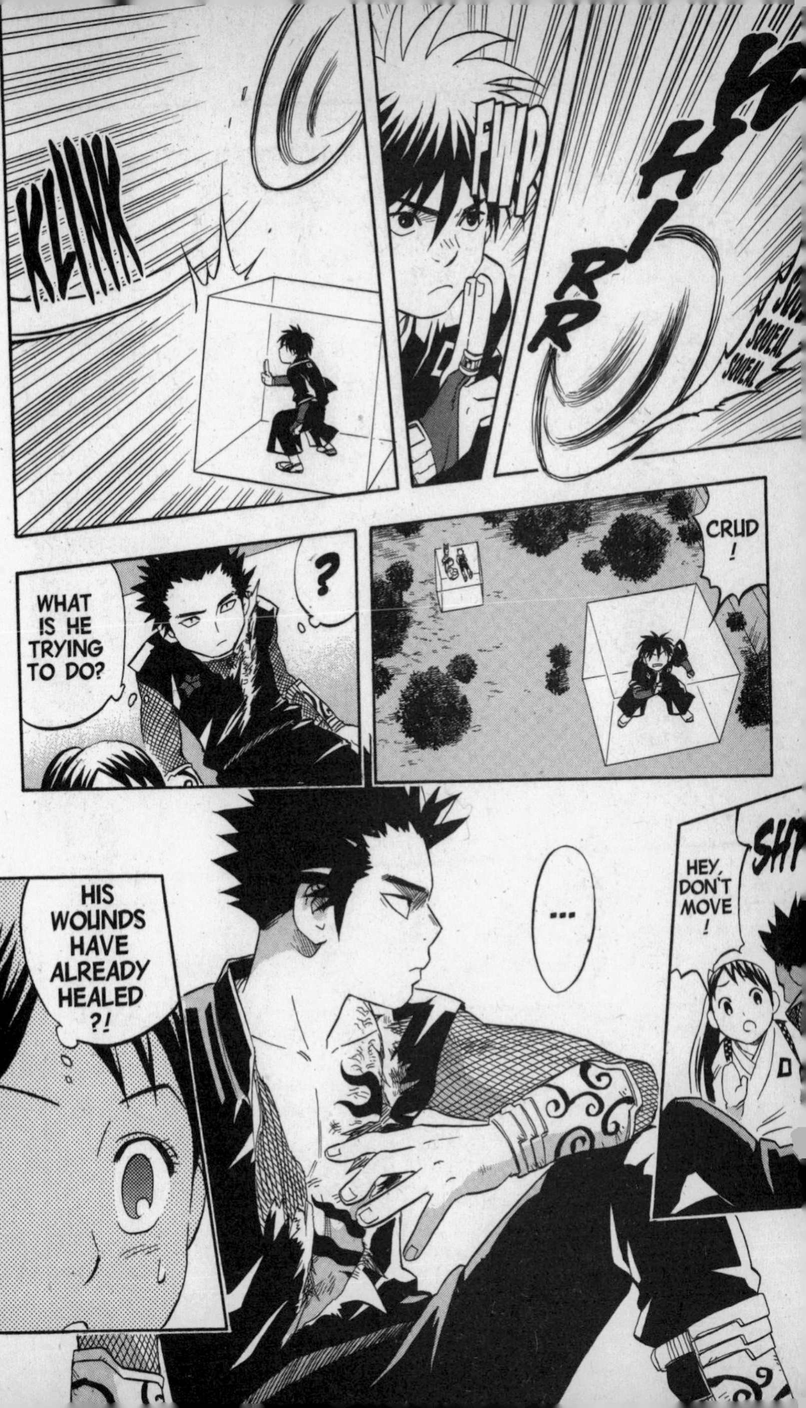
WHIRR
SQUEAL SQUEAL SQUEAL
FWIP
KLINK
CRUD!
?
WHAT IS HE TRYING TO DO?
SHP
HEY, DON'T MOVE!
...
HIS WOUNDS HAVE ALREADY HEALED?!

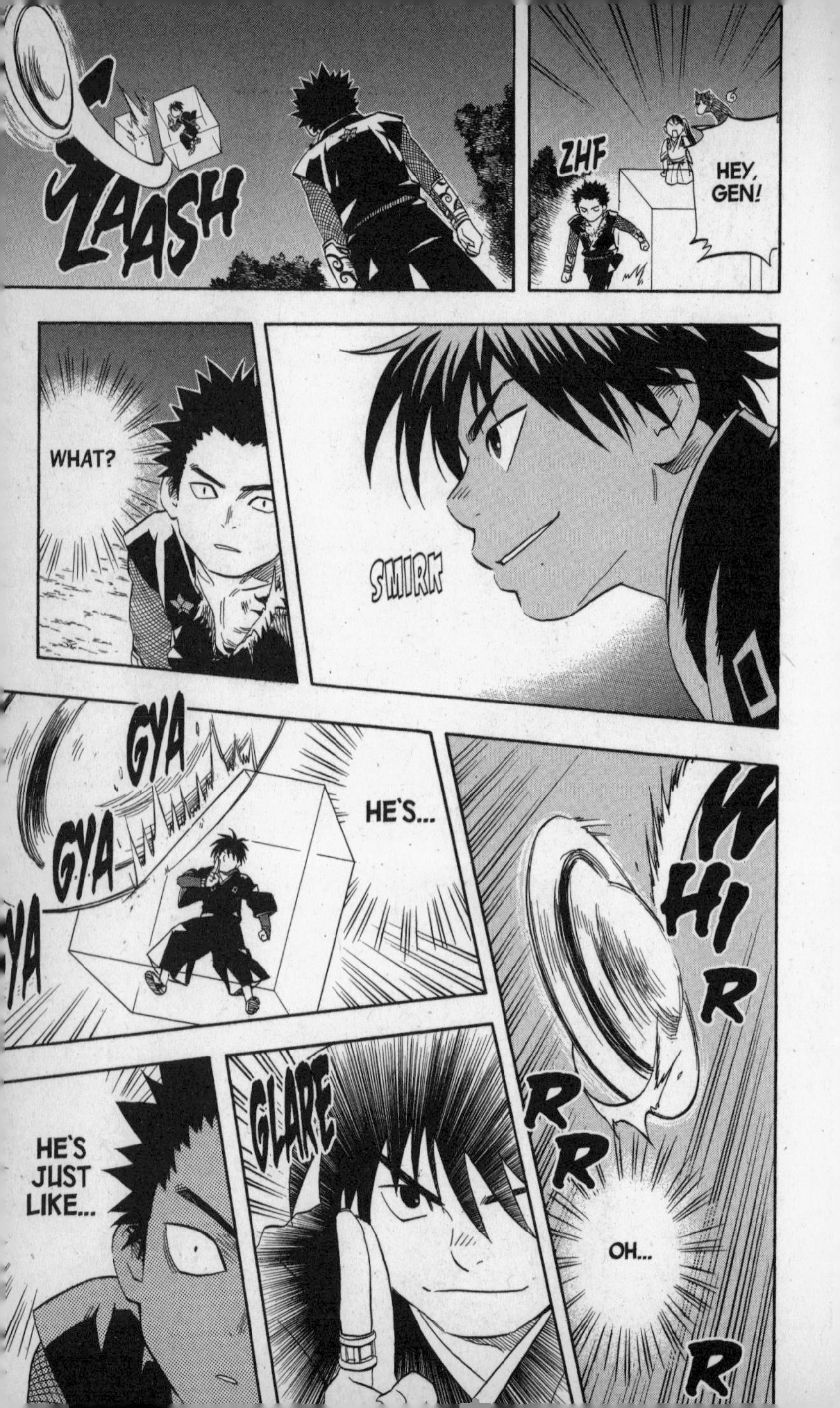
HEY, GEN!
ZHF
ZAASH
SMIRK
WHAT?
WHIRRRR
OH...
GYA GYA YA
HE'S...
GLARE
HE'S JUST LIKE...

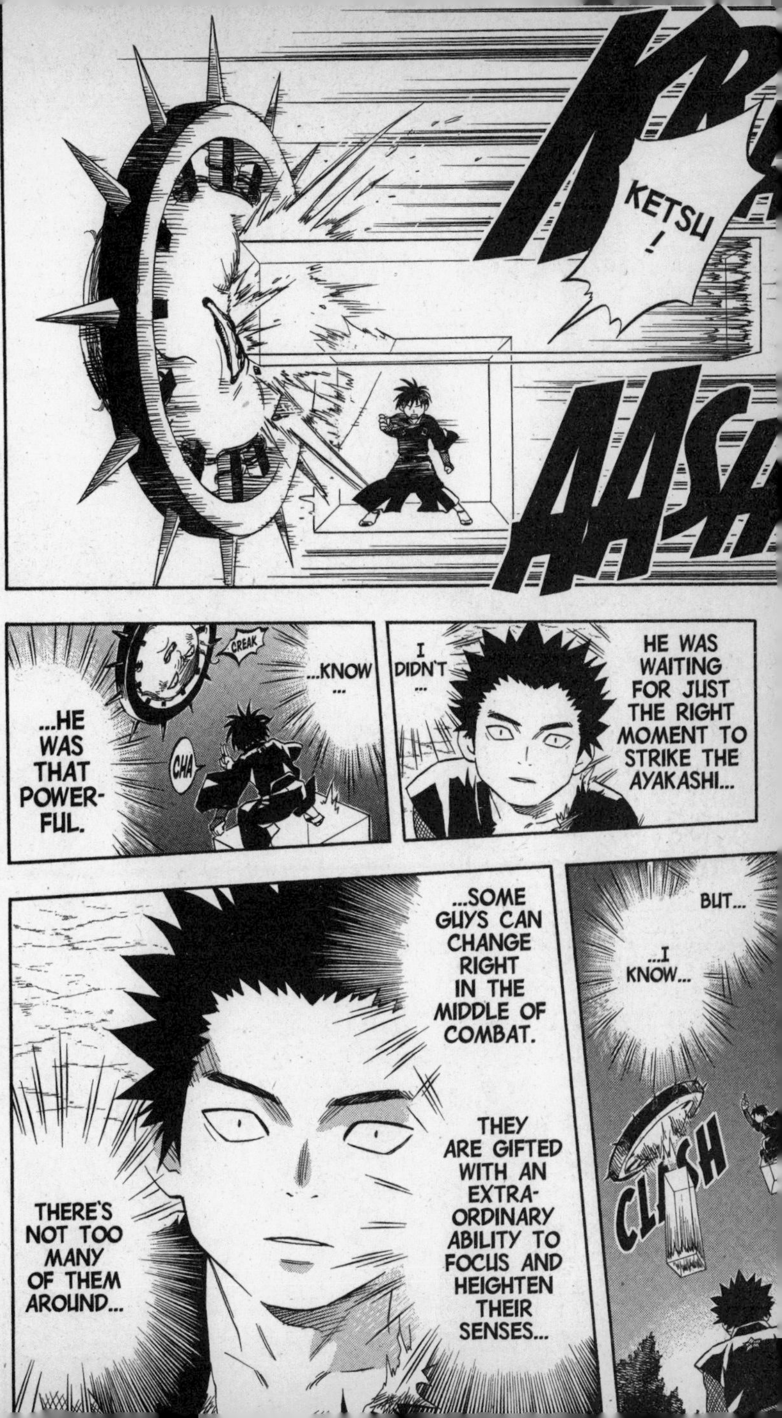
KETSU!
HE WAS WAITING FOR JUST THE RIGHT MOMENT TO STRIKE THE AYAKASHI...
I DIDN'T ...
...KNOW ...
CREAK
...HE WAS THAT POWERFUL.
CHA
BUT...
...I KNOW...
CLASH
...SOME GUYS CAN CHANGE RIGHT IN THE MIDDLE OF COMBAT.
THEY ARE GIFTED WITH AN EXTRAORDINARY ABILITY TO FOCUS AND HEIGHTEN THEIR SENSES...
THERE'S NOT TOO MANY OF THEM AROUND...

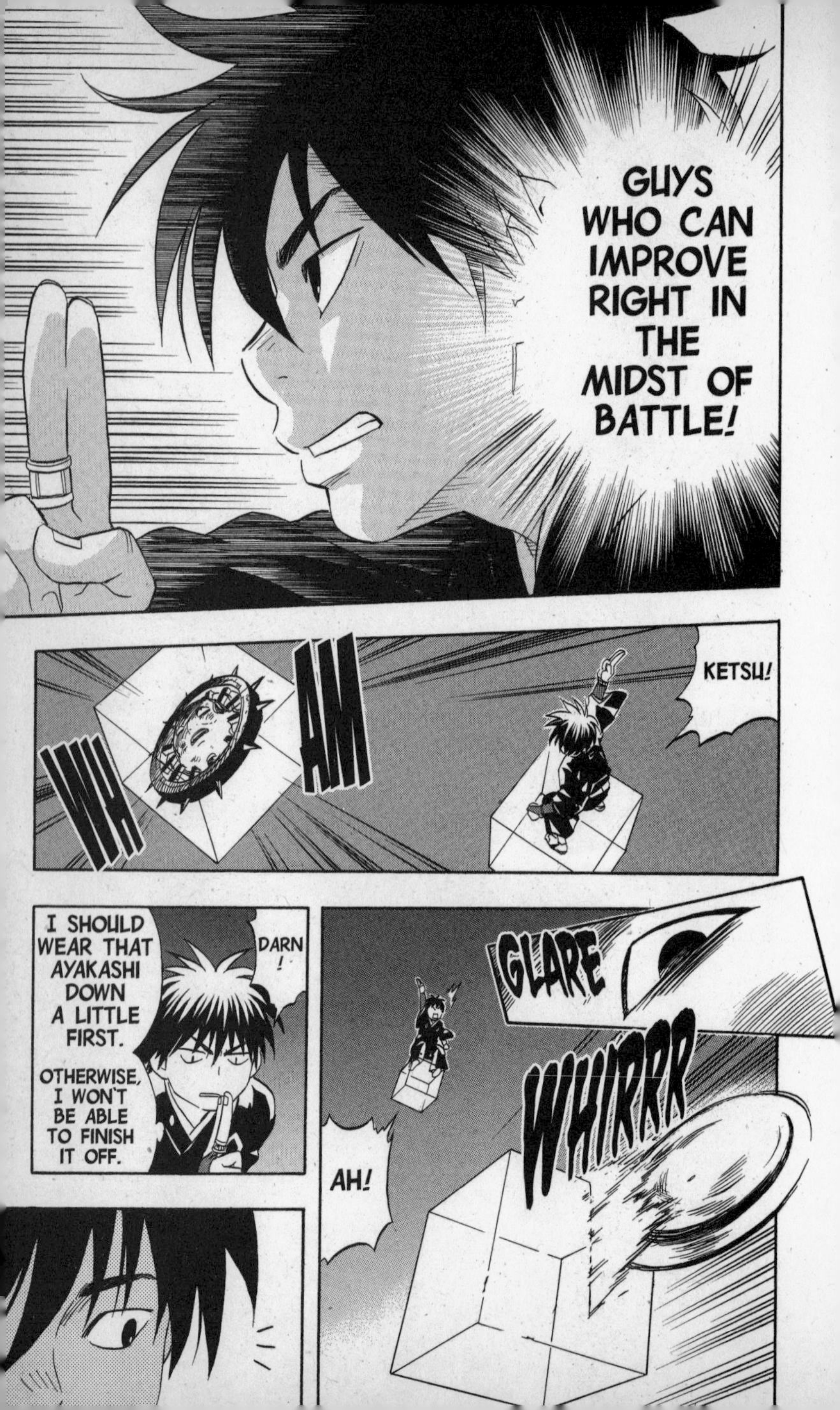
GUYS WHO CAN IMPROVE RIGHT IN THE MIDST OF BATTLE!
KETSU!
WHAM
GLARE
WHIRRR
AH!
DARN!
I SHOULD WEAR THAT AYAKASHI DOWN A LITTLE FIRST.
OTHERWISE, I WON'T BE ABLE TO FINISH IT OFF.

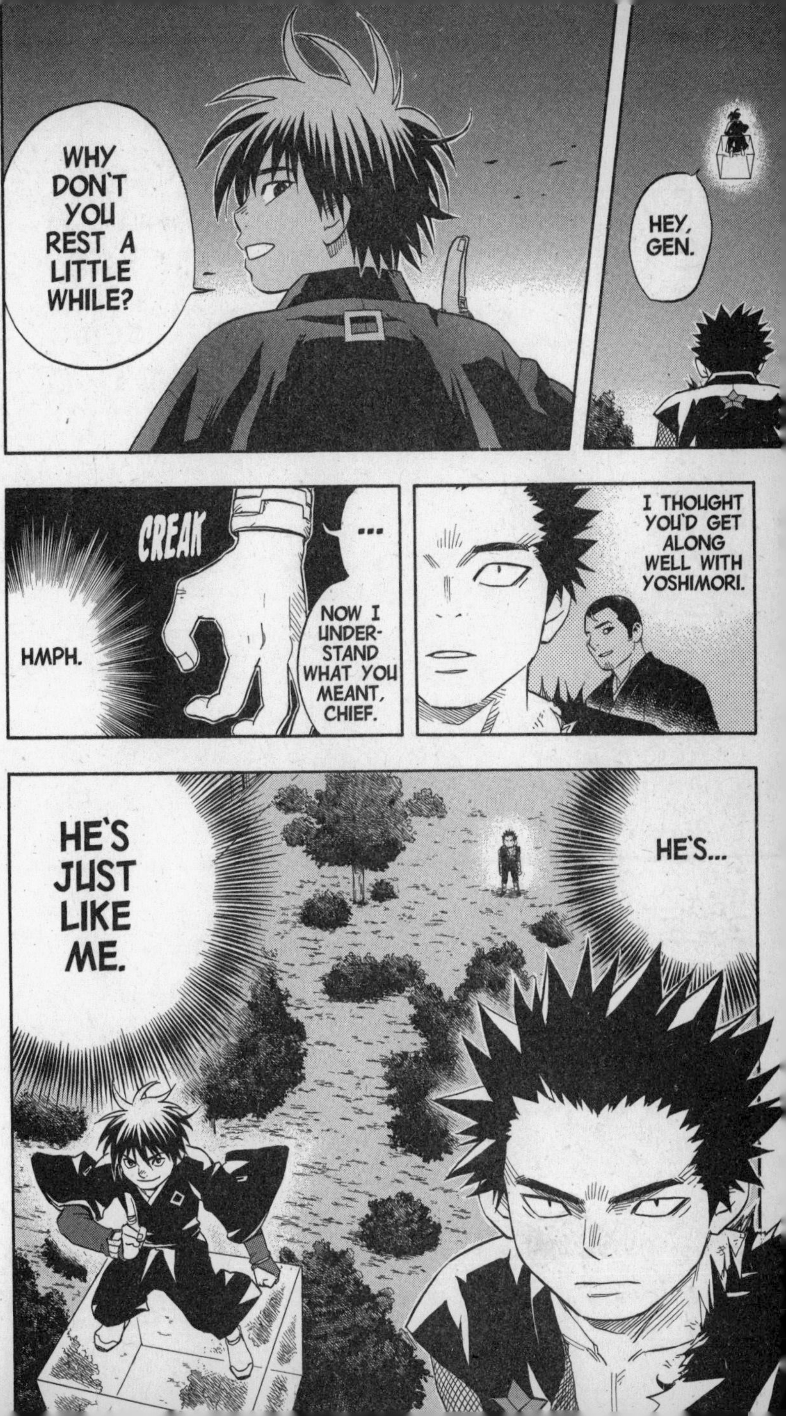
HEY, GEN.
WHY DON'T YOU REST A LITTLE WHILE?
I THOUGHT YOU'D GET ALONG WELL WITH YOSHIMORI.
...
NOW I UNDER-STAND WHAT YOU MEANT, CHIEF.
CREAK
HMPH.
HE'S...
HE'S JUST LIKE ME.

Chapter 54: Legitimate Heir

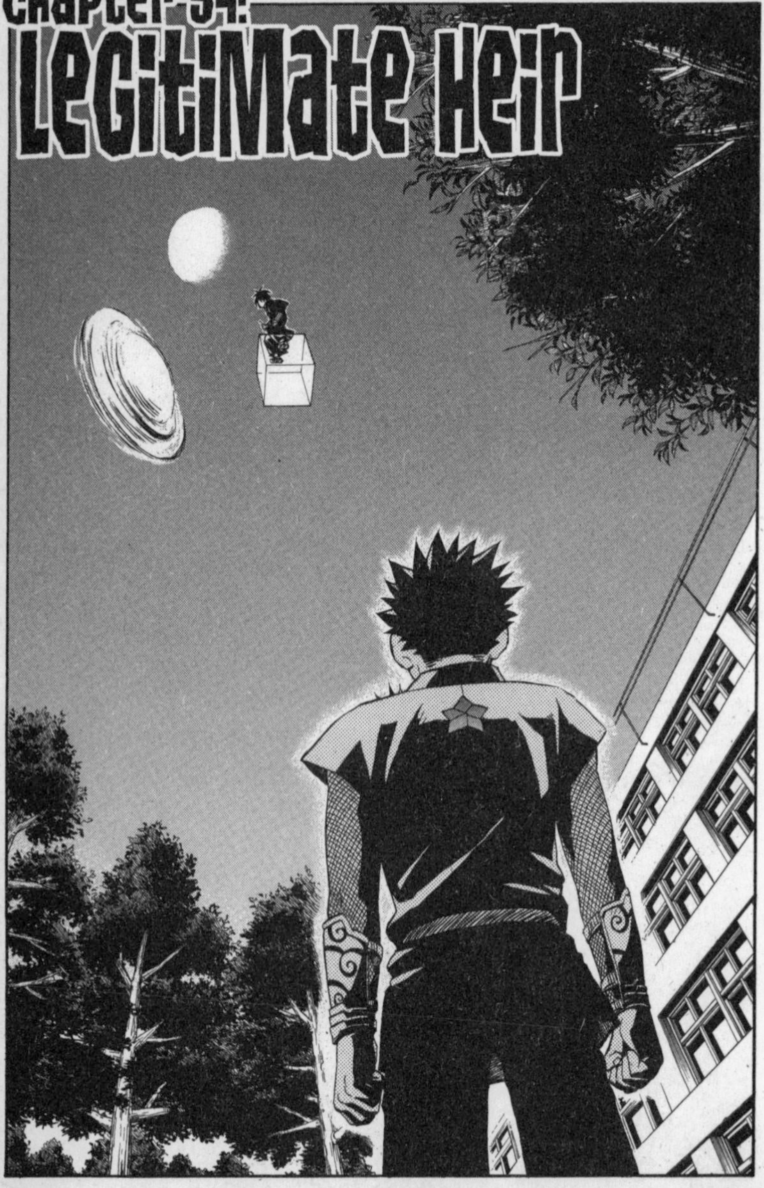

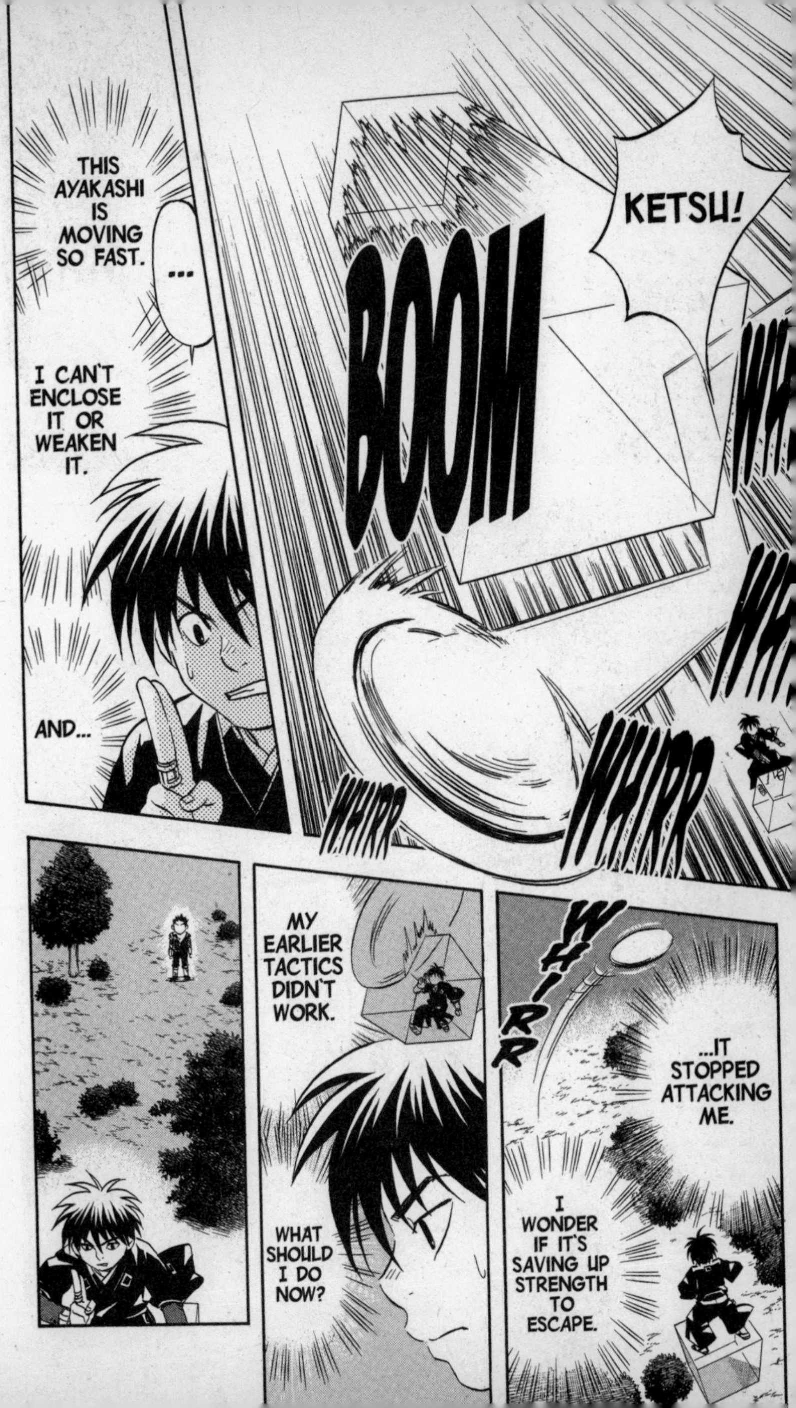
KETSU!
BOOM
WHIRR
WHIRR
THIS AYAKASHI IS MOVING SO FAST.
...
I CAN'T ENCLOSE IT OR WEAKEN IT.
AND...
WHIRR
...IT STOPPED ATTACKING ME.
I WONDER IF IT'S SAVING UP STRENGTH TO ESCAPE.
MY EARLIER TACTICS DIDN'T WORK.
WHAT SHOULD I DO NOW?

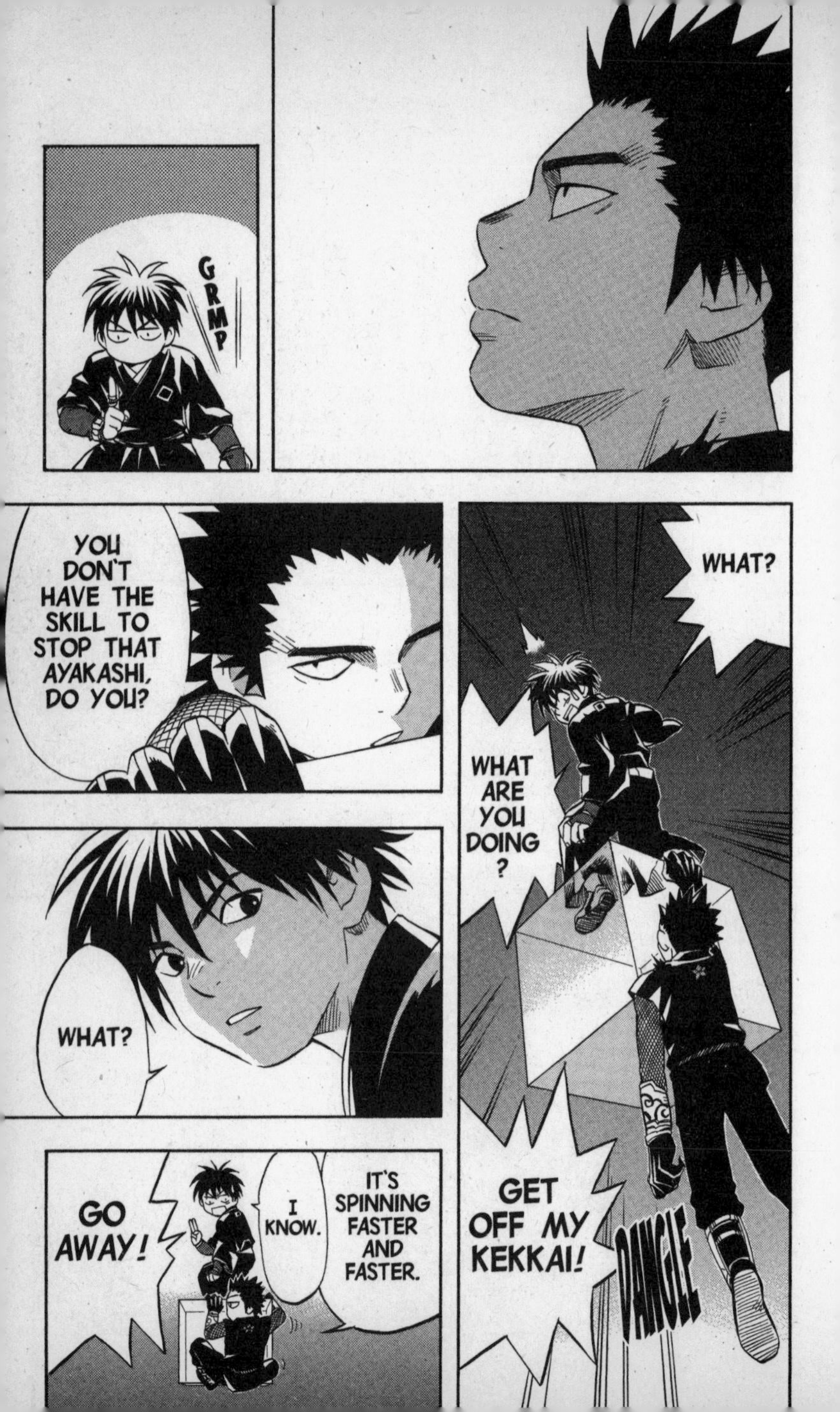
GRMP
WHAT?
WHAT ARE YOU DOING?
GET OFF MY KEKKAI!
DANGLE
YOU DON'T HAVE THE SKILL TO STOP THAT AYAKASHI, DO YOU?
WHAT?
IT'S SPINNING FASTER AND FASTER.
I KNOW.
GO AWAY!

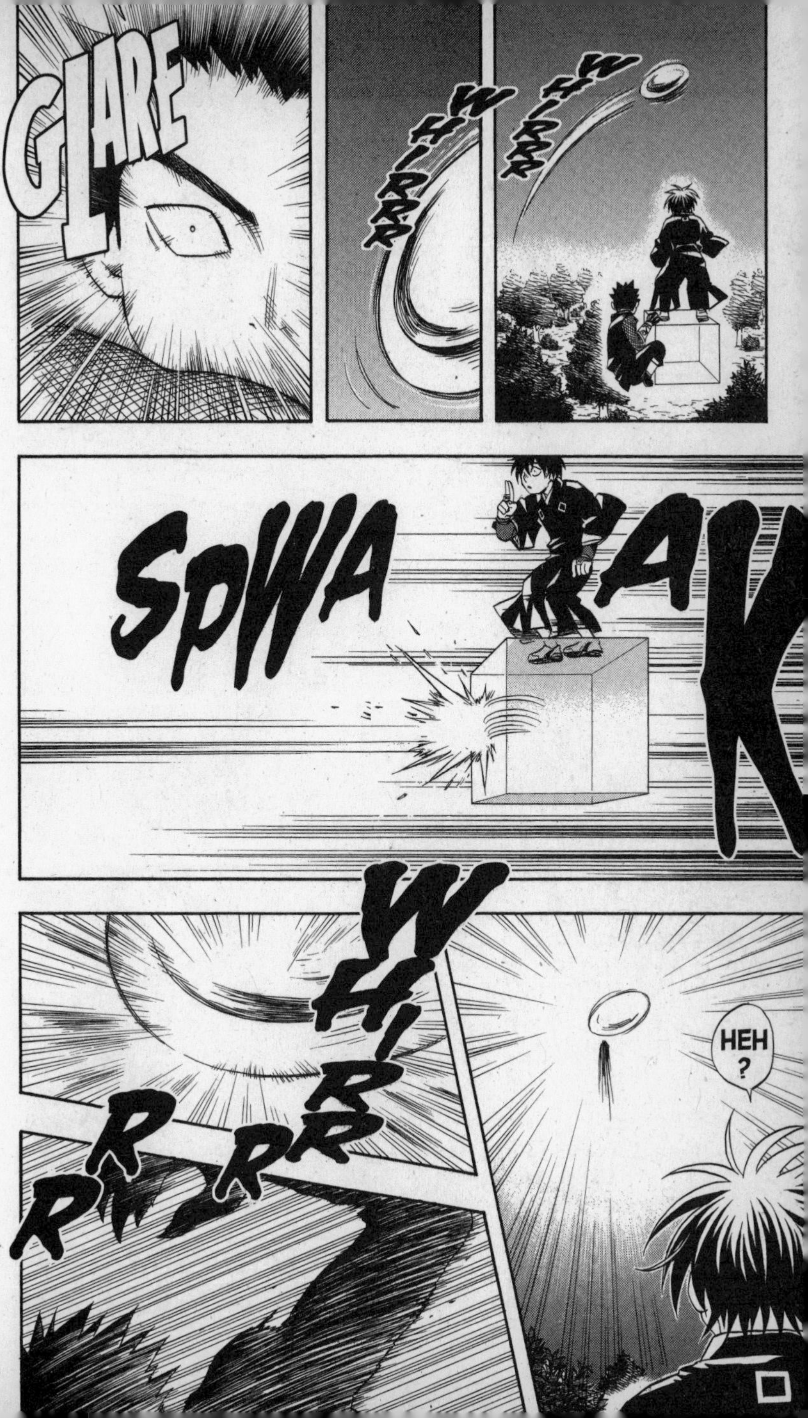
WHIRRR
WHIRRR
GLARE
SPWAAK
HEH?
WHIRRRRRR

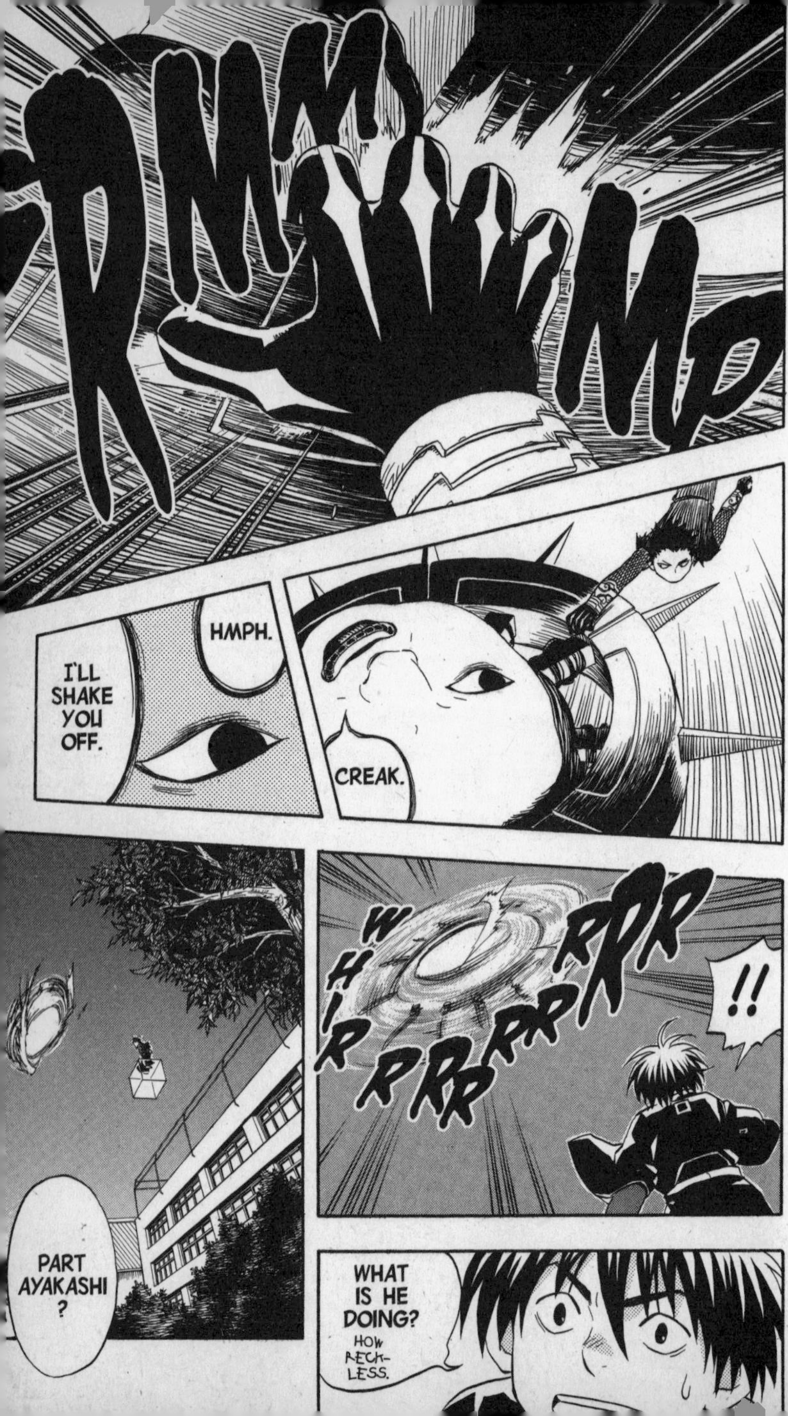
CREAK.
HMPH.
I'LL SHAKE YOU OFF.
WHIRRRRRRRRRRRR
!!
WHAT IS HE DOING?
HOW RECK-LESS.
PART AYAKASHI?

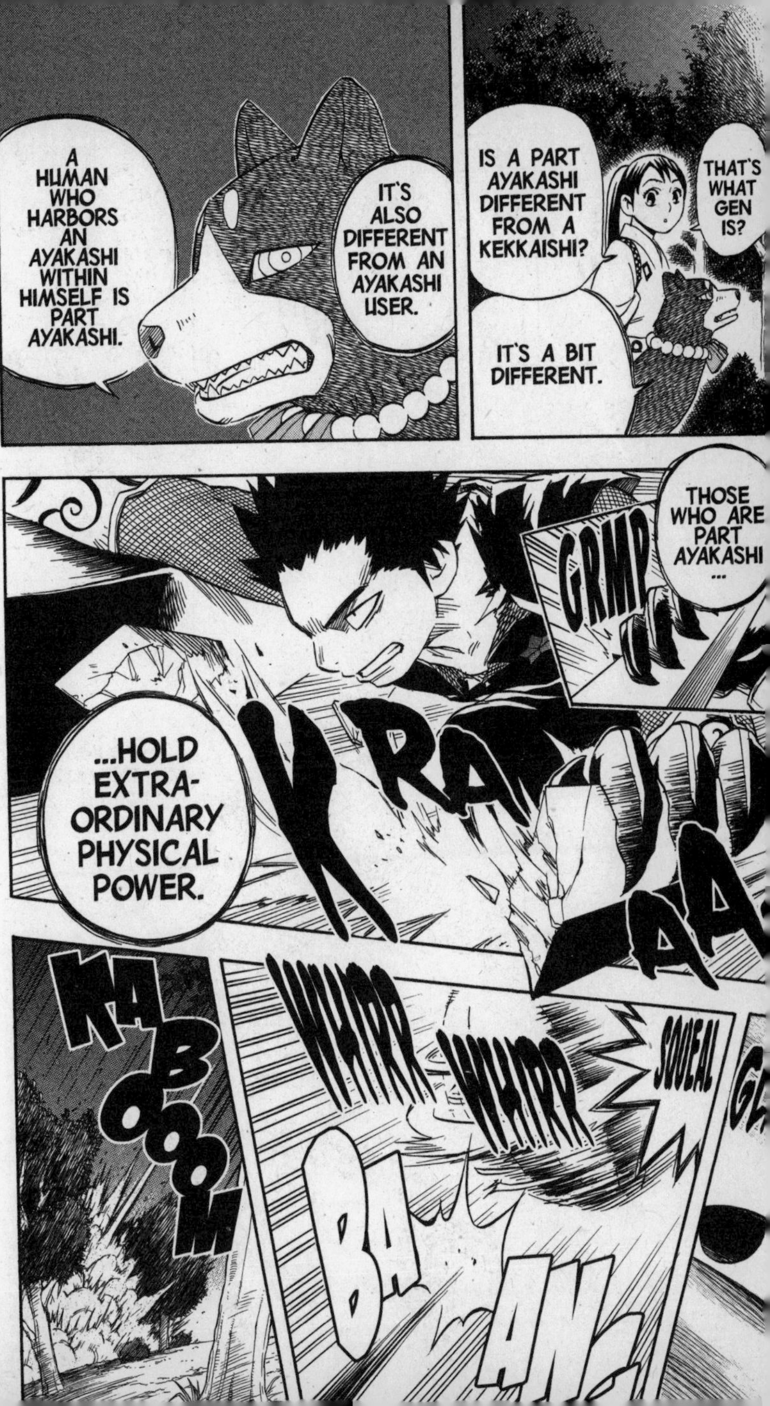
THAT'S WHAT GEN IS?
IS A PART AYAKASHI DIFFERENT FROM A KEKKAISHI?
IT'S A BIT DIFFERENT.
IT'S ALSO DIFFERENT FROM AN AYAKASHI USER.
A HUMAN WHO HARBORS AN AYAKASHI WITHIN HIMSELF IS PART AYAKASHI.
THOSE WHO ARE PART AYAKASHI ...
GRMP
...HOLD EXTRA-ORDINARY PHYSICAL POWER.
SQUEAL
WHIRR
WHIRR
KABOOOM

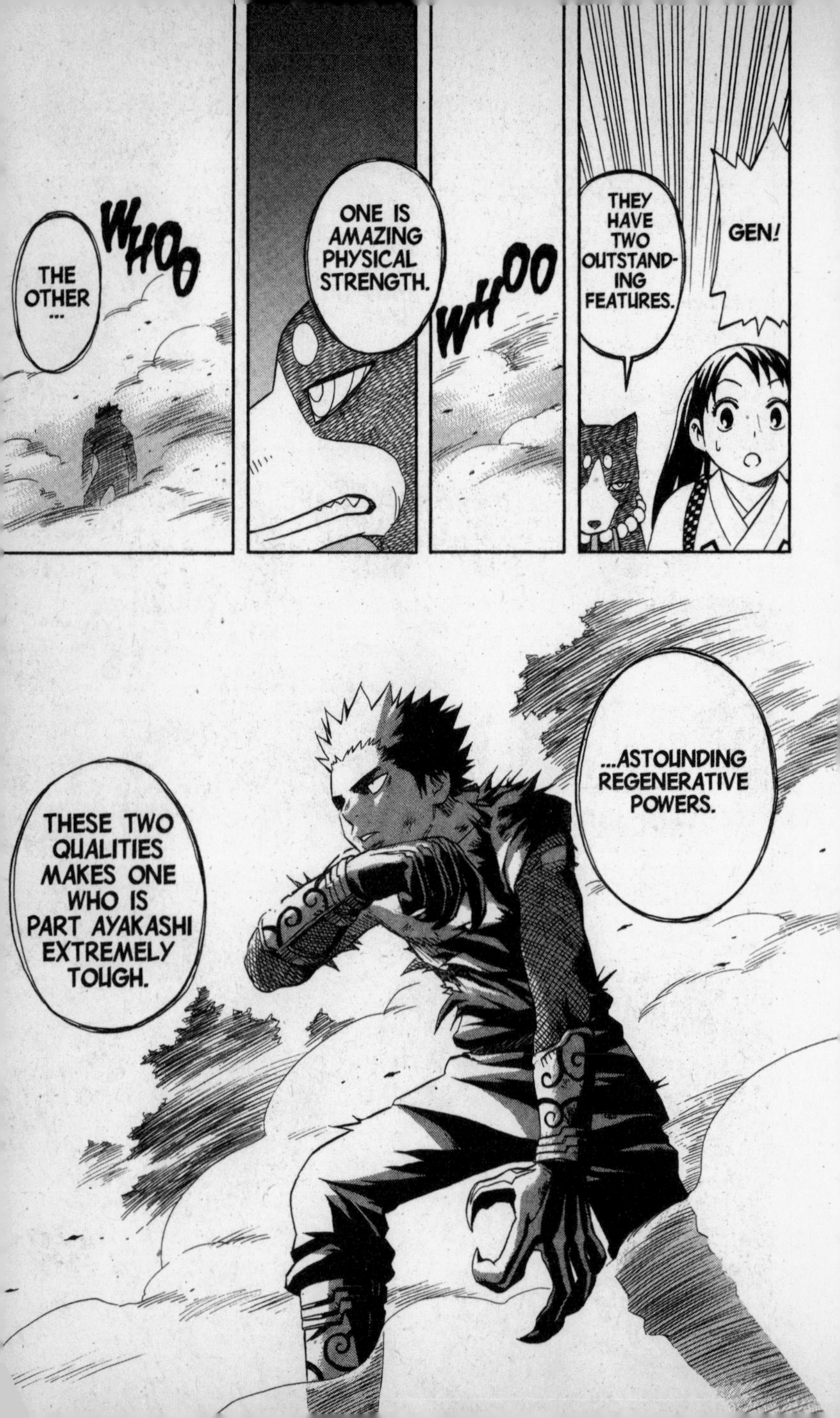
GEN!
THEY HAVE TWO OUTSTAND-ING FEATURES.
WHOO
ONE IS AMAZING PHYSICAL STRENGTH.
WHOO
THE OTHER ...
...ASTOUNDING REGENERATIVE POWERS.
THESE TWO QUALITIES MAKES ONE WHO IS PART AYAKASHI EXTREMELY TOUGH.

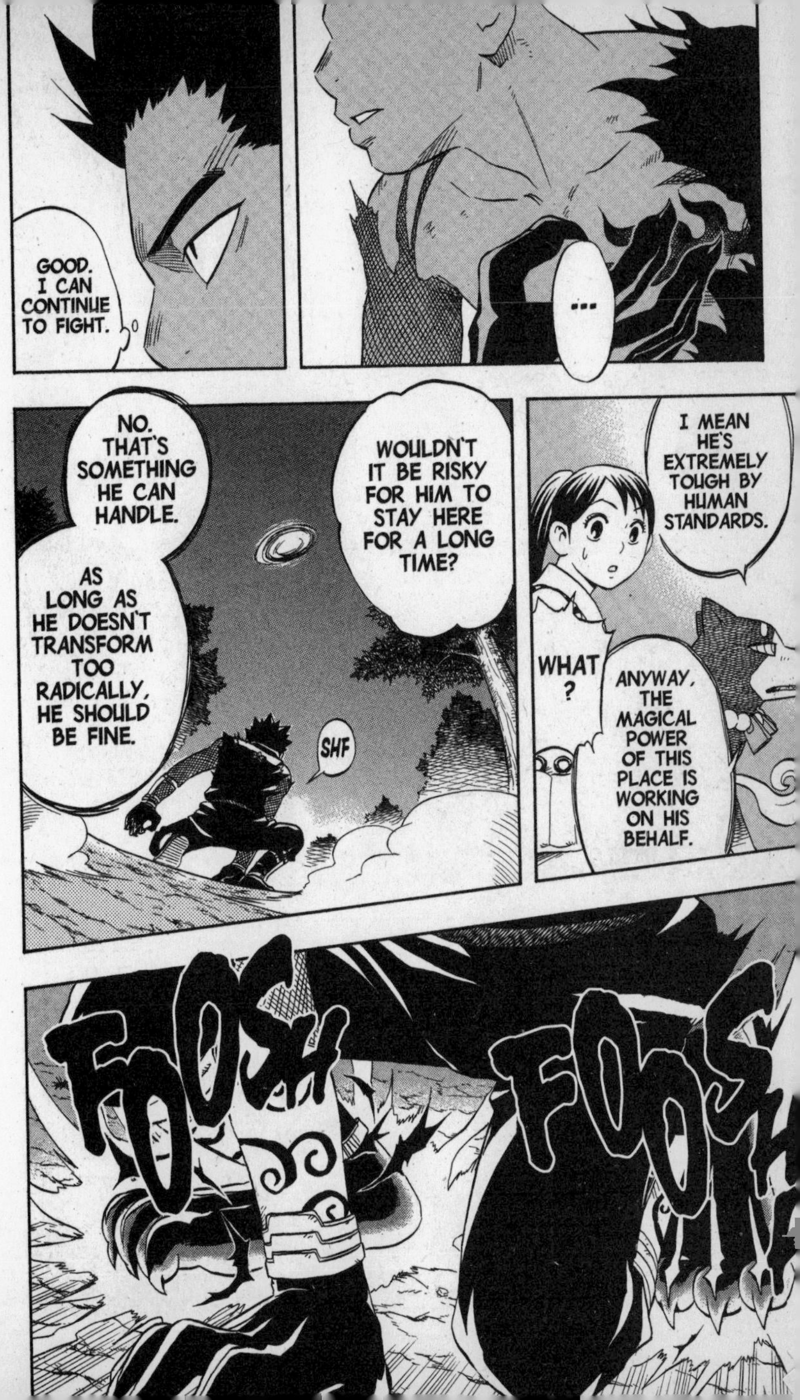
...
GOOD. I CAN CONTINUE TO FIGHT.
I MEAN HE'S EXTREMELY TOUGH BY HUMAN STANDARDS.
WHAT?
ANYWAY, THE MAGICAL POWER OF THIS PLACE IS WORKING ON HIS BEHALF.
WOULDN'T IT BE RISKY FOR HIM TO STAY HERE FOR A LONG TIME?
NO. THAT'S SOMETHING HE CAN HANDLE.
AS LONG AS HE DOESN'T TRANSFORM TOO RADICALLY, HE SHOULD BE FINE.
SHF
FOOSH
FOOSH

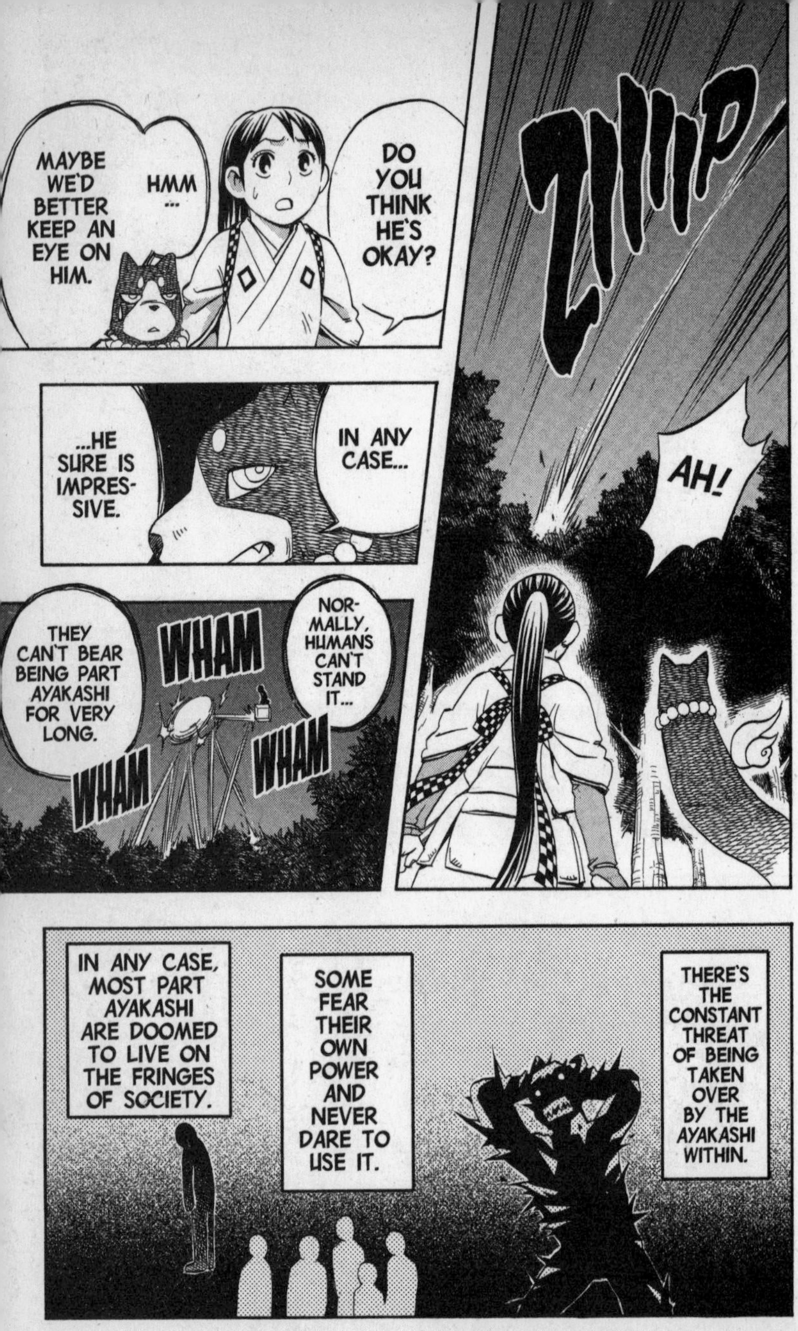
ZIIIIP
AH!
DO YOU THINK HE'S OKAY?
HMM...
MAYBE WE'D BETTER KEEP AN EYE ON HIM.
IN ANY CASE...
...HE SURE IS IMPRESSIVE.
NORMALLY, HUMANS CAN'T STAND IT...
WHAM
WHAM
WHAM
THEY CAN'T BEAR BEING PART AYAKASHI FOR VERY LONG.
THERE'S THE CONSTANT THREAT OF BEING TAKEN OVER BY THE AYAKASHI WITHIN.
SOME FEAR THEIR OWN POWER AND NEVER DARE TO USE IT.
IN ANY CASE, MOST PART AYAKASHI ARE DOOMED TO LIVE ON THE FRINGES OF SOCIETY.

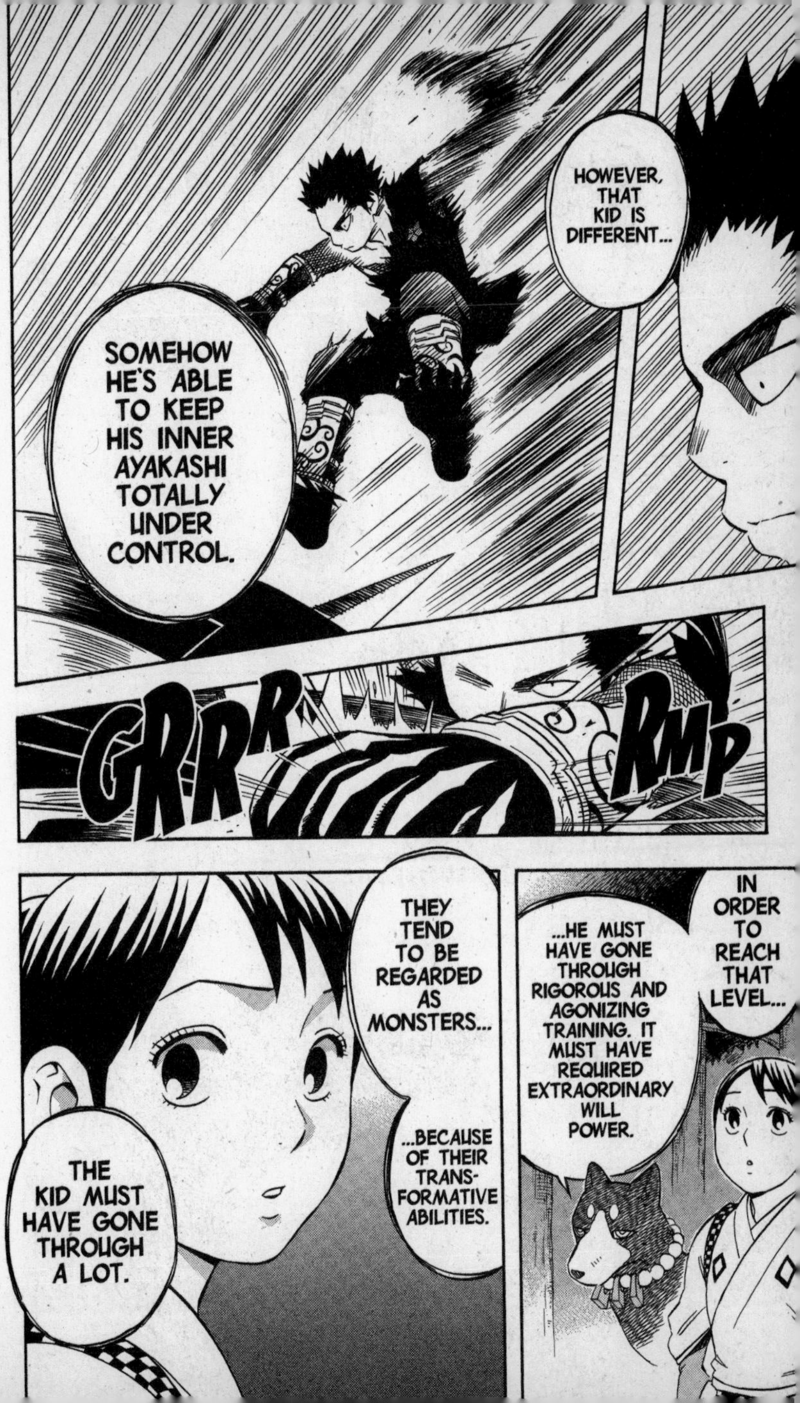
HOWEVER, THAT KID IS DIFFERENT...
SOMEHOW HE'S ABLE TO KEEP HIS INNER AYAKASHI TOTALLY UNDER CONTROL.
GRRR... RMP
IN ORDER TO REACH THAT LEVEL...
...HE MUST HAVE GONE THROUGH RIGOROUS AND AGONIZING TRAINING. IT MUST HAVE REQUIRED EXTRAORDINARY WILL POWER.
THEY TEND TO BE REGARDED AS MONSTERS...
...BECAUSE OF THEIR TRANS-FORMATIVE ABILITIES.
THE KID MUST HAVE GONE THROUGH A LOT.

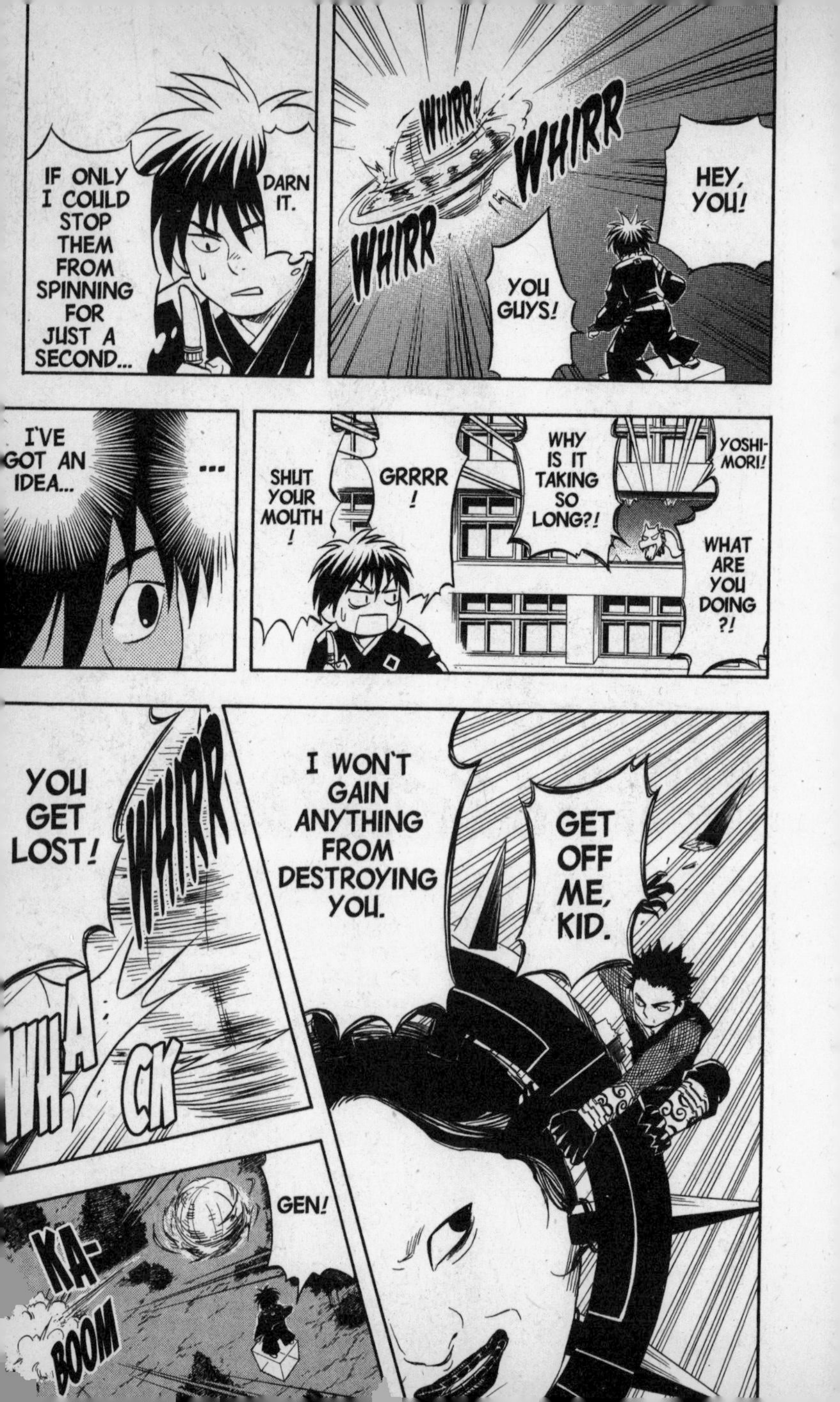
HEY, YOU!
WHIRR
WHIRR
WHIRR
YOU GUYS!
DARN IT.
IF ONLY I COULD STOP THEM FROM SPINNING FOR JUST A SECOND...
YOSHI-MORI!
WHAT ARE YOU DOING?!
WHY IS IT TAKING SO LONG?!
GRRRR!
SHUT YOUR MOUTH!
...
I'VE GOT AN IDEA...
GET OFF ME, KID.
I WON'T GAIN ANYTHING FROM DESTROYING YOU.
YOU GET LOST!
WHIRR
WHACK
GEN!
KA-BOOM

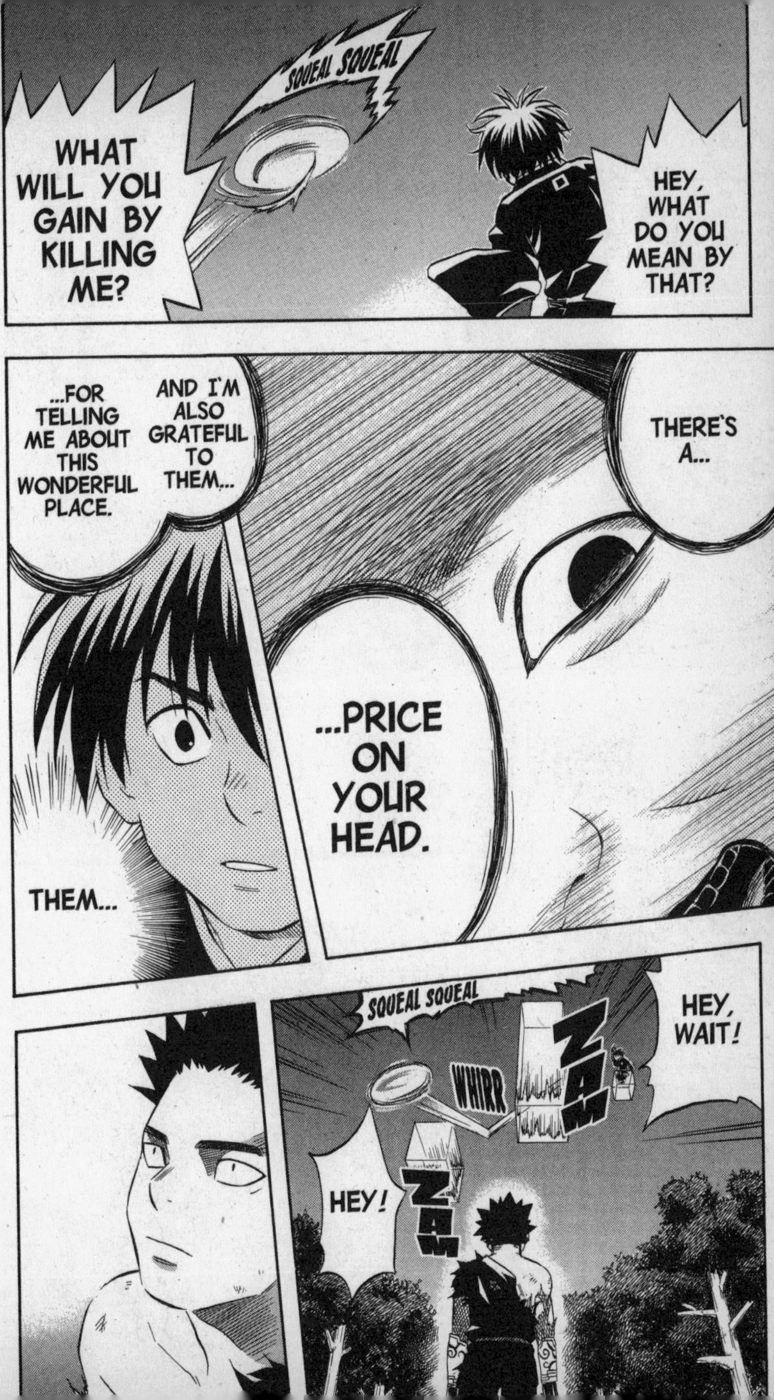
SQUEAL SQUEAL
HEY, WHAT DO YOU MEAN BY THAT?
WHAT WILL YOU GAIN BY KILLING ME?
THERE'S A...
...PRICE ON YOUR HEAD.
AND I'M ALSO GRATEFUL TO THEM...
...FOR TELLING ME ABOUT THIS WONDERFUL PLACE.
THEM...
HEY, WAIT!
SQUEAL SQUEAL
ZAM
WHIRR
HEY!
ZAM

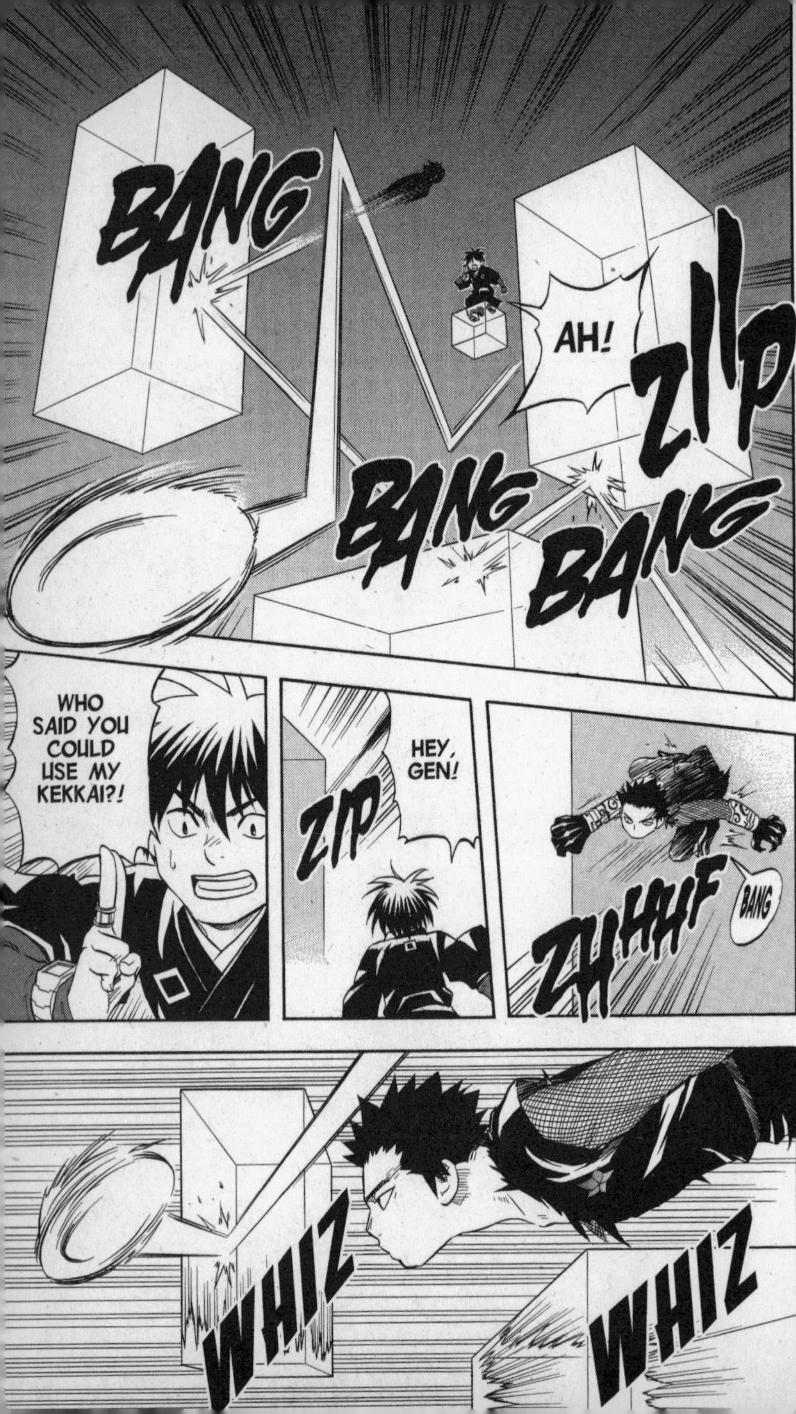
ZIP
AH!
BANG
BANG
BANG
ZHHHF
BANG
HEY, GEN!
ZIP
WHO SAID YOU COULD USE MY KEKKAI?!
WHIZ
WHIZ

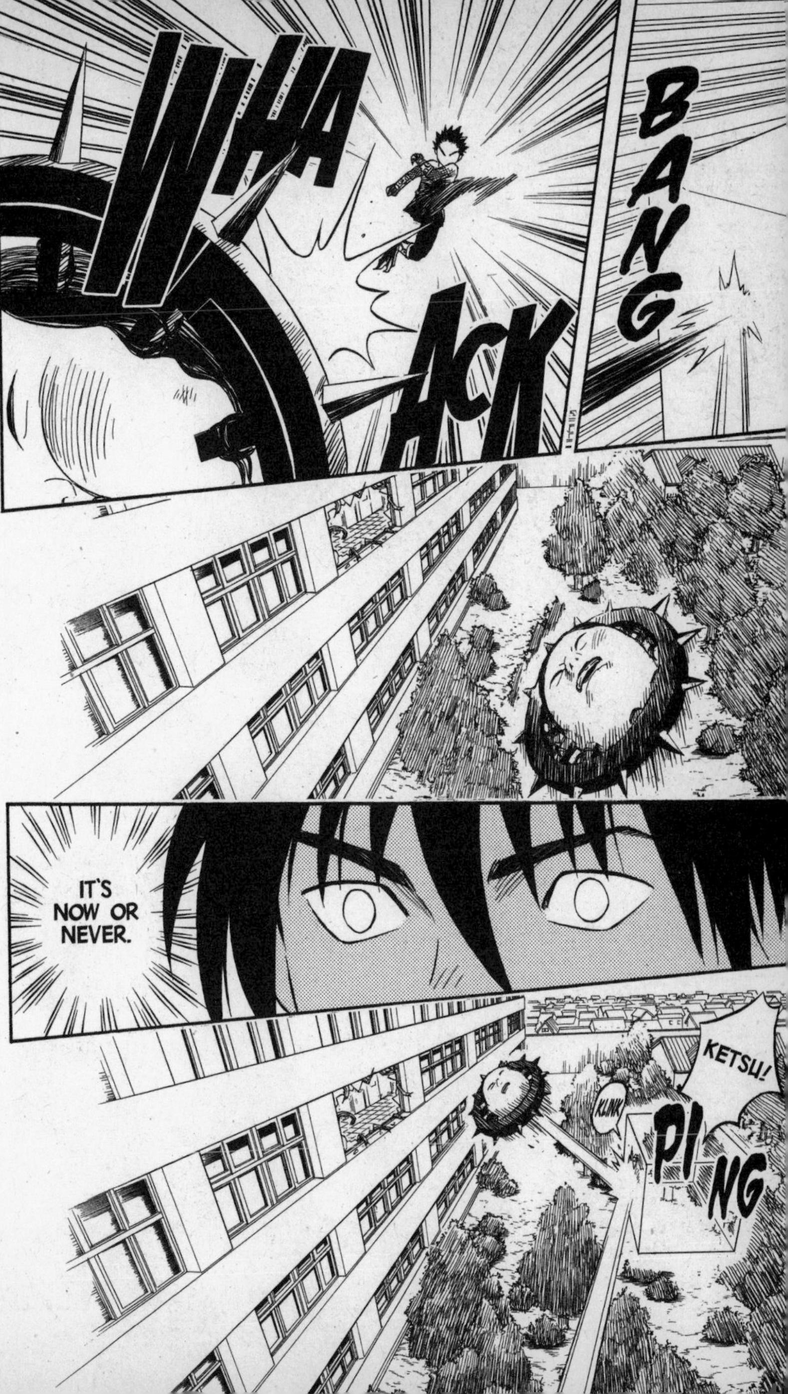
BANG
WHA
ACK
IT'S NOW OR NEVER.
KETSU!
KLINK
PI
NG

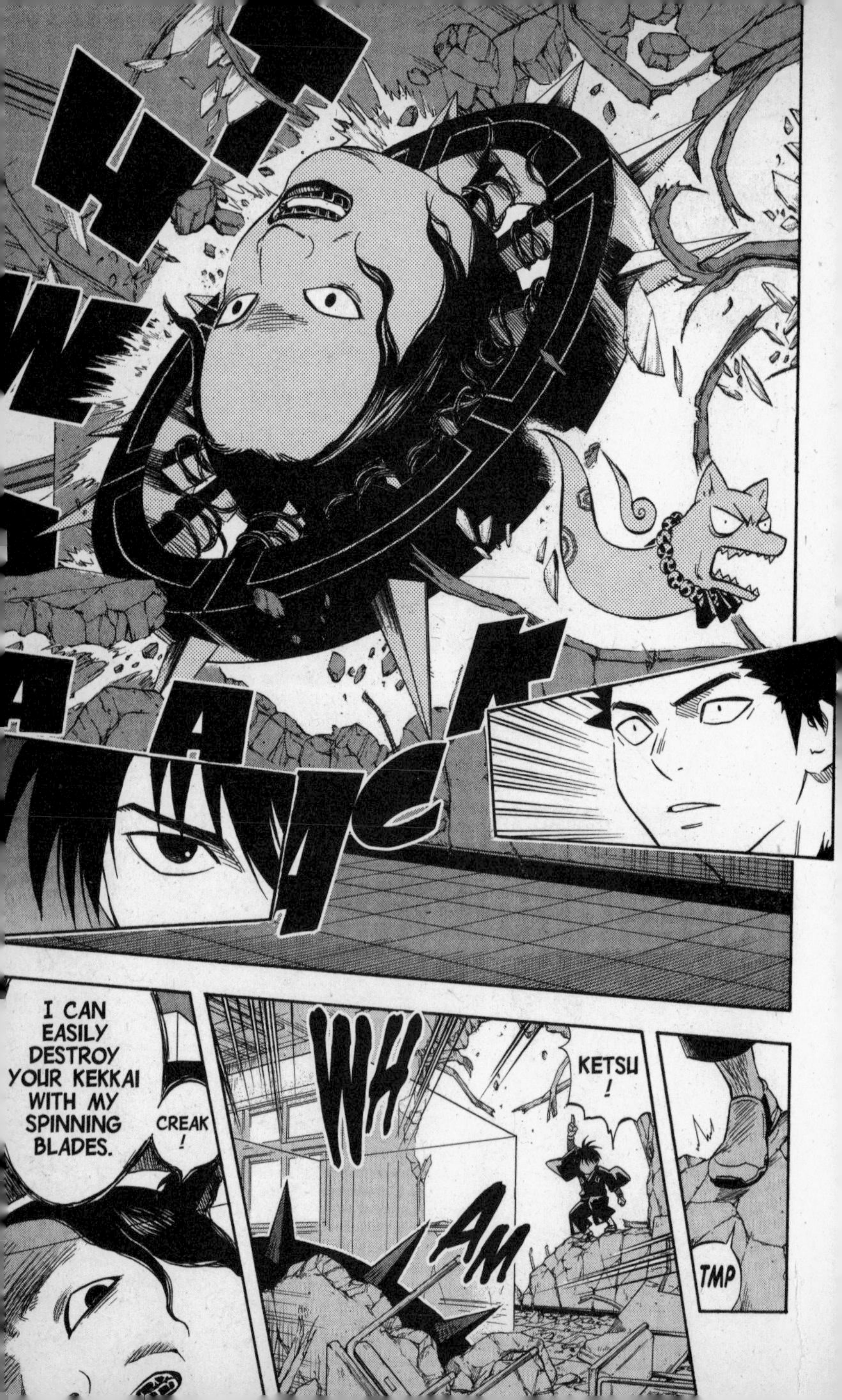
TMP
KETSU!
WHAM
CREAK!
I CAN EASILY DESTROY YOUR KEKKAI WITH MY SPINNING BLADES.

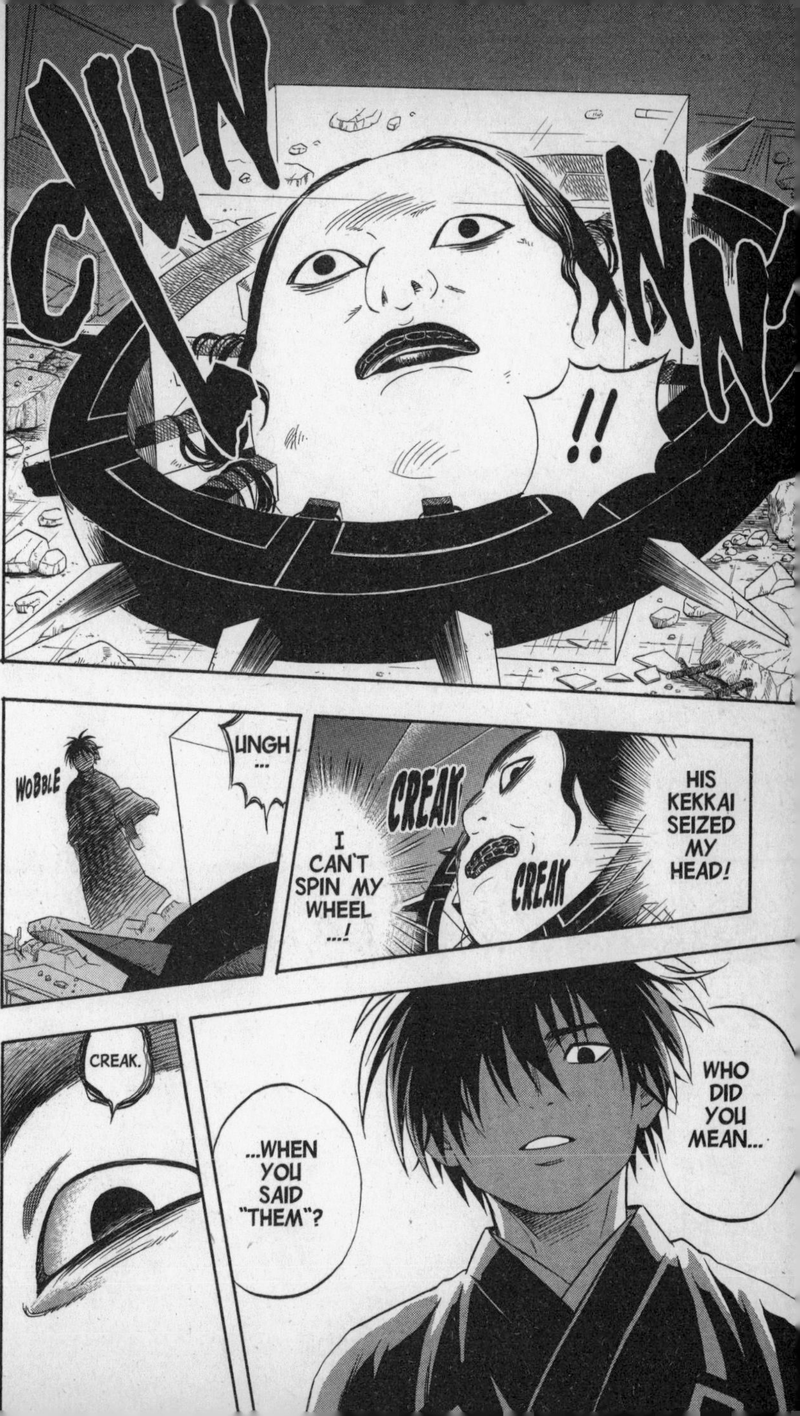
CHUN
!!
HIS KEKKAI SEIZED MY HEAD!
CREAK
CREAK
I CAN'T SPIN MY WHEEL ...!
UNGH ...
WOBBLE
WHO DID YOU MEAN...
...WHEN YOU SAID "THEM"?
CREAK.

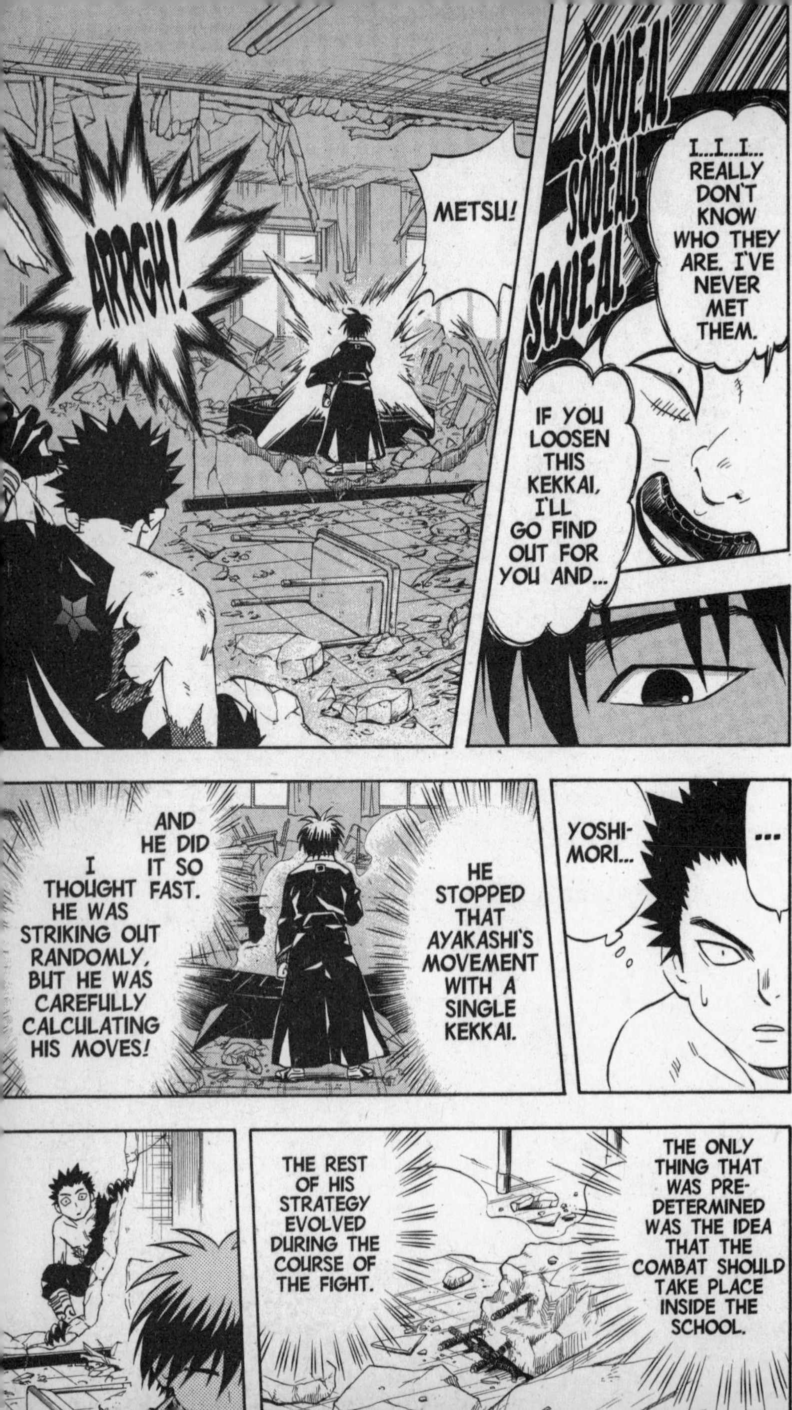
SQUEAL SQUEAL SQUEAL SQUEAL
I...I...I... REALLY DON'T KNOW WHO THEY ARE. I'VE NEVER MET THEM.
IF YOU LOOSEN THIS KEKKAI, I'LL GO FIND OUT FOR YOU AND...
METSU!
ARRGH!
...
YOSHI-MORI...
HE STOPPED THAT AYAKASHI'S MOVEMENT WITH A SINGLE KEKKAI.
AND HE DID IT SO FAST.
I THOUGHT HE WAS STRIKING OUT RANDOMLY, BUT HE WAS CAREFULLY CALCULATING HIS MOVES!
THE ONLY THING THAT WAS PRE-DETERMINED WAS THE IDEA THAT THE COMBAT SHOULD TAKE PLACE INSIDE THE SCHOOL.
THE REST OF HIS STRATEGY EVOLVED DURING THE COURSE OF THE FIGHT.

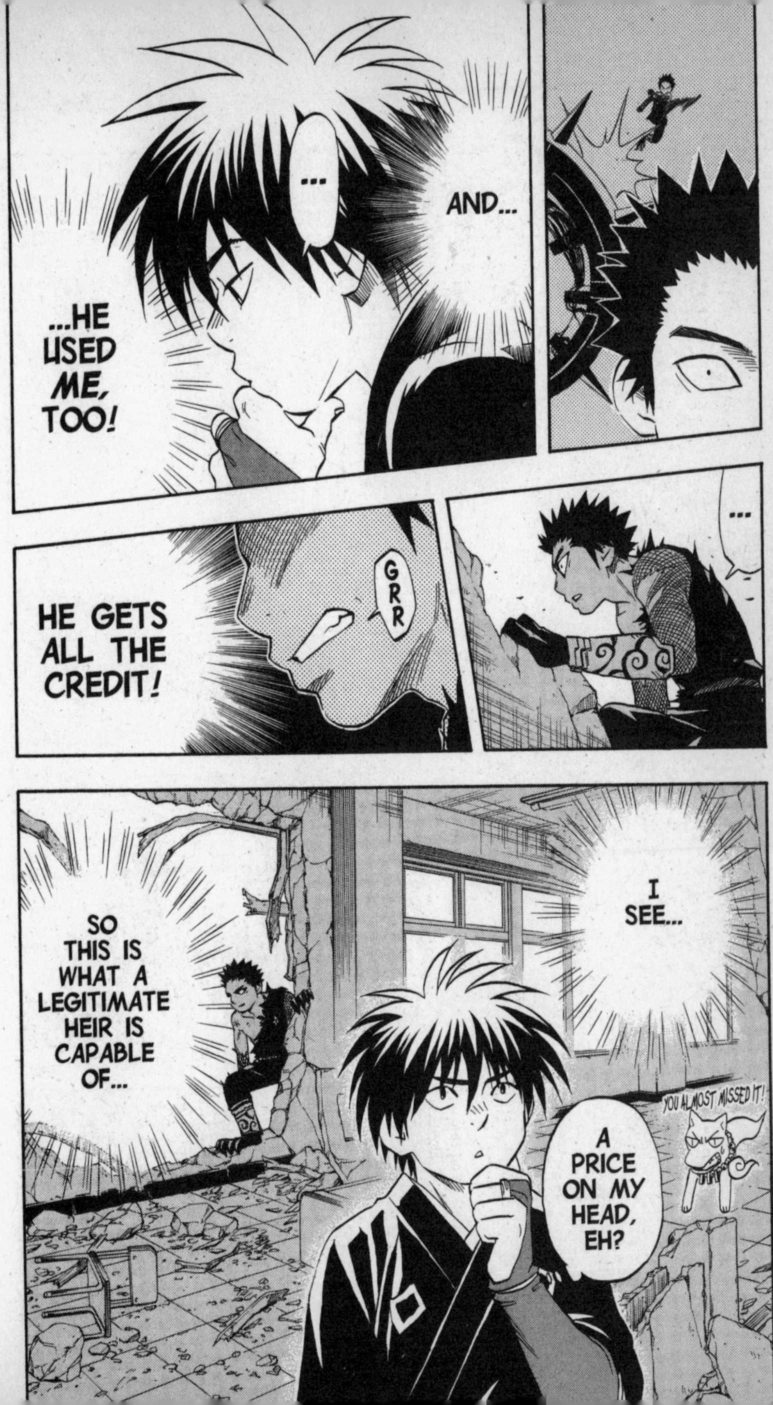
...
AND...
...HE USED ME, TOO!
...
GRR
HE GETS ALL THE CREDIT!
I SEE...
YOU ALMOST MISSED IT!
A PRICE ON MY HEAD, EH?
SO THIS IS WHAT A LEGITIMATE HEIR IS CAPABLE OF...

Chapter 55: Reward

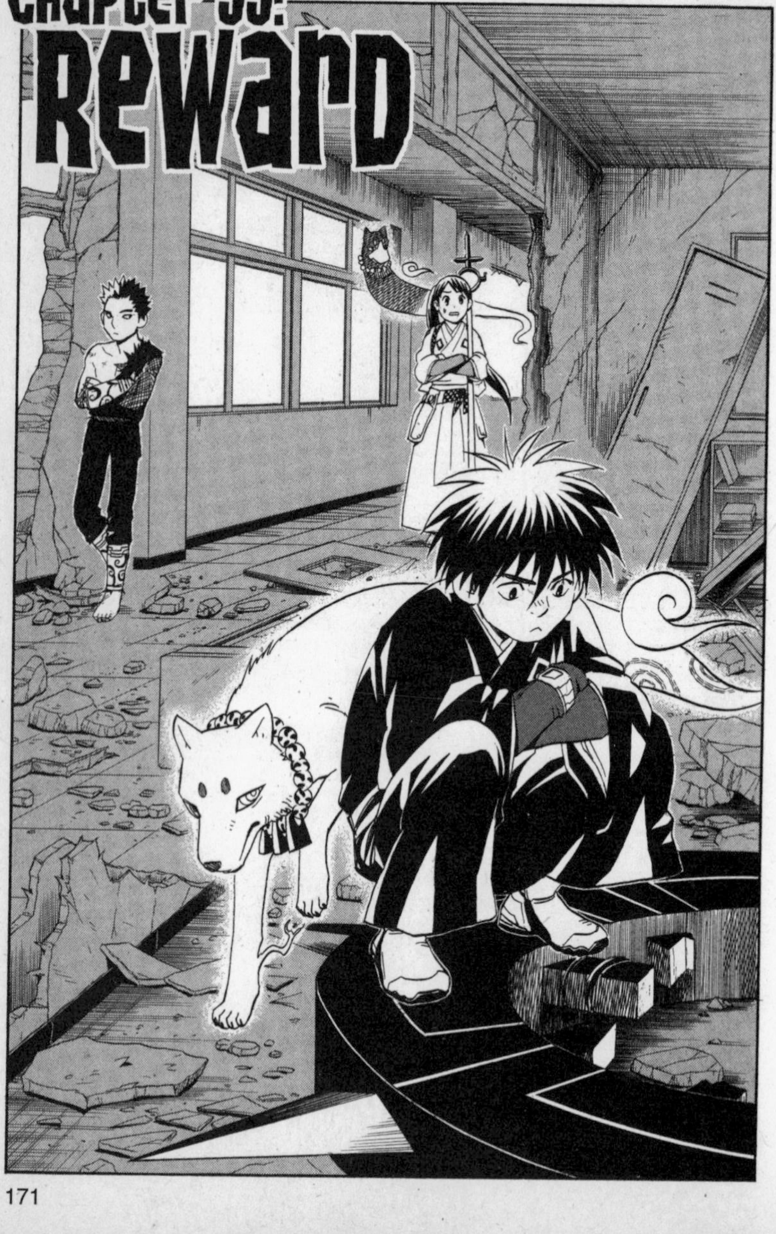

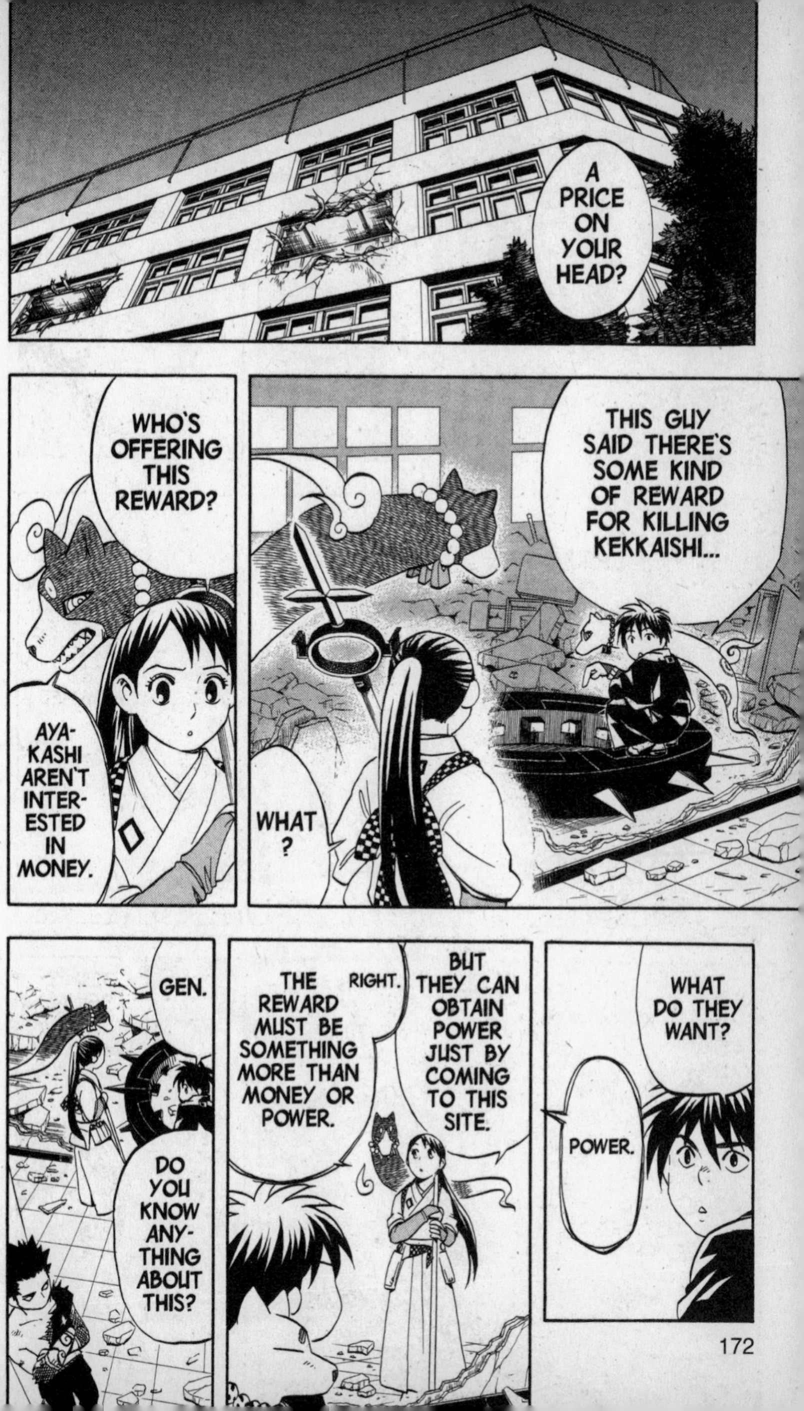
A PRICE ON YOUR HEAD?
THIS GUY SAID THERE'S SOME KIND OF REWARD FOR KILLING KEKKAISHI...
WHAT?
WHO'S OFFERING THIS REWARD?
AYAKASHI AREN'T INTERESTED IN MONEY.
WHAT DO THEY WANT?
POWER.
BUT THEY CAN OBTAIN POWER JUST BY COMING TO THIS SITE.
RIGHT.
THE REWARD MUST BE SOMETHING MORE THAN MONEY OR POWER.
GEN.
DO YOU KNOW ANYTHING ABOUT THIS?

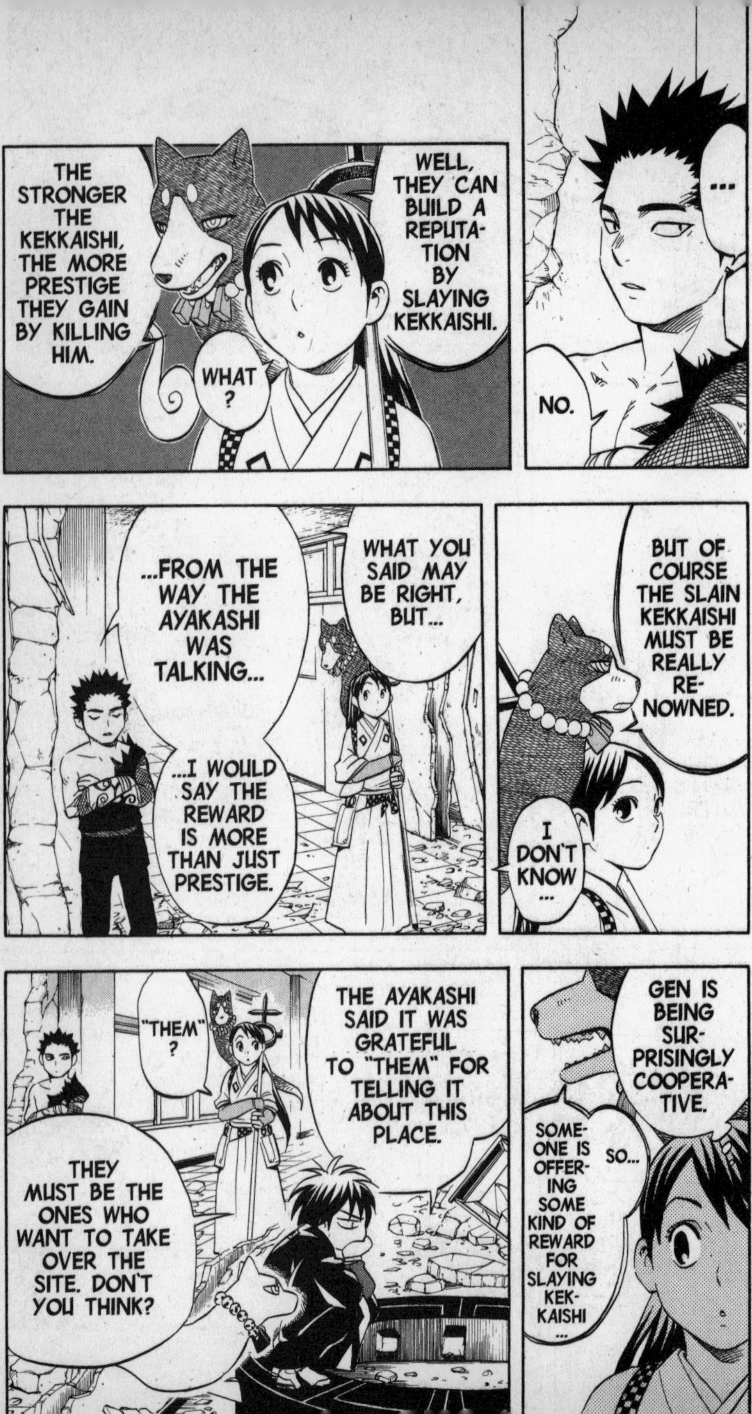
...
NO.
WELL, THEY CAN BUILD A REPUTATION BY SLAYING KEKKAISHI.
THE STRONGER THE KEKKAISHI, THE MORE PRESTIGE THEY GAIN BY KILLING HIM.
WHAT?
BUT OF COURSE THE SLAIN KEKKAISHI MUST BE REALLY RENOWNED.
I DON'T KNOW...
WHAT YOU SAID MAY BE RIGHT, BUT...
...FROM THE WAY THE AYAKASHI WAS TALKING...
...I WOULD SAY THE REWARD IS MORE THAN JUST PRESTIGE.
GEN IS BEING SURPRISINGLY COOPERATIVE.
SO...
SOMEONE IS OFFERING SOME KIND OF REWARD FOR SLAYING KEKKAISHI...
THE AYAKASHI SAID IT WAS GRATEFUL TO "THEM" FOR TELLING IT ABOUT THIS PLACE.
"THEM"?
THEY MUST BE THE ONES WHO WANT TO TAKE OVER THE SITE. DON'T YOU THINK?

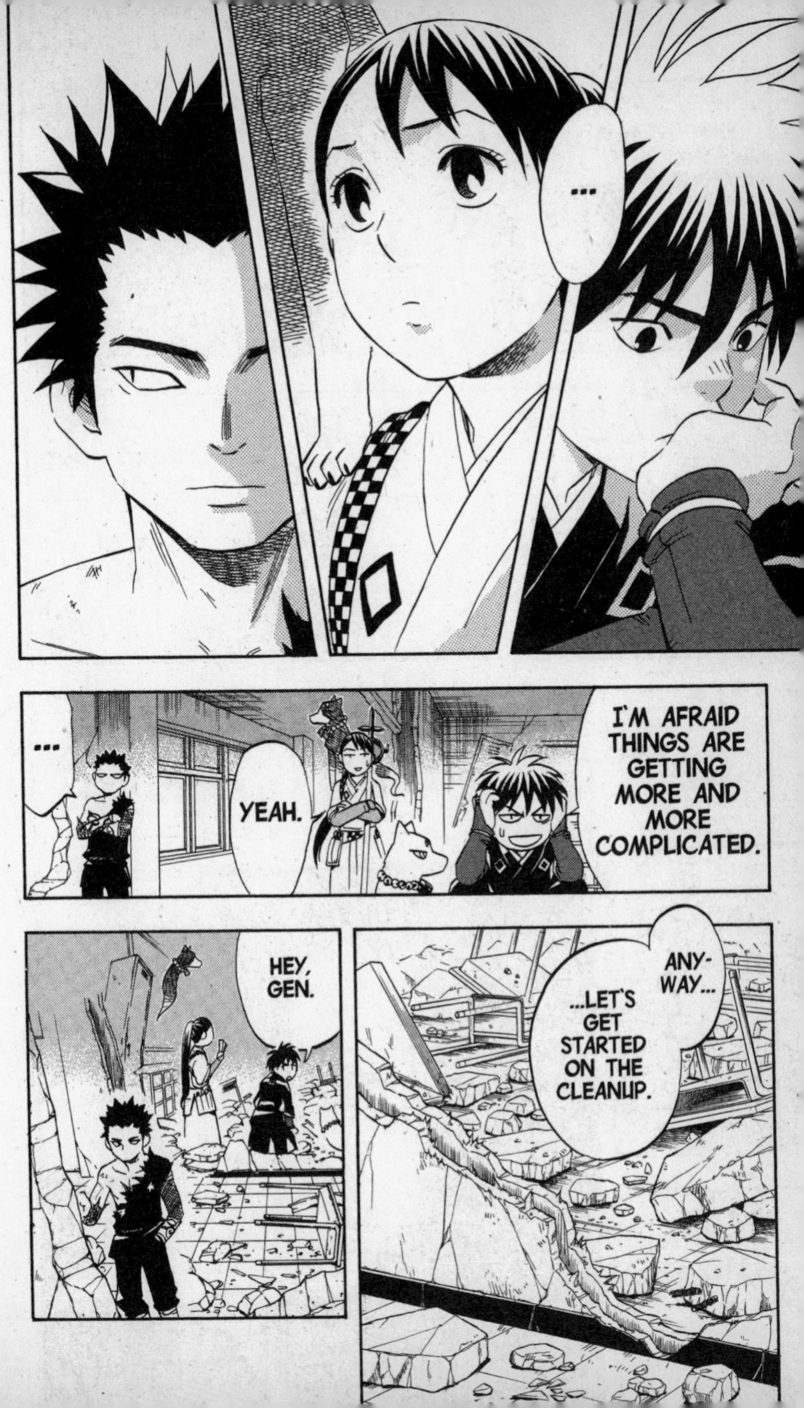
...
I'M AFRAID THINGS ARE GETTING MORE AND MORE COMPLICATED.
YEAH.
...
ANY-WAY...
...LET'S GET STARTED ON THE CLEANUP.
HEY, GEN.

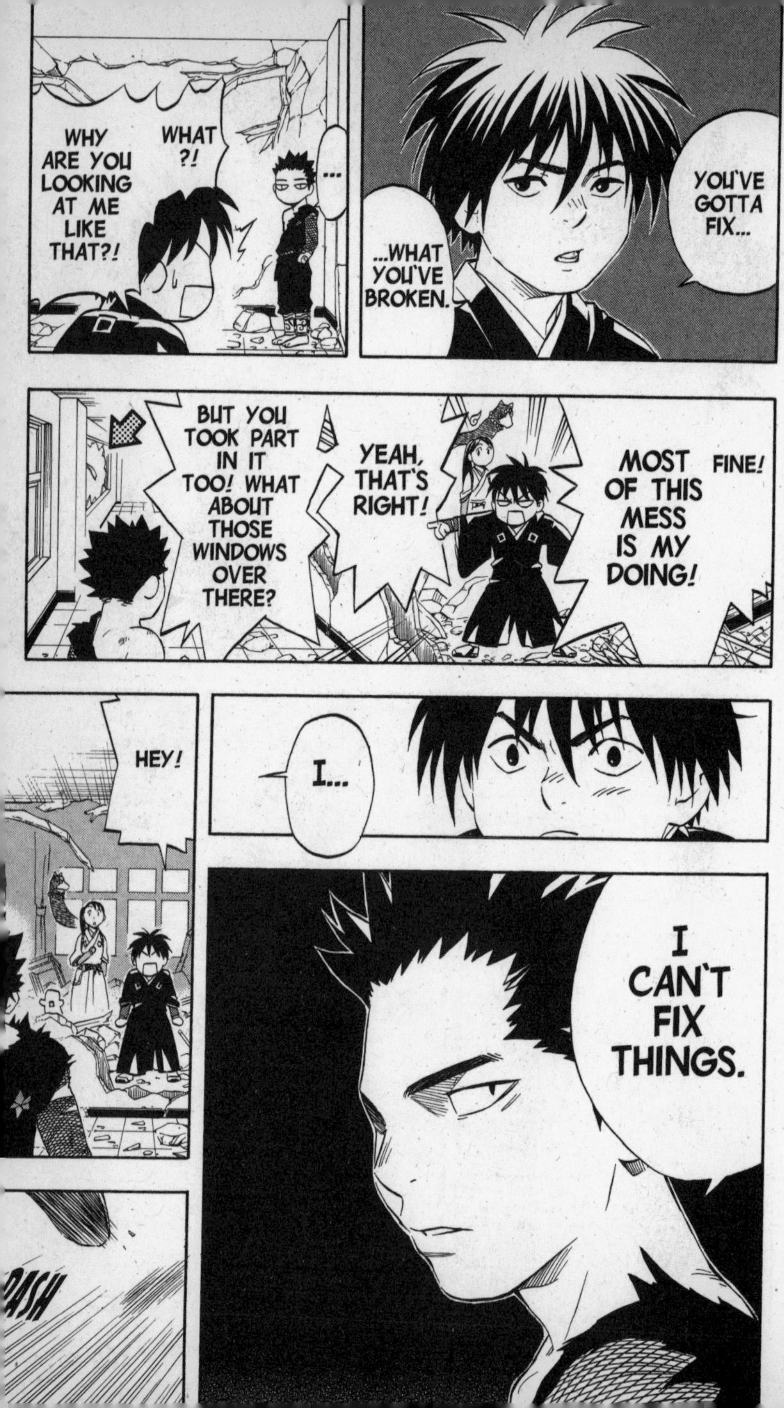
YOU'VE GOTTA FIX...
...WHAT YOU'VE BROKEN.
...
WHAT ?!
WHY ARE YOU LOOKING AT ME LIKE THAT?!
FINE!
MOST OF THIS MESS IS MY DOING!
YEAH, THAT'S RIGHT!
BUT YOU TOOK PART IN IT TOO! WHAT ABOUT THOSE WINDOWS OVER THERE?
I...
I CAN'T FIX THINGS.
HEY!
DASH

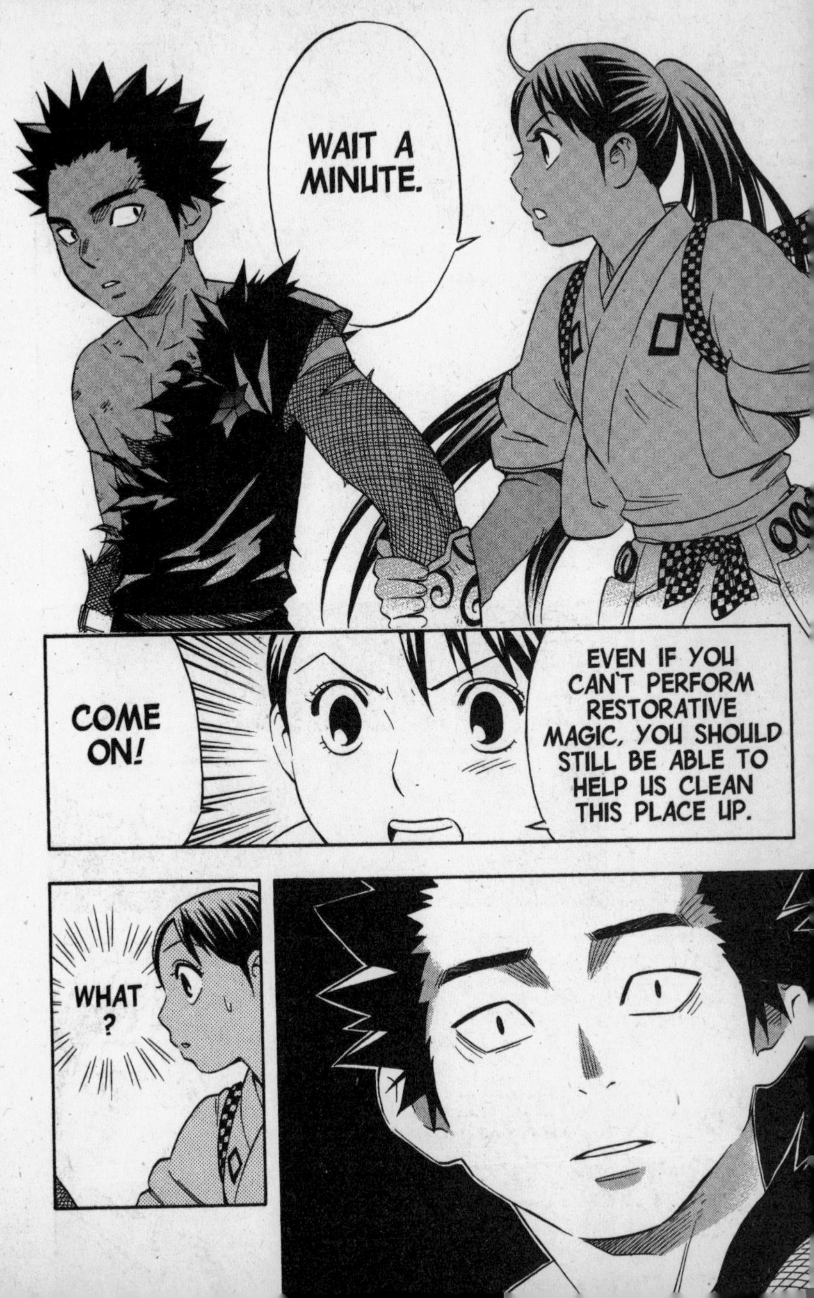
WAIT A MINUTE.
EVEN IF YOU CAN'T PERFORM RESTORATIVE MAGIC, YOU SHOULD STILL BE ABLE TO HELP US CLEAN THIS PLACE UP.
COME ON!
WHAT ?

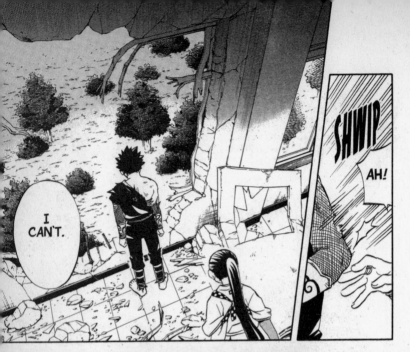

I CAN'T.

SHWIP

AH!

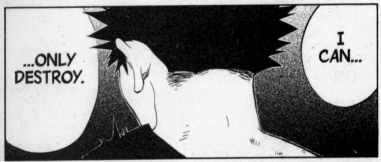

I CAN...

...ONLY DESTROY.

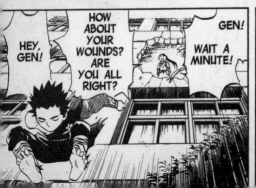

HEY, GEN!

HOW ABOUT YOUR WOUNDS? ARE YOU ALL RIGHT?

GEN!

WAIT A MINUTE!

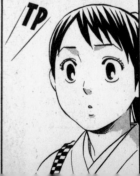

TP

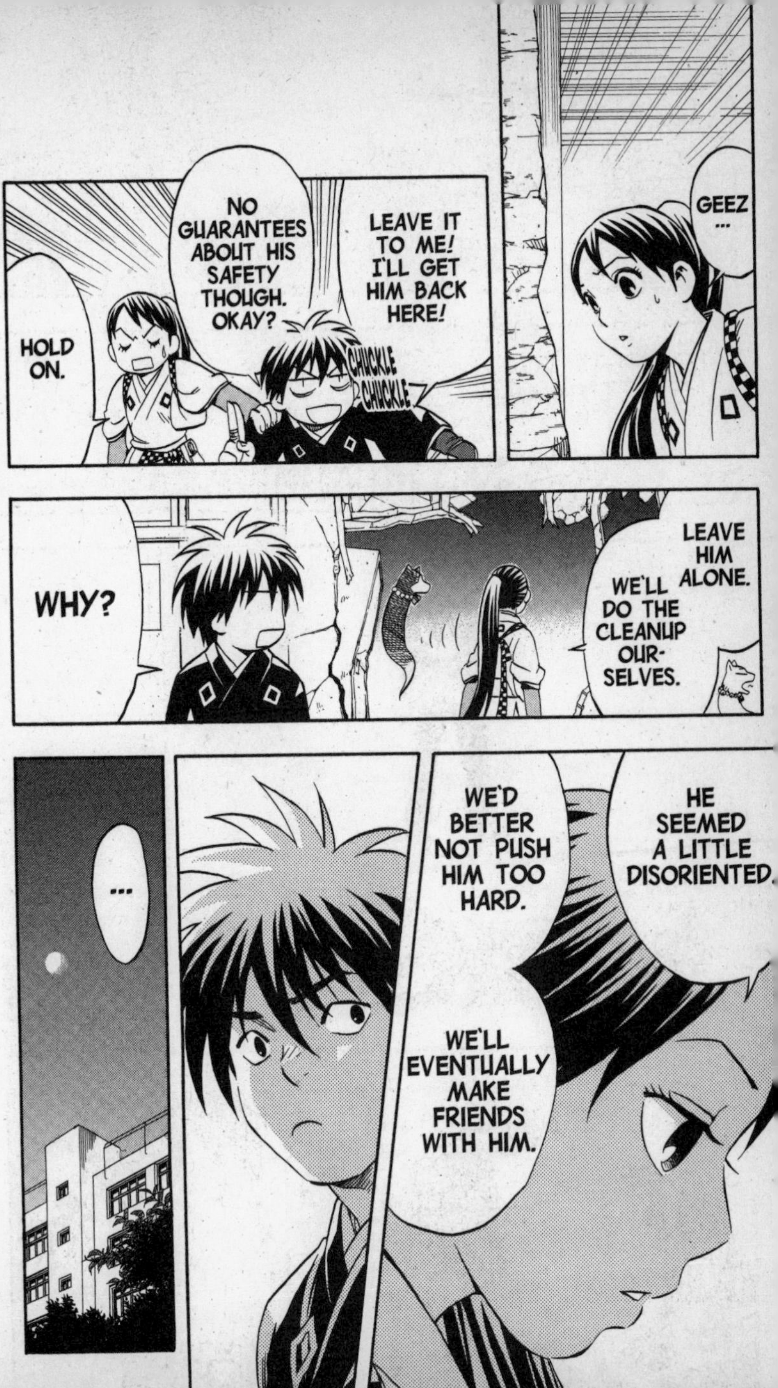
GEEZ ...
LEAVE IT TO ME! I'LL GET HIM BACK HERE!
CHUCKLE CHUCKLE
NO GUARANTEES ABOUT HIS SAFETY THOUGH. OKAY?
HOLD ON.
LEAVE HIM ALONE.
WE'LL DO THE CLEANUP OUR-SELVES.
WHY?
HE SEEMED A LITTLE DISORIENTED.
WE'D BETTER NOT PUSH HIM TOO HARD.
WE'LL EVENTUALLY MAKE FRIENDS WITH HIM.
...

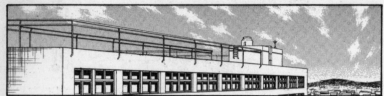

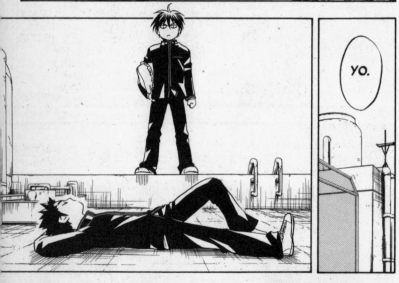

YO.

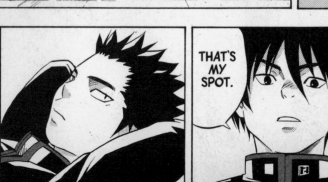

THAT'S MY SPOT.

HEY...

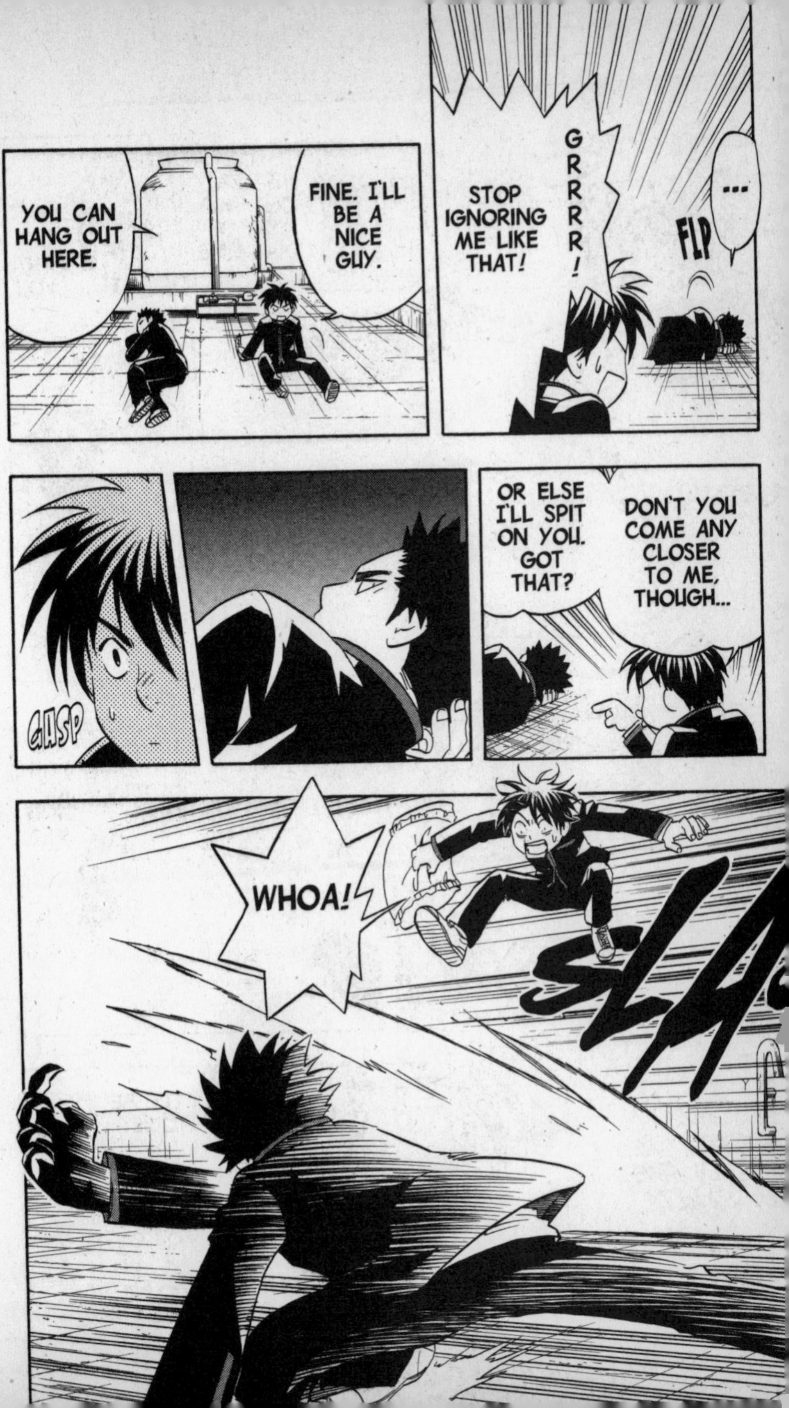
...
FLP
GRRRR!
STOP IGNORING ME LIKE THAT!
FINE. I'LL BE A NICE GUY.
YOU CAN HANG OUT HERE.
DON'T YOU COME ANY CLOSER TO ME, THOUGH...
OR ELSE I'LL SPIT ON YOU. GOT THAT?
GASP
WHOA!

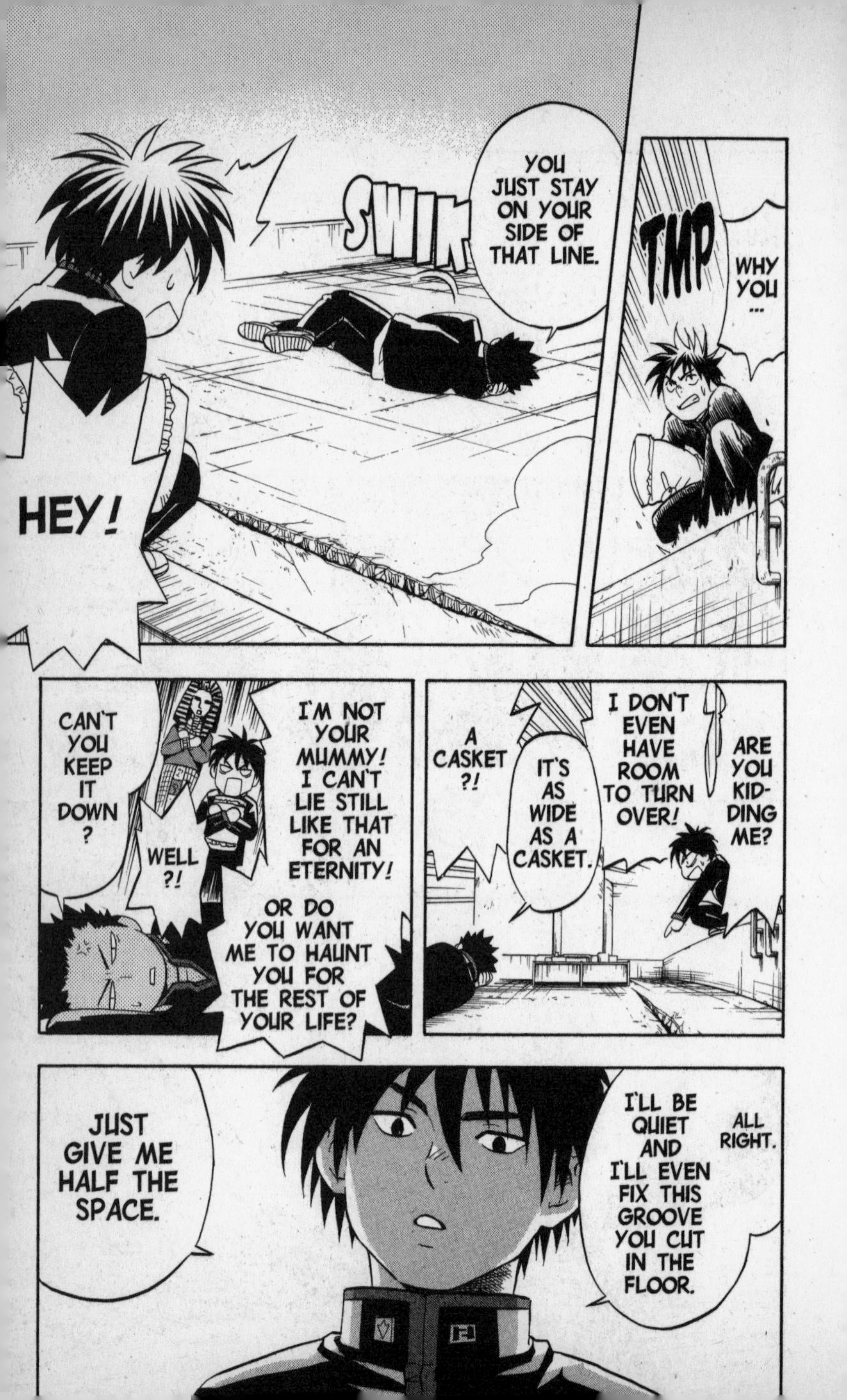
TMP
WHY YOU ...
YOU JUST STAY ON YOUR SIDE OF THAT LINE.
SWIN
HEY!
ARE YOU KID-DING ME?
I DON'T EVEN HAVE ROOM TO TURN OVER!
IT'S AS WIDE AS A CASKET.
A CASKET ?!
I'M NOT YOUR MUMMY! I CAN'T LIE STILL LIKE THAT FOR AN ETERNITY!
CAN'T YOU KEEP IT DOWN ?
WELL ?!
OR DO YOU WANT ME TO HAUNT YOU FOR THE REST OF YOUR LIFE?
ALL RIGHT.
I'LL BE QUIET AND I'LL EVEN FIX THIS GROOVE YOU CUT IN THE FLOOR.
JUST GIVE ME HALF THE SPACE.

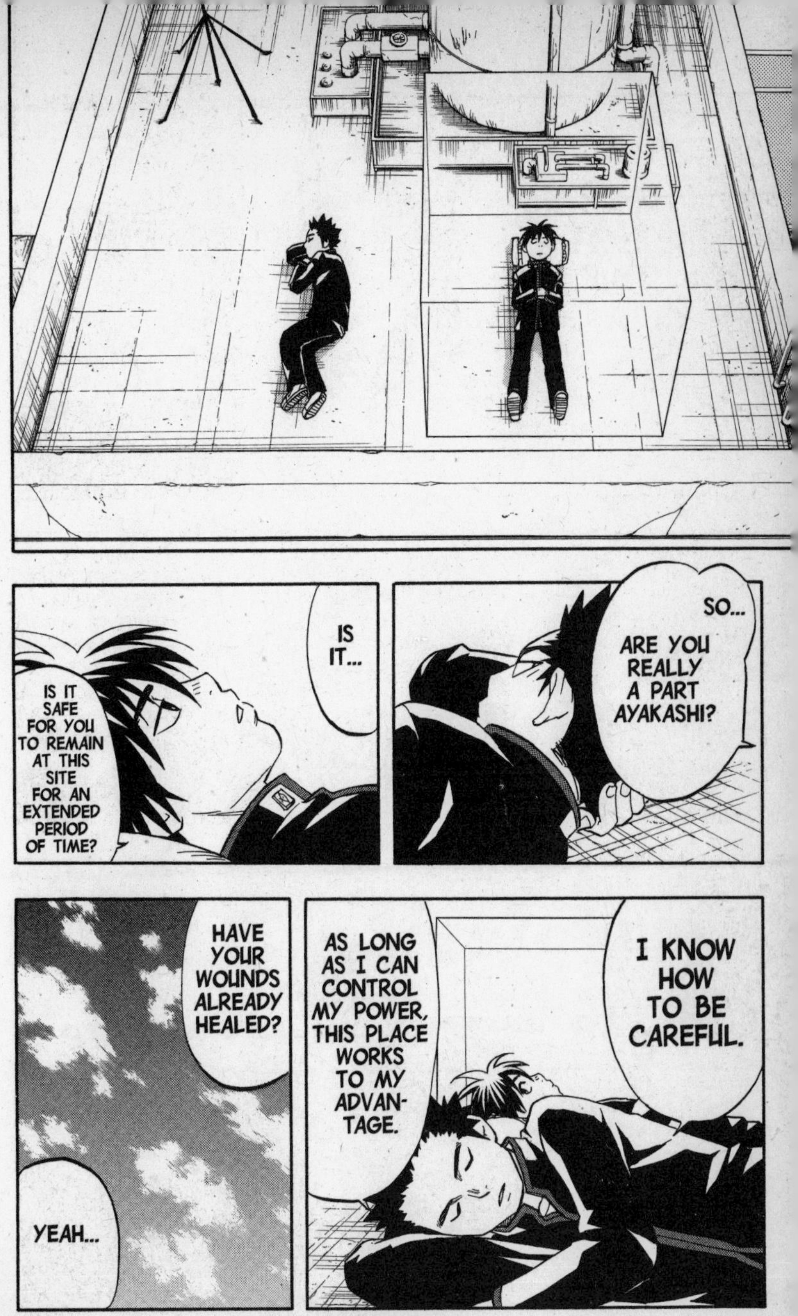
SO...
ARE YOU REALLY A PART AYAKASHI?
IS IT...
IS IT SAFE FOR YOU TO REMAIN AT THIS SITE FOR AN EXTENDED PERIOD OF TIME?
I KNOW HOW TO BE CAREFUL.
AS LONG AS I CAN CONTROL MY POWER, THIS PLACE WORKS TO MY ADVANTAGE.
HAVE YOUR WOUNDS ALREADY HEALED?
YEAH...

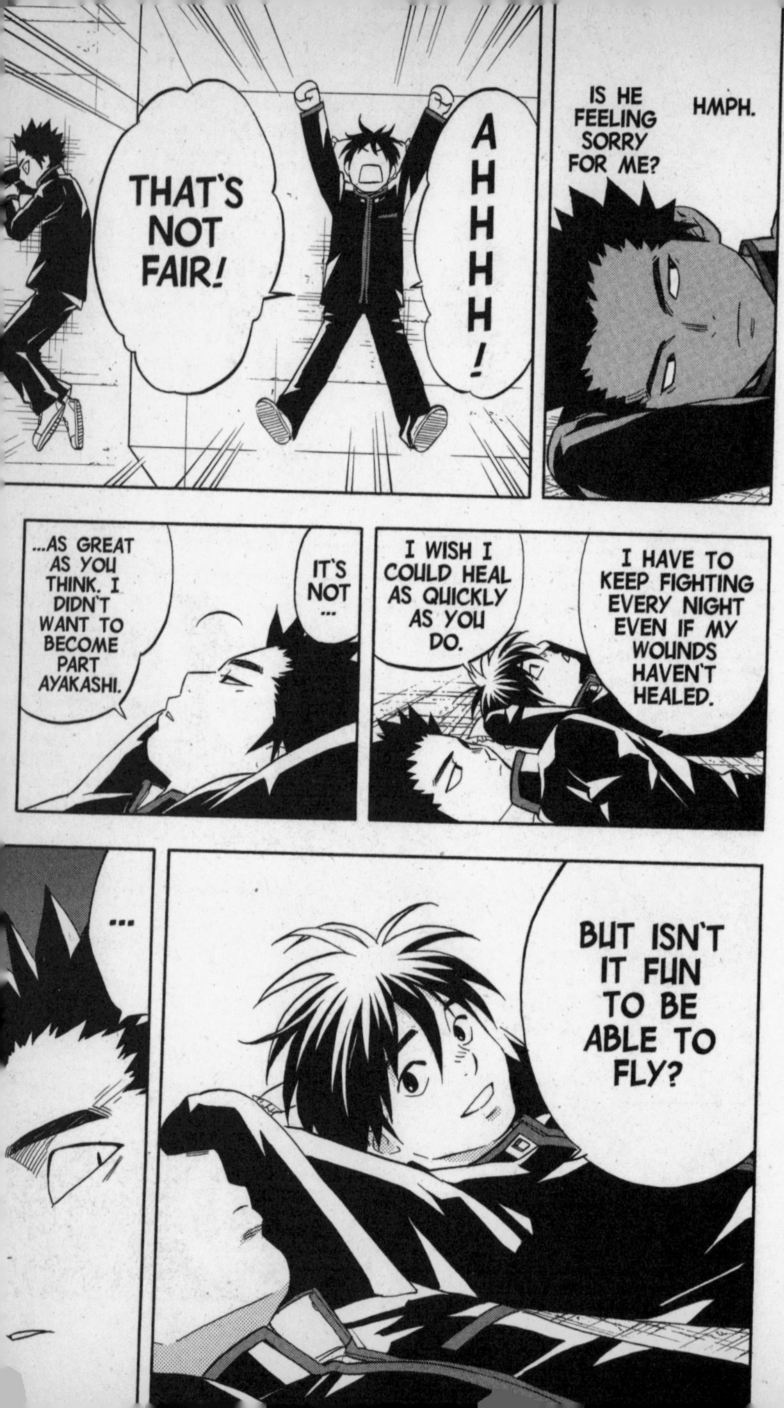
HMPH.
IS HE FEELING SORRY FOR ME?
AHHHH!
THAT'S NOT FAIR!
I HAVE TO KEEP FIGHTING EVERY NIGHT EVEN IF MY WOUNDS HAVEN'T HEALED.
I WISH I COULD HEAL AS QUICKLY AS YOU DO.
IT'S NOT ...
...AS GREAT AS YOU THINK. I DIDN'T WANT TO BECOME PART AYAKASHI.
BUT ISN'T IT FUN TO BE ABLE TO FLY?
...

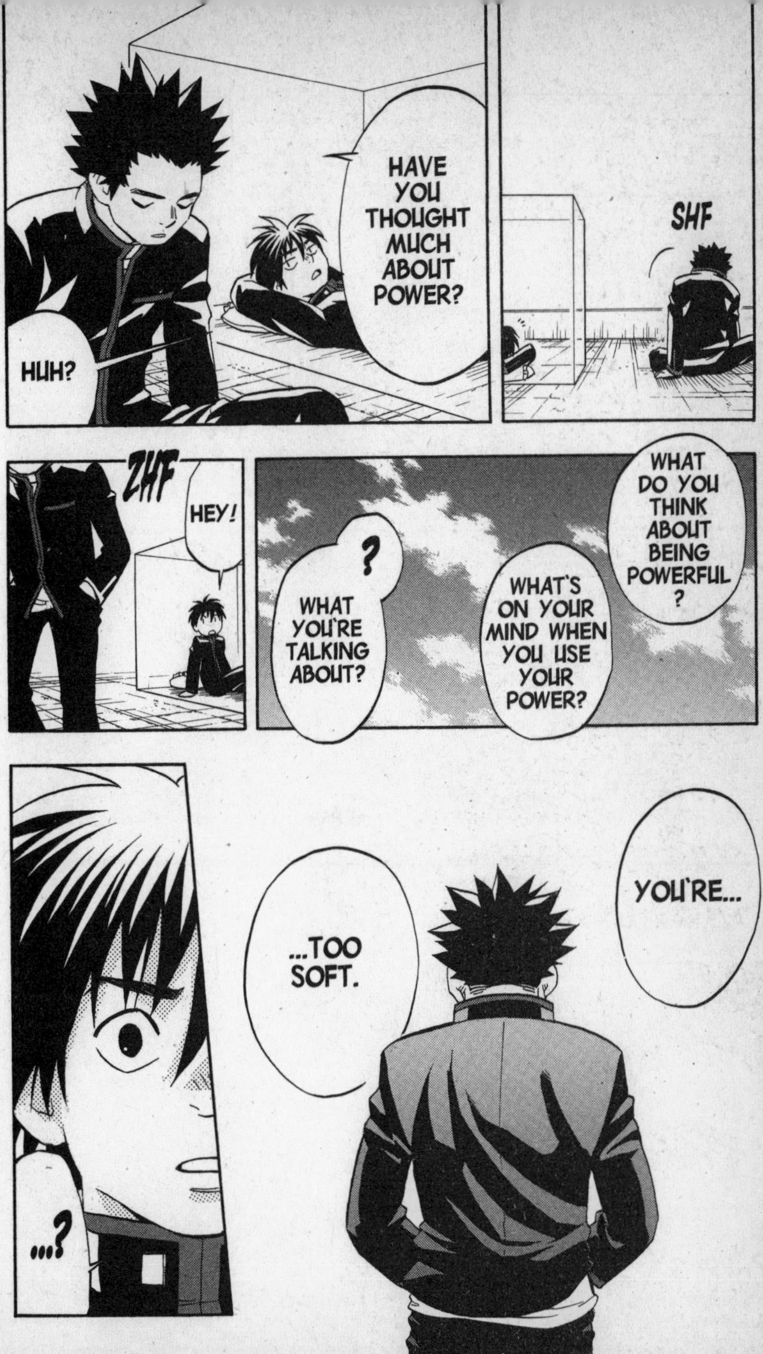
SHF
HAVE YOU THOUGHT MUCH ABOUT POWER?
HUH?
WHAT DO YOU THINK ABOUT BEING POWERFUL?
WHAT'S ON YOUR MIND WHEN YOU USE YOUR POWER?
?
WHAT YOU'RE TALKING ABOUT?
ZHF
HEY!
YOU'RE...
...TOO SOFT.
...?

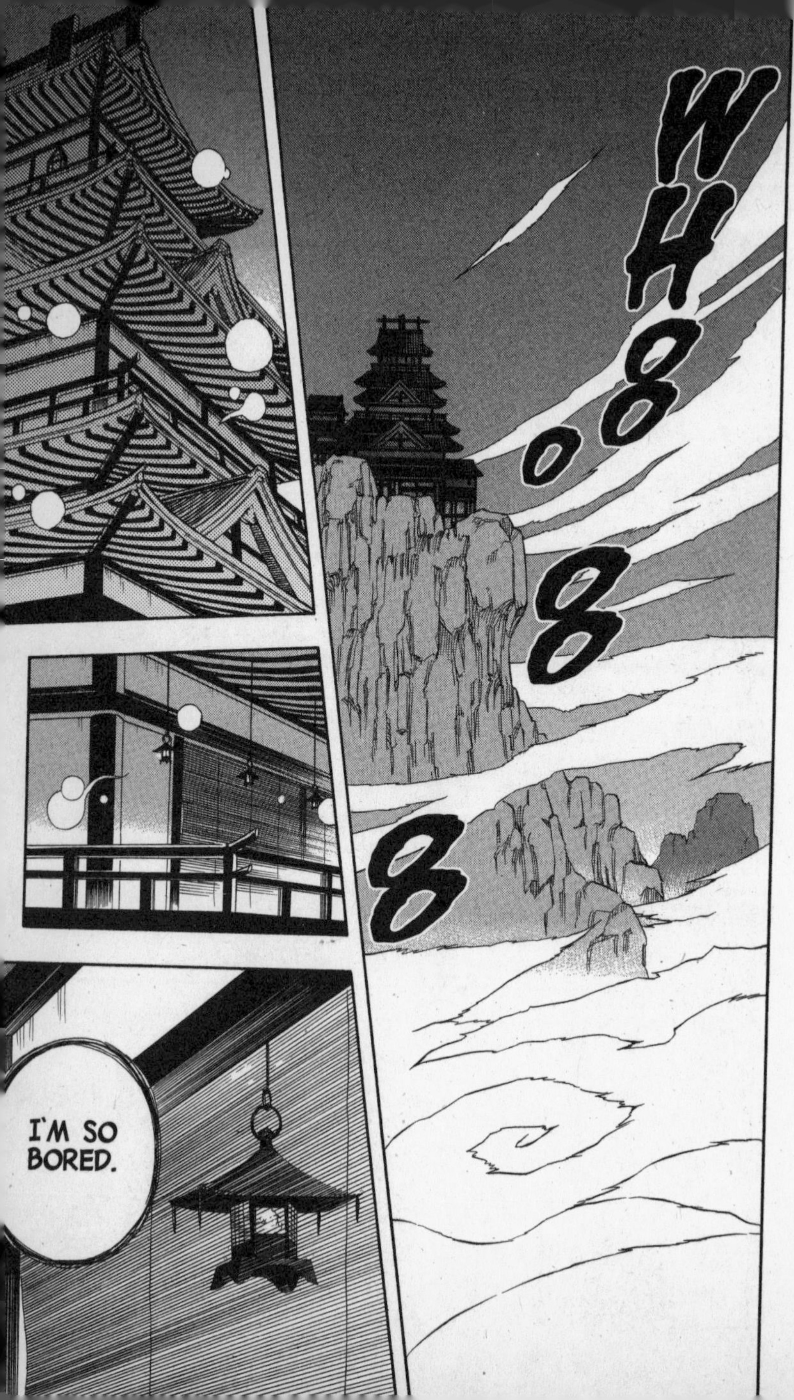
WHOOOO
I'M SO BORED.

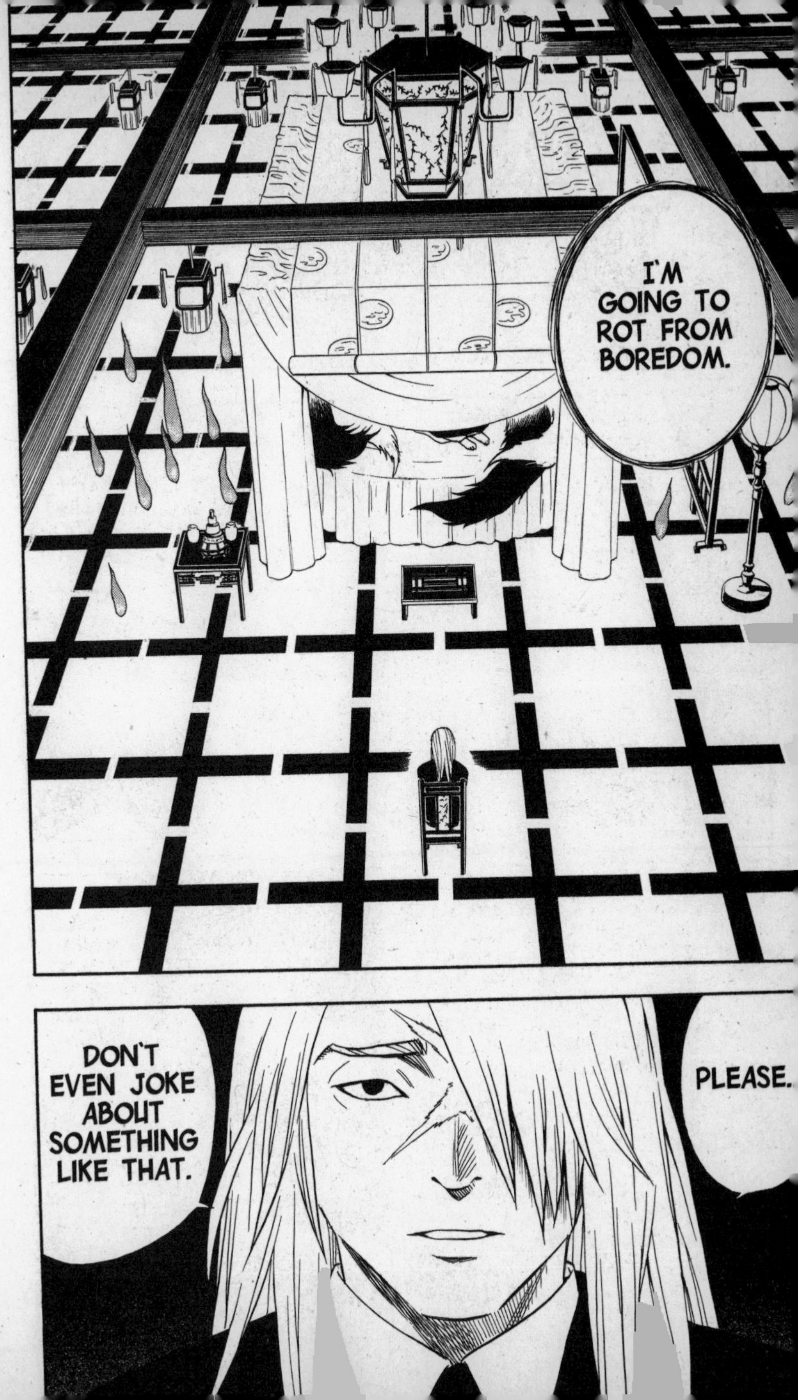
I'M GOING TO ROT FROM BOREDOM.
PLEASE.
DON'T EVEN JOKE ABOUT SOMETHING LIKE THAT.

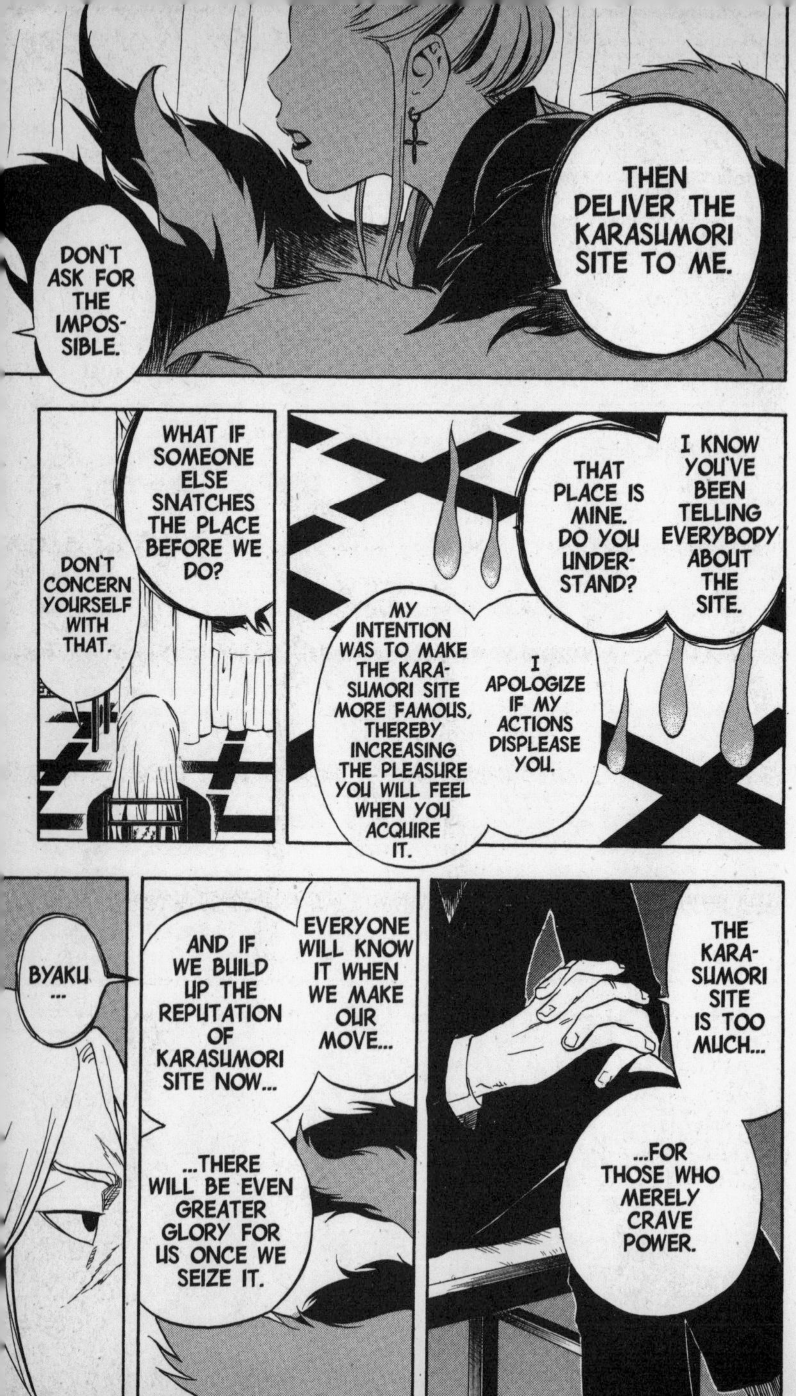
THEN DELIVER THE KARASUMORI SITE TO ME.
DON'T ASK FOR THE IMPOSSIBLE.
I KNOW YOU'VE BEEN TELLING EVERYBODY ABOUT THE SITE.
THAT PLACE IS MINE. DO YOU UNDERSTAND?
I APOLOGIZE IF MY ACTIONS DISPLEASE YOU.
MY INTENTION WAS TO MAKE THE KARASUMORI SITE MORE FAMOUS, THEREBY INCREASING THE PLEASURE YOU WILL FEEL WHEN YOU ACQUIRE IT.
WHAT IF SOMEONE ELSE SNATCHES THE PLACE BEFORE WE DO?
DON'T CONCERN YOURSELF WITH THAT.
THE KARASUMORI SITE IS TOO MUCH...
...FOR THOSE WHO MERELY CRAVE POWER.
EVERYONE WILL KNOW IT WHEN WE MAKE OUR MOVE...
AND IF WE BUILD UP THE REPUTATION OF KARASUMORI SITE NOW...
...THERE WILL BE EVEN GREATER GLORY FOR US ONCE WE SEIZE IT.
BYAKU ...

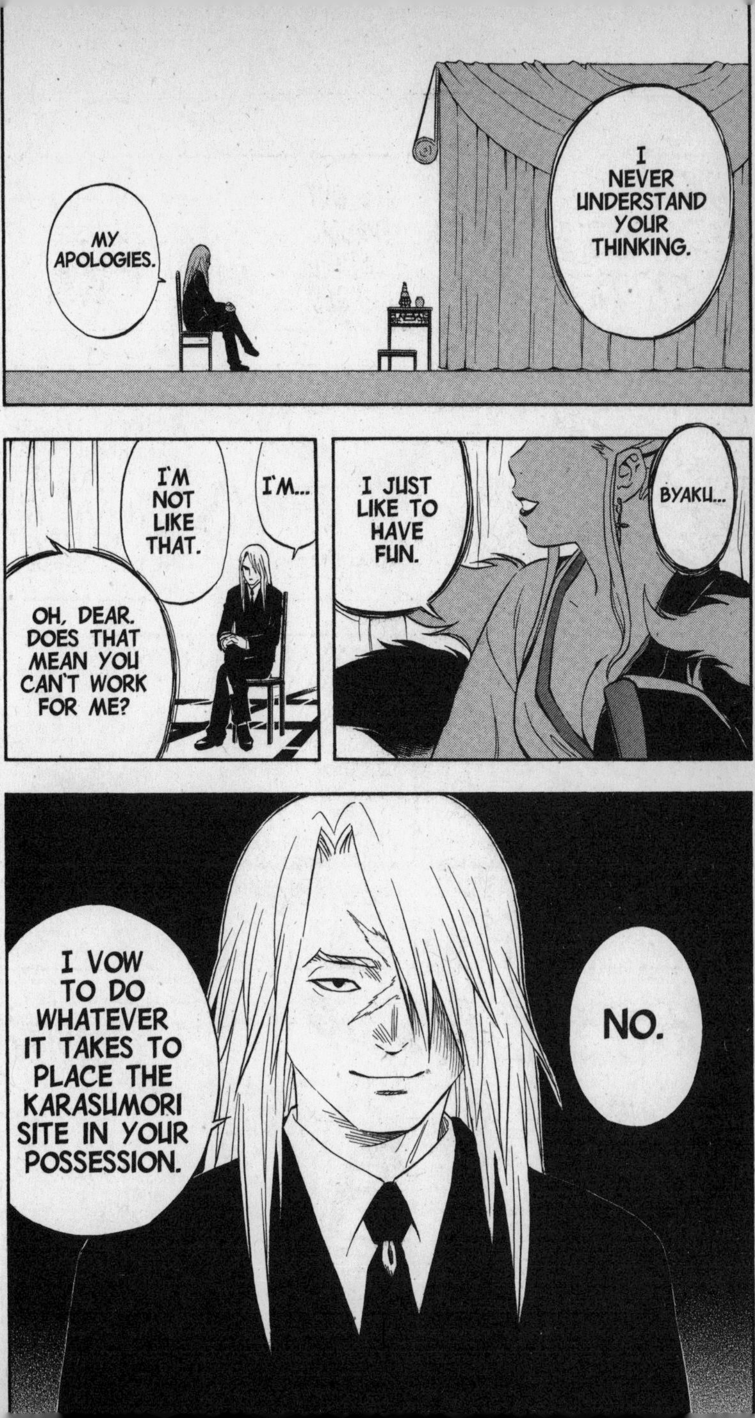
I NEVER UNDERSTAND YOUR THINKING.
MY APOLOGIES.
BYAKU...
I JUST LIKE TO HAVE FUN.
I'M...
I'M NOT LIKE THAT.
OH, DEAR. DOES THAT MEAN YOU CAN'T WORK FOR ME?
NO.
I VOW TO DO WHATEVER IT TAKES TO PLACE THE KARASUMORI SITE IN YOUR POSSESSION.

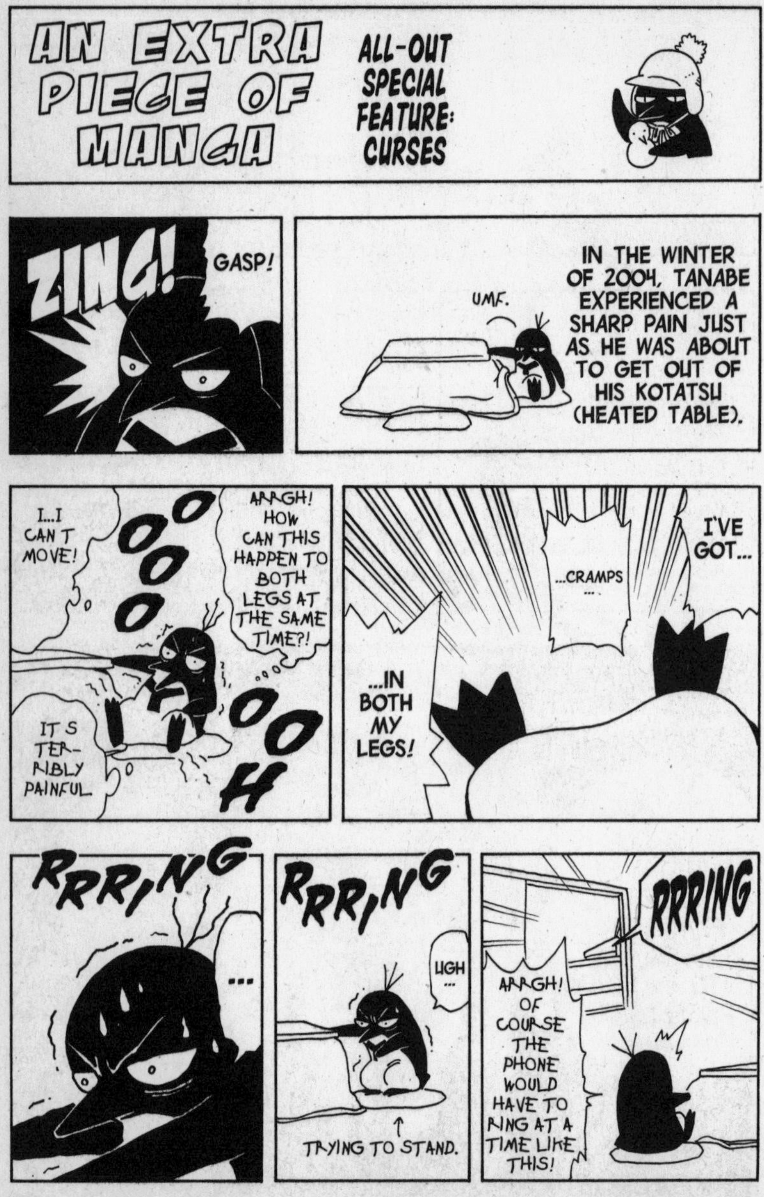
AN EXTRA PIECE OF MANGA
ALL-OUT SPECIAL FEATURE: CURSES
IN THE WINTER OF 2004, TANABE EXPERIENCED A SHARP PAIN JUST AS HE WAS ABOUT TO GET OUT OF HIS KOTATSU (HEATED TABLE).
UMF.
ZING!
GASP!
I'VE GOT...
...CRAMPS...
...IN BOTH MY LEGS!
ARRGH! HOW CAN THIS HAPPEN TO BOTH LEGS AT THE SAME TIME?!
OOOOOOOH
I...I CAN T MOVE!
IT S TERRIBLY PAINFUL
RRRING
ARRGH! OF COURSE THE PHONE WOULD HAVE TO RING AT A TIME LIKE THIS!
RRRING
UGH...
TRYING TO STAND.
RRRING
...

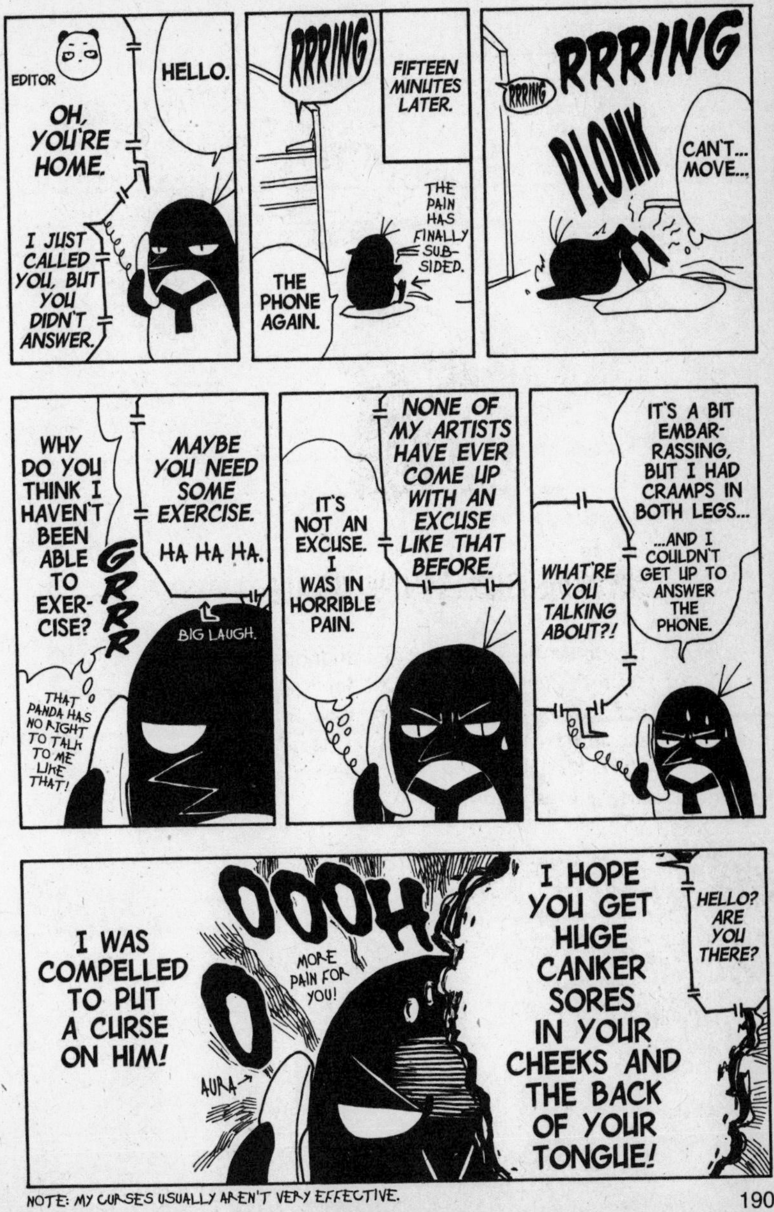
RRRING
RRRING
PLONK
CAN'T... MOVE...
RRRING
FIFTEEN MINUTES LATER.
THE PAIN HAS FINALLY SUBSIDED.
THE PHONE AGAIN.
HELLO.
EDITOR
OH, YOU'RE HOME.
I JUST CALLED YOU, BUT YOU DIDN'T ANSWER.
IT'S A BIT EMBARRASSING, BUT I HAD CRAMPS IN BOTH LEGS...
...AND I COULDN'T GET UP TO ANSWER THE PHONE.
WHAT'RE YOU TALKING ABOUT?!
NONE OF MY ARTISTS HAVE EVER COME UP WITH AN EXCUSE LIKE THAT BEFORE.
IT'S NOT AN EXCUSE. I WAS IN HORRIBLE PAIN.
MAYBE YOU NEED SOME EXERCISE.
HA HA HA.
BIG LAUGH.
WHY DO YOU THINK I HAVEN'T BEEN ABLE TO EXERCISE?
GRRR
THAT PANDA HAS NO RIGHT TO TALK TO ME LIKE THAT!
HELLO? ARE YOU THERE?
I HOPE YOU GET HUGE CANKER SORES IN YOUR CHEEKS AND THE BACK OF YOUR TONGUE!
OOOH
MORE PAIN FOR YOU!
AURA
I WAS COMPELLED TO PUT A CURSE ON HIM!

NOTE: MY CURSES USUALLY AREN'T VERY EFFECTIVE.

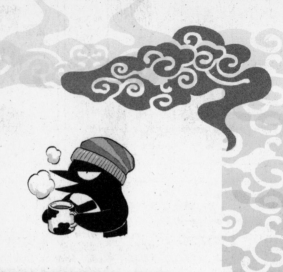

MESSAGE FROM YELLOW TANABE

I prefer coffee over tea. I like to drink strong coffee with milk, but I don't take it with sugar. This really doesn't have much of a connection with Yoshimori liking his coffee-milk drink. I also drink tea with milk. Maybe I just like milk.

KEKKAISHI

VOLUME 6

VIZ MEDIA EDITION

STORY AND ART BY YELLOW TANABE

Translation/Yuko Sawada
Touch-up Art & Lettering/Stephen Dutro
Cover Design & Graphic Layout/Amy Martin
Editor/Andy Nakatani

Managing Editor/Annette Roman
Editorial Director/Elizabeth Kawasaki
Editor in Chief/Alvin Lu
Sr. Director of Acquisitions/Rika Inouye
Senior VP of Marketing/Liza Coppola
Exec. VP of Sales & Marketing/John Easum
Publisher/Hyoe Narita

Published by VIZ Media, LLC
P.O. Box 77010
San Francisco, CA 94107

10 9 8 7 6 5 4 3 2 1
First printing, August 2006

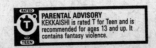

PARENTAL ADVISORY
KEKKAISHI is rated T for Teen and is
recommended for ages 13 and up. It
contains fantasy violence.

www.viz.com

store.viz.com

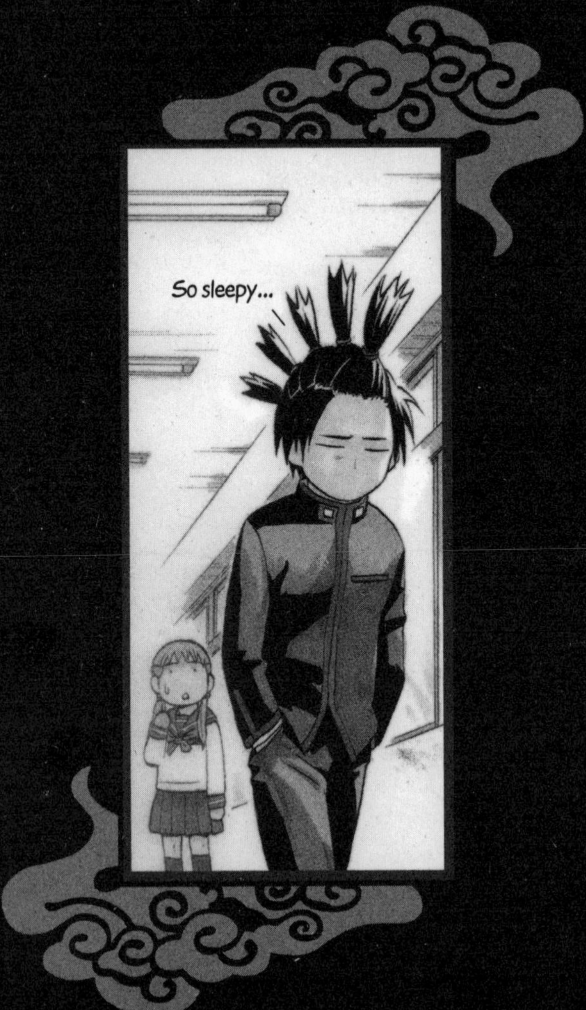
So sleepy...

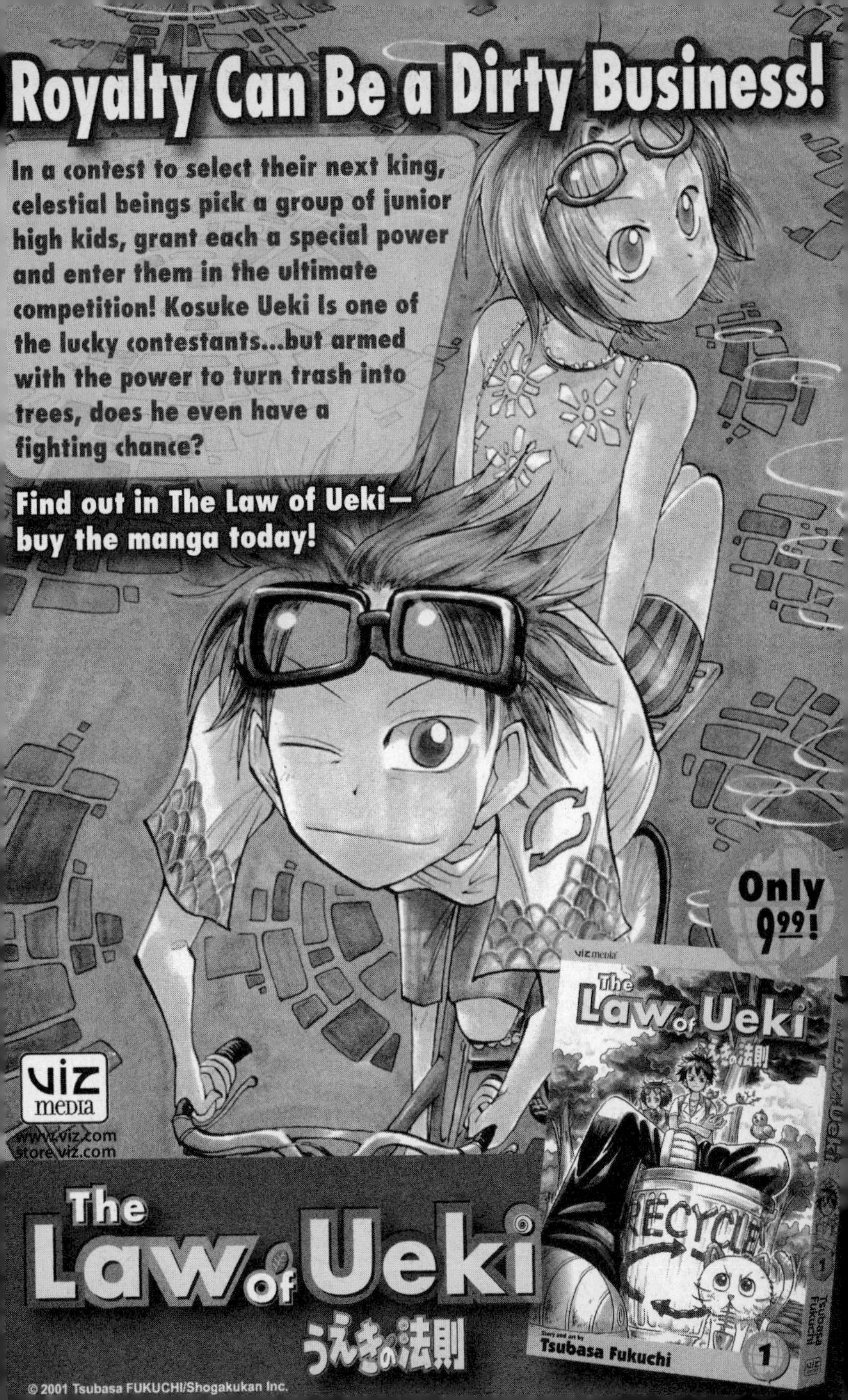
Royalty Can Be a Dirty Business!
In a contest to select their next king, celestial beings pick a group of junior high kids, grant each a special power and enter them in the ultimate competition! Kosuke Ueki is one of the lucky contestants...but armed with the power to turn trash into trees, does he even have a fighting chance?
Find out in The Law of Ueki—buy the manga today!
Only 9.99!
VIZ media
www.viz.com
store.viz.com
The Law of Ueki
うえきの法則
viz media
The Law of Ueki
うえきの法則
RECYCLE
Story and art by
Tsubasa Fukuchi
1
© 2001 Tsubasa FUKUCHI/Shogakukan Inc.

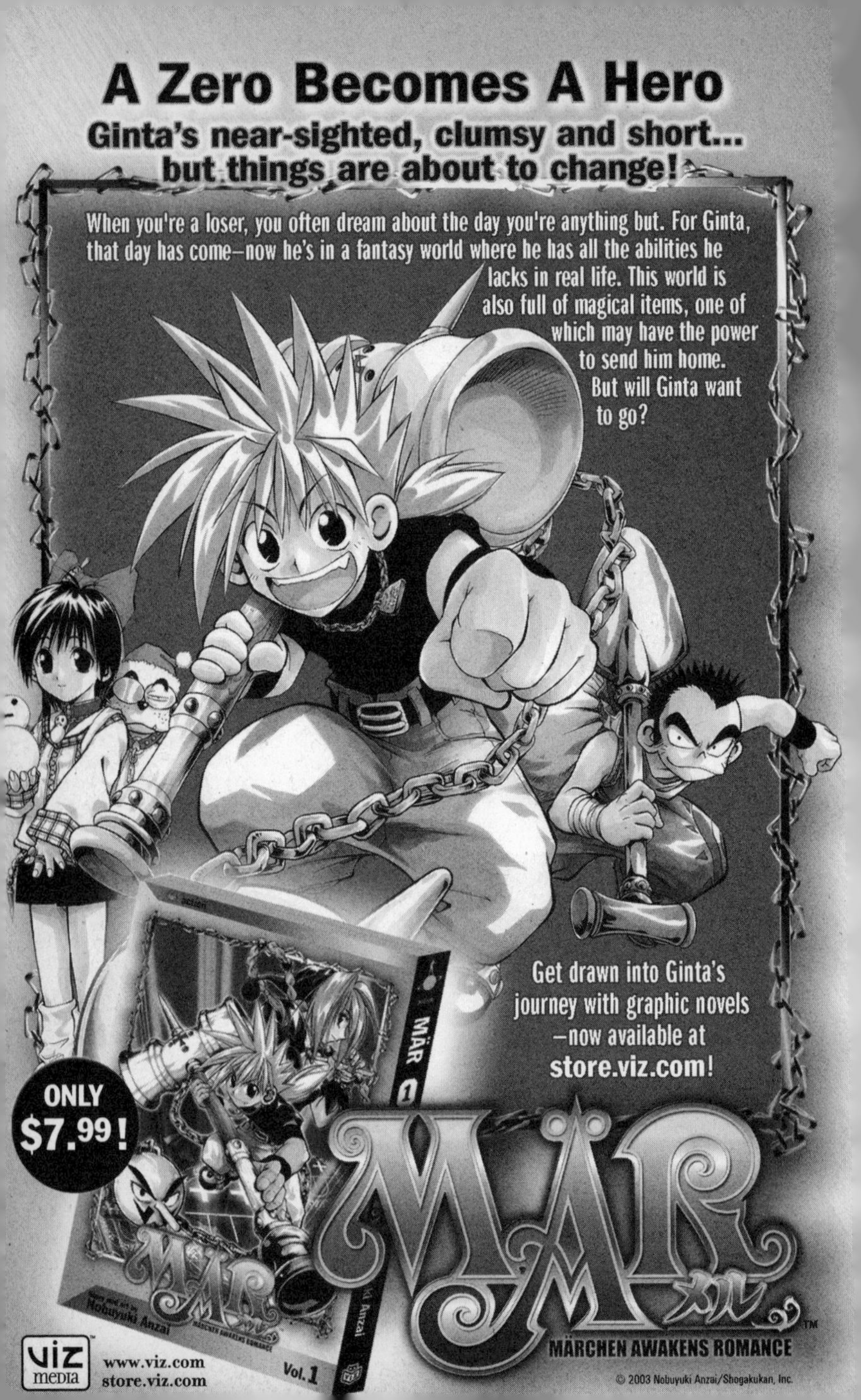
A Zero Becomes A Hero
Ginta's near-sighted, clumsy and short...
but things are about to change!
When you're a loser, you often dream about the day you're anything but. For Ginta, that day has come—now he's in a fantasy world where he has all the abilities he lacks in real life. This world is also full of magical items, one of which may have the power to send him home. But will Ginta want to go?
Get drawn into Ginta's journey with graphic novels —now available at store.viz.com!
ONLY $7.99!
MÄR
Nobuyuki Anzai
Vol. 1
MÄR
MÄRCHEN AWAKENS ROMANCE
viz media
www.viz.com
store.viz.com
© 2003 Nobuyuki Anzai/Shogakukan, Inc.

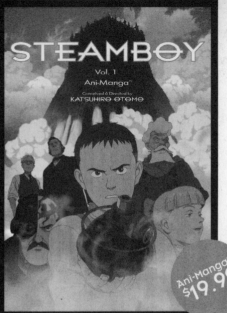
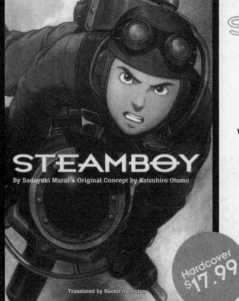

The Evolution of Science... The Downfall of Man?

Based on the hit movie from Katsuhiro Otomo

STEAMBOY

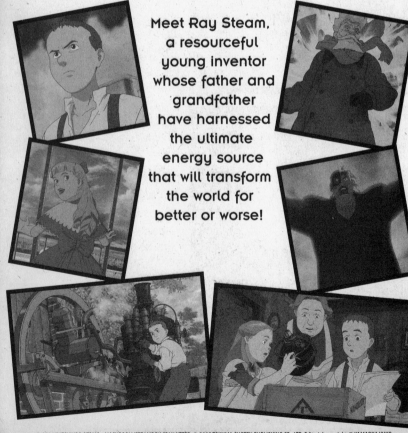

Meet Ray Steam, a resourceful young inventor whose father and grandfather have harnessed the ultimate energy source that will transform the world for better or worse!

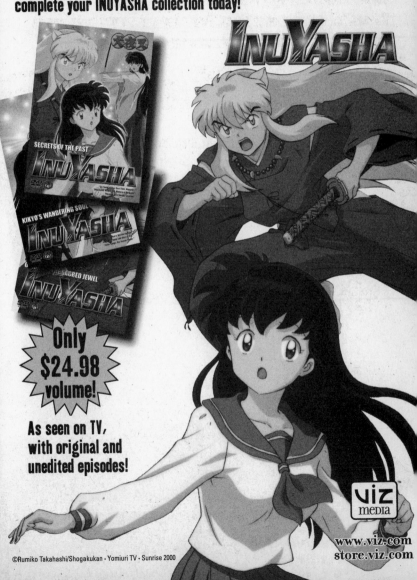

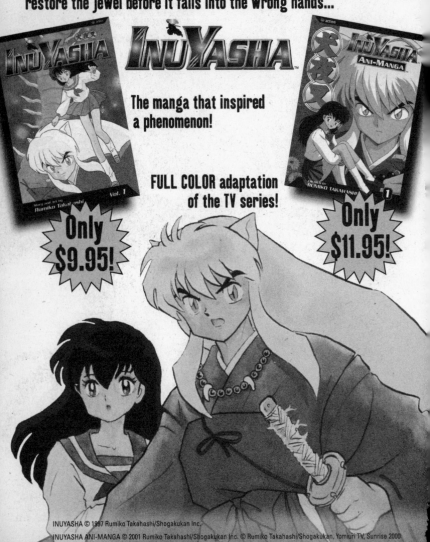

LOVE MAN
LET HINK!

IS NOW
ASE VISIT:
URVEY

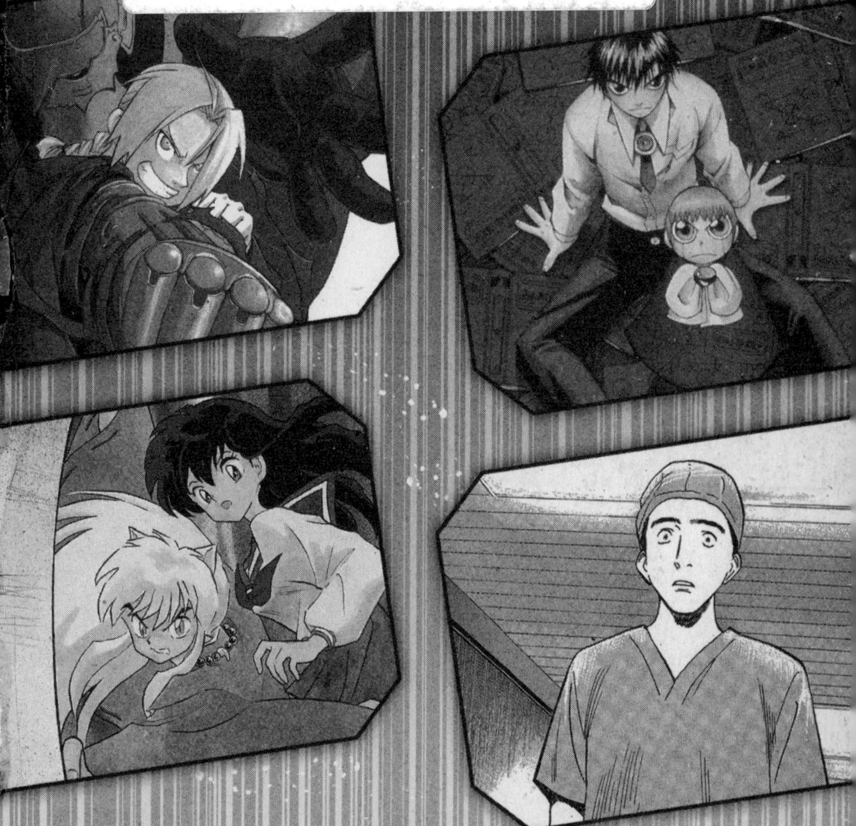

HELP US MAKE THE MANGA YOU LOVE BETTER!